Ten Good Governance Tips from Sarbanes-Oxley Lawyers

Sarbanes-Oxley (SOX) provides a legal model for running corporations of all sizes, regardless of whether or not they're publicly traded and technically subject to SOX. The best legal minds agree that good liability-limiting governance after SOX requires corporations to do the following:

- **Evaluate your board members.** After SOX, shareholders expect the directors who sit on the boards that run companies to be independent and financially literate. Chapter 8 explains what these new requirements mean, and what to do if your board members don't quite measure up.

- **Create the correct kinds of committees.** After SOX, well-governed companies of all sizes break their board members up into audit committees, nominating committees, compensation committees, and maybe even disclosure committees. (For committee coverage, check out Chapters 7, 8, and 9.)

- **Get good counsel for corporate officers.** The legal trend is that chief executive officers (CEOs) and chief financial officers (CFOs) are held responsible for everything that appears on financial statements. CEOs and CFOs need good legal counsel inside and outside the company to help them ask questions and spot issues necessary to reasonably protect these officers from liability.

- **Set defensive communication standards.** When a legal battle ensues, communications processes within the company are scrutinized. Establish clear communication procedures that reflect responsibility and accountability within the company.

- **Know the "hidden" risks to board members.** Board members are responsible to shareholders and third parties that rely on the company's financials. Even in small, private companies, board members can be sued by creditors and third parties that rely on the financial statements.

- **Know when to say "No" to a Section 404 auditor.** Attorneys can be instrumental in cutting Section 404 costs in a company's first year of 404 compliance by identifying areas in which legal liabilities and exposures are minimal.

- **Get all the deadlines straight.** Don't confuse the deadlines for implementing the different requirements under SOX. For example, although companies with revenues of less than $75 million don't have to comply with SOX Section 404 until after July 15, 2007, their CEOs and CFOs must begin certifying financial statements long before that.

- **Don't treat whistle-blowers like whiners.** Whistle-blowers are people who alert the company to breaches of internal policy and government regulations, and they must be treated with special care after SOX (see Chapter 16).

- **Know when to file an 8-K report.** SOX Section 404 contains a list of seemingly routine events in the life of a corporation (such as changes in management and loss of a major client that trigger real time disclosure) that call for the filing of an 8-K report. Know these triggering events.

- **Figure out whether your company needs an SAS 70 Form.** Even small companies that technically don't have to comply with SOX Section 404 may be asked to provide certifications about their internal control to their clients who do have to comply using this form.

For Dummies: Bestselling Book Series for Beginners

What Every Company in America Should Do After SOX

Sarbanes-Oxley (SOX) was passed to combat corruption at big public companies like Enron, WorldCom, Tyco, Adelphia, Global TelLink, HealthSouth, and Arthur Andersen. But small and not-for-profit companies are finding they have no choice but to adopt many of the same standards if they want to get insurance, attract investors and donors, and repel lawsuits. SOX compliance is becoming a portfolio building block that no company can ignore.

- **Form an audit committee.** Your company's audit committee should consist of independent directors who sit on the board and ensure the integrity of your company's audit process. After SOX, it's tough to explain to investors and regulatory authorities why your company never got around to convening an audit committee. Chapter 7 explains how to form an audit committee, and Chapter 19 gives you a checklist of audit committee basics.

- **Combat Section 404 audit-chondria and policy paranoia.** Auditors and governance officers want to shine by conscientiously complying with SOX Section 404. However, they have to do their jobs within the bounds of budget and reason. Not every audit issue deserves full-throttle testing, and not every trivial process needs accompanying policies and controls. Chapter 11 gives you guidance on how to curb Section 404 costs without cutting controls.

- **Prevent whistle-blower complaints from becoming lawsuits.** Every company has its share of complainers and malcontents. However, when employee or vendor complaints regard matters than can affect the company's financial statements, the issues need to be fully documented and vetted (see Chapter 16).

- **Keep a lid on insurance premiums.** Increasingly, insurance companies are looking at SOX compliance as an unofficial underwriting criterion in quoting officers' and directors' liability policies and other coverage relative to companies' exposure. Put simply, SOX compliance can save premium dollars.

- **Be credible in raising capital.** No investor or donor wants to assume unnecessary risk. Documenting your company's compliance with the relevant aspects of SOX shows creditors and donors that your company operates in an ethical, controlled environment and that its future growth is a good bet.

- **Deal with real data in making decisions.** No company can make good decisions if its financial data is speculative and its procedures are hazy. The good news about SOX is that it has created spinoff software tools and checklists to help your CEOs, CFOs, and other management team members get a handle on what's happening with your company. Chapter 15 covers simple software tools (some are only a couple thousand dollars) and tells where to find checklists for the latest standards.

- **Figure out if SAS 70 applies to you (even if the rest of SOX doesn't).** If your company provides services to publicly traded companies, your clients may be asking you for an SAS 70 report. Even if you don't have to comply with SOX, your customers may have to document that they only outsource to service providers with good internal controls in place and may be looking for you to provide the appropriate SAS 70 documentation.

- **Communicate about control.** When a company experiences a breach of ethics or internal control, it's important to be able to trace the company communications to see where the breakdown occurred. Clear communications about controls, procedures, and ethics can protect conscientious management and employees at all levels while laying the blame on those attempting to circumvent SOX standards. The SOX spinoff market has produced tools and checklists to test communication as well as other types of control.

- **Prepare management for new levels of liability.** SOX places more responsibility (and potential liability) on management than ever before. Management needs to understand what it can no longer delegate under SOX and develop a strategy for maintaining control over what can be handed off to others.

- **Adopt a code of ethics, and mean it.** Every company should adopt a simple code of ethics (as discussed in Chapter 10) and communicate it to everyone in the organization. In any company, new situations that aren't covered by specific policies will arise. However, in the post-Enron era of SOX, the company's code of ethics should cover everything.

For Dummies: Bestselling Book Series for Beginners

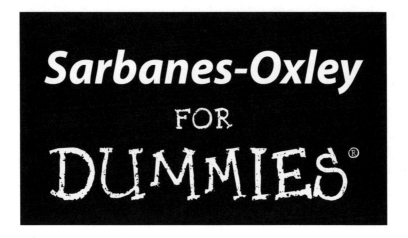

Sarbanes-Oxley FOR DUMMIES®

by Jill Gilbert Welytok, JD, CPA

WILEY

Wiley Publishing, Inc.

Sarbanes-Oxley For Dummies®

Published by
Wiley Publishing, Inc.
111 River St.
Hoboken, NJ 07030-5774
www.wiley.com

For general information on our other products and services, please contact our Customer Care Department within the U.S. at 800-762-2974, outside the U.S. at 317-572-3993, or fax 317-572-4002.

For technical support, please visit www.wiley.com/techsupport.

Wiley also publishes its books in a variety of electronic formats. Some content that appears in print may not be available in electronic books.

Library of Congress Control Number: 2005937351

ISBN-13: 978-0-471-76846-3

ISBN-10: 0-471-76846-4

Manufactured in the United States of America

10 9 8 7 6 5 4 3 2

1O/RS/QW/QW/IN

WILEY

About the Author

Jill Gilbert Welytok, JD, CPA, LLM, practices in the areas of corporate, non-profit law, and intellectual property. She is the founder Absolute Technology Law Group, LLC (www.abtechlaw.com). She went to law school at DePaul University in Chicago, where she was on the Law Review, and picked up a Masters Degree in Computer Science from Marquette University in Wisconsin where she now lives. Ms. Welytok also has an LLM in Taxation from DePaul. She was formerly a tax consultant with the predecessor firm to Ernst & Young. She frequently speaks on nonprofit, corporate governance and taxation issues and will probably come speak to your company or organization if you invite her. You may e-mail her with questions you have about Sarbanes-Oxley or anything else in this book at jwelytok@abtechlaw.com. You can find updates to this book and ongoing information about SOX developments at the author's Web site located at www.abtechlaw.com.

Dedication

To Tara, Julia, and Daniel.

Author's Acknowledgments

Several exceptional professionals (whom I call The SOX SWAT Team) contributed their time and expertise reviewing and making technical edits to this book. Feel free to e-mail or call them with questions you may have about Sarbanes-Oxley that weren't answered in this book.

Daniel S. Welytok, JD, LLM — Whyte Hirschboeck Dudek S.C. Dan is a partner in the business practice group of Whyte Hirschboeck Dudek S.C., where he concentrates in the areas of taxation and business law. Dan advises clients on strategic planning, federal and state tax issues, transactional matters and employee benefits. He represents clients before the IRS and state taxing authorities concerning audits, tax controversies, and offers in compromise. He has served in various leadership roles in the American Bar Association and as Great Lakes Area liaison with the IRS. He can be reached at dsw@whdlaw.com.

Ronald Kral, CPA, CMA — Candela Solutions, LLC. Ron knows auditing and consulting well, having assisted over 200 clients as a Principal Consultant at PricewaterhouseCoopers and as the Managing Director of a statewide CPA firm where he worked extensively with Ernst & Young. Ron is a nationally recognized speaker on governance, business ethics, internal controls, and the Sarbanes-Oxley Act of 2002, including the COSO and COBIT frameworks, NYSE and NASDAQ requirements, PCAOB standards, and SEC regulations. Ron is also a Director of Financial Executives International's Milwaukee Chapter. He can be reached at rkral@candelasolutions.com.

Richard Kranitz, JD — Kranitz & Philipp Rich has been an attorney in private practice since 1970, emphasizing securities, banking, and business law. He has served as venture capital consultant to, and director of, various private companies and a number of professional, civic, and charitable organizations.

Bill Douglas — Cost Advisors, Inc. Bill is the president of Cost Advisors, Inc., a financial project management firm he founded in 1999. Over the last 3 years, Cost Advisors project teams have assisted numerous companies in complying with the Sarbanes-Oxley Act. Building on his firm's experience, Bill designed SarbOxPro (www.SarbOxPro.com).

Publisher's Acknowledgments

We're proud of this book; please send us your comments through our Dummies online registration form located at `www.dummies.com/register/`.

Some of the people who helped bring this book to market include the following:

*Acquisitions, Editorial,
and Media Development*

Senior Project Editor: Tim Gallan

Acquisitions Editor: Kathy Cox

Copy Editor: Elizabeth Rea

Editorial Program Coordinator: Hanna K. Scott

Technical Editors: Daniel S. Welytok, Ronald Kral, Richard Kranitz

Editorial Manager: Christine Meloy Beck

Editorial Assistants: Erin Calligan, David Lutton, Nadine Bell

Cartoons: Rich Tennant
(`www.the5thwave.com`)

Composition Services

Project Coordinator: Maridee Ennis

Layout and Graphics: Carl Byers, Andrea Dahl, Lauren Goddard, Joyce Haughey, Stephanie D. Jumper, Julie Trippeti

Proofreaders: Leeann Harney, TECHBOOKS Production Services

Indexer: TECHBOOKS Production Services

Publishing and Editorial for Consumer Dummies

 Diane Graves Steele, Vice President and Publisher, Consumer Dummies

 Joyce Pepple, Acquisitions Director, Consumer Dummies

 Kristin A. Cocks, Product Development Director, Consumer Dummies

 Michael Spring, Vice President and Publisher, Travel

 Kelly Regan, Editorial Director, Travel

Publishing for Technology Dummies

 Andy Cummings, Vice President and Publisher, Dummies Technology/General User

Composition Services

 Gerry Fahey, Vice President of Production Services

 Debbie Stailey, Director of Composition Services

Contents at a Glance

Introduction 1

Part 1: The Scene Before and After SOX 7

Chapter 1: The SOX Saga 9

Chapter 2: SOX in Sixty Seconds 25

Chapter 3: SOX and Securities Regulations 39

Chapter 4: SOX and Factual Financial Statements 59

Part 11: SOX in the City: Meeting New Standards 73

Chapter 5: A New Audit Ambience 75

Chapter 6: A Board to Audit the Auditors 89

Chapter 7: The Almighty Audit Committee 99

Chapter 8: Building Boards That Can't Be Bought 111

Chapter 9: SOX: Under New Management 123

Chapter 10: More Management Mandates 139

Part 111: Surviving Section 404 149

Chapter 11: Clearing Up Confusion About Control 151

Chapter 12: Surviving a Section 404 Audit 165

Chapter 13: Taking the Terror Out of Testing 179

Part 1V: Software for SOX Techies 195

Chapter 14: Surveying SOX Software 197

Chapter 15: Working with Some Actual SOX Software...........211

Part V: To SOX-finity and Beyond 227

Chapter 16: Lawsuits Under SOX..229

Chapter 17: The Surprising Scope of SOX 245

Part VI: The Part of Tens 251

Chapter 18: Ten Ways to Avoid Getting Sued or Criminally Prosecuted
Under SOX...253

Chapter 19: Ten Tips for an Effective Audit Committee...............259

Chapter 20: Ten Smart Management Moves 265

Chapter 21: Ten Things You Can't Ask an Auditor to Do After SOX........271

Chapter 22: Top Ten Places to Get Smart About SOX............277

Part VII: Appendixes 283

Appendix A: The Entire Sarbanes-Oxley Act..........................285

Appendix B: Sample Certifications..................................319

Appendix C: Sample Audit Committee Charter 323

Appendix D: Sample Audit Committee Report 333

Appendix E: Sample Corporate Governance Principles 335

Appendix F: Sample Code of Ethics 341

Appendix G: Sample SAS 70 Report 349

Index 351

Table of Contents

Introduction 1

About This Book...1
What I Assume About You...2
Conventions Used in This Book 3
How This Book Is Organized..3
    Part I: The Scene Before and After SOX..........................3
    Part II: SOX in the City: Meeting New Standards 4
    Part III: Surviving Section 404 4
    Part IV: Software for SOX Techies 4
    Part V: To SOX-finity and Beyond..................................4
    Part VI: The Part of Tens 4
    Part VII: Appendixes..5
Icons Used In This Book..5
Where to Go from Here...5
Feedback, Please 6

Part 1: The Scene Before and After SOX 7

Chapter 1: The SOX Saga 9

The Politics of SOX 9
    A loophole under prior law..10
    New ammunition for aggrieved investors 12
    Corporate America after SOX 12
Who Combats Corruption under SOX?....................................12
    The independent audit board......................................13
    Evolving auditors 13
    Lawyers' noisy new liability...15
    CEOs and CFOs 15
    Small businesses and nonprofits in the headlights 15
    The rank-and-file 16
    New high–paid governance gurus 16
A Summary of SOX: Taking It One Title at a Time.......................16
    Title I: Aiming at the audit profession 17
    Title II: Ensuring auditor independence 18
    Title III: Requiring corporate accountability.....................18
    Title IV: Establishing financial disclosures, loans, and
        ethics codes..19

Title V: Protecting analyst integrity 20
Title VI: Doling out more money and authority............................20
Title VII: Supporting studies and reports 21
Title VIII: Addressing criminal fraud and whistle-blower
    provisions 21
Title IX: Setting penalties for white-collar crime 21
Title X: Signing corporate tax returns..................................22
Title XI: Enforcing payment freezes, blacklists, and prison
    terms 22
Some Things SOX Doesn't Say: SOX Myths..................................22
Myth #1: Auditors can't provide tax services............................23
Myth #2: Internal control means data security 23
Myth #3: The company isn't responsible for functions it
    outsources 23
Myth #4: My company met the deadline for Section 404 first-year
    compliance. We're home free! 24

Chapter 2: SOX in Sixty Seconds **25**
The Pre-SOX Scandals..25
Enron events everyone overlooked 26
More tales from the corporate tabloids 29
Four Squeaky Clean SOX Objectives.......................................30
How SOX Protects the Investing Public 31
Creating a Public Company Accounting Oversight Board 32
Clamping down on auditors...32
Rotating auditors...33
Creating committees inside companies 33
Making management accountable...34
Taking back bogus bonuses 35
Banning blackouts...35
Ratcheting up reporting 35
Purging company conflicts of interest..................................36
Exercising internal control 36
Looking at lawyers 37
Waiting seven years to shred..37
Putting bad management behind bars 37
Freezing bonuses 38
Blackballing officers and directors 38
Providing whistle-blower protection 38
Rapid Rulemaking Regrets 38

Chapter 3: SOX and Securities Regulations **39**
Pre-SOX Securities Laws...39
The Securities Act of 1933: Arming investors with information.....41
The Securities Exchange Act of 1934: Establishing the SEC 42
Other securities laws 44

The Scope of SOX: Securities and Issuers.................................45
    What is a "security"?...45
    Who is an "issuer"?..46
    The SOX surprise..48
The Post-SOX Paper Trail...50
    Form 10-K...50
    Form 10-Q...51
    Form 8-K...51
Behind the 8-K Ball After SOX..51
    Adding new events to the list 52
    Shuffling events from the 10-K and 10-Q...................53
    Creating four-day reporting events............................53
    Providing protection in the safe SOX harbor............53
Annual SEC Scrutiny After SOX..54
    Mandatory review rule 54
    Remedies for inaccurate registration materials...........54
Why Privately Held Companies Care About SOX..................56
    Bolstering the bottom line 56
    Defending company practices in court 57
    The prospect of going public......................................57

Chapter 4: SOX and Factual Financial Statements **59**
Looking for Cooked Books After SOX..................................60
    What the income statement reveals 60
    Balance sheet (and off–balance sheet) transactions.....62
    Looking for funky footnotes.......................................63
    Complying with GAAP and GAAS 64
Finding Financial Information...65
    The free stuff..65
    The stuff you get for a fee...66
Accessing Annual Reports 67
    The glossy pictures and the real figures 68
    Management's Discussion and Analysis......................70
Surfing SEC Filings..70
    10-K reports..70
    Other useful forms on EDGAR 72

Part II: SOX in the City: Meeting New Standards...........**73**

Chapter 5: A New Audit Ambience **75**
How SOX Rocks the Accounting Profession 75
An Example of Audit Failure: Arthur Andersen....................76
    Chronology of a collapse...76
    A vindicating verdict . . . years later 77
    Bridging the GAAP..78

SOX as a Substitute for Self-Regulation 78
    Shifting the role of the AICPA..79
    Whose turn is it to watch the CPA? 81
Is There an Independent Auditor in the House? 82
    The importance of audit independence 83
    Every auditor's dilemma 83
What SOX Says to CPAs 83
    Give the whole team a cooling-off period.............................84
    Prohibit services that cause conflicts 84
    Get prior permission for potential conflicts 85
    Everybody change partners!...86
    Wait seven years to shred 86
    Recognize when auditors are "impaired" 86
Section 404: The Sin Eater Provision 87
    CEOs and CFOs signing off 87
    Compliance dates and delays 87
    CPAs certifying the certifications..88

Chapter 6: A Board to Audit the Auditors 89
Taking a New Approach to Audit Oversight 89
    The old ad hoc system of accounting oversight 90
    Alphabet soup of accounting regulation 90
Primary Purposes of the PCAOB 91
    Goals of the PCAOB...92
    The seven statutory duties of the PCAOB 93
Some Practical PCAOB Matters...93
    Who's on the board? 93
    Who pays for the PCAOB? 94
PCAOB Rules: Old Meets New 94
    Sticking to the ol' standby rules 94
    Adjusting to some new rules...95
Evolving PCAOB Policies and Issues 96
    Sanctioning sloppy auditors 97
    Keeping an eye on small CPA firms 97
    Extending authority internationally......................................97
    Communicating with the SEC..98
When the PCAOB Doesn't Perform 98

Chapter 7: The Almighty Audit Committee 99
Deliver or De-list..99
From Audit Committee Annals 100
    Mr. Leavitt's Blue Ribbon panel..101
    Enron impetus..101
    The quest for consistent committee rules..........................101

Starting with a Charter 102
The Audit Committee Interface 102
Some Stricter NYSE Rules 103
Membership Requirements 104
    A few independent members 104
    Figure in a financial expert 105
Day-to-Day Committee Responsibilities 105
    Monitoring events and policing policies 105
    Interfacing with the auditors 106
    Preapproving nonaudit services 107
    Handling complaints 108
    Receiving CEO and CFO certifications 108
    Monitoring conflicts and cooling-off periods 109
    Ferreting out improper influence 109
    Rotating the audit partners 109
    Engaging advisors 109
    Providing recognition in annual reports 110
Audit Committee Rules for Private Companies...........................110
Foreign Company Committee Issues 110

Chapter 8: Building Boards That Can't Be Bought **111**
Some Background about Boards..112
    What does a director do? 112
    Looking at some bad, bad boards 113
In Search of Independent Directors 115
    No relationships with related companies 115
    Three-year look-back period 115
    Prohibited payments...116
    Family ties 116
Mandatory Meetings under SOX 117
Forming Committees for Nominating Directors...........................117
    NYSE nominating procedures 118
    NASDAQ nominating rules 118
Regulating Director Compensation...118
    Making governance guidelines public 119
    Evaluating the board's performance...119
Some Exempt Boards . . . For the Moment....................................120
    Nonpublic companies 120
    Nonprofit corporations...121
    Other exempt companies 121

Chapter 9: SOX: Under New Management **123**
Chiefly Responsible: CEOs and CFOs 123
    CEO: The chief in charge 124
    CFO: The financial fact finder 124
    Three SOX sections for the chiefs...125

A Section 302 Certification Checklist..126
  Paragraph 1: Review of periodic report 127
  Paragraph 2: Material accuracy..127
  Paragraph 3: Fair presentation of financial information 127
  Paragraph 4: Disclosure controls and procedures........................127
  Paragraph 5: Disclosure to auditors 128
  Paragraph 6: Changes in internal controls..............................129
Clearing Up Common Section 302 Questions 129
  What companies are required to file certifications under
    Section 302?...130
  What are the filing deadlines for Section 302?.........................130
  Which reports get certified? 131
Viewing Control as a Criminal Matter: Section 906..............................131
More Reporting Responsibilities for Management: Section 404 133
  What management has to do under Section 404........................133
  What the auditors need from management 134
The Benefits of Internal Control from a Management Perspective........134
  Considering the auditor's perspective 134
  What the SEC says...135
  Management standards criteria for controls 135
Seeking Out Subcertifications 136
Some Good Advice for CEOs and CFOs..136
  Establish a disclosure committee 137
  Take an inventory..137
  Woo the whistle-blowers 137

Chapter 10: More Management Mandates .139
Codifying the Corporate Conscience..139
  Explaining the code...140
  Establishing worthwhile objectives...................................140
  Realizing one code doesn't fit all companies.........................141
  Disclosing amendments and waivers 141
  Expecting ethics on the exchanges...................................141
  A checklist of code contents...142
New Rules for Stock Selling and Telling 142
  Faster disclosure 143
  More disclosure..143
Prohibiting Personal Loans...144
Banning Blackout Trading..144
  Avoiding media images of stricken retirees..........................145
  Making some necessary exceptions 145
Making Managers Pay Personally 145
  The freeze factor..146
  The danger of disgorgement 146
Stopping Audit Inference..147
  Identifying audit interlopers 147
  Suing audit interlopers 148

Part III: Surviving Section 404 149

Chapter 11: Clearing Up Confusion About Control 151

The Nuts and Bolts of Section 404 152
What Section 404 says 152
What Section 404 really does..153
SEC Rules Under Section 404 153
PCAOB participation in the Section 404 process 153
When Do Companies Have to Comply with Section 404? 154
Section 302 "Internal Control" versus Section 404 "Internal
Control"..156
Defining "disclosure controls and procedures" under
Section 302...156
Interpreting "internal control over financial reporting" under
Section 404...158
Controlling the Cost of Compliance...159
Cost-cutting measures by the PCAOB 160
Section 404 sticker shock..161
Decreasing costs in year two 161

Chapter 12: Surviving a Section 404 Audit 165

Dividing Up Responsibilities in a Section 404 Audit..............................165
Management's role 166
The independent auditor's role..166
What the Auditors Are Looking For 167
What Is (and Is Not) Related to the Audit..167
Complying with Audit Standard No. 2 168
Evaluating management's assessment 168
Walking through the controls in place..169
Identifying assertions and significant accounts...............................170
Evaluating the design of controls..171
Taking the "top-down" approach 172
Testing operating effectiveness...172
Timing the testing 173
Relying on other peoples' work..173
Identifying control deficiencies 174
Working with the audit committee...174
Forming an opinion and reporting 175
Flunking a 404 Audit...176
How to flunk a Section 404 audit 176
What to do if your company flunks..177

Chapter 13: Taking the Terror Out of Testing **179**

The Price of the Project..180
    The six most common Section 404 project costs........................180
    Meeting massive manpower requirements 181
    The social challenges of Section 404 182
Hail to the Documenters 182
    The right documentation skills 182
    Getting the documentation down 183
    Time tracking...184
    Scoping out savings 184
    Taking an inventory of your company processes 185
    Organizing the documentation: Why form is
        equal to substance 188
Caveats about Controls 189
    Key controls 190
    Some common key controls...190
Ogling the Outside Vendors: SAS 70 Reports 191
Evaluating Control with the COSO Framework 192
    How COSO breaks down companies' controls 192
    COSO guidance for your company..193
A Bit about COBIT 194

Part IV: Software for SOX Techies...............................195

Chapter 14: Surveying SOX Software **197**

Some SOX Software Trends...197
Identifying the Types of Software on the Market 199
Shopping for SOX Software..202
SOX Meets Cousin IT 203
    Collecting scattered company data 204
    Evaluating your company's existing IT systems: A checklist 204
The COSO Standards for Software 207
    What COSO says 207
Complying with COBIT 210
Will SOX Software Pay for Itself? 210

Chapter 15: Working with Some Actual SOX Software **211**

Doing Your Research Before a Software Installation 211
    Tracking the flow of information in your company 212
    Following the trial balance trail..214
Getting to Know SarbOxPro..216
    The SarbOxPro checklist...216
    Hey, this looks familiar: The SarbOxPro data tree 216
    SarbOxPro stages 218

Opting for Other Types of Software Solutions 223
 Looking at a general information management tool 223
 Using Web-based compliance tools 225

Part V: To SOX-finity and Beyond 227

Chapter 16: Lawsuits Under SOX 229

The Smoking Gun: Knowledge 229
The First Big SOX Trial: Richard Scrushy 230
 The squishy Scrushy facts 231
 The Scrushy post-game recap 232
 What's next: Scrushy civil suits 232
The "Ignorance" Defense of Kenneth Lay 233
Timing Is Everything: Andersen, Ernst, and KPMG Litigation
 Outcomes 235
 Andersen's victory: Three years too late 236
 An Ernst error 236
 Kid gloves for KPMG? 237
The Gemstar Case: Interpreting Section 1103 238
Suing Under SOX Section 304 239
Suing Under Section 806: The Whistle-Blower Provision 239
 Blowing the whistle before and after SOX 240
 What happens when the whistle blows? 240
 Tips for defending against whistle-blower suits 243

Chapter 17: The Surprising Scope of SOX 245

Outsourcing Under SOX 245
 Summarizing SAS 70 246
 Sidestepping SAS 70 247
Extending SOX Principles to Not-for-Profits 247
 Altruism is not enough 247
SOX and Foreign Companies 249

Part VI: The Part of Tens 251

Chapter 18: Ten Ways to Avoid Getting Sued or Criminally Prosecuted Under SOX 253

Chapter 19: Ten Tips for an Effective Audit Committee 259

Chapter 20: Ten Smart Management Moves 265

Chapter 21: Ten Things You Can't Ask an Auditor to Do After SOX . . .271

Chapter 22: Top Ten Places to Get Smart About SOX 277

Part VII: Appendixes *283*

Appendix A: The Entire Sarbanes-Oxley Act .285

Appendix B: Sample Certifications 319

Appendix C: Sample Audit Committee Charter 323

Appendix D: Sample Audit Committee Report 333

Appendix E: Sample Corporate Governance Principles 335

Appendix F: Sample Code of Ethics 341

Appendix G: Sample SAS 70 Report 349

Index *351*

Introduction

⦁ ⦁

*W*elcome to *Sarbanes-Oxley For Dummies*. This book takes you on a tour of post-Enron corporate America. Whether you're a CEO, governance officer, CPA, manager, entrepreneur, file clerk, or cleric, this book is for you. It's designed to tell you where you fit into the grand scheme of corporate compliance and why you're being asked to do what you do by your board of directors, banker, customers, and clients.

Having the big picture straight in your mind helps ensure that you won't lose track of the minutiae and details that accompany the sweeping piece of legislation that is Sarbanes-Oxley, whether you're gearing up for initial compliance or attempting to streamline in subsequent years. If you're part of a private company or not-for-profit, a special congratulations to you. You know that Sarbanes-Oxley is here to stay and is becoming the gold standard for fair, ethical, and efficient business practices.

About This Book

The Sarbanes-Oxley Act, or SOX, as it's affectionately called in the world of corporate governance, is a responsive piece of legislation. Like the securities laws passed in the 1930s, SOX was passed in response to a real crisis and genuine public outrage. It sailed through Congress on a wave of bipartisan support surprisingly free of lobbying and loophole legislating. Instead, Congress left the details to the Securities and Exchange Commission (SEC) and the newly created Public Company Accounting Oversight Board (PCAOB). This book walks you through SOX's rather piecemeal rules and pronouncements and gives you a sense of how to anticipate future trends and traps in this area of the law.

The goal of *Sarbanes-Oxley For Dummies* is to give you a helicopter view of the regulatory terrain while helping you focus a beam on the key details of the legislation. This book is intended to give you a sophisticated understanding of the purpose and structure of the legislation as it affects many disciplines and areas of the law. *Sarbanes-Oxley For Dummies* will empower you with the level of insight you need for practical, cost-effective decision making.

This book will assist you in

- ✔ **Understanding why SOX was passed:** Looking at the kind of conduct SOX was intended to combat can help you create meaningful standards for the company with which you work or are affiliated.

- ✔ **Instituting cost-effective compliance with SOX:** This book's practical view of the legislation can keep you from becoming bogged down in regulatory details and allowing lawyers and accountants to go off on expensive tangents that have little to do with the essence of SOX.

- ✔ **Finding answers on specific SOX issues:** This book explains how and where to find SEC rules and pronouncements critical to implementation of SOX and translates those rules into plain English.

- ✔ **Avoiding lawsuits and regulatory actions:** This book, although not intended as a substitute for a good securities lawyer or a CPA, takes a hard look at who gets sued under SOX and how you can avoid having your company or yourself added to the list of litigants.

- ✔ **Anticipating future rules and trends:** SEC rules and PCAOB pronouncements under SOX continue to be issued with regularity. But with a comprehensive understanding of what the law is designed to do, you'll be less surprised by what's ultimately issued.

What I Assume About You

In writing this book, I had to make a few assumptions about who my readers would be and what kind of information they'd be looking for. First of all, I assume you want to understand the Sarbanes-Oxley Act in a way you can't achieve by suffering through the 80-some pages of the statute and 1,000 or so pages of related congressional hearings. You want to make sure you have a handle on the important aspects of the legislation, how it affects you and your company, and how companies can comply most cost-effectively.

Secondly, if you're a service provider such as a lawyer or CPA, I assume you're looking for insight into the following tasks — insights you would glean from the legal and accounting professionals involved in writing this book (whose credentials and accomplishments are listed on the acknowledgments page):

- ✔ Recognizing and creating a legally effective, fully compliant corporate governance framework

- ✔ Determining what aspects of SOX apply to your company or should be voluntarily adopted by your company (whether it's publicly traded, privately held, or not-for-profit)

✔ Managing and streamlining Section 404 compliance, as well as seizing opportunities and benefiting from information resulting from the unprecedented testing and documentation of business processes all across the United States

✔ Interpreting media accounts, court cases, and economic projections involving SOX

Conventions Used in This Book

It's unfortunate, but understanding SOX means that you're going to run into lots of legal jargon and accounting minutiae. To give you a jump start, I define some legal and accounting terms in this book and use *italics* to make such terms stand out a bit.

Also, I occasionally wander off-topic to discuss something historical, technical, or interesting (or, at least, interesting *to me!*). In these instances, I set the discussions apart by placing them in *sidebars,* which are the gray boxes you'll see from time to time throughout the book. Because the text in sidebars is nonessential, feel free to skip it if it doesn't interest you.

How This Book Is Organized

Sarbanes-Oxley is an extremely broad piece of legislation, spanning legal, accounting, and information technology disciplines. The index and table of contents will help you find your way. The chapters in this book treat each topic independently without assuming you've read previous chapters (as a textbook might), so you can use them as references and jump around to find what you need. *Sarbanes-Oxley For Dummies* is divided into six parts, which I explain in the following sections.

Part I: The Scene Before and After SOX

This part of the book starts at the beginning, explaining why SOX was passed and taking you on a tabloid tour of the corporate scandals — Enron, WorldCom, Adelphi, Global Crossing, and more — that inspired it. These chapters shock you with tales of greed and manipulation and then walk you section-by-section through the legislation, explaining what each provision is intended to accomplish.

Part II: SOX in the City: Meeting New Standards

The chapters in this part spell out who's affected by which provisions. You find out why the accounting profession is no longer self-regulating and are introduced to the new audit ambience. You also get a good look at what SOX means for management, including what's expected of boards and the committees formed under their direction.

Part III: Surviving Section 404

SOX Section 404 is a big enough deal to warrant its own part in this book. These chapters take you by the hand and guide you through the dreaded Section 404 audit process. They tell you how to manage a Section 404 project and when and how to cut compliance costs without cutting corners.

Part IV: Software for SOX Techies

This part of *Sarbanes-Oxley For Dummies* is all about software. It explains how software can help you comply with SOX and what to look for when investing in information technology to carry out SOX objectives. These chapters also sample some of the more cost-effective products on the market and suggest particularly useful systems for small to mid-size companies.

Part V: To SOX-finity and Beyond

This part looks at the future of SOX and corporate governance. These chapters take you into the courtroom to see who's getting sued under SOX and what the outcomes are. This part also looks at what SOX means for outsourced services and service providers and explains when special SAS 70 reports are required (as well as when they aren't).

Part VI: The Part of Tens

The chapters in this part provide the skinny on important subjects such as what every audit committee absolutely must undertake, how to avoid getting sued under SOX, and even how to save money with SOX. In essence, this part of the book is about taking control and proceeding confidently under SOX.

Part VII: Appendixes

The appendixes in the book contain useful reference materials and forms you can actually put to use in your company. It also contains a teeny-tiny version of the entire Sarbanes-Oxley Act. (Don't worry, more user-friendly, searchable versions of SOX are located online at www.findlaw.com and on the Securities and Exchange Web site at www.sec.gov.)

Icons Used In This Book

For Dummies books use little pictures, called *icons,* to flag parts of text that stand out from the rest for one reason or another. Here's what the icons in this book mean:

 Time is money. When you see this icon, your attention's being directed to a compliance shortcut or timesaving tip.

 This icon signals the type of advice you may get in a lawyer's office if your company were paying the exorbitant going rates. Of course, the information highlighted by this icon is no substitute for sound legal advice from your own company attorney, who actually knows the facts of your individual situation.

 This icon indicates you're getting the kind of tip your audit or CPA firm might dispense. Of course, you should actually consult a real accounting professional before acting on anything that follows this icon.

 This is a heads-up warning to help you avoid compliance mistakes, legal traps, and audit imbroglios.

 This icon flags particularly noteworthy information — stuff you shouldn't forget.

Where to Go from Here

Because I wrote each chapter of this book as a stand-alone treatment of the topic covered, you can start with Chapter 1 and read the whole book, or you can skip around and brush up only on the topics that interest you at the moment. If you're new to SOX, I recommend you start with Part I. If you're hip to securities law in general and SOX in particular, skip ahead to the parts in the book that address your particular needs or concerns.

Feedback, Please

I'm always interested in your comments, suggestions, or questions, so I'd love to hear from you. Send me an e-mail message at jgilbert@abtechlaw.com, or visit my Web site at www.abtechlaw.com. On that site, you'll find a link to a special update page for this book as well as contact information for all the great legal and accounting professionals who helped with this book (I've included their credentials and accomplishments on the acknowledgments page).

Part I

The Scene Before and After SOX

The 5th Wave   By Rich Tennant

"Cooked books? Let me just say you could serve this profit and loss statement with a fruity Zinfandel and not be out of place."

In this part . . .

The Sarbanes-Oxley Act, or SOX, didn't pop up out of nowhere. Rather, its passage is rooted in some steamy corporate scandals. This part examines how Congress responded to events surrounding Enron, Tyco, WorldCom, Gobal, TelLink, and Adelphia in a bipartisan whirlwind. This part also looks at how this far-reaching legislation affects existing securities legislation, what it says, what it certainly doesn't say, and how it has spawned some mighty media myths.

Chapter 1

The SOX Saga

In This Chapter

▶ Riding the wave of political support for SOX

▶ Looking at the loopholes SOX closed

▶ Surveying SOX's impact

▶ Debunking some common media myths about SOX

*I*n response to a loss of confidence among American investors reminiscent of the Great Depression, President George W. Bush signed the Sarbanes-Oxley Act into law on July 30, 2002. SOX, as the law was quickly dubbed, is intended to ensure the reliability of publicly reported financial information and bolster confidence in U.S. capital markets. SOX contains expansive duties and penalties for corporate boards, executives, directors, auditors, attorneys, and securities analysts.

Although most of SOX's provisions are mandatory only for public companies that file a Form 10-K with the Securities and Exchange Commission (SEC), many private and nonprofit companies are facing market pressures to conform to the SOX standards. Privately held companies that fail to reasonably adopt SOX-type governance and internal control structures may face increased difficulty in raising capital, higher insurance premiums, greater civil liability, and a loss of status among potential customers, investors, and donors.

In this chapter, I take a look at the political impetus for SOX and summarize some key provisions of the SOX statute in plain English. I also dispel a few common SOX myths.

The Politics of SOX

SOX passed through both houses of Congress on a wave of bipartisan political support not unlike that which accompanied the passage of the U.S. Patriot Act after the terrorist attacks of 2001. Public shock greased the wheels of the political process. Congress needed to respond decisively to the Enron media fallout, a lagging stock market, and looming reelections (see Chapter 2 for details). SOX passed in the Senate 99–0 and cleared the House with only three dissenting votes.

Because political support for SOX was overwhelming, the legislation was not thoroughly debated. Thus, many SOX provisions weren't painstakingly vetted and have since been questioned, delayed, or slated for modification.

For the past 70 years, U.S. securities laws have required regular reporting of results of a company's financial status and operations. SOX now focuses on the accuracy of what's reported and the reliability of the information-gathering processes. After SOX, companies must implement internal controls and processes that ensure the accuracy of reported results.

Prior to SOX, the Securities Act of 1933 was the dominant regulatory mechanism. The 1933 Act requires that investors receive relevant financial information on securities being offered for public sale, and it prohibits deceit, misrepresentations, and other fraud in the sale of securities.

The SEC enforces the 1933 Act requiring corporations to register stock and securities they offer to the public. The registration forms contain financial statements and other disclosures to enable investors to make informed judgments in purchasing securities. (For more about the securities registration process, flip to Chapter 3.) The SEC requires that the information companies provide be accurate and certified by independent accountants.

SEC registration statements and prospectuses become public shortly after they're filed with the SEC. Statements filed by U.S. domestic companies are available on the EDGAR database accessible at www.sec.gov.

A loophole under prior law

SOX provides that publicly traded corporations of all sizes must meet its requirements. However, not all securities offerings must be registered with the SEC. Some exemptions from the registration requirement include:

- ✔ Private offerings to a limited number of persons or institutions
- ✔ Offerings of limited size
- ✔ Intrastate offerings
- ✔ Securities of municipal, state, and federal governments

The SEC exempts these small offerings to help smaller companies acquire capital more easily by lowering the cost of offering securities to the public.

In contrast, SOX provides that publicly traded corporations of all sizes must meet certain specific requirements depending on the size of the corporation.

Not everyone's a SOX fan

Only three Congressmen opposed the 2002 passage of SOX: GOP Representatives Ron Paul of Texas, Jeff Flake of Arizona, and Mac Collins of Georgia. Congressman Flake observed:

> *Obviously there are businesses that were acting in a fraudulent manner. We still have that today, and there are laws on the books that thankfully are being used more aggressively today to get at these businesses. But when we react so quickly, sometimes without the best knowledge of how to do this, without some of these investigations taking their course, without these enforcement agencies giving us full recommendations, then we have unintended consequences.*

In the years after SOX, many businesses and politicians are echoing the sentiments of Congressman Flake. The greatest criticism has been the financial burden imposed on small companies. The SEC received so many complaints about the disproportionately high costs of compliance for smaller public companies that it convened an Advisory Committee on Smaller Public Companies to investigate them. In response, the SEC has voted twice to extend the compliance deadline for Section 404 smaller public companies, called *non-accelerated filers,* primarily because it has acknowledged that the costs of compliance for smaller companies greatly exceeded estimates. (Section 404 is discussed in Chapter 11.)

The SEC extended the deadline for small-cap companies by one year, voting in March 2005 to push the compliance date to July 2006. When this extension failed to stop the grumbling about costs and confusion about compliance, the SEC decided in September 2005 that small companies wouldn't be required to comply with the Section 404 requirements until their first fiscal year ending on or after July 15, 2007.

In addition to the burden on small business, SOX is criticized for the sheer confusion it has created. SOX requires accounting firms and companies to simultaneously monitor several evolving sets of interpretive standards from the SEC and the Public Company Accounting Oversight Board (PCAOB). Early attempts to implement SOX have been accompanied by more resignations within regulatory agencies than shake-ups in corporate boardrooms. (The PCOAB is on its third chairman in as many years, as discussed in Chapter 6, and turnover at the SEC has been equally eventful since SOX.) most studies have shown that SOX has impacted the composition and behavior of corporate boards, to date, less than expected.

Regulatory confusion isn't the only culprit; many companies have contributed to their own SOX woes by simply failing to plan properly. The start-up costs of any initiative are always highest in the beginning; however, many companies simply panicked, hiring teams of expensive consultants and launching overlapping and ill-conceived projects to document their controls under SOX. This initial "spare-no-expense" approach may have helped some companies meet a deadline, but it also established the framework for new internal bureaucracy.

A final, broader criticism waged against SOX is its effect on the competitiveness of U.S. businesses. Many argue that SOX is a major distraction from the core activities of businesses, making them less viable in a global marketplace. Management must spend more time jumping through regulatory hoops and less time innovating. Arguably, SOX also makes it more difficult and costly for technologically innovative companies to raise capital by selling their stock on U.S. exchanges because of the increased regulatory burden. (See Chapter 3 for an explanation of securities registration requirements and stock exchanges.)

New ammunition for aggrieved investors

SOX now gives public companies specific directives as to how financial information offered to the public must be compiled, yet, as Chapter 16 discusses, it stops short of giving investors a right to sue companies privately for failing to meet these standards. Rather, with the exception of SOX Section 306 (dealing with stock trading during pension fund blackout periods), investors must wait for the SEC and Justice Department to bring actions against companies for SOX violations. Investors can't hire their own lawyers to initiate action on their behalf.

Although there's no "private right" to sue directly under SOX, shareholders and litigants are in a much stronger position after SOX than under the old federal and state statutes. Prior to SOX, federal and state laws didn't establish specific standards for corporations in *compiling* the information they fed to the public in their financial reports. In the event that investors were damaged or defrauded, the investors themselves were responsible for persuading judges the information they had received wasn't truthful or accurate, without reference to any specific standards. Aggrieved investors had only an amorphous body of analogous facts from prior court cases to try to convince courts to apply their specific situation. Now plaintiffs may strengthen their claims and arguments by referencing the standards set forth in SOX.

Corporate America after SOX

SOX goes where the federal government has never gone before. Although federal regulation of the sale of securities to protect the public is nothing new, SOX goes beyond simply prohibiting deceptive conduct and misrepresentations — it actually tells public corporations how they must run themselves, and creates a new environment for nonpublic companies and nonprofits.

SOX defines specific duties for employees and board members and dictates the structure of boards of directors. It even tells corporations how they have to conduct their day-to-day operations to prevent theft and misappropriation, requiring them to maintain adequate internal controls. (I talk more about internal controls in Chapter 11.) SOX also elbows out state governments in their traditional roles of governing corporations, making corporate law in the United States much more federalized.

Who Combats Corruption under SOX?

SOX is a multidisciplinary piece of legislation that regulates several professions simultaneously. Board members, auditors, attorneys, management, small business owners, and even rank-and-file employees all have their own statutorily scripted roles to play.

The independent audit board

One of the most significant reforms introduced by SOX is the advent of the independent audit board. SOX requires corporations to have audit committees made up solely of *independent* directors. Board members are considered independent in the sense that they receive no salary or fees from the company other than for services as directors.

The audit committee is responsible for obtaining information from management relevant to the audit and otherwise assisting in the audit process. It's viewed as an important part of a company's internal control because it provides a company presence entirely independent from management and interfaces with the independent auditors (from an outside firm). For more coverage of the audit committee's responsibilities, check out Chapter 7.

Ironically, one firm that would have been able to comply with the SOX director independence requirements *before* the law was passed was Enron. Eighty-six percent of Enron's board was independent. A former dean of the Stanford Business School and professor of accounting chaired its audit committee. Yet when the scandal broke, the professor claimed he didn't understand the audit documentation.

SOX presumes that boards made up of independent directors will look out for shareholders' interests and ask auditors to more carefully review management policies and decisions that can affect profitability. However, in the end, an independent audit committee isn't a panacea and doesn't guarantee objectivity in the audit process. The committee, the board, and the auditors all must rely on the accuracy of the information they get from management and on management to recognize, anticipate, and prevent problems.

SOX regulates the membership composition of boards but doesn't specifically regulate their behavior.

Evolving auditors

Auditors are the traditional arbiters of accurate information within a company. They're the accountants responsible for testing the accounting data gathered from management and from rank-and-file employees. Auditors may be either internal employees of a company or independent auditors working for an outside firm.

Both internal and independent auditors adhere to Generally Accepted Accounting Principles (GAAP). GAAP is a term that refers to the rules established by the Financial Accounting Standards Board, the American Institute of Certified Public Accountants, and the SEC, which is the standard-setting body for publicly traded U.S. companies and the exchanges that list their stock.

GAAP contains a number of provisions designed to ensure auditors' independence, objectivity, and professionalism. An auditor must certify that a company's financial statements are fairly presented in accordance with GAAP and contain no material irregularities that would adversely affect reported results.

Traditionally, auditors have been viewed as pretty trustworthy people. The Enron scandal that led to the demise of the nation's largest independent auditing firm, Arthur Andersen, changed all that. Congress and the public were shocked that one of the world's largest corporations (Enron) could collapse within five months of receiving a clean opinion from its auditors (Andersen). (I talk more about the Enron and Arthur Andersen stories in Chapters 2 and 5.)

At the Enron trials, senior managers testified that the auditors never brought material issues to the managers' attention. The managers claimed that although they had ultimate responsibility for what was included in the financial statements with the SEC, they couldn't know what the auditors didn't tell them or failed to bring to their attention. It also came to light that the so-called independent auditors weren't so independent. In addition to providing audit services, they provided a myriad of highly lucrative consulting, tax, and other support services to Enron, which meant that the audit firm had tremendous financial incentives to stay on good terms with Enron, rather than being vocal about the company's accounting flaws.

Enron wasn't the only scandal that tainted the audit industry. During the Savings and Loan (S&L) crisis of the 1980s, auditors failed to take into account the industry's shift from home loans to riskier real estate ventures and junk bonds. As a result, many S&Ls went bankrupt just months or even weeks after getting clean opinions from their auditors.

To resolve problems associated with self-regulation (which had previously been the norm for the accounting profession), SOX creates the Public Company Accounting Oversight Board (PCAOB), a regulatory oversight board. This board is charged with the enormous responsibilities of setting ethics and conflict of interest standards as well as disciplining accountants and conducting annual reviews of large accounting firms. (For more on the PCAOB, turn to Chapter 6.)

Not only has the accounting profession suffered the loss of the right to regulate itself, but it can no longer market and compete for business in the same way. SOX makes it unlawful for a registered audit firm to provide many types of nonaudit services to its clients that were formally its bread-and-butter. For example, an audit firm can't provide bookkeeping, financial information systems design, appraisal, evaluation, actuarial, or investment services to clients it audits. (However, audit firms can make up some, if not all, of this lost income by performing internal control audits under Section 404 of SOX; see Chapter 12.)

According to a survey of 32 mid-sized companies by the law firm Foley & Lardner, accounting, audit, and legal fees also doubled under Sarbanes-Oxley. The costs of directors' liability insurance skyrocketed from $329,000 to $639,000.

Lawyers' noisy new liability

Incident to its authority to make rules under SOX, the SEC has proposed a controversial *noisy withdrawal* rule for attorneys. The rule would require a lawyer who learns of a corporate client's wrongdoing to alert SEC regulators to the nature of any ongoing fraud before withdrawing from representation. Attorneys who are unable to persuade a corporate client to mend its ways would be required to notify the SEC that they are withdrawing from representation. Not surprisingly, opponents have argued that the rule violates traditional concepts of attorney-client privilege. However, the American Bar Association has taken the position that noisy withdrawal doesn't violate the privilege.

CEOs and CFOs

SOX forces chief executive officers (CEOs) and chief financial officers (CFOs) of corporations to take responsibility and possibly face criminal penalties for earnings misstatements. They're required to certify in writing that the information appearing in the company's report is a fair and accurate representation of the company's financial status and activity.

Not only do criminal penalties apply if officers and directors misstate financial information, but these individuals also can be required to give back their bonuses to compensate the company for the costs of redoing the financial statements. (For more on the consequences officers and directors face for misstatements, check out Chapter 2.) Under SOX, each member of management is expected to certify that he or she runs a clean ship — no excuses.

Small businesses and nonprofits in the headlights

Although SOX was passed to deal with mega-scandals like Enron and WorldCom, it's becoming a catastrophe for American small business. As of this writing, although the wording of the SOX statute technically applies only to publicly traded corporations, it's the benchmark against which every privately held company's financial and corporate governance practices are measured.

Banks and insurance companies report that they now ask small, privately held companies about their internal controls and audit procedures. Failure to answer convincingly can result in more costly credit or higher insurance premiums.

Nonprofits, which can't afford a hint of scandal that may ruin their credibility with donors, are rushing to adopt governance and conflict-of-interest policies in line with SOX.

Start-ups and new ventures are facing increased hurdles as they attempt to "go public" by becoming eligible to list their stock on exchanges.

The rank-and-file

SOX imposes new burdens on rank-and-file employees, often requiring them to adhere more carefully to company procedures or to complete additional documentation to carry out new internal control measures. However, SOX empowers blue-collar and other nonmanagerial employees in other ways:

- ✔ Section 301(4) requires publicly traded companies to collect, retain, and resolve complaints from employees.
- ✔ Section 806 specifically protects whistle-blowers who report violations of law or company policy from suffering retaliation by the company.

New high–paid governance gurus

Nearly every public company has designated specific management or legal personnel responsible for overseeing corporate governance policies. A 2005 survey posted on Salary.com reported compensation for many top global ethics and compliance executives to be approaching $750,000.

A Summary of SOX: Taking It One Title at a Time

The SOX statute is more or less an outline, with full details coming in the form of Securities Exchange Commission (SEC) rules for implementation as well as pronouncements from the newly created Public Company Accounting Oversight Board (PCAOB). Most of SOX's provisions currently apply to public companies that file Form 10-K with the SEC; however, more and more companies are opting for voluntary compliance to insulate themselves from future litigation risks and unforeseen management liabilities.

This section is intended to give you a broad view of what the new law contains and what it requires of today's companies in the United States.

Title 1: Aiming at the audit profession

At its outset, SOX establishes a five-member Public Company Accounting Oversight Board (PCAOB) that lets auditors know what they're supposed to be evaluating and sets rules about the relationships and ties auditors can have with the companies they audit. Title I provides for change in six major areas:

- **The PCAOB:** The SEC oversees the PCAOB, which is funded through fees collected from issuers. The PCAOB (affectionately nicknamed "Peek-a-boo" by many auditors, attorneys, and other professionals) has the following responsibilities:

  - **To oversee the audit of public companies:** The accounting profession used to regulate itself through a voluntary organization known as the American Institute of Certified Public Accountants (AICPA), but Enron proved that the old system didn't work very well.

  - **To establish audit report standards and rules:** Auditors wait avidly for the issue of these standards and rules to clear up confusion and aid them in performing their day-to-day duties after SOX.

  - **To register audit firms:** The PCAOB is in charge of registering, inspecting, investigating, and enforcing compliance of public accounting firms as well as CPAs and other people in the profession. Any public accounting firm that participates in any audit for a company covered by SOX is required to register with the PCAOB.

  Critics have noted the Public Company Accounting Oversight Board would have been more appropriately named the Public Company *Auditing* Oversight Board.

- **Work paper retention:** Title I contains some new administrative requirements for auditors, including a rule that audit firms retain all their work papers for seven years.

- **Two-partner requirement:** Two partners now have to sign off on every audit, as discussed further in Chapter 5.

- **Evaluation of internal control:** Auditors must evaluate whether the companies they audit have internal control structures and procedures that ensure that their financial records accurately reflect transactions and disposition of assets. Auditors must also assess whether the companies appropriately authorize receipts and expenditures and verify that transactions are made only with authorization of senior management. If companies don't have adequate internal controls in place, the auditors must describe any material weaknesses in the internal control structures and document instances of material noncompliance.

> ✔ **Inspections of audit firms:** Auditors must submit to continuing inspections by the PCAOB. Firms that provide audit reports for more than 100 public companies get inspected once a year. Firms that audit fewer than 100 companies get reviewed every three years.

Title I of SOX also empowers the PCAOB to impose disciplinary or remedial sanctions upon audit firms.

Title II: Ensuring auditor independence

Title II of SOX focuses on conflicts of interests arising from close relationships between audit firms and the companies they audit; namely, it prohibits auditors from performing certain nonaudit services to clients they audit. However, SOX allows *audit committees* (internal committees charged with overseeing the audit process within publicly traded companies) to approve some activities for nonaudit services that aren't expressly forbidden by Title II of SOX (see Chapter 7 for more on audit committees and nonaudit services).

To further protect against conflicts of interest, audit partners must be rotated to prevent individuals from getting too close to the companies they audit. Specifically, a partner is prevented from being the lead or reviewing auditor for more then five consecutive years. Also, an auditor faces a one-year prohibition if the company's senior executives were employed by that audit firm during the one-year period preceding the audit initiation date. Title II also requires auditors to report to the audit committee on accounting policies used in the audit and document communications with management.

Title III: Requiring corporate accountability

This section of SOX focuses on the company's responsibility to ensure that the financial statements it distributes to the public are correct. Its two main provisions include:

> ✔ **Establishment of audit committees:** SOX requires each company subject to SOX to form a special audit committee. Each member of the audit committee must be a member of the board of directors but otherwise *independent* in the sense that he or she receives no other salary or fees from the company.

> ✔ **Management certification:** Title III requires CEOs and CFOs to certify:
>> • That periodic financial reports filed with the SEC don't contain untrue statements or material omissions
>>
>> • That financial statements fairly present, in all material respects, the financial conditions and results of operations

- The company's chief executive and chief financial officers are responsible for internal controls, and that the internal controls are designed to ensure that management receives material information regarding the company and any consolidated subsidiaries

- That internal controls have been reviewed within 90 days prior to the report

- Whether there have been any significant changes to the internal controls

Title III also makes it unlawful for corporate personnel to exert improper influence upon an audit for the purpose of rendering financial statements materially misleading.

✔ **Bonuses:** Title III requires a company's CEO and CFO to forfeit certain bonuses and compensation received if the company has to issue corrected financial statements (called *restatements*) due to noncompliance with SEC rules.

✔ **Bans on stock trades during blackout periods:** Title III bans directors and executive officers from trading their public company's stock during pension fund blackout periods. It also obligates attorneys appearing before the SEC to report violations of securities laws and breaches of fiduciary duty by a public company. For the benefit of victims of securities violations, Title III creates a special disgorgement fund that's funded by the fines companies have to pay to the SEC.

Title IV: Establishing financial disclosures, loans, and ethics codes

This section contains several key SOX provisions, including:

✔ **Disclosure of adjustments and off–balance sheet transactions:** Financial reports filed with the SEC must reflect all material corrections to the financial statements made in the course of an audit. Title IV also requires disclosure of all material off–balance sheet transactions and relationships that may have a material effect upon the financial status of an issue.

✔ **Prohibition of personal loans extended by a corporation to its executives:** Such loans are prohibited if they're subject to the insider lending restrictions of the Federal Reserve Act.

✔ **Disclosure of changes to inside stock ownership:** Senior management, directors, and principal stockholders have to disclose changes in their ownership of corporate stock within two business days of making the transaction.

✔ **Internal control certification:** The now-famous Section 404 provides that annual reports filed with the SEC must include an internal control report stating that management is responsible for the internal control structure and procedures for financial reporting. The report should also state that management assesses the effectiveness of the internal controls for the previous fiscal year.

✔ **Code of ethics:** Companies subject to SOX must disclose whether they have adopted a code of ethics for their senior financial officers and whether their audit committees have at least one member who is a financial expert. (For more on the financial expert requirement, flip to Chapter 7.)

✔ **Regular SEC review:** Article IV requires regular SEC reviews of the disclosure documents companies file each year with the SEC.

Title V: Protecting analyst integrity

This section of SOX is aimed at preventing several types of conflicts of interest; among other things, it restricts the ability of investment bankers to preapprove research reports and ensures that research analysts aren't supervised by persons involved in investment banking activities. Title V prohibits employer retaliation against analysts who write negative reports, and it requires specific conflict of interest disclosures by research analysts who make information available to the public.

Title VI: Doling out more money and authority

This section authorizes the SEC to spend at least $98 million to hire at least 200 qualified professionals to oversee auditors and audit firms.

Title VI also gives the SEC the authority to

✔ Censure persons appearing or practicing before it for unethical or improper professional conduct. Title VI also directs federal courts to prohibit persons from participating in small (penny) stock offerings if the SEC initiates proceedings against them.

✔ Consider orders of state securities commissions when deciding whether to limit the activities, functions, or operations of brokers or dealers.

Title VII: Supporting studies and reports

This section of SOX funds and authorizes a number of reports and studies that, for example,

- ✔ Look at factors leading to the consolidation of public accounting firms and its impact on capital formation and securities markets.
- ✔ Address the role of credit-rating agencies in the securities markets.
- ✔ Examine whether investment banks and financial advisors assisted public companies in earnings manipulation and obfuscation of financial conditions.

Title VIII: Addressing criminal fraud and whistle-blower provisions

Title VIII imposes criminal penalties (maximum 10 years in prison) for knowingly destroying, altering, concealing, or falsifying records with intent to obstruct or influence a federal investigation or bankruptcy matter. It also imposes sanctions on auditors who fail to maintain for a five-year period all audit or review work papers pertaining to securities issuers. It makes certain debts incurred in violation of securities fraud laws nondischargeable in bankruptcy.

Title VIII also extends the statute of limitations for private individuals to sue for securities fraud violation. Individuals can sue no later than two years after the violation is discovered or five years after the date of the violation.

Finally, Title VIII provides whistle-blower protection by prohibiting a publicly traded company from retaliating against an employee who assists in a fraud investigation; executives who target whistle-blowers are subject to fines or imprisonment of up to 25 years. (For more on the whistle-blower provision, check out Chapter 16.)

Title IX: Setting penalties for white-collar crime

This section increases penalties for mail and wire fraud from 5 to 20 years in prison and penalties for violations of the Employee Retirement Income Security Act of 1974 to up to $500,000 and 10 years in prison.

In particular, Title IX establishes criminal liability for corporate officers who fail to certify financial reports, including maximum imprisonment of 10 years for knowing that the periodic report doesn't comply with SOX and 20 years imprisonment for willfully certifying a statement known to be noncompliant.

Title X: Signing corporate tax returns

This section of SOX expresses that a corporation's federal income tax return "should" be signed by its chief executive officer.

Title XI: Enforcing payment freezes, blacklists, and prison terms

Title XI adds to the criminal penalties aimed at fraud that are established by SOX's other sections. This section amends federal criminal law to establish a maximum 20-year prison term for tampering with a record or otherwise impeding an official proceeding. It also authorizes the SEC to seek a temporary injunction to freeze "extraordinary payments" to corporate management or employees under investigation for possible violations of securities law. Currently, there's no specific definition as to what constitutes an "extraordinary payment." However, Chapter 16 discusses some interesting litigation in this area (particularly the Gemstar case). This section also prohibits persons who violate state or federal laws governing manipulative, deceptive devices and fraudulent interstate transactions from serving as officers or directors of publicly traded corporations.

Finally, Title XI increases penalties for violations of the Securities Exchange Act of 1934 to up to $25 million dollars and up to 20 years in prison.

Some Things SOX Doesn't Say: SOX Myths

Although SOX costs corporations billions of dollars and diverts massive resources from production and profit-generating activities, it's not all bad. In fact, there are things it doesn't require; this section puts to rest four common SOX myths.

Myth #1: Auditors can't provide tax services

SOX doesn't segregate to absurd extremes the services accountants can provide to companies. For example, in passing SOX, Congress recognized that in many cases it's practical and cost-efficient for audit firms to prepare tax returns.

Although SOX precludes auditors from providing certain services to their clients to prevent Enron-type conflicts of interest, the legislation doesn't ban tax preparation services outright. Rather, the company's audit committee is charged with the responsibility of determining who provides tax services. However, some caveats must be considered in each case; for example, SOX's ban on software consulting may sound a death knell for audit firms that sell tax software to their audit clients and provide consulting services to support it.

Myth #2: Internal control means data security

Internal control refers to financial controls that impact financial statements, not data security. SOX doesn't specifically spell out any data security requirements for companies. Other legislation, such as the Health Insurance Portability and Accountability Act of 1996 (HIPAA), has rules about data security, but SOX is silent on things like password protection and encryption standards. This myth likely results (at least in part) from SOX's emphasis on internal control, which is a term sometimes used by information technology professionals.

Myth #3: The company isn't responsible for functions it outsources

Not true. Under SOX Section 404, it doesn't matter whether you outsource a system, process, or control or handle it internally — if it impacts the financial statements, the reporting company is on the line. This means you may have to directly test the controls at your outside service providers. Or, in some circumstances, you may be able to get a special type of report called an SAS 70 (type 2) from the service provider; this report documents the effectiveness of the provider's internal controls. (For more on the SAS 70 report, flip to Chapter 13.)

Myth #4: My company met the deadline for Section 404 first-year compliance. We're home free!

Sorry, 404 certification is an annual event. And when it comes to Section 404 compliance, a corporation is never "done." Compliance is a continual and ongoing process. Your systems must evolve as the company evolves, and so must the tests that are performed on those systems.

Chapter 2

SOX in Sixty Seconds

....

In This Chapter

▶ Reviewing the events that led up to SOX

▶ Identifying the abuses SOX is supposed to remedy

▶ Evaluating the key provisions of SOX

▶ Speculating on the future interpretation of some sections

....

*U*nquestionably, corporate America had a major case of "the uglies" as the calendar turned on the new millennium. Long-buried losses, financial shell games, corrupt practices, and secret self-dealings were suddenly thrust into the light of day and became front-page news.

The Sarbanes-Oxley Act, or SOX, was signed into law by President Bush on July 30, 2002, and passed through Congress on a wave of bipartisan support. The implications of SOX are staggering, and it will be years before they're fully understood.

This chapter takes a look at some of the biggest bankruptcies of the Enron era. It also covers what legislators were hoping to accomplish with SOX, points out the blatant conflicts that SOX is supposed to clarify, and explains the rationale behind key elements of the statute.

The Pre-SOX Scandals

SOX raises — and attempts to answer — more questions about companies than were ever considered before: Are there adequate financial controls and processes? Are there off–balance sheet transactions that don't make it onto the financials the public relies on? Are there any shake-ups in management or ethical lapses that signal a tenuous future?

Enron events everyone overlooked

Major credit reporting agencies failed to identify the events leading up to the collapse of Enron, which was at the time the largest bankruptcy in history. Moody's Investors' Service, Standard & Poor's Corporation, and Fitch Rating Services all gave Enron good credit ratings a mere two and a half months prior to Enron filing Chapter 11. (The story of Enron's demise is discussed in detail in the sidebar "A brief chronology of the Enron collapse.")

The key omens that foreshadowed Enron's implosion, which SOX reporting standards now address, include:

- ✓ **Successive resignations of key management:** On August 14, 2001, CEO Jeff Skilling resigned after being in the position only six months. On October 16, 2001, coinciding with a huge restatement of third-quarter earnings, Enron announced that its CFO, Andrew Fastow, would also be replaced. SOX now requires corporations to report changes in management on Form 8-K within four days after they occur (as discussed in Chapter 2).

  Prior to SOX, changes in key management weren't required to be announced to the public, nor did they justify scrutiny by the SEC.

- ✓ **Inaccurate and unreliable financial statements:** On October 16, 2001, Enron announced third-quarter earnings that reflected an unexpected $544,000 earnings change and a $1.2 million change in stockholders' equity. On November 8, 2001, Enron further announced that it needed to restate its financial statements for the first and second quarters of 2001 and for the four years prior, 1997 through 2000. The grand total of over-stated income was $586 million. Several sections of SOX now place responsibility on management and auditors for the accuracy of information used to prepare the financial statements. (See Chapters 5 and 10 for a discussion of these provisions.)

- ✓ **CEO stock sales during a blackout period:** During the period from October 29 to November 12, 2001, Enron employees were prohibited from selling the plummeting Enron stock in their 401(k) plans. (The average employee retirement had 63 percent invested in Enron stock.) During this period, CEO Ken Lay sold most of his company stock. SOX prohibits preferential treatment of management during blackout periods.

- ✓ **Nondisclosure of earlier CEO stock sales:** In addition to selling stock during a blackout period, CEO Ken Lay also reportedly sold large amounts of Enron stock earlier in 2001. At the time, SEC requirements didn't technically require the reporting of these sales. (Chapter 2 explains the new post-SOX reporting requirements for such provisions.)

- ✓ **Off–balance sheet transactions to hide losses:** A big factor in Enron's eventual collapse was the use of so-called *special purpose entities,* which were separate companies set up to hide Enron losses on their own financial statements. This arrangement ensured that the losses didn't see the light of day on Enron's books. (Off–balance sheet transactions are explained in Chapter 8.)

Essentially, Enron got banks to advance funds to off–balance sheet entities non-recourse to Enron, which meant Enron could not be held liable for the debt, and therefore it did not have to be disclosed on the Enron's financial statements. Instead, the debt was collateralized by shares of appreciating Enron stock. The deal unraveled when the shares began declining in value. Then, to placate the banks, Enron began to guarantee the debt. However, since Enron hadn't reported this obligation previously, the financials were deemed fraudulent.

✔ **Document destruction:** On January 10, 2002, Enron's audit firm, Arthur Andersen, admitted to Congress that it had destroyed or shredded an undisclosed number of documents related to Enron's use of special purpose entities to hide losses and related matters. At the time, no one within Andersen questioned or took steps to stop the shredding.

✔ **Rigging the ratings:** During the congressional hearings, it was revealed that Enron had contacted the agencies responsible for maintaining its credit rating to persuade them to alter their ratings. The rapidly declining Enron retained its investment grade rating up until three weeks before it filed for Chapter 11 bankruptcy protection. SOX Section 501 now provides stronger conflict-of-interest rules that prohibit companies from retaliating if they're adversely reviewed.

A brief chronology of the Enron collapse

Prior to filing bankruptcy in late 2001, Enron had revenues of around $101 billion and was one of the world's largest energy companies, providing electricity and natural gas. The company branched out into financial and risk management service. *Fortune* magazine had named Enron "America's Most Innovative Company" for six previous consecutive years.

Many experts attribute the initial financial troubles of Enron to its launch of EnronOnline. EnronOnline was an innovative Web-based transaction system that allowed selling and trading of commodities products (such as gas and electricity) online. However, the system was neither profitable nor attractive to customers. The online encyclopedia Wikipedia (at www.wikipedia.com) surmises that due to

"the giant cash needs of EnronOnline and the company wasting money in other areas such as broadband, Azurix, Enron Energy Services, and shutting down the original pipeline service which generated cash flow, Enron virtually drained itself of cash." As a result, Wikipedia concludes, "The Enron Global Finance department had to keep working up more and more creative financing moves to keep the company up and running."

During 2001, the company became tainted by corporate scandal. Enron shares fell from over $90 per share to about 30 cents per share.

The following are some key events chronicling the roles of Enron management in the energy giant's rise and fall:

(continued)

(continued)

1997: Chief Financial Officer Andrew Fastow creates the first in a series of partnerships, which are established for the purpose of keeping debt from showing up Enron's balance sheet.

August 2000: Enron shares reach their peak price of $90.

December 2000: Enron announces Jeffrey Skilling is appointed CEO. Skilling resigns after six months.

August 2001: Founder of Enron, Kenneth Lay, is named CEO of Enron (for the second time). Finance executive Sherron Watkins meets with Ken Lay after submitting an anonymous memo saying, "I am incredibly nervous that we will implode in a wave of accounting scandals." Watkins later becomes a role model for corporate whistle-blowers and ethicists.

October 2001: Enron reports a $638 million third-quarter loss and discloses a $1.2 billion reduction in shareholder equity, mostly due to the partnerships run by Fastow to hide debt. Fastow is fired.

November 2001: Enron files documents with the SEC revising its financial statements for the last five years to reflect previously undisclosed losses of $586 million.

December 2001: Enron files for bankruptcy protection and lays off thousands of workers.

January 2002: The Justice Department announces it's conducting a criminal investigation of Enron. Lay resigns as chairman and CEO of Enron and several weeks later resigns from the board of directors.

March 2002: Enron's audit firm, Arthur Andersen LLP, is indicted for destroying Enron-related documents.

June 15, 2002: Andersen is convicted of obstruction of justice and fined the maximum amount allowed by statute, which is $500,000.

August 21, 2002: Michael Kopper, a former top aide to Fastow, strikes a deal with prosecutors. He pleads guilty to money laundering and conspiracy and identifies a web of partnerships designed to make Enron appear profitable and to financially benefit Fastow and other Enron management.

October 2002: Fastow is indicted for 78 charges of conspiracy, money laundering, and various types of fraud.

May 2003: Andrew Fastow's wife Lea is charged with participating in some of her husband's deals.

September 2003: Former Enron treasurer Ben Glisan Jr. strikes his deal with prosecutors. He receives a five-year sentence for one count of conspiracy to commit securities and wire fraud, and he agrees to cooperate with prosecutors.

January 2004: Fastow pleads guilty to conspiracy, receives a ten-year sentence, and agrees to help the prosecution.

February 2004: A 42-count indictment charges former CEO Jeffrey Skilling with 35 counts of conspiracy, fraud, and insider trading.

July 2004: Enron CEO Kenneth Lay is indicted for participating in a conspiracy to manipulate Enron's quarterly financial results, making false statements about Enron's financial performance and omitting facts necessary to make financial statements accurate and fair. Lay pleads innocent.

More tales from the corporate tabloids

When a public company's stock plummets because of a scandal, the event has a distinctly human element. Employees of that corporation and members of the public at large may have invested substantial retirement funds and life savings in the stock, and the betrayal of the public trust fuels an outrage that transcends partisan politics. Ultimately, it's the kind of event that made possible the rapid and near unanimous passage of SOX in 2002.

This section touches on a few headline stories that came after Enron's collapse and prompted Congress and the SEC to unite in legislative and rule-making initiatives in order to calm the public.

Global Crossing

Just three months after the Enron scandal, Global Crossing, Ltd, a high-speed Internet company, also filed bankruptcy in the largest filing ever by a telecommunications company. The company concealed its ailing financial condition by swapping fiber-optic network capacity with other companies and deluded the public by improperly recognizing the revenue. Also, Global Crossing chairman Gary Winnick reportedly reaped $734 million from the sale of his company stock before it became virtually worthless.

WorldCom

On July 25, 2002, the second largest long-distance and Internet carrier in the country became the subject of an accounting scandal. An SEC investigation disclosed that WorldCom had overstated its earnings by $3.8 billion. The SEC called the revelation one of the largest cases of "false bookkeeping ever" and lamented its "unprecedented magnitude."

The House Financial Services Committee immediately called for pubic hearings into the matter. However, WorldCom CEO Bernard Ebbers and other key management enraged the public by invoking the Fifth Amendment protection against self-incrimination and refusing to testify. WorldCom had loaned Ebbers over $366 million and even issued loan guarantees to cover his potential losses in WorldCom stock!

Tyco

In 2002, Tyco International, Ltd. became embroiled in a controversy about millions of dollars in questionable bonuses, loans, and other payments to its CFO, CEO, and others. In one instance, Tyco paid an outside director $10 million and paid $10 million to the director's charity.

Socking it to the spouse

In one of the more interesting legal maneuvers employed under SOX, the Justice Department indicted Lea Fastow, the wife of Enron CFO Andrew Fastow. The charges were seen by many as an attempt to pressure her husband to cooperate with investigators. Andrew Fastow ultimately pleaded guilty to two conspiracy charges in exchange for ten years in prison.

Lea Fastow was originally charged with six tax felonies emanating from her knowledge of her husband's activities at Enron and for disguising money from an Enron side deal as gifts. She planned to plead guilty to one felony, but changed her plea when the presiding judge refused to accept a five-month prison deal prosecutors recommended in the plea bargain.

The judge who sentenced Lea Fastow admitted she was a prime candidate for a less restrictive minimum-security camp but refused to allow her to serve her sentence under the usual conditions given to other first-time tax offenders but did not publicly state why.

In the Tyco case, the public accounting firm PricewaterhouseCoopers was on the hot seat. As Tyco's auditors, the firm had to answer questions about whether its audit had disclosed such bonuses and why the auditors had signed off on them.

Adelphia

On March 27, 2002, Adelphia Communications Corporation, the nation's sixth largest cable television company, disclosed the existence of $2.3 billion in off–balance sheet transactions. The Rigas family, which had founded Adelphia and taken it public, controlled the corporation and had co-borrowed the $2.3 billion debt and couldn't provide much detail about the transactions to the SEC. The company's founder, John Rigas, and his two sons were eventually convicted of defrauding the company of over $1 million. John was sentenced to 15 years in jail, while his son, Tim, received a 20-year sentence. Additionally, the Rigas family was ordered to turn over most of their assets, estimated to be about $1.5 billion, to a "disgorgement fund" to help compensate defrauded investors.

Adelphia stock plummeted 33 percent in May 2002, when Adelphia announced to a scandal-sensitive public that it was delaying its 10-K filing and restating its earnings.

Four Squeaky Clean SOX Objectives

In the months subsequent to the Enron collapse, no less than two dozen SOX-related bills were proposed in Congress. The SEC issued a comprehensive response during a February 2002 press release, and President Bush announced his own "ten-point plan." The following objectives emerged from the extensive testimony, press conferences, and thick packets of proposed legislation and protracted hearings that ensued:

- ✔ **Make management accountable.** Several provisions of SOX seek to ensure that management, accountants, and attorneys are held directly accountable for information that makes it onto a company's financial statements on their watches.

- ✔ **Enhance disclosure.** SOX's provisions address the fact that several key events and relatively shocking transactions having to do with corporate scandal escaped scrutiny simply because they weren't required to be disclosed to the public.

- ✔ **Conduct regular reviews by the SEC.** SOX requires the SEC to look at companies more often and more closely, a reaction to the SEC's declining to review Enron's records for several years preceding its bankruptcy filing and consequential loss to investors.

- ✔ **Make accountants accountable.** SOX seeks to purge the accounting industry of the conflicts of interest, financial self-dealing, and plain-old poor judgment that placed the investing public at risk when relying on "certified" financial statements.

How SOX Protects the Investing Public

It used to be that corporations were fixated on reporting results and the investing public was obsessed with reading them. Prior to SOX, the general view was that if companies provided regular financial statements, the public could simply examine them and make informed investment decisions. However, when Enron and WorldCom and other companies' financial statements had to be restated because they were off by millions, the public felt they had been duped. Congress and the SEC decided that requiring regularly filed financial statements wasn't enough to protect the public. There needed to be much stricter regulation as to how information included on the financial statements was compiled.

Because reporting problems can trigger serious and tragic consequences for investors, SOX focuses both on how companies arrive at the results they report and the reliability and credibility of the reporting process. It also holds management, directors, attorneys, and auditors accountable for the end product. This section breaks down those objectives, further explaining the different sections of SOX.

Creating a Public Company Accounting Oversight Board

One of the key components of the Enron crisis was the demise of the nation's largest public accounting firm, Arthur Andersen. In response to perceived lapses in judgment and objectivity of the accounting profession as a whole, SOX establishes a Public Company Accounting Oversight Board (PCAOB), which I discuss in Chapter 6. The PCAOB is charged with the following tasks:

- Register public accounting firms
- Make rules for "auditing, quality control, ethics, independence, and other standards relating to the preparation of audit reports for issuers"
- Conduct inspections of accounting firms
- Perform investigations and disciplinary proceedings and impose appropriate sanctions on firms that violate the rules established for their conduct
- Enforce compliance with SOX professional standards, securities laws, and other board rules
- Set the board's budget and manage its staff
- Perform such other duties or functions as necessary or appropriate

Under SOX, the board is required to have five full-time, financially-literate members who are appointed for five-year terms. Two of the members must be or must have been CPAs, and the remaining three must not be CPAs. The chair of the board can be a CPA but cannot have practiced as one in the prior five years.

Clamping down on auditors

An *audit* isn't necessarily an adversarial process, but it's supposed to be an objective one. An audit is a process of verifying information and identifying information that isn't consistent with Generally Accepted Auditing Standards, or GAAS (see Chapter 5). One purpose of an audit is so that accountants can *certify* financial statements that are prepared in accordance with Generally Accepted Accounting Principles (GAAP); certification assures anyone who reviews them that the statements are GAAP-compliant.

SOX addresses the issue of auditors becoming too chummy with the clients they're auditing. Accounting firms, like any service company, have a financial incentive to cater to clients that pay their fees. A tense audit could strain the client relationship and result in the accounting firm getting fired. This conflict of interest is exacerbated if the accounting firm provides other lucrative services to the client besides the audit.

Accordingly, SOX Section 201 limits the scope of services that can be performed by auditors (see Chapter 5 for coverage of prohibited services). SOX provides that it's unlawful for a registered public accounting firm to provide any nonaudit service to an issuer contemporaneously with the audit, including:

- ✔ Bookkeeping or other services related to the accounting records or financial statements of the audit client

- ✔ Financial information systems design and implementation

- ✔ Appraisal or valuation services, fairness opinions, or contribution-in-kind reports

- ✔ Actuarial services

- ✔ Internal audit outsourcing services

- ✔ Management or human resources functions

- ✔ Broker, dealer, investment advisor, or investment banking services

- ✔ Legal and expert services unrelated to the audit

- ✔ Any service that the board determines, by regulation, is impermissible

SOX does allow accounting firms to perform services that aren't included in the above list. For example, accountants traditionally perform tax return preparation services. (See Chapter 1 for more about the myth about auditors and tax services.)

Rotating auditors

SOX presumes that an auditor's long-time familiarity with a company compromises the quality of an audit rather than makes the process more efficient each year. SOX presumes that auditors lose their objectivity when they develop a close and comfortable relationship with the client. Accordingly, SOX Section 203 provides that the lead and concurring audit partners must rotate off the audit every five years

Creating committees inside companies

SOX creates a new class of worker bees within public companies. Section 301 requires that public companies, which are listed with the national securities exchanges and associations, form *audit committees.* These audit committees are responsible for working with the independent auditors and getting them the information they need, as well as for establishing procedures on related issues such as record retention and hearing complaints.

Each member of the audit committee must be a member of the board of directors of the issuer and must be independent. Accountants and attorneys are prime prospects for board membership. Also, audit committee members can receive compensation for serving on the committee.

The audit committee of an issuer is "directly responsible" for the appointment, compensation, and oversight of the work of any registered public accounting firm hired by the company to audit its financial statements. It's also the audit committee's job to establish procedures for the "receipt, retention, and treatment of complaints" received by the issuer regarding accounting, internal controls, and auditing concerns.

SOX requires that companies pay the costs of audit committees and give them the authority to hire independent counsel or other advisors to carry out committee functions.

Making management accountable

CEOs and CFOs are likely to be much more proactive in making sure their companies' financial statements are accurate now that they have to personally vouch for the statements and risk doing time if they're not accurate.

SOX Section 302 provides that CEOs and CFOs must personally certify the "appropriateness of the financial statements and disclosures contained in the periodic report, and that those financial statements and disclosures fairly present, in all material respects, the operations and financial condition of the issuer." A violation of this section must be knowing and intentional to give rise to liability.

In addition, Section 302 requires that the CEO and CFO disclose all significant deficiencies and material weaknesses in controls over financial reporting to both the independent accountants and the audit committee. Disclosure prevents management from taking a passive attitude toward serious weaknesses.

SOX also suggests — but doesn't require — that a corporation's federal income tax return be signed by the CFO of the corporation in order to emphasize its accuracy.

SOX Section 303 now specifically provides that it is "unlawful" for any officer or director of an issuer to take any action to fraudulently influence, coerce, manipulate, or mislead any auditor engaged in the performance of an audit for the purpose of rendering the financial statements materially misleading. (How could anyone ever think this type of thing was *lawful?*)

Taking back bogus bonuses

CEOs and CFOs may be required to give back their bonuses if financial statements have to be restated (changed) after an audit due to "material noncompliance" with financial reporting requirements due to fraudulent activity. SOX Section 304 provides that CEOs and CFOs must "reimburse the issuer for any bonus or other incentive-based or equity-based compensation received" during the 12 months following the issuance or filing of the noncompliant document and "any profits realized from the sale of securities of the issuer" during that period.

Banning blackouts

SOX Section 306 prohibits officers and directors from pulling "a Fastow." Officers, directors, and other insiders aren't allowed to sell their stock during blackout periods, as Kenneth Lay did during Enron's blackout period when its stock plummeted more than $5 per share.

Any profits resulting from sales in violation of this Section are recoverable by the issuing company. If the company fails to sue under this provision, a suit can be initiated by "the owner of any security of the issuer," meaning any shareholder.

SOX Section 306 is the only section of the statute that shareholders may use to sue a company directly on their own behalf. Under other sections of SOX, only the SEC may initiate a lawsuit against a company.

Ratcheting up reporting

Federal securities law is based on the premise that investors in a public company have a right to know the facts and circumstances that would reasonably and fairly influence their decisions to invest in the company.

SOX attempts to ensure that investors are fairly well-informed by adding the following provisions to existing law:

- **Reflection of accounting adjustments:** SOX Section 401(a) requires that companies' financial reports "reflect all material correcting adjustments . . . that have been identified by a registered accounting firm."

- **Disclosure of off–balance sheet transactions:** SOX requires that a company's annual and quarterly financial reports disclose all material off–balance sheet transactions and other relationships with "unconsolidated entities" that may have a material current or future effect on the company's financial condition. Chapter 4 contains more coverage of off–balance sheet transactions.

✔ **Real-time reporting of key events:** Companies need to disclose information on material changes in their financial conditions or operations on a rapid and current basis on Form 8-K reports (see Chapter 3).

Purging company conflicts of interest

Under SOX, auditors cannot accept jobs with their clients until they have taken off a complete audit cycle. This restriction makes sense because an auditor may otherwise hesitate to alienate a prospective employer.

Under SOX Section 206, CEOs, controllers, CFOs, chief accounting officers, and persons in equivalent positions can't have been employed by the company's audit firm during the one-year period preceding the audit.

It's also unlawful under SOX Section 402(a) for a company to lend money to any director or executive officer. Under Section 403, directors, officers, and 10-percent owners must report designated transactions by the end of the second business day following the transaction so that the public can follow what the "insiders" are doing.

Exercising internal control

The dreaded SOX Section 404 requires that companies include in their Form 10-K annual reports an *internal control report* that states:

✔ Management's responsibility for establishing and maintaining an adequate internal control structure and procedures for financial reporting.

✔ Management's assessment of the effectiveness of the internal control structure and procedures of the issuer for financial reporting. The assessment must include disclosure of any identified "material weakness" in the company's internal control over financial reporting existing at the company's fiscal year-end.

✔ The framework used by management to evaluate the effectiveness of their controls.

✔ That the company's auditor has attested to the adequacy of management's assessment and the company's internal control over financial reporting.

Chapter 11 covers these requirements of Section 404 in-depth.

Looking at lawyers

SOX was one scandal in which lawyers weren't directly implicated — no high-profile ones went to jail or had to do the perp walk on the 6 o'clock news, but that doesn't mean they emerged unscathed. SOX increases the level of regulation, which applies to them as well.

Section 602(d) establishes rules setting minimum standards for professional conduct for attorneys practicing before the SEC.

Waiting seven years to shred

Under SOX Section 802(a), it's a felony to knowingly destroy or create documents to "impede, obstruct, or influence" any existing or contemplated federal investigation. This is a SOX section that impacts the criminal provisions of the law and thus impacts all organizations, not just public companies.

Auditors are required to maintain "all audit or review work papers" for seven years from the dates their reports are issued.

Putting bad management behind bars

SOX subjects white-collar criminals to the same tough-sentencing trends that have been imposed on other types of criminals for some time. It also enhances some existing penalties, such as increasing maximum penalties for mail and wire fraud from five to ten years.

Criminal penalties including fines up to $5 million and prison terms of up to 20 years for securities fraud are imposed for the following:

- ✔ It's a crime under SOX to tamper with a record or otherwise impede an "official proceeding" (that is, to shred documents).

- ✔ Individuals who misstate financial statements filed with the SEC can expect maximum penalties for "willful" violations.

- ✔ Sections of SOX impose prison time of up to 20 years and fines for persons who corruptly alter, destroy, mutilate, or conceal any document with the intent to impair the object's integrity or availability.

SOX extends the statute of limitations on civil fraud claims to the earlier of five years from the fraud, or two years after the fraud was discovered. (Prior to that it was three years from the fraud or one year from discovery.)

Freezing bonuses

The SEC is authorized to freeze an extraordinary payment to any director, officer, partner, controlling person, agent, or employee of a company during an investigation of possible violations of securities laws.

Blackballing officers and directors

The SEC may issue an order to prohibit, conditionally or unconditionally, permanently or temporarily, any person who has committed securities fraud (specifically, violated Section 10(b) of the Securities and Exchange Act of 1934) from acting as an officer or director of a public company if the SEC has found that his or her conduct "demonstrates unfitness" to serve as an officer or director.

Providing whistle-blower protection

Whistle-blowers are employees who report information about corporate fraud or mismanagement. Under SOX, employees of issuers and accounting firms are extended *whistle-blower protection.* These protections prohibit employers from taking certain actions against employees who disclose information to, among others, parties in a judicial proceeding involving a fraud claim. Whistle-blowers are also granted a remedy of special damages and attorney's fees. (For more on whistle-blowers, check out Chapter 16.)

Rapid Rulemaking Regrets

With the passage of SOX, Congress required the SEC to make substantive rules to be enforced by the agency in 19 major areas. This requirement meant that there was an abbreviated period for both public commentary and the drafting process itself. Undoubtedly, many aspects of these rules will be subject to interpretation or revision as enforcement efforts unfold.

Chapter 3

SOX and Securities Regulations

● ●

In This Chapter

▶ Summarizing 70 years of securities law

▶ Figuring out which companies must comply with SOX

▶ Understanding why private companies should "SOX-ify"

▶ Complying with enhanced reporting requirements under SOX

▶ Surveying the SEC's review procedures

● ●

*T*he Sarbanes-Oxley Act, or SOX, passed in 2002 is the most far-reaching attempt to protect investors since Franklin Delano Roosevelt's 1933 Securities Act following the Great Depression. Like the New Deal securities laws of the 1930s, SOX comes on the heels of widespread disillusionment about corporate integrity. It signals a new era in the relationship among business, government, and the investing public.

SOX isn't a stand-alone piece of legislation: It's part of the complex tapestry of federal securities regulations and statutes that have been carefully woven by Congress over the last seven decades.

This chapter gives you an overview of securities law and the important historical context of SOX. Understanding the objectives of securities law and how SOX serves those objectives can help you better understand your company's current reporting obligations and prepare for future legislative trends.

Pre-SOX Securities Laws

To develop a sound SOX strategy for your company, you need to be aware of the securities laws that define the legal context of SOX and are altered by its provisions. SOX amends many of the securities laws discussed in this section.

Disclosure and merit at the state level

It's important to understand that the 1933 Act has always been exclusively based on disclosure and not merit. As one federal judge aptly put it, any company has the right to offer and investors to buy any "hair-brained investment scheme" as long as it's accurately described. According to Richard Kranitz, a securities attorney with over 30 years of experience, "State merit review laws have generally been repealed because voters over time recognized that regulators were no better than investors at picking winning stocks."

The federal National Securities Markets Improvements Act (NSMIA), passed in 1996, encourages the elimination of merit review, and now only a few states still have those rules in effect. The NSMIA preempted state regulation of national offerings but preserved the role of states in prosecuting fraud cases.

In the 1930s, the idea of laws to protect the investing public took hold among a hardworking generation that had known the devastation of a stock market crash. Just prior to his 1932 reelection bid, President Franklin Delano Roosevelt assigned a former Federal Trade Commissioner, Huston Thompson, the task of drafting a securities law proposal to woo a depression-dazed electorate on the campaign trail.

Mr. Huston and the committee that convened to review his draft were faced with an early dilemma: Should the role of government be to protect the public from poor investments (a *merit system*) or to simply to make sure that the public had enough information to evaluate investments on their own (a *disclosure system*)? In the end, the draft legislation opted for the disclosure approach, which is still used today. (For more on the disclosure system, see the sidebar "Disclosure and merit at the state level.")

The laws that ultimately emerged from Mr. Huston's draft are the Securities Act of 1933 (also known as the 1933 Act) and the Securities Exchange Act of 1934 (also known as the 1934 Act). Decades after their drafting, these two statutes remain the backbone of the federal securities regulation system. The objective of these laws goes beyond simply ensuring companies fill out the right forms; the disclosures required are designed to provide all the information necessary for an investor to determine the true value of an investment offered to the public.

SOX is an attempt to modernize existing securities laws to ensure that they continue to meet the statutes' objective in the 21st century. The premise of federal securities law, then and now, is that government plays an important role in protecting the investing public from shaky securities.

The Securities Act of 1933: Arming investors with information

The Securities Act of 1933 is sometimes referred to as the "truth in securities" law because it requires that investors receive adequate and thorough financial information about significant aspects of securities being offered for public sale. It expressly prohibits deceit, misrepresentation, and other fraud in the sale of securities. The 1933 Act contains a detailed registration process that companies must comply with before they can offer securities to the public. The burden and expense of completing the forms is the responsibility of the registering company, which is referred to as *the issuer.*

The Securities and Exchange Commission (SEC) examines all registration documents for compliance with the 1933 Act. If the SEC determines information is missing or inaccurate, the issuer may be denied registration and the right to sell its securities in the United States. (Section 5(a) of the 1933 Act provides that it's "unlawful" to offer to sell a security to the public unless a registration statement is in effect.)

Companies undergoing the registration process are required to provide information about:

- ✔ The company's properties and business
- ✔ The types of securities to be offered for sale, as in stocks, bonds, shares indentures, partnership interests, and so on
- ✔ Background on the management of the company

The registration statement must also include financial statements certified by independent accountants. (The requirements for audited financial statements for these statements are discussed more fully in Chapter 4.)

In order to comply with disclosure requirements, companies generally distribute a document called a *prospectus* to potential investors. The content of the prospectus is governed by the 1933 Act, which provides that "a prospectus shall contain the information contained in the registration statement." This instruction is somewhat misleading because companies usually create these documents in reverse — drafting a prospectus prior to preparing a registration statement and then including a copy of the prospectus in the registration statement filing.

The Securities Exchange Act of 1934: Establishing the SEC

Although the 1933 Act set ambitious goals and standards for disclosure (see the preceding section), it was silent on the practical aspect of enforcement. To plug this hole, Congress passed the Securities Exchange Act of 1934, which established the Securities and Exchange Commission (SEC) to implement the 1933 Act.

Overview of the 1934 Act

The 1934 Act established the ground rules under which the purchasers of securities may resell and trade shares by:

- ✓ Requiring sellers of securities to register as broker dealers
- ✓ Creating regulated securities exchanges
- ✓ Defining the duties of companies whose securities are traded among investors

In effect, the 1934 Act requires a company to make certain information available to the public so that company shareholders may resell their stock to members of the general public.

Half of all securities sold in the U.S. are private placement offerings, which are not subject to registration under the 1933 Act but are subject to the civil liability and anti-fraud provisions of the 1934 Act. (For more information about private placements, see the sidebar "Keeping offerings private under Regulation D.")

Powers given to the SEC

Under the 1934 Act, the SEC has the power to register, regulate, and oversee brokerage firms, transfer agents, and clearing agencies as well as the nation's securities stock exchanges.

Periodic reporting requirements under the 1934 Act require full disclosure of facts subsequent to filing that are material or significant enough to affect investors' decision-making processes. The 1934 Act also identifies and prohibits certain types of conduct in the markets, such as insider trading and market manipulation, and provides the SEC with disciplinary powers over regulated entities and persons associated with them.

The SEC's rulemaking authority for SOX

The 1934 Act gives the SEC the authority to supplement securities laws by making its own rules for carrying them out. The SEC passes its own regulations, which have the same force, effect, and authority as laws passed by Congress.

Keeping offerings private under Regulation D

The term *private placement* refers to the offer and sale of any security by a brokerage firm to certain investors but not to the general public.

Private offerings are "exempt from registration under the 1933 Act, subject to specific exemptions contained in Sections 3(b) 4(2) of the 1933 Act as interpreted by SEC Regulation D." However, private placements may still be subject to portions of the 1934 Act and to state securities laws requiring registration as well as to certain provisions of SOX.

Regulation D Sections 504–506 establish three types of exemptions from the registration requirements of the 1933 Act:

✔ **Rule 504 applies to transactions in which no more than $1 million of securities are sold in any consecutive 12-month period.** Rule 504 doesn't limit the number of investors. These types of offerings remain subject to federal anti-fraud provisions and civil liability provisions of the 1934 Act if they raise more than $1 million.

✔ **Rule 505 applies to transactions in which not more than $5 million of securities are sold in any consecutive 12-month period.** Sales of the security cannot be made to more than 35 "non-accredited" investors but can be made to an unlimited number of accredited investors. An issuer under this section can't use any general solicitation advertising to sell its securities.

✔ **Rule 506 has no dollar limitation of the offering.** An exemption under this section is available for offerings sold to not more than 35 non-accredited purchasers and an unlimited number of accredited investors. Rule 506 requires an issuer to make a subjective determination that at the time the shares are sold, each non-accredited purchaser meets a certain sophistication standard.

For purposes of Regulation D, an *accredited investor* is defined in Rule 501(a) as someone who has the following characteristics:

✔ Is a director, executive officer, or general partner of the issuer

✔ Has a net worth either individually or jointly with their spouse that equals or exceeds $1 million

✔ Has income in excess of $200,000 per year (or $300,000, jointly with spouse) for each of the two most recent years and reasonably expects an income in excess of $200,000 in current year

Accordingly, the SEC is in charge of making rules to implement the broad statutory provisions of the Sarbanes-Oxley Act. In fact, SOX specifically requires that the SEC make rules in 19 different areas! Congress required that rules in 12 of these areas by passed within 12 months of the date SOX was enacted in 2002. As a result, many SOX analysts worry that with so little time for public comment, the rapid rulemaking will give rise to interpretive issues in the future.

Periodic reporting under the 1934 Act

The Securities Exchange Act of 1934 directs the SEC to require periodic reporting of information by companies with publicly traded securities. These companies must submit 10-K annual reports, 10-Q quarterly reports, and

Form 8-K for significant events. These reports are made available to the public through the SEC's EDGAR database located at www.sec.gov. (I discuss the 10-K, 10-Q, and 8-K in more detail in the section "The Post-SOX Paper Trail" later in this chapter.)

Additionally, the 1934 Act imposes special reporting requirements on companies in the following contexts:

- ✔ **Proxy solicitations:** The SEC uses a procedure called *proxy* to allow geographically distant shareholders to participate in elections without attending meetings. Naturally, persons seeking control, including insiders hoping to retain control, solicit those proxies for their candidates. Companies must file materials with the SEC in advance of any such solicitations.

- ✔ **Tender offers:** The 1934 Act requires disclosure of important information by anyone seeking to acquire more than 5 percent of a company's securities by direct purchase, also known as a *tender offer.*

- ✔ **Exchanges and associations:** The 1934 Act requires that exchanges, brokers and dealers, transfer agents, and clearing agencies report to the SEC.

The 1933 Act covers offers and sales by *issuers* (companies whose securities are offered), while the 1934 Act defines what information those companies must make available to permit their shareholders to trade company shares after purchasing them.

Insider trading provisions

Section 16 of the Securities Exchange Act of 1934 establishes that it's illegal for management, directors, and other people having "inside" knowledge about a company to use that information themselves or pass it on to others so that they can use it improperly to gain a financial benefit for themselves. Every member of the public should have an equal advantage when it comes to investing in public companies.

SOX Section 403(a) strengthens Section 16 of the 1934 Act by requiring company insiders to disclose to the SEC information about their stock transactions within two business days of when they occur. These disclosures are made on an 8-K filing, which I explain in the "The Post-Sox Paper Trail" section later in the chapter.

Trading securities while in possession of information that's not available to the public is illegal if that information is material to the value of the investment.

Other securities laws

As part of an overall regulatory scheme to protect investors, the Sarbanes-Oxley Act impacts disclosures required under the following laws:

✔ **The Trust Indenture Act of 1939:** Contains requirements on debt securities such as bonds, debentures, and notes that are offered for public sale. Most of the SOX provisions amending the 1934 Act apply to securities governed under this provision.

✔ **Investment Company Act of 1940:** Regulates mutual funds and companies that invest in other companies and whose own securities are offered to the investing public. SOX's accounting disclosure and management certification requirements specifically apply to investment companies defined in this act.

✔ **Investment Advisers Act of 1940:** Requires that firms or sole practitioners who have at least $25 million in assets and advise others about securities investments register with the SEC. (Instead of selling a security as a broker, the advisor recommends the purchase of the security.) SOX's prohibitions on accountants performing nonaudit services (see Chapter 5) directly affect the services that can offered by many of the firms registered under this act. Also related to this act, SOX provides criminal provisions that directly apply to investment advisors.

The Scope of SOX: Securities and Issuers

To understand which parts of SOX apply to your company, you need to understand what type of investments are considered securities and which types of issuers are subject to or exempt from SOX.

For example, Section 807 creates a new securities fraud provision that appears in the criminal code. This provision makes it a crime "to defraud any person in connection with a security" or to obtain "by means of false or fraudulent pretenses, representations or promises, any money or property in connection with the sale or purchase of any security." In order to determine whether you've broken the law under Section 807 and can be sent to jail, you need to know if the transaction you've conducted involves a security. If it doesn't, you may still be sued in a civil action for fraud but won't serve time in a federal penitentiary under this provision.

What is a "security"?

SOX makes reference to the Securities Act of 1933 and the Securities Exchange Act of 1934 for purposes of defining what is and is not a security. Both acts contain similar specific definitions. The 1933 Act uses the following language:

[T]he term "security" means any note, stock, treasury stock, bond, debenture, security, future, evidence of indebtedness, certificate of interest or participation in any profit-sharing agreement . . . , pre-organization certificate or subscription, transferable share, investment contract, voting trust certificate, certificate of deposit for a security . . . or warrant or right to subscribe to or purchase, any of the foregoing

There has long been confusion about the term *investment contract* as it's used in the definition of a security along with all the other terms. The use of this particular phrase has really extended the scope of transactions the statute covers. Those words don't have any real meaning in a commercial context, so the courts have had to interpret them in deciding when an agreement between two or more parties constitutes an investment contract that's subject to the registration and reporting requirements of federal securities law.

A famous Supreme Court case in the 1940s, *SEC v. WJ Howey Co.,* made it clear that federal securities law covers a broad scope of commercial transactions. In this case, the court held that companies that offered sections of orange groves for sale along with contracts to harvest the oranges and distribute the profits were indeed selling investment contracts subject to federal securities law and had to register such contracts with the SEC.

In the *Howey* case, the Supreme Court stated that the test for whether the securities laws apply in a given transaction is "whether the scheme involves an investment of money in a common enterprise with profits to come solely from the efforts of others." Although this is a pretty broad definition, not all investments are considered securities under SOX. For example, courts have also held that transactions such as purchasing a share in a cooperative housing project or participating in a pension plan funded solely by employers (with no employee contribution) aren't securities.

Under the *Howey* case, the key questions to ask in determining whether a particular transaction may be a security subject to SOX are:

- ✔ Is there an investment of money?
- ✔ Is this a common enterprise?
- ✔ Is there expectation of profits?
- ✔ Do profits come solely from the investments of others?

Who is an "issuer"?

SOX provides that issuers of all stock in all publicly traded corporations of all sizes must meet its requirements — that's a lot of issuers. *Issuer* is the term used to refer to companies that sell securities to the public and either are required to register with the SEC or meet the requirements for an exemption from registration.

Your company is required to register its securities if they're going to be traded on a securities exchange or if the company meets certain criteria with respect to the number of shareholders and the amount of assets held.

Section 207(a) of SOX identifies the types of issuers that are subject to SOX, including:

- **Companies whose securities trade on a securities exchange:** Companies that offer stock to the public though the New York Stock Exchange (NYSE) or other stock exchange must register securities under Section 12(b) of the Securities Exchange Act of 1934. (For more about stock exchanges, see the sidebar "How stock exchanges work.")

- **Companies with more than 500 investors and $10 million in assets:** SOX requires issuers with over $10 million in assets to register securities that are held by at least 500 persons, regardless of whether the securities are traded on a securities exchange. These companies are required to register under Section 12(g) of the 1934 Act.

- **Companies with more than 300 investors:** Some companies aren't required to file under 12(g) of the 1934 Act because they have less than 500 shareholders. However, if these companies have more than 300 securities holders (and therefore don't qualify for a specific registration exemption), they must file under Section 15(d) of the 1934 Act. This category of issuers often includes companies that have privately held stock but offer debt instruments (such as bonds) to the public. Offering debt pushes them over the 300-investor mark.

- **Voluntary filers:** Some companies decide to file reports with the SEC for a variety of reasons even though they're not legally required to do so. For example, to trade stocks on NASDAQ (which isn't technically a stock exchange), a company must file SEC disclosures even if it isn't otherwise required to do so.

- **Companies with registrations pending:** A company conducting an initial public offering of equity or debt securities must file a registration statement on one of the public offering forms, one of the S-series forms, or one of the SB-series forms. Then the company must file three 10-Qs and one 10-K in the first year (even if it hasn't filed under the 1934 Act). Upon filing these statements these companies become subject to many provisions of SOX.

When interpreting the requirements of SOX, it's important to look at each particular statutory provision for definitions and criteria identifying to whom that particular statute applies. Some sections of SOX apply to management, and others apply to auditors or benefit plan administrators.

How stock exchanges work

After a company decides to go public, it has some important decisions to make about how to market its shares to the public: Should it register to sell the shares on a stock exchange? If so, which exchange?

In 1792, 24 men signed an agreement to sell securities among themselves, thus creating the New York Stock Exchange (NYSE). Today, the United States has several competing exchanges. The NYSE is home to some of America's best-known corporations, including General Electric, Exxon, Wal-Mart, America Online, IBM, and Lucent Technologies. NASDAQ is a competing stock exchange on which the stock of some equally impressive companies is traded. It includes many high-tech companies such as Microsoft, Cisco Systems, and Intel. Other exchanges available to companies include the NASDAQ SmallCap Market and the American Stock Exchange (AMEX).

Companies don't directly sell shares on an exchange; rather, they're permitted to list shares on an exchange, selling them through licensed professionals.

Each stock exchange has its own listing requirements, which may include:

✔ Levels of pretax income

✔ Market value and share

✔ Net assets

✔ Number of shareholders

✔ Share price

In general, requirements for listing on the NASDAQ are less restrictive than those for the NYSE, which is why many newer high-tech companies elect to list with the NASDAQ.

For example, the NYSE requires companies to have either $2.5 million before federal income taxes for the most recent year and $2 million pretax for each of the preceding two years or an aggregate of $6.5 million for the three most recent fiscal years. All three of those years must be profitable. In contrast, the NASDAQ requires only $1 million in pretax income in two of the last three fiscal years. It also offers some alternative standards to pretax income that are easier for emerging companies to meet; these standards are based on factors such as assets, revenues, operating history, and market value. As for the NASDAQ SmallCap Market and the AMEX, both have low threshold requirements for listing with them.

When a company elects to list on an exchange, it must register the class of securities under the Securities Exchange Act of 1934, agreeing to make public information available and follow the other requirements of the 1934 Act. In addition to complying with federal securities law, the company may also have to comply with state securities laws, known as *blue sky laws*, in at least one state.

The SOX surprise

Because they're not required to register with the SEC, some companies have been surprised to learn that parts of the Sarbanes-Oxley Act apply to them. However, the fact that a company is exempt from registering with the SEC doesn't mean it's exempt from complying with SOX.

The end of some old exemptions

Historically, the 1933 Act and the SEC have held the authority to exempt certain types of small companies and securities and offerings from SEC registration in order to help them acquire capital more easily by lowering the cost of offering securities to the public.

Exemptions are based on the type of security (for example, a bank is regulated by the Banking Commission, so bank stock is exempt) or on the type of transaction (for example, sales of under $1 million are exempt from federal registration under Rule 504 of Regulation D, promulgated under the 1933 Act). Most states exempt offers and sales to only a limited number of investors (for example, 25 persons in a single offering in Wisconsin). In 1996, Congress passed the National Securities Markets Improvements Act, which requires states to impose a uniform exemption under Rule 506 of Regulation D, which all states must obey. (For more about Regulation D, see the sidebar "Keeping offerings private under Regulation D.")

Prior to SOX, these exemptions and waivers left a regulatory gap in the securities field and meant that many companies in which the public was investing didn't have to go through the registration process and little other government oversight occurred. Arguably, some shaky companies were exempted from tough scrutiny to the detriment of the investing public. The types of offerings exempt from regulatory oversight included:

- Private offerings to a limited number of persons or institutions
- Offerings of limited size
- Intrastate offerings
- Securities offerings of municipal, state, and federal governments

SOX doesn't have any direct effect on registration exemptions. The vast majority of small offerings are exempt from registration (see the sidebar "Keeping offerings private under Regulation D"). As of this writing, proposals are on the table to exempt even more companies. For example, one proposal would exempt from federal registration any state-registered offering of up to $10 million in size.

According to 30-year veteran securities attorney, Richard Kranitz, "Even the most carefully planned and highly funded start-ups involve great risk, but also potential reward. They also are the source of around 60 percent of all new jobs in the U.S. and most of its economic growth. They need to be able to issue securities to raise capital to survive, to grow, and to prosper."

Some universal SOX provisions

Congress has made clear that it intends some provisions of SOX to apply to all companies that sell their securities, regardless of whether these companies are required to register with the SEC.

These catch-all provisions are

- **Section 1107,** employee and whistle-blower protections
- **Sections 802 and 1102,** recordkeeping requirements (see Chapter 5)
- **Sections 807 and 902,** criminal provisions requiring jail time for securities fraud and conspiracy

Although many provisions of SOX technically apply only to publicly traded companies, securities law experts expect that courts and legislatures will apply the standards of the statute in a variety of litigation contexts and legal actions brought by investors.

The Post-SOX Paper Trail

Registration with the SEC is a milestone for companies going public, but it's only the beginning of the reporting relationship. After a company's registered as an issuer of securities, it's subject to annual and periodic reporting requirements that extend over the life of the company. SOX dramatically changes the content, depth, and frequency of reports — the 10-K, 10-Q, and 8-K — that must be filed with the SEC.

SOX shortens the deadlines for filing annual and quarterly reports for a certain class of large public companies referred to as *accelerated filers.* These shortened deadlines require that reports be filed within 60 days rather than 90 days after the close of the reporting period.

Form 10-K

Form 10-K is an annual report that companies must provide to their investors and make publicly available on the SEC database (see the sidebar "Researching SEC filings online"). Many companies seize the opportunity to make their annual reports glossy marketing tools, touting the growth and accomplishments of the company over the past year. They know their 10-Ks will be reviewed by existing and prospective investors as well as securities rating companies.

SOX-mandated enhancements to 10-K annual reports include:

- An internal control report that states the management is responsible for the internal control structure and procedures for financial reporting and assesses the effectiveness of the internal controls for the previous fiscal year

✔ A requirement that all financial reports filed with the SEC reflect corrections and adjustments made to the financial statements by the company's auditors

✔ Disclosure of all material off–balance sheet transactions and relationships that may have a material effect upon the financial status of an issue

✔ Disclosures of changes in securities ownership by management, directors, and principal stockholders, and information on whether these individuals have adopted a code of ethics

Form 10-Q

Form 10-Q is a quarterly supplement to the annual 10-K report; it contains updates to the annual disclosures. 10-Q reports provide a more current view of financial performance than annual reports, and analysts often compare the actual data contained within the 10-Q to prior projections that may have been released by overly optimistic corporate management.

Form 8-K

Form 8-K is a short and simple form that a company must file when certain types of events occur, such as the ceasing of a commercial activity or the departure of company officers or directors. The list of events that trigger the filing of an 8-K has grown over the years, particularly as a result of SOX. The content of Form 8-K is limited to some salient facts abut the triggering event. For more on the 8-K, see the next section "Behind the 8-K Ball After SOX."

Behind the 8-K Ball After SOX

The SEC has always required disclosure of events that are "clearly material" to the public using Form 8-K. The important change in this area is that SOX now requires earlier and more pro-active disclosure of material events to the investing public.

SOX adds several new events to the list of material events, moves other events to the 8-K from the 10-Q and 10-K forms, and imposes a special four-day rule for other events. Each of these categories of SOX–specific 8-K events is covered in this section.

The enhanced 8-K requirements are a legacy of the Enron scandal, which I cover in Chapter 1. Many of the events that foreshadowed Enron's demise but escaped public disclosure would now trigger 8-K filing obligations under the four-day rule.

Adding new events to the list

Form 8-K disclosures play an important role in keeping the public informed about occurrences in small companies that may not capture the attention of the media.

Under new rules mandated by SOX, the following events appear on the list of 8-K triggering disclosures:

- **Entry into or termination of a material agreement:** This provision is a response to the pre-Enron practice of burying such news, such as the losses of clients and contracts, in the cheery language of glossy annual reports.

- **Creation of a new material obligation:** This requirement applies to obligations of the issuer that are either direct or arise contingently out of an off–balance sheet arrangement. Enron's off–balance sheet transactions (discussed in Chapter 2) epitomize the extent to which pre-SOX management was able to conceal a company's ailing financial position while paying themselves large salaries.

- **Defaulting on a financial obligation or moving up the date when an obligation is due:** A company's inability to pay its bills and the acceleration of an obligation by a nervous creditor are deemed events that the public should know about.

- **Ceasing a commercial activity:** Investors have a right to know what business enterprises they're investing in and when those enterprises change.

- **Write-offs:** Reportable write-offs include disposing of or materially adjusting the value of a company asset or taking action that will result in a material write-off on the company's balance sheet. Rather than allowing such information to be buried in the balance sheet, SOX mandates that investors be informed about material write-offs on an 8-K.

- **Failure to meet stock exchange reporting requirements:** Investors have a right to know about this type of event because the inability to buy and sell their stock on an exchange can dramatically impact a company's liquidity.

- **Restating previously issue financial statements:** If a company makes a decision to restate, or redo, financial statements it has already issued to the public, rules under SOX say investors have a right to know the source of the error.

- **Departing directors and officers:** When key players are bailing, investors may want to as well.

Shuffling events from the 10-K and 10-Q

Certain events that companies used to report quarterly on Forms 10-K and 10-Q now must be reported more currently. Companies can't lump the following events with other reports but instead must put them on their 8-Ks:

- **Significant sales:** The sale of more than 1 percent of the outstanding securities or the new issuing of that amount of securities must be reported on the 8-K.

- **Changes in shareholder rights:** Shareholders of stock, debt, and all other types of securities must get notice of any *material modifications,* or significant changes, to their rights.

- **Amendments to bylaws and articles:** If bylaws or articles of incorporation are amended, shareholders are entitled to an 8-K.

Creating four-day reporting events

Some events are subject to a requirement that they be disclosed to the investing public within four days of when they occur. Events that call for these real-time disclosures include:

- Bankruptcy or *receivership* (a process in which a bankruptcy trustee manages assets of an indebted individual or entity)

- Purchase of significant financial assets

- Changes in auditors

- Changes in financial control policies

- Suspensions of employee rights to transfer 401(k) plan assets

- Changes or waivers of ethics policies for financial officers

Providing protection in the safe SOX harbor

To keep lawsuits from clogging the courts, the SEC contains a safe harbor for companies that fail to file their 8-Ks in the required time frames. As long as the disclosure is made in the company's next periodic report, the SEC will not prosecute or allow a cause of action to be made under the fraud provisions of the Securities Exchange Act of 1934. The SEC also doesn't allow parties to sue a company simply because it failed to file an 8-K.

This safe harbor doesn't apply to material misstatements or omissions, and companies that don't file 8-Ks are still subject to SEC penalties for failing to meet their reporting obligations. Reporting failures also may cause the SEC to more carefully review and scrutinize the future activities of a company, as I explain in the next section.

Annual SEC Scrutiny After SOX

SEC Chairman Arthur Leavitt championed many of the SOX reforms long before they were enacted. However, in the late 1990s, the SEC (under Leavitt's watch) declined to review Enron's books for the prior three years and even gave Enron specific exemptions from securities laws. "Never again," said Congress and the SEC. New rules now make periodic review by the SEC mandatory.

Mandatory review rule

SOX requires the SEC to review a public company's annual and quarterly reports at least once every three years. Taking things a step further, the SEC has publicly stated that the largest public companies can look forward to being audited as often as once every year. It's up to the SEC to exercise its discretion in deciding how and when to conduct its review process.

SOX Section 408 provides that the SEC will use the following criteria in determining how often to review a company:

- ✔ Whether the issuer has had to make substantial corrections (restatements) to previously issued financial statements
- ✔ Whether the company has experienced a lot of volatility in its stock price
- ✔ How many shares are issued and the cost per share (referred to as *the size of the issue*)
- ✔ The disparity of the company's stock price to its earnings (called the *price to earning ratio*)
- ✔ The influence the issuer can exert over a particular segment of the economy
- ✔ Other factors the SEC considers relevant

Remedies for inaccurate registration materials

By law, the SEC requires that the information provided in the publicly disclosed registration documents be accurate. However, the SEC doesn't guarantee that companies always follow this rule, so you can't sue the agency for failing to do its job if a problem arises.

Researching SEC filings online

Registration statements and information documents, which are sometimes also called *prospectuses,* become public shortly after filing with the SEC. You can access these documents for free on the EDGAR database located on the SEC Web site at www.sec.gov. The figure in this sidebar shows a portion of an 8-K statement for Toys "R" Us, Inc. on the database.

You can search the database for any of the following filings for a specific company:

✔ Prospectuses

✔ Annual reports (Form 10-K)

✔ Quarterly reports

✔ Proxies solicitations

✔ Tender offer disclosures

✔ Filings by mutual fund companies

The EDGAR database is surprisingly current: You can retrieve 8-Ks and other documents that were filed as recently as the previous week.

Tip: Your search on a particular company may pull up hundreds of documents, so it's helpful to limit your search to a particular time period.

Investors who purchase securities and suffer losses must prove in court that the registration documents or periodic filings included incomplete or inaccurate information. This cause of action, generally, is limited to suing the company and not the federal government.

Why Privately Held Companies Care About SOX

Think that only publicly traded companies need to worry about SOX? This may not be the case. Private companies that fail to concern themselves early on with the standards set by SOX may significantly limit their growth potential and find themselves on the losing side of court controversies. This section looks at a couple of reasons why a privately held company may want to be SOX compliant as it grows.

Bolstering the bottom line

SOX is becoming a model for governing corporations of all sizes. SOX provides nonpublic companies with a template of "best practices" so they don't have to develop structures from scratch as they grapple with governance issues.

Adopting SOX standards can ratchet up a company's credibility because SOX structures and procedures are easily recognizable in today's financial and business environment. This familiarity inspires trust for investors, creditors, prospective purchasers, and joint venture partners.

Privately held companies that voluntarily adopt SOX standards can expect to realize financial benefits that bolster their profits as a result of the following dynamics:

- **Financial institutions and lenders may rely on the company's internal control and governance systems in streamlining their own due diligence process.** Companies with good governance and internal control are attractive to institutions that have to assess these processes and procedures as part of their decision-making process. Good governance and internal controls inspire the confidence of lenders, investors, and other decision makers.

- **Insurance companies may offer lower premiums for officers and directors.** Good governance and internal control are rapidly becoming an unofficial underwriting criteria that allows companies to shop for more competitive rates.

- **It may be easier to attract qualified board members who are wary of serving on boards of companies that lack adequate controls.** No board member wants to feel like he's just stepped into a quicksand of questionable practices and lax controls by agreeing to serve on a board. SOX ensures that good procedures are in place, which can help the company recruit more qualified board members.

✔ **A company with good governance structures and internal control is more attractive to a prospective purchaser.** A purchase involves considerable due diligence, and adopting SOX standards reassures prospective buyers that the company's financial statements can be relied upon.

✔ **The company may be more desirable as a candidate to participate in joint ventures when adequate internal control is a selection criterion.** No company wants to be affiliated with a scandal-ridden partner in a joint venture situation. These joint ventures can be particularly lucrative to small companies. Nonpublic companies can more effectively compete for joint venture deals by voluntarily adopting SOX standards, a practice that may make them stand out among other competing companies.

Defending company practices in court

Even if your company has no imminent plans to go public, it may want to adopt SOX standards in order to posture and present itself in court should the unfortunate need ever arise.

In civil lawsuits and criminal litigation, courts must develop and apply standards of conduct. Courts are likely to look to SOX in evaluating the conduct of privately held companies and in developing judicial standards. If your company is sued, undoubtedly it will fare better before a judge or jury if it has embraced the principles and objectives of SOX, such as adequate financial controls and management accountability.

Moreover, several provisions of SOX, such as its criminal and whistle-blower protections, apply to companies that aren't publicly traded in the traditional sense.

The prospect of going public

Most budding entrepreneurs dream of developing a business that's so successful they can earn the prestige of *going public,* or selling shares of the business's stock. As soon as a company realizes this dream, it comes under the scope of SOX and, more specifically, Section 404's compliance requirements.

According to securities law expert, Richard Kranitz, Section 404 is the single biggest concern of most small companies, and as of this writing, implementation has been postponed because the SEC fears that requiring 404 compliance by small firms may harm those firms severely.

Why would a company want to go public? For those that satisfy the SEC registration requirements and willingly submit to SOX standards, the payoff can have the following advantages:

- ✔ **Consistent capital (if a liquid market for the securities can be achieved):** Many successful businesses survive their early years on successive rounds of borrowed funds. A successful public offering may yield important working capital needed to expand the business.

- ✔ **Control:** In the early stages of business, venture capitalists may want significant control of a company in exchange for their financial contributions. A public offering can represent an important opportunity for a company's founders to raise necessary cash without relinquishing or concentrating significant control in the hands of a small group of investors.

- ✔ **Compensation:** For an entrepreneur living on a shoestring budget while developing a business that's worth a lot of money, the prospect of going public can represent the opportunity to cash in on the success of the enterprise by selling some of his or her stock in the business.

- ✔ **Acquisitions:** A public company that wants to acquire another company can do so by issuing stock to finance the acquisition rather than financing through borrowing.

Taking a company public can cost hundreds of thousands — or even millions — of dollars in legal and underwriting fees and millions more to comply with ongoing SEC reporting requirements. And if a company isn't in compliance with SOX at the time of registration, taking the necessary steps to comply can delay the registration and significantly increase the costs associated with it. On the other hand, if a company has already been implementing practices consistent with SOX, the process can be simplified (although still expensive).

Chapter 4

SOX and Factual Financial Statements

In This Chapter

▶ Understanding the information on financial statements

▶ Ferreting out a public company's hidden weaknesses

▶ Investigating financial information about public companies

▶ Looking up SEC filings and disclosures

*T*he wave of corporate scandals that began 2001 revealed that publicly traded corporations like Enron and WorldCom were routinely leaving critical information off their financial statements or burying it the footnotes. This practice meant that revenue was overstated by hundreds of millions of dollars, massive losses were concealed, and investors could not possibly be informed about the company's performance or financial condition.

The Sarbanes-Oxley Act (SOX) arms the investing public with several methods for obtaining better information about the companies in which they invest. Great emphasis is now placed on companies' internal control over the accuracy of the information that appears on its financial statements, as discussed in Chapter 11. Additionally, the Securities and Exchange Commission (SEC) increased other types of public disclosures that companies must make. Companies are now required to file reports on Form 8-K for events that may result in exposure to their companies, such as lawsuits or losses of major contracts.

This chapter explains how to critically review the information on financial statements, both from the perspective of an investor and from the perspective of a company attempting to make sound judgments about its required financial statement disclosures after SOX. It also explains how to research the new wealth of information about companies available on the SEC Web site.

Looking for Cooked Books After SOX

U.S. businesses prepare two major types of financial statements — the income (profit and loss) statement and the balance sheet. The *income statement* is supposed to fairly reflect the income and expenses of the company, while the *balance sheet* discloses assets and liabilities. However, as this section discusses, even after SOX, many companies may have liabilities, risks, and exposures that don't show up in the account balances on these statements.

This section shares some basic information to help you read both types of statements with some healthy post-SOX skepticism.

What the income statement reveals

Most income statements follow a variation of the general format that follows:

```
Sample Income Statement for ABC Company
December 31, 2007

Income from Operations
Net Revenue

Less: Cost of Goods sold

        Minus: Expenses from Operations
        Minus: General and Administrative Expenses

= Operating Profit
        Minus: Interest Expenses
        Plus: Other Revenue or Gains
        Minus: Other Expenses or Losses

= Earnings Before Taxes
        Minus: Taxes
= Earnings Before Irregular Items
        Plus/Minus: Discontinued Operations
        Plus/Minus: Extraordinary Items
        Plus/Minus: Adjustments for Changes in
        Accounting Principle

= Net Income
        Retained Earnings
        Earnings Per Share
```

The income statement (also called the *profit and loss statement)* is a financial report that covers the business's revenues and expenses over the fiscal year. SOX is intended to ensure that this information is accurately reported and that profits aren't inflated with false promises to lure investors.

A new income statement is prepared at the end of each fiscal year. This means that companies start with a fresh income statement each accounting period, and each account on the statement has a zero balance at the beginning of the year.

Some key sections and terms disclosed on the income statement include the following:

- ✔ **The income section:** The income section may include information about returns, allowances, discounts, and cost of goods sold. Generally Accepted Accounting Principles (GAAP) allows these items to be shown as part of the income section of the profit and loss statement when your company feels that such placement makes the information easier to understand.

- ✔ **Net revenue:** This is usually the company's sales, presented as its total (gross) sales minus sales discounts, returns, income statement template, and allowances.

- ✔ **Cost of goods sold:** This is the amount it costs the company to make a product.

- ✔ **Income from operations:** The number you get when you subtract sales, general, and administrative expenses from net income is sometimes referred to as *income from operations.* This is income earned in the normal course of doing business.

- ✔ **Expenses from operations:** The expense section of the income statement shows the costs of goods and services used by the company to produce income or revenue. This section includes sales, general, and administrative expenses.

- ✔ **Retained earnings:** The profit or loss at the end of each year is summarized in the retained earnings account.

- ✔ **The "other" income and expense categories:** Sometimes a company has income from events that are not a normal or ongoing part of its business, such as the sale of an asset. These items may be shown as "other revenue and expenses" to give investors a clearer picture of the company's performance.

Some common financial statement terms

The following are some common terms you'll see on financial statements and in the media when it reports on a corporate scandal:

- **Discontinued operations:** This is where income or expenses from shifting a business location or permanently discontinuing production appear.

- **Extraordinary items:** This section reflects accounting events that are both unusual and infrequent. Examples include natural disasters, government expropriation, or changes in laws.

- **Changes in accounting principle:** These are changes in income that result from changing a method of accounting. For example, a company's change in the method of computing depreciation could affect income.

- **Earnings per share (EPS):** EPS is the amount of income per share of stock. It can be computed in several ways using the average shares outstanding or by some other method. For example, "diluted" EPS is a calculation that includes convertible stock options in the calculation.

- **Nonoperating expenses:** Large expenses unrelated to the operations of the company (such as legal fees) can be a red flag signaling future losses or lagging profits. Look for an explanation in the footnotes.

Balance sheet (and off–balance sheet) transactions

One of the major aspects of the Enron fraud was the existence of so-called *off–balance sheet transactions*. Sham foreign subsidiaries were created, and Enron's losses were recorded on the subsidiaries' books instead of its own, thus inflating both income and owners' equity.

The information shown on a balance sheet is always presented in a specific order: assets, then liabilities, and finally the owner's equity accounts. The information shown on the balance sheet should reflect this equation:

Assets + Liabilities = Owner's Equity

The year-end balance in the net income account shown on the income statement is added to the retained earnings account in the equity section of the balance sheet. The equity section (which is sometimes called *stockholders' equity*) reflects the value of the shareholders' ownership interest in the company.

Here's a very simple balance sheet format:

```
Balance Sheet Format
December 31, 2007

ASSETS

Current Assets
Checking/Savings
Accounts Receivable
Other Current Assets
Total Current Assets
Fixed Assets

= TOTAL ASSETS

LIABILITIES AND EQUITY

Liabilities
Current Liabilities
Accounts Payable
Credit Cards
Other Current Liabilities
Total Liabilities
Equity

= TOTAL LIABILITIES AND EQUITY
```

Looking for funky footnotes

Companies love to bury unfavorable information in the footnotes to their financial statements, whenever the law permits them to do so. Footnotes on financial statements can include important information that doesn't show up in a company's income and balance sheet accounts but nevertheless affects the financial condition of the company:

For example, the footnotes to financial statements may reveal information about:

- **Pending litigation and other contingent liabilities:** If a company is being sued or expects to be sued, the legal exposure that it faces does not show up on its income or balance sheet. There is no actual transaction or reduction in assets to record. Rather, information about the company's financial exposure to these sorts of events usually appears in the footnotes.

- **Outstanding debt:** Financial accounts show the existence of a debt but not how soon it's due. Large debts due before revenues are expected to come in obviously signal trouble for any business.

- ✔ **The accounting methods used on the financials:** Footnotes explain the major accounting policies of the business, such as how inventory costs and asset values are determined, as well as any other significant accounting policies that the company feels shareholders should know about.

- ✔ **Special disclosures:** Footnotes may provide information about exposures and financial deficiencies that don't fit in the financials. For example, a footnote may disclose underfunded pension plan liabilities or anticipated business interruptions.

Complying with GAAP and GAAS

Each type of business has its own peculiar types of transactions, investments, and subsidiaries. However, all financial statements filed with the United States Securities Exchange Commission (SEC) must adhere to Generally Accepted Accounting Principles (GAAP) and Generally Accepted Auditing Standards (GAAS), which are set by the American Institute of Certified Public Accountants (AICPA).

Some fuzzy footnote language

A problem with footnotes is that they aren't required to be presented in any standard format, which means that companies may try to obscure disclosures using highly technical terms and jargon. Here are few examples of footnotes meant to obfuscate and confuse:

- ✔ *We have received informal inquiries from the staff of the Securities and Exchange Commission (the "SEC") with respect to the accounting treatment and disclosures . . .*

  Translation: The company may be facing a costly SEC investigation.

- ✔ *We received a request from the United States Justice Department for the voluntary production of documents and information concerning . . .*

  Translation: The company may be facing a criminal investigation.

- ✔ *A number of purported class action complaints were filed by holders of our equity and debt securities against us, our directors, and certain of our senior officers during 2001 . . . made false or misleading statements.*

  Translation: A lot of our shareholders are suing the company (so many that they aren't suing us in their individual capacities but have banded together and met the complicated legal requirements for forming a "class").

- ✔ *We may be unable to prevent our competitors from selling unlawful goods bearing our trademark . . .*

  Translation: We can't protect ourselves from illegal knock-offs that cut into our revenues so significantly that we have to disclose it on our financial statements.

GAAP embodies all the written and unwritten pronouncements and policies of the following:

✔ American Institute of Certified Public Accountants (AICPA)

✔ Financial Accounting Standards Board (FASB)

✔ Securities and Exchange Commission (SEC)

✔ American Accounting Association (AAA)

✔ Other bodies such as the Financial Executives Institute (FEI)

✔ National Association of Accountants (NAA) and state boards that regulate the accounting profession

GAAS is a set of systematic guidelines used by auditors when conducting audits. GAAS is designed to ensure the accuracy, consistency, and verifiability of auditors' actions and reports.

Adherence to these standards makes it possible for investors to look at a company's financial statements and understand and compare that company's performance to others. (For more on GAAP and GAAS, turn to Chapter 5.)

Finding Financial Information

Investors can get your company's financial information from a variety of sources, both free and for a fee. The primary advantage of using fee-based services is that they sometimes present the data users want in a more convenient report format than the free services provide. However, the public can generally get much the same information about your company using the free resources available to them.

This section examines both types of resources and gives you tips on finding the information you seek.

The free stuff

If the company is a public company required to register with the Securities and Exchange Commission (SEC), investors can find its financial information on EDGAR, the SEC's Electronic Data Gathering, Analysis, and Retrieval System. EDGAR's Web site, shown in Figure 4-1, is located at www.sec.gov/EDGAR.

All SEC-registered companies, whether foreign or domestic, are required to file registration statements, periodic reports, and other forms electronically through EDGAR. Anyone can access and download this information for free.

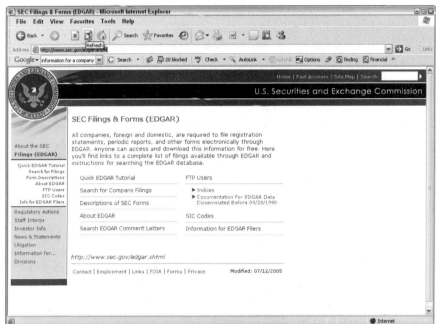

Figure 4-1:
The SEC
EDGAR
database.

Investors can also get a wealth of information from a company's own Web site. Many companies, like the one for this book's publisher, John Wiley & Sons, Inc. (see Figure 4-2), put special links on their home pages for investors (or prospective investors) to access the companies' annual reports. For more on annual reports, see the section "Accessing Annual Reports" later in this chapter.

The stuff you get for a fee

The fee-based information services are particularly useful for your company's creditors, competitors, or people who want to obtain marketing-related information about a company. Many of these services have tools to help you search for a number of companies that meet certain criteria. Some of the more popular fee-based Web sites for obtaining financial information include:

- **Dun & Bradstreet:** D&B reports provide a summary analysis of a company's financial position based on the information you would find on the SEC Web site if you were to search it. You can order D&B reports from the firm's Web site, located at www.smallbusiness.dnb.com. As of this writing, reports cost about $139 each.

✔ **Hoovers Online:** This subscription-based service features special tools to help you search for companies that meet specific criteria and evaluate potential new markets. You can access this resource by visiting `www.hoovers.com`.

✔ **Morningstar:** This resource, located at `www.morningstar.com`, is a favorite among investors for its wealth of services. It provides analyst reports, portfolio management tools, and popular stock and fund screening tools that can help you identify stocks and funds that meet criteria you select.

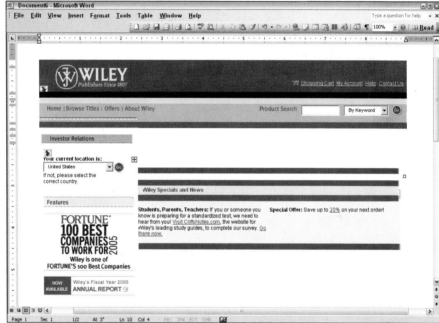

Figure 4-2: Many companies have investor information and annual report links on their Web sites.

Accessing Annual Reports

Every public company issues an annual report, which it sends (free) to its shareholders and to anyone else who requests one. Most companies also post copies of their annual reports on their Web sites, with links to the reports on their home pages.

The glossy pictures and the real figures

The annual report is primarily useful to tell you about the company's goals, vision, and future product lines, but most annual reports look more like magazines than financial documents. They're usually slick-looking promotional documents with lots of color and hype about the growth and future prospects of the company. A copy of the cover of the annual report for John Wiley & Sons, Inc. appears in Figure 4-3.

Reports often address various aspects of a company's business, including goals and products, as you can see from the example in Figure 4-4. Since the passage of SOX, most annual reports also contain information about corporate governance and ethical issues (see Figure 4-5).

Generally, problems such as declining revenues or cash flows are downplayed in the glossy part of the annual report. However, they can't be hidden in the financial statements, which must be prepared according to GAAP and GAAS, as discussed in Chapter 5. The company's financial statements also appear in its annual report, further back from the promotional part at the beginning.

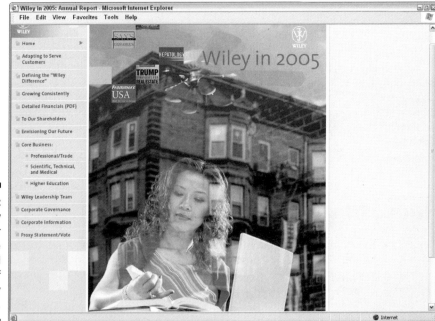

Figure 4-3: The glossy photo-cover of the annual report of John Wiley & Sons, Inc.

Figure 4-4:
This annual report excerpt contains information about the company's products, customers, and brands.

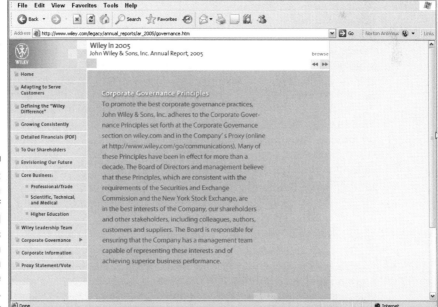

Figure 4-5:
Since the passage of SOX, annual reports often contain governance information.

Management's Discussion and Analysis

Accompanying the financial statements in an annual report is a section labeled *Management's Discussion and Analysis* (MDA). This section, which was required long before SOX was passed, summarizes the company's results for the year — it's sort of a combination of the glowing optimism of the glossy part of the annual report and the reality of the financial statements. The MDA gives you management's spin on the financials and contains information such as:

- ✔ Discussion of risks
- ✔ Year-to-year comparisons
- ✔ Breakdowns of financial results according to sectors and geographic locations

Surfing SEC Filings

The Securities Act of 1933 requires that companies that accept investments from the public make their financial information public, and the Securities Exchange Act of 1934 created the SEC to monitor this process. (For more on securities legislation, turn to Chapter 3.) The SEC requires publicly traded companies to issue reports at regular intervals, providing financial data and other relevant information to investors.

Twenty-four hours after they're filed with the SEC, these documents are accessible online through EDGAR. You can access and download a company's financial information for free through EDGAR's Web site, `www.sec.gov/edgar.shtml`; on the site, you can either run through the quick EDGAR tutorial or move straight to searching for company filings. Figure 4-6 shows the EDGAR Web site for this book's publisher, John Wiley & Sons, Inc., with links to the documents the company has filed with the SEC.

This section covers some of the specific and particularly useful documents you can find on the EDGAR Web site.

10-K reports

Every company has to file a 10-K report with the SEC each year. The 10-K is a more objective version of the annual report, without smiling photos and glossy graphics (see "Accessing Annual Reports" earlier in the chapter). The 10-K is likely to contain more complete financial statements than the annual report, and those statements may contain critical footnotes pertaining to issues such as pensions, contingent liabilities, and taxes.

Figure 4-7 shows a portion of the Form 10-K for John Wiley & Sons, Inc., found both on the company's Web site and on the EDGAR site.

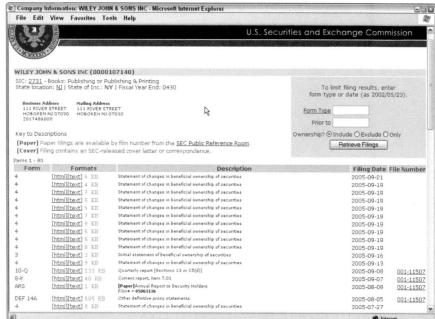

Figure 4-6:
The EDGAR database provides links to all documents John Wiley & Sons, Inc. has filed with the SEC.

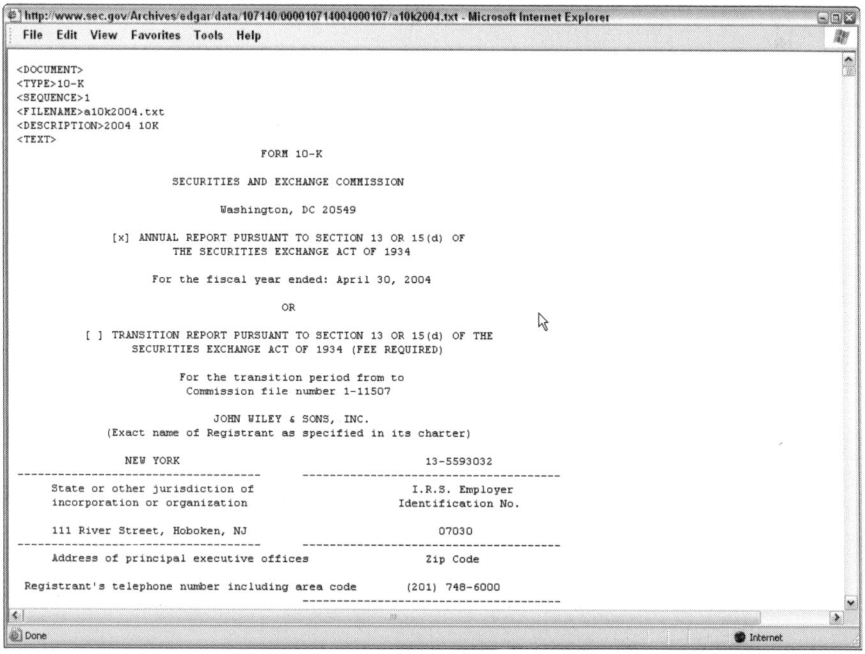

Figure 4-7:
An annual report Form 10-K such as this one appears on the EDGAR Web site for every publicly traded company as well as companies that voluntarily file with the SEC.

The 10-K requires several types of information that aren't included in the company's annual report:

- **Detailed business description:** A breakdown of the company's performance by geographical region and business segment and a detailed description of its business. (The business description is always at the beginning of the 10-K.)

- **Disclosure of legal proceedings:** A description of any legal proceedings in which the company is involved. (This disclosure is especially important in industries such as tobacco and pharmaceuticals.)

- **How much everyone gets paid:** A list of all the company's executives and how much they're paid.

- **The competition:** Detailed discussion of the risks involved in the company's business and the major sources of competition it faces.

- **Legal documents:** The company bylaws and other legal documents.

Other useful forms on EDGAR

In each of the three quarters that a company doesn't have to file a 10-K, it has to file a quarterly report, or 10-Q, with the SEC. The 10-Q doesn't contain as much general information as the 10-K but rather updates the financial statements and the MDA.

In addition to the 10-Q, other useful documents you can find on the SEC Web site include:

- **Form 8-K:** This form of interim report announces any material events or corporate changes that occur between quarterly reports. SOX has substantially expanded the number of events that require the filing of an 8-K, as discussed in Chapter 3.

- **Prospectus (S-1) Form:** The S-1 Form is a prospectus for a stock offering. Reviewing the information on this form is particularly helpful if you're evaluating an initial public offering because the S-1 discloses the amount of stock being offered for sale and what the company plans to do with the proceeds.

- **Form 20-F:** This is the annual report form that foreign companies are required to file with the SEC.

- **Form 13-D:** This form discloses information about ownership of a firm's shares. Any person or people who acquire more than 5 percent of a class of the company's stock must file a Form 13-D within ten days of the acquisition.

Part II

SOX in the City: Meeting New Standards

The 5th Wave   By Rich Tennant

"Thanks to Sarbanes-Oxley, we've got more internal controls than a warehouse full of Imodium."

In this part . . .

SOX is a major piece of legislation, so it shouldn't be surprising that it's chock-full of reforms to the corporate status quo. This part takes a look at the reforms carried out under SOX and outlines what's required of companies, committees, and boards of directors. The chapters in this part also address the consequences of noncompliance and the possible collateral benefits for those companies who do embrace the ethical governance principles of SOX.

Chapter 5

A New Audit Ambience

In This Chapter

▶ Changing the audit profession

▶ Making auditors independent from the clients they audit

▶ Looking out for what happened to Arthur Andersen

▶ Replacing accounting self-regulation

*B*eginning in 2002, a wave of accounting scandals, including Enron, WorldCom, Adelphia, and Global Crossing, prompted Congress and the public to ask "Where are the auditors?" The CPAs who performed audits on the scandal-ridden companies and failed to detect financial impropriety were blamed (and sued) for profiting while fraud flourished under their watches.

This chapter explores how the audit profession as a whole came to be viewed as ethically ailing and incapable of self-regulation following waves of scandal. It explains how standards set by SOX and the SEC regulations impact the audit profession.

How SOX Rocks the Accounting Profession

Both SOX and the 2003 SEC rules passed to further the legislation fundamentally change the accounting profession. These rules take aim at auditors who accepted large fees from corrupt corporate clients and performed inadequate audit testing before signing off on the engagement. SOX now mandates the following:

> ✔ **Audit of internal control:** Under SOX Section 404, the company's independent auditors must conduct an audit on the company's internal control practices over financial reporting resulting in two opinions; one on management's assessment, and another on the effectiveness of the company's internal control over financial reporting.

✔ **New standards for auditor independence:** SOX introduces a new set of independence rules and regulations that affect accounting professionals performing audits, including a list of prohibited services.

✔ **Shift from self-regulation:** SOX signals a fundamental shift in regulating the accounting industry, from a primarily self-regulated environment to a public approach (see "SOX as a Substitute for Self-Regulation" later in this chapter).

✔ **Establishment of a public oversight board (PCAOB):** This board has the direct authority to oversee and discipline the accounting profession.

✔ **Record retention rules:** Auditors must save and store all records related to an audit for seven years.

An Example of Audit Failure: Arthur Andersen

In March 2002, Arthur Andersen, one of the world's largest and most prestigious audit firms, was indicted by the U.S. Department of Justice on charges of obstructing the course of justice in the Enron case. The Justice Department claimed that Andersen personnel shredded many documents related to its work for Enron while Enron was being investigated by the SEC.

By the end of 2002, Arthur Andersen had ceased operations and was a mere line on a resume for hundreds of out-of-work accountants, consultants, and support staff. The firm has come to symbolize the unethical environment in which audit firms operated in the 1990s and the pervasive conflicts that were deemed acceptable in the audit industry to the detriment of the investing public.

Chronology of a collapse

The following are the key events in Andersen's downfall:

1. **The shredding policy memo:** On October 19, 2001, just as Enron's collapse became public, Nancy Temple, a lawyer for Andersen, sent an e-mail to employees reminding them of the company's policy of "routine" document shredding. Two tons of documents were destroyed just prior to Andersen receiving notification that it was under investigation by the SEC.

2. **The criminal indictment:** On March 14, 2002, the Justice Department announced the criminal indictment of Arthur Andersen. The indictment

contained a single count of obstruction of justice based on Arthur Andersen's destruction of Enron documents.

3. **The criminal conviction:** On June 15, 2002, the jury handed down a guilty verdict on the charge of obstruction of justice.

4. **Disbanding of the firm:** In response to the criminal conviction, Arthur Andersen announced it would cease operations as of August 12, 2002.

5. **The vindication:** In June 2005, the U.S. Supreme Court overturned the criminal conviction against Andersen.

The court fined Andersen only $500,000, the maximum criminal penalty permitted under the statute. However, the fine was miniscule compared to the exposure Andersen faced from pending civil lawsuits emanating from its audits of Enron, Global Crossing, WorldCom, and other former clients plagued by accounting scandals. The criminal conviction in the Enron case virtually assured huge verdicts against the firm in all of these cases.

A vindicating verdict . . . years later

Ultimately, in 2005, the Supreme Court overturned the Andersen verdict on the basis of faulty instructions given to the jury by the federal judge in the case. The nine Supreme Court justices concluded that the jury in the Andersen case had been given vague and overly broad instructions by the presiding federal judge.

Because of the faulty instructions, the court concluded Andersen was convicted without legal proof that its document shredding was intended to undermine the pending SEC investigation. The Supreme Court held that the jury should have been instructed that the law required the government to prove that Andersen knew it was breaking the law and acted intentionally.

Unfortunately, the successful Supreme Court appeal came three years too late to save Andersen and prevent the "big five" audit firms in the United States from becoming "the big four." At the time of its 2002 conviction, over 28,000 professionals were employed by the company. By the time of the verdict, Andersen had a staff of only 200.

On the brighter side, the favorable appeal may help Andersen and its malpractice insurers defend the firm in pending shareholder suits related to its work for Enron, Global Crossing, and other former clients. It also may help some individuals defend or fight criminal prosecution.

Some lawyers speculate that the Supreme Court's 2005 decision to overturn the Arthur Andersen conviction reflects concern about the provisions of SOX, which allow the government to aggressively prosecute CPAs and audit firms.

Bridging the GAAP

During 1997 congressional hearings on SOX, Congress was outraged to learn that Enron's auditors at Arthur Andersen had suggested several adjustments to the company's financial statements. Anderson had indicated it was unwilling to give Enron an "unqualified" opinion that its financial statements were prepared in accordance *Generally Accepted Accounting Principles,* or GAAP. (As I explain in the section "The GAAP all financial statements must fall into" later in this chapter, an unqualified opinion is the type most firms need to have.)

The adjustments proposed by the auditors would have reduced Enron's reported net income for the year from $104 million to $54 million. When Enron's management refused to make the adjustments, Andersen capitulated and eventually certified the financial statements anyway.

In response to this revelation, SOX amends the Securities and Exchange Act of 1934 to deter auditors from capitulating to clients in the future. The revised law states what perhaps should have been assumed from the very beginning:

> *ACCURACY OF FINANCIAL REPORTS — Each financial report that contains financial statements, and that is required to be prepared in accordance with (or reconciled to) generally accepted accounting principles under this title and filed with the Commission shall reflect all material correcting adjustments that have been identified by a registered public accounting firm in accordance with generally accepted accounting principles and the rules and regulations of the Commission.*

SOX as a Substitute for Self-Regulation

Prior to SOX, the accounting profession was self-regulated in that CPAs formed an organization known as the *American Institute of Certified Public Accountants* (AICPA). One of this organization's main functions was to set rules and standards for its own members, which it did by maintaining its Generally Accepted Accounting Principles (GAAP) and Auditing Standards (GAAS) as well as a Code of Professional Conduct.

Not surprisingly, Congress and the SEC viewed the events tied to Enron, WorldCom, Adelphia, and Global Crossing as evidence that the self-regulation system didn't work and established a new government entity to take over the task.

Congress decided it needed to do more than make a lot of new rules for audi-tors to apply to themselves. It created the *Public Company Accounting Oversight Board* (PCAOB) to fill the regulatory gap.

The standards set by the PCAOB not only impact large accounting firms, but they also apply to any CPA actively providing an audit opinion to a publicly traded company. The five-member PCAOB has the authority to set and enforce the following standards for auditors of public companies:

✔ Auditing

✔ Attestation

✔ Quality control

✔ Ethics (including independence)

Many of the PCAOB's responsibilities overlap with the AICPA, including:

✔ Registering public accounting firms that issue audit reports for publicly traded companies

✔ Establishing auditing, quality control, ethics, independence, and other standards for audit firms relating to their preparation of audit reports

✔ Conducting inspections of registered public accounting firms

✔ Conducting investigations and disciplinary proceedings and imposing appropriate sanctions on audit firms and auditors

The powers, duties, and procedures are discussed in more detail in Chapter 6.

Shifting the role of the AICPA

Despite the establishment of the PCAOB, the AICPA continues to play a critical role in setting GAAP and GAAS that the PCAOB enforces. The AICPA remains primarily responsible for establishing critical day-to-day accounting and stan-dards for the profession. The difference is that it now answers to the PCAOB in deciding how to apply and enforce those standards.

As of April 16, 2003, the PCAOB essentially adopted all GAAS by the AICPA as of April 16, 2003, as interim standards for audits of public companies. However, the PCAOB also announced on the same day that it would not rely on the AICPA in the future but would instead be preparing its own standards.

The AICPA continues to set standards for CPAs in the U.S., the District of Columbia, Guam, Puerto Rico, and the Virgin Islands. By creating the PCAOB (see preceding section), Congress and the SEC weren't suggesting that AICPA rules and standards should be abandoned. Rather, Congress took the position that the profession needed outside intervention to enforce them.

The GAAP all financial statements must fall into

In reviewing a company's financial statements, auditors render opinions that are included as part of the company's required SEC disclosures. (See Chapter 2, where I discuss the documents companies must file with the SEC.) The auditor's opinion, along with the other SEC documents, is made available to the public.

Auditors can be sued by investors, creditors, and other parties who rely upon financial statements they've audited.

The AICPA Code of Professional Conduct dictates that licensed CPAs must strictly adhere to GAAP in rendering their opinions. An *unqualified opinion* (which is the kind every company ultimately aspires to get) means that the CPA has found that the financial statements or other financial data is "presented fairly . . . in conformity with generally accepted accounting principles." If any information contains any departures from GAAP, the CPA must either render a *qualified opinion* explaining the departures from GAAP or refuse to render an opinion at all.

GAAP is particularly concerned with issues of consistency. An audit opinion not only must state whether the financial statements have been prepared in conformity with GAAP but also must address whether or not these principles have been applied consistently from one year to the next.

If the auditors aren't confident that a company's financial statements "present fairly" all the necessary information that the public and the SEC need in order to be informed, management may be asked to make *audit adjustments,* adjusting or adding information to financial statements before the auditors issue an unqualified opinion.

Footnotes often contain the information auditors require companies to include because they think it is necessary for the reader to properly interpret the financial statements. A great deal of important information (such as long-term obligations or pending lawsuits) may be "buried" in the footnotes.

If the auditors can't issue an unqualified opinion, they may instead render a qualified or adverse opinion or disclaim an opinion. The basic format for each type of opinion is pretty much the same, except that in a qualified or adverse opinion, an additional paragraph is added for each problem found within the financial statements. A disclaimer of opinion is issued when auditors are unable to complete the entire audit for some reason.

The GAAS audits run on

Generally Accepted Auditing Standards have been around since 1941, when the president of a large drug company, McKesson & Robbins, Inc., and his three brothers embezzled company funds. A very public investigation ensued.

In response to the McKesson case, the AICPA developed GAAS for auditors to follow while conducting the audit of a company's or government entity's financial statements. These standards are maintained and updated by the AICPA to this day, and because of SOX, the PCAOB helps enforce the standards and discipline accountants who disobey them.

GAAS are divided into three categories:

- ✔ **General Standards:** Deal with technical training and proficiency, independence, and due professional care
- ✔ **Standards of Fieldwork:** Address issues pertaining to the planning, supervision, examination, and evaluation of internal controls
- ✔ **Standards of Reporting:** Are concerned with the auditor's function of determining whether the financial statements are presented in accordance with GAAP

Whose turn is it to watch the CPA?

Under GAAS, an auditor must remain independent of the client at all times and avoid any situations that may jeopardize that independence. These standards are short on specifics, so SOX and the SEC have concentrated considerable effort to clarify them.

Figure 5-1 shows how CPAs, the PCAOB, and the AICPA fit into the overall regulatory process established by SOX.

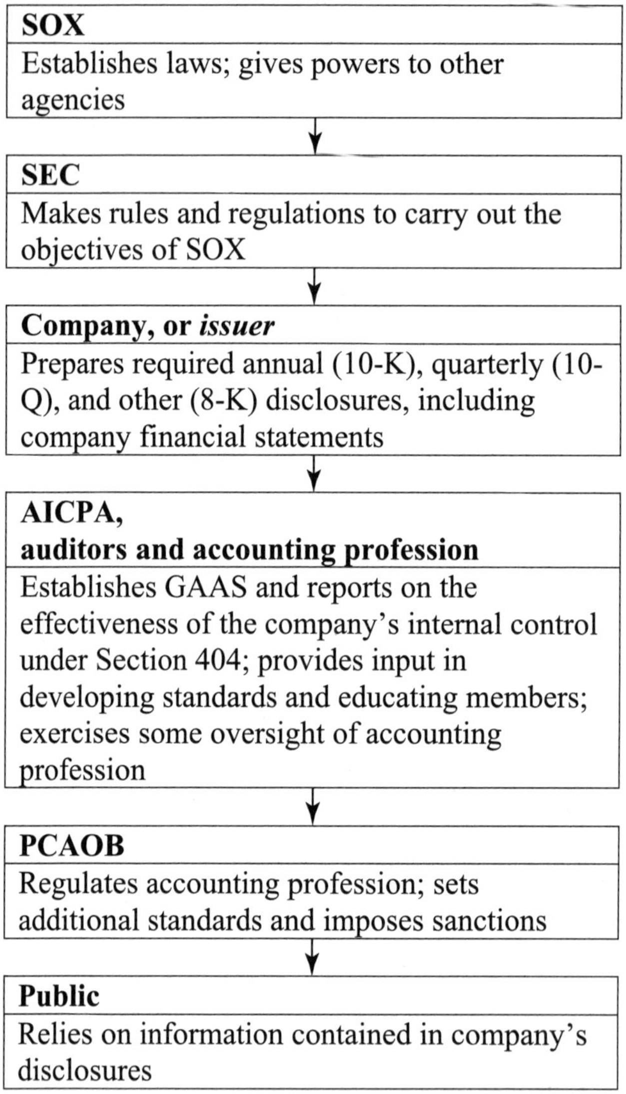

SOX
Establishes laws; gives powers to other agencies

↓

SEC
Makes rules and regulations to carry out the objectives of SOX

↓

Company, or *issuer*
Prepares required annual (10-K), quarterly (10-Q), and other (8-K) disclosures, including company financial statements

↓

AICPA, auditors and accounting profession
Establishes GAAS and reports on the effectiveness of the company's internal control under Section 404; provides input in developing standards and educating members; exercises some oversight of accounting profession

↓

PCAOB
Regulates accounting profession; sets additional standards and imposes sanctions

↓

Public
Relies on information contained in company's disclosures

Figure 5-1:
The overall regulatory process established by SOX.

Is There an Independent Auditor in the House?

During their exhaustive hearings on the objectives of SOX, Congress and the SEC identified *auditor independence* (or the lack of thereof) as the smoking gun in many major accounting scandals.

The importance of audit independence

Auditors are the arbiters of integrity when it comes to financial statements; they certify that the financial reports and disclosures fairly reflect the financial picture of a company and were prepared in accordance with GAAP.

It's an anomaly of the U.S. financial reporting system that auditors are hired and paid for performing an audit by the very companies they're auditing. Despite this symbiotic relationship, an auditor is expected to remain distanced from the client/auditee both in appearance and in fact.

Some of the ways Congress and the SEC seek to ensure auditor independence involve imposing the following general restrictions on the profession:

- ✔ Banning auditors from performing certain types of nonaudit services to audit clients
- ✔ Requiring auditors to get preapproval from the company's audit committee before doing nonaudit services not banned by SEC rules
- ✔ Mandating the rotation of the lead partner on a company's audit every five years
- ✔ Requiring a five-year timeout period for members of an audit engagement team before they can work for an audit client

Every auditor's dilemma

Accounting firms don't live on audits alone. Virtually all accounting firms perform some sort of consulting or advisory services (such as tax-related work) in addition to carrying out the audit function.

When these advisory services are rendered, the question of independence emerges. Can an audit firm objectively examine financial statements prepared by management while relying upon management to renew a lucrative consulting contract? This is an ongoing dilemma that SOX attempts to address.

The auditor independence provisions of SOX were strongly influenced by the fact that Arthur Andersen received $25 million in audit fees and $27 million in consulting fees from Enron in the years prior to its bankruptcy filing.

What SOX Says to CPAs

The SEC has high expectations for the accounting profession and views the auditor's opinion as an important instrument in protecting the public.

The agency has stated that the auditor's opinion "furnishes investors with critical assurance that the financial statements have been subjected to rigorous examination by an objective, impartial and skilled professional, and that investors, therefore, can rely upon them."

In order to ensure that auditors are "objective, impartial and skilled," SOX and the corresponding SEC rules impose upon them the requirements that I cover in this section.

Give the whole team a cooling-off period

It used to be that accounting clients openly recruited members of an outside audit staff to fill positions in their own accounting departments, which explains why a lot of CFOs and controllers started as auditors.

Now both SOX and corresponding SEC final rules require a one-year cooling-off period before any member of an audit engagement team can go to work for a former audit client. This cooling-off period is intended to prevent undue influence on audit quality. The concern is that a former member of the audit team may attempt to influence that team in order to benefit his or her new employer.

Prohibit services that cause conflicts

After SOX, many auditors find that they may have to choose between performing an audit or performing other equally lucrative services for a client. Most banned services are related to consulting or advisory services that could create a conflict of interest for independent auditors.

Under SOX Section 201 and SEC Regulation SX Rule 2-1(c) (4), auditors are no longer permitted to provide the following types of services to the clients they're auditing:

- **Bookkeeping:** Auditors can't keep books, maintain accounting records, or provide other related services to a client. Doing so destroys the auditor's independence, as defined by SOX and SEC rules. If bookkeeping services weren't prohibited, auditors would potentially be auditing records and financial statements they themselves prepared.

- **Information systems:** An auditor can't help a company design or implement financial information systems because ultimately the auditor must evaluate those same systems for control and compliance.

   Prior to SOX, installing and maintaining computerized accounting systems for large clients were very lucrative consulting services offered by many big accounting firms. Since this activity was first banned in 2000 (prior to SOX), many accounting firms have sold off their computer consulting divisions.

- ✔ **Appraisal and valuation services:** These systems involve determinations of fairness and reasonableness of exchanges of property and money. The value assigned to these assets directly affects the balance sheet and other financial statements.

- ✔ **Actuarial services:** Because actuarial services involve a determination of amounts recorded in the financial statements, auditor involvement can lead to a conflict of interest if questions regarding the audit arise.

- ✔ **Internal audit outsourcing services:** Sometimes a company needs extra manpower to perform its accounting functions and may hire a third-party service provider for this purpose. Examples of outsourced services include payroll, internal audit functions, or financial information gathering. Because these outsourced services are related to some of the information that must be audited, auditors can no longer perform them for the clients they audit.

- ✔ **Management functions:** Auditors can't act temporarily or permanently as directors, officers, or employees of an audit client.

- ✔ **Human resources:** Auditors can't act as so-called headhunters and help the client company find or do background checks on candidates for positions in managerial, executive, or director positions.

- ✔ **Broker-dealer, investment advisor, or investment banking services:** Auditors can't act as brokers, promoters, or underwriters on behalf of a client they're auditing, nor can they assist in making investment decisions.

- ✔ **Legal services:** Auditors can't provide any service to audit clients that could be provided only by someone licensed to practice law.

- ✔ **Expert services unrelated to audit:** Auditors can't give their clients expert opinions on matters that may be the subject of the audit. For example, an auditor can't write his client a memo containing his opinion about a regulatory issue.

All these prohibited service areas are covered in more detail in Chapter 21.

What economic impact does the list of prohibited services have on the accounting profession as a whole? In the end, it means that the large accounting firms simply work for more companies, and the companies themselves work with multiple accounting firms.

Get prior permission for potential conflicts

Services not banned outright by SOX Section 201 and the SEC rules may be permitted if auditors jump through the right hoops. If a service isn't on the prohibited list, such as tax services, for example, it's permitted if the auditor gets permission from the client's audit committee before doing the work. (Services that are banned outright are covered in the preceding section.)

The SEC rules require that the company disclose on its financial statements *any* fees it pays to its auditors. Companies must separately disclose fees they pay their auditors to perform audit and nonaudit services.

Tax services are one area in which audit firms have been given some leeway. Generally, an audit firm may give tax-planning services and advice to a client but can't represent the client in a pending tax proceeding.

Everybody change partners!

Both SOX and SEC rules prohibit long-term client/auditor relationships. Specifically, they limit the time that a partner can serve on a client's audit to five consecutive years. Apparently, the SEC and Congress have determined that the value of experience is outweighed by the risk of losing one's objectivity.

Wait seven years to shred

SOX introduces a seven-year storage rule for accounting firms; they must retain all records relevant to the audits and reviews of any companies that file reports with the SEC.

Records that can't be purged or shredded under SOX Rule 802 include work papers as well as electronic records that contain conclusions, opinions, analyses, and financial data related to the audit or review. Specifically, the SEC requires accounting firms to retain any documentation that's "inconsistent" with conclusions reached by the auditors in the course of the audit.

Recognize when auditors are "impaired"

It's the job of a company's audit committee to identify situations in which an auditor's independence is impaired and recommend appropriate action. Under the new stringent standards introduced by SOX, what happens to auditors whose independence is somehow compromised? A violation of the independence rules (see the section "Is There an Independent Auditor in the House?" earlier in this chapter) may result in a company being forced to change auditors midstream, before the audit is complete. This interruption in the process can result in considerable cost to the company for duplicative services.

If the auditor's impairment isn't remedied during the audit, the consequences may be even worse — financial statements may be required to be restated or reissued.

Section 404: The Sin Eater Provision

SOX requires CEOs and CFOs to certify that financial sins haven't been committed on their watches at the expense of shareholders. It further requires that the auditors certify management's reports. Two levels of review and accountability mean more professionals and their malpractice insurers share any potential liability for corporate wrongdoing.

CEOs and CFOs signing off

Section 404 of SOX requires CEOs to evaluate and report on the effectiveness of their company's internal control. This report is included in the company's Form 10-K annual report, which is filed with the SEC.

The SEC has passed rules to specifically implement the requirements of Section 404. The concept of internal control and the specific contents of management's report are discussed more fully in Chapter 9.

In addition to providing the required report on internal control, the company's CEO and CFO are required to sign certifications that are attached to the company's 10-K and 10-Q quarterly reports.

Compliance dates and delays

Large companies with annual market capitalization in excess of $75 million (referred to by the SEC as *accelerated filers*) were required to comply with Section 404 for their first fiscal year ending on or after November 15, 2004. (The deadline was originally June 15, 2004, but the SEC extended it.)

Smaller companies with revenues under $75 million and certain foreign companies that do business in the U.S. and must file disclosures with the SEC were given two extensions by the SEC to comply with Section 404. These companies are called *nonaccelerated filers,* and they must begin to comply with the requirements for the first fiscal year ending on or after July 15, 2007. (The original date set by Congress was April 15, 2005.)

The SEC decided to give small companies a break because the costs of compliance were deemed "disproportionately high" for smaller companies (and by at least one SEC commissioner's estimate were 22 times higher than expected by the SEC). The SEC also wanted to give COSO, the standard-setting body for Section 404 compliance (discussed in Chapter 13) more time to establish standards applicable to smaller companies.

CPAs certifying the certifications

The PCAOB issues standards for auditors to follow in certifying management's report on internal controls. The new PCAOB Auditing Standard No. 2, *An Audit of Internal Control Over Financial Reporting Performed in Conjunction With an Audit of Financial Statements,* is a 250-page standard that will become effective upon approval by the SEC. The standard spells out the work required by a company's external auditor to audit internal controls over financial reporting and a company's financial statements as a whole. You can view the document online at www.pcaobus.org.

Chapter 6

A Board to Audit the Auditors

In This Chapter

▶ Understanding the creation of the Public Company Accounting Oversight Board

▶ Pondering the PCAOB's role

▶ Identifying sources of accounting standards

▶ Gauging the PCAOB's effect on firms large and small

▶ Checking up on the PCAOB's performance

*A**uditors** are arbiters of fairness and accuracy in the world of securities and investing. Their job is to ensure that the information that appears on a corporation's financial statements is an accurate, objective reflection of its financial operations.

The Sarbanes-Oxley Act (SOX) ends an era of self-regulation previously enjoyed by the accounting firms that audit public companies. Specifically, it creates a new *Public Company Accounting Oversight Board* (PCAOB) to register, supervise, and discipline these firms. When you really get down to it, the PCAOB has the enormous task of overseeing ethics and conflict-of-interest issues in the audit world.

In this chapter, I take a look at the reasons for establishing a special oversight body for the auditing profession, which has historically regulated itself.

Taking a New Approach to Audit Oversight

The need for increased auditor oversight became a potent political mantra in the United States during congressional hearings in the post-Enron era (around 2001). The media ran heavy coverage of a flawed audit process followed by the demise of public companies. The public questioned why accountants had been permitted to govern themselves for decades through their own professional organizations and affiliations without government intervention. As the expected response to these questions and concerns, SOX established unprecedented government oversight of the accounting profession by the SEC, through its newly created arm, the Public Company Accounting Oversight Board, or PCAOB.

Unfortunately, the PCAOB got off to an inauspicious start. The first guy appointed to head the board, Harvey Pitt, resigned after it came to light that he was director of a board under investigation. So the PCAOB held its first meeting without a chair (during which it voted on a $400,000 salary for each member). Subsequently, William J. McDonough, current chair, was ensconced only to resign two years later.

This section looks at some history of accounting oversight, including the responsibilities held by the Securities and Exchange Commission (SEC), in order to further highlight the need for the PCAOB and closer government monitoring of accounting firms.

The old ad hoc system of accounting oversight

Prior to SOX, the SEC, individual states, and the accounting profession shared regulatory authority over accounting firms that audited public companies. Their influence broke down as follows:

- ✔ **The SEC** maintained standards for financial statements submitted with filings required by the Securities Act of 1933 and the Securities Exchange Act of 1934 (as discussed in Chapter 3). It also prohibited certified public accountants (CPAs) from practicing if they weren't in good standing.

- ✔ **The states** held the responsibility of licensing and registering CPAs.

- ✔ **The accounting profession** established the American Institute of Accountants, which later became the American Institute of Certified Public Accountants (AICPA). This private entity developed standards for certifying accountants, governing the profession, the content of financial statements, and the conduct of audits. The AICPA's standards were followed by most states admirably and without incident until the major corporate scandals of the new millennium (see Chapter 16 for details).

Alphabet soup of accounting regulation

The SEC has only gotten involved in the business of setting accounting or auditing standards on a sort of peripheral basis, leaving most of the job to the accountants themselves via the AICPA. To a great extent, the PCAOB is expected to defer to AICPA standards rather than rewrite them. This section offers an aerial view of the patchwork landscape of regulations in place before the PCAOB came on the scene.

FASB pronouncements

In 1973, the AICPA created an independent body with the responsibility of crafting accounting standards. The seven-member Financial Accounting Standards Board (FASB) is administered by a not-for-profit organization called the Financial Accounting Foundation (FAF), which appoints FASB members and funds that board's activities. SOX creates a mandatory funding scheme for the FAF and FASB but doesn't otherwise alter the authority or function of FASB or the weight that its pronouncements carry.

ASB standards

The AICPA established the Accounting Standards Board (ASB) in 1978 to provide technical assistance and support to the accounting profession. The ASB issues publications that provide "auditing, attestation and quality control standards and guidance." *Attestation* refers to the process of verifying the information reported on financial statements or in other documents. The SEC has traditionally deferred to the ASB's auditing standards and is expected to continue to do so after SOX.

The prior POB: An oversight debacle

An interesting note in the annals of accounting self-regulation is the fate of the Public Accounting Oversight Board (POB), an ill-fated predecessor to the PCAOB. The POB was created by the SEC in 1978 to enhance audit quality and help ensure adequate internal control within audit firms. The POB was intended, among other things, to administer peer review and quality control programs within the profession. Under POB standards, accounting firms that audited the financial statements of public companies were required to go through a peer review process conducted by another audit firm every three years.

When many accounting firms balked at the cost of paying for the peer review process, the POB lacked the support necessary to enforce its policies. Frustrated with its own ineffectiveness, the POB voted itself out of existence in 2002.

Primary Purposes of the PCAOB

For the majority of public companies, accounting firms, and auditors, self-regulation was a concept that worked remarkably well. That's why much of the new Public Company Accounting Oversight Board's function is to promote public trust and a sense that the government is monitoring the accounting profession. While the PCAOB provides an added layer of enforcement, it continues to look to the profession itself to suggest and maintain technical standards for conducting audits and reporting financial information.

The PCAOB's role is primarily one of enforcement, added analysis, and discipline. The SOX sections that create the PCAOB are directed at sorting out the profession's bad apples and aren't by any means focused on overall accounting standards or procedures.

It only makes sense that the PCAOB not scrap the accounting profession's well-defined standards that have taken decades to develop. Rather, the focus is on shoring up enforcement of these existing standards and tightening them as necessary. After all, who understands the nuances of the accounting profession better than the accountants themselves?

Goals of the PCAOB

The functions and scope of the PCAOB were hotly debated and extensively discussed during congressional hearings on SOX. In the end, Congress, the SEC, and, to some extent, the accounting profession agreed on the following objectives for the PCAOB:

- **Revamp standards for the accounting profession.** The PCAOB takes a good look at the standards the AICPA has put into place for accountants over the last several decades and decides which standards stay, which ones go, and what new rules should be imposed.

- **Investigate questionable conduct by auditors.** Prior to the PCAOB, the accounting profession investigated its members by way of a loose system largely based on volunteer committees within the AICPA that were assisted by a few paid staff whose salaries were funded with members' dues. The disciplinary process was perceived by many as subject to cronyism and arbitrariness, with small firms far more likely to be sanctioned and CPAs in large firms left alone. During the post-Enron hearings, Congress seemed to take the view that as a volunteer organization, the AICPA lacked resources, training, and government support to police the entire profession.

- **Discipline errant auditors.** In its capacity as the new disciplinary authority for errant CPAs, the PCAOB is charged with administering sensible sanctions in an even-handed manner.

- **Ensure the auditing profession keeps up with changing times.** As information technology and the nature of business conducted by public companies evolves and in response to the increasing globalization of the U.S. economy, the PCAOB faces the challenge of making sure the auditing profession doesn't fall behind the times.

The seven statutory duties of the PCAOB

Administrative agencies often have overlapping functions and therefore can be prone to turf wars with other agencies. To avoid having the PCAOB step on the toes of other state and federal regulatory bodies, Congress carefully spells out what it actually intended the PCAOB to do — and not to do. SOX Section 101(c) lays out the following seven statutory duties of the PCAOB:

✔ Register public accounting firms that prepare audit reports

✔ Establish, or adopt, by rule, "auditing, quality control, ethics, independence, and other standards relating to the preparation of audit reports for issuers"

✔ Conduct inspections of accounting firms

✔ Conduct investigations and disciplinary proceedings, and impose appropriate sanctions

✔ Enforce compliance with the Sarbanes-Oxley Act, the rules of the PCAOB, professional standards, and the securities laws relating to the preparation and issuance of audit reports and the obligations and liabilities of accountants with respect thereto

✔ Set the budget and manage the operations of the PCAOB and its staff

✔ Perform such other duties or functions as necessary or appropriate

Some Practical PCAOB Matters

The Public Company Accounting Oversight Board (PCAOB) is the child of the Securities and Exchange Commission (SEC). In its capacity of protecting the investing public, the SEC appoints members of the board and oversees them. In turn, the PCAOB works with the AICPA to ensure the quality of audits and financial statements.

Who's on the board?

The PCAOB is required to have five full-time, financially literate members who are appointed for five-year terms. *Financially literate* generally means able to understand and assess the information in the financial statements based on professional experience doing so. To balance the perspective of the board, two of the members must have backgrounds as CPAs (either currently holding that job or held in the past), and the remaining three members must *not* be CPAs. The board chairperson can be a CPA, but he or she can't have practiced as one in the prior five years.

SOX also stipulates that no member of the PCAOB is permitted to "share in any of the profits of, or receive payments from, a public accounting firm."

Who pays for the PCAOB?

Under SOX, an accounting firm must register with the PCAOB and pay registration and annual fees before it can audit a public company. Essentially, auditors are paying for their own PCAOB audits through these mandatory fees. This arrangement has a certain logic to it; public companies currently pay the bill for their own audits. The PCAOB is authorized to set these fees at amounts that are sufficient to recover the costs of processing and reviewing applications and annual reports.

The mandatory dues also pay the costs of setting standards and disciplining the profession. The PCAOB needs research and support staff in order to issue standards or adopt standards set by other groups or organizations, and PCAOB dues fund inspections and investigations of public accounting firms as well as disciplinary hearings and proceedings.

In addition to mandatory registration and annual fees, the PCAOB also establishes by rule a reasonable *annual accounting support fee* as may be necessary or appropriate to maintain the board. This fee is assessed on issuers only.

PCAOB Rules: Old Meets New

Under SOX, the PCAOB is required to "cooperate on an on-going basis" with designated professional groups of accountants. The PCAOB also has the authority to amend, modify, repeal, and reject any standards it doesn't like, which includes deciding which FASB and AICPA rules and pronouncements to keep.

The PCAOB must report its standard-setting activity to the SEC on an annual basis.

Sticking to the ol' standby rules

The PCAOB, technically, gets to pick and choose which rules of the FASB, ASB, and other AICPA-created bodies it wants to keep "to the extent that it determines appropriate." However, the SEC, which oversees the PCAOB, is separately authorized to "recognize, as 'generally accepted' . . . any accounting principles" that are established by a standard-setting body that meets SOX's criteria. To be considered *standard-setting,* a body must:

- ✔ Be a private entity (as opposed to a public charity or not-for-profit organization)

- ✔ Be governed by a board of trustees (or equivalent body), the majority of whom are not or have not been associated with a public accounting firm for the past two years

- ✔ Be funded in a manner similar to the PCAOB

- ✔ Have adopted procedures to ensure prompt consideration of changes to accounting principles by a majority vote

- ✔ Consider, when adopting standards, the need to keep them current and the extent to which international convergence of standards is necessary or appropriate

For the short term, at least, the PCAOB is expected to hang onto existing standards in each of the following areas:

- ✔ **Auditing:** Generally Accepted Auditing Standards (GAAS) developed by the AICPA and the ASB remain in force.

- ✔ **Attestation and quality control:** The PCAOB continues to use the Statements of Position developed by the ASB for engagements that require auditors to attest to the accuracy of documents.

- ✔ **Ethics and independence:** The PCAOB relies heavily on the AICPA's existing Code of Professional Conduct, which covers recommendations on things such as an auditor's obligations to third parties who may be relying upon financial statements and when impermissible conflicts of interest may arise in particular situations.

Adjusting to some new rules

New boards bring new rules, and thanks to the PCAOB, not everything is business as usual for the accounting profession. As I explain in Chapter 5, CPAs have many new burdens, obligations, PCAOB pronouncements, and SEC rules to follow. The PCAOB is directly involved in implementing the changes covered in this section.

Inspections of registered public accounting firms

Public accounting firms are subject to regular inspections with respect to their audits of public companies. The frequency of the inspections depends on how many public companies a firm audits:

- ✔ Firms that audit more than 100 public companies are inspected annually.

- ✔ Firms that audit fewer than 100 companies are inspected every three years.

In addition, the SEC or the PCAOB may order a special inspection of any firm at any time.

Maintenance of work paper trails

The PCAOB is responsible for making sure that registered public accounting firms "prepare, and maintain for a period of not less than 7 years, audit work papers, and other information related to any audit report, in sufficient detail to support the conclusions reached in such report."

Supervision of internal quality standards and reviews

The PCAOB is in charge of ensuring that accounting firms carry out certain SOX mandates with respect to public accounting firms' internal supervision and review. Namely, SOX requires that a second partner review and approve audits of reports and that each accounting firm adopt its own quality control standards.

Standards for reviews of 404 audits

SOX requires the PCAOB to oversee and implement standards for public accounting firms to use as they conduct Section 404 audits, a special type of audit that pertains to a company's internal control (see Chapter 9).

Section 404 requires auditors to:

- ✔ Evaluate whether the internal control structure and procedures include records that accurately and fairly reflect the transactions of the company
- ✔ Provide reasonable assurance that the transactions are recorded in a manner that will permit the preparation of financial statements in accordance with Generally Accepted Accounting Principles (GAAP)
- ✔ Include a description of any material weaknesses in the internal controls

Evolving PCAOB Policies and Issues

The practical implications of establishing the PCAOB as an unprecedented arm of the SEC are ongoing. The public and the accounting profession can expect further SEC rules to delineate the PCAOB's powers and limitations. More importantly, pronouncements issued by the new PCAOB profoundly impact the accounting profession in a direct way. This section highlights a few key policies that have emerged with respect to the role of the PCAOB.

Sanctioning sloppy auditors

The PCAOB is empowered to police public accounting firms with an unprecedented range of enforcement and oversight mechanisms. As directed by SOX, the PCAOB regularly inspects registered accounting firms' operations and follows up to investigate potential violations of securities laws and accounting standards.

The PCAOB has the authority to conduct full-blown investigations and hearings, including requiring testimony or documentation, to determine if an accounting firm has committed a violation. The PCAOB also can refer matters to the SEC for investigation, or, with the SEC's approval, to the Department of Justice, state attorneys general, or state boards of accountancy.

If the PCAOB decides to conduct the investigation itself, it can directly impose an array of formidable sanctions, including civil penalties, revoking or suspending an accounting firm's registration, and prohibiting the CPA firm from auditing public companies.

If an accounting firm violates rules passed by the PCAOB, it's subject to the same penalties imposed for violations of SEC rules under the Securities Exchange Act of 1934. (For more on this legislation, check out Chapter 3.)

Keeping an eye on small CPA firms

Even accounting firms that don't audit any public companies may be subject to the long arm of the PCAOB if their state laws permit. Under SOX, state regulators are directed to independently decide whether PCAOB standards should apply to small and mid-size nonregistered accounting firms within their borders.

Extending authority internationally

Sometimes foreign accounting firms perform all or part of an audit. This arrangement may be the case, for example, when foreign subsidiaries or operations are reported on a company's U.S. financial statements.

SOX provides that foreign accounting firms that "prepare or furnish" audit reports involving U.S. registrants are subject to the authority of the PCAOB. Additionally, if a U.S. accounting firm relies on some or all the work of a foreign accounting firm, the foreign firm's audit work papers must be supplied to the PCAOB upon request.

Communicating with the SEC

The PCAOB is required to notify the SEC of pending investigations involving potential violations of the securities laws and coordinate its investigation with the SEC Division of Enforcement as necessary to protect ongoing SEC investigations.

The PCAOB also must notify the SEC when it imposes "any final sanction" on any accounting firm or associated person because the board's findings and sanctions are subject to review by the SEC. The SEC may enhance, modify, cancel, reduce, or require remission of such sanctions.

When the PCAOB Doesn't Perform

SOX is a piece of legislation that leaves nothing to chance with respect to accounting oversight and regulation. The statute even provides for the contingency that the PCAOB may become compromised or ineffectual; it states that the SEC shall have "oversight and enforcement authority over the board," which means that the SEC can require the board to retain certain records and can inspect the PCAOB itself.

Also, the SEC may, by order, "censure or impose limitations upon the activities, functions, and operations" of the PCAOB if it finds that the board has violated the securities laws or has failed to ensure that accounting firms comply with applicable rules.

Chapter 7

The Almighty Audit Committee

In This Chapter
- ▶ Defining the role of the audit committee
- ▶ Creating an effective audit committee
- ▶ Including private and foreign companies as a result of committee requirements

SOX requires the board of directors of every public company to form an audit committee. These audit committees have direct responsibility for monitoring the independent CPA firm that conducts the audit of the company, which includes hiring, firing, preapproving services and fees, resolving disputes with management, and monitoring the quality of the audit. Under SOX, audit committee members are required to be independent from management as well as "financially literate." In many respects, they're intended to be the moral compasses of corporations.

This chapter explores how companies implement new standards for audit committee independence, expertise, and objectivity.

Deliver or De-list

Stock exchanges, such as the NYSE, AMEX, and NASDAQ, traditionally have had their own rules and requirements that companies must meet before they can list their stock on the exchange. (The NASDAQ rules are more liberal and easily met by smaller companies, as discussed in Chapter 3.) When it comes to audit committees, the NYSE and NASDAQ require corporations listed with them to have independent audit committees. Under SOX, the SEC requires the exchanges to impose specific standards for audit committees of publicly traded companies and increases the exchanges' supervisory role over audit committees.

Under the Securities Exchange Act of 1934, the SEC is responsible for supervising the NYSE, NASDAQ, and other exchanges. For further discussion of exchange history and securities legislation, check out Chapter 3.

The Cynthia Cooper story

In 1997, Cynthia Cooper, the General Auditor for WorldCom, made a startling discovery. Her small audit team uncovered billions of dollars of operating fee expenses paid to local telephone companies. Instead of correctly reporting these expenses in the company's profits and losses, the company executives moved them to the balance sheet, treating them as assets, or *capitalizing* them.

Ms. Cooper and her audit team realized that WorldCom management had perpetrated an accounting fraud of massive proportions on the investing public. She confronted CEO Bernard Ebbers with her findings and then alerted the company's audit committee. Ms. Cooper was promptly terminated.

Incidents such as this underscore the importance of independent audit committees within the corporate structure.

SOX Section 301 amends the Securities Exchange Act of 1934 to include specific requirements for audit committees, which I cover in more detail later in this chapter:

- ✓ **Independence:** Audit committee members must be selected from members of the company's board of directors and can't be compensated by the company or its affiliates for any reason other than for serving as directors.

- ✓ **Complaint procedures:** Every audit committee must have procedures in place for receiving and handling complaints about the company's "accounting, internal accounting controls or auditing matters," including procedures for "the confidential, anonymous submission by the employers . . . of concerns regarding questionable accounting or auditing matters."

- ✓ **Authority to engage advisors:** A company must permit its audit committee to bring on board independent auditors it "determines necessary to carry out its duties" and pay the cost of hiring such advisors.

- ✓ **Company funding:** Companies have to pay for the operations of their audit committees.

From Audit Committee Annals

The need for more effective auditor oversight didn't go entirely unnoticed before SOX. In 1998, SEC Chairman Arthur Leavitt expressed uneasiness over the rather capricious oversight corporate boards of directors exercised over the audit process, but it wasn't until the corporate scandals of 2001 and 2002 that Mr. Leavitt's concerns struck a chord with Congress and the public.

Mr. Leavitt's Blue Ribbon panel

At the urging of Arthur Leavitt, chairman of the SEC, the NYSE, AMEX, and NASDAQ sponsored a Blue Ribbon Committee on Improving the Effectiveness of Corporate Audit Committees in 1998. This panel suggested a number of changes that became the basis for SEC, NYSE, and NASDAQ rule changes in the following year and later for the statutory mandates of SOX.

Stock exchanges, such as the NYSE, AMEX, and NASDAQ, traditionally have all had their own rules and requirements for companies to be permitted to trade stock on them. The NASDAQ rules are more liberal and easily met by smaller companies.

Enron impetus

The Senate subcommittee investigating Enron in 2001 concluded that the company's audit oversight committee didn't oversee much. Expert witnesses at the hearings testified that the audit committee had not challenged management's refusal to make recommended adjustments to correctly reflect earnings and losses or management's omission of significant loss transactions from the company's financial statements.

The quest for consistent committee rules

In 2002, at the request of the chairman of the SEC, the SEC, the NYSE, and NASDAQ took steps to harmonize their rules on corporate governance and, in particular, the required policies for corporate audit committees. In 2003, the SEC approved the new NASDAQ and NYSE rules, which were drafted to correspond to the standards set forth in SOX.

SOX Section 301 reflects many of the policies and practices established by the stock exchanges as well as the recommendations made by the Blue Ribbon panel that convened in 2003. The Senate version of SOX gave a nod to the Blue Ribbon panel, stating, "[C]onsistent with their recommendations, the bill enhances audit committee independence by barring audit committee members from accepting consulting fees, or being affiliated with persons of the issuer or the issuer's subsidiaries other than in the member's capacity as a member of the board of directors or any board committee."

Starting with a Charter

The NYSE and NASDAQ both require audit committees of publicly traded companies to adopt written charters. A committee's charter is a set of rules and guidelines intended to direct the committee in performing its oversight function.

The NYSE and NASDAQ rules require an audit committee's written charter address the committee's:

- ✔ **Purpose:** SOX states that this purpose "at minimum" must be to ensure the integrity of the company's financial statements, its compliance with legal and regulatory requirements, and the independent auditor's competence and independence.

- ✔ **Role within the company:** The charter must spell out the specific duties of the audit committee with respect to ensuring the quality of the company's audited financial statements.

- ✔ **Policies:** The charter must address the audit committee's policies with respect to risk assessment and management.

A sample audit committee charter appears in Appendix C.

The Audit Committee Interface

Based on revelations that audit committees at WorldCom, Global Crossing, and other companies tended to see themselves as extensions of management, Congress and the SEC enacted legislation to clarify the role of the audit committee as distinct from management.

Audit committees are responsible for evaluating management and auditors and must retain objectivity about both. The committee monitors management's effectiveness in providing auditors with information needed to determine whether the company's financial statements are prepared in accordance with Generally Accepted Accounting Principles (GAAP) and Generally Accepted Auditing Standards (GAAS), as discussed in Chapter 4.

Audit committees should not get involved in performing audits; rather, they should facilitate them. The internal audit committee provides an essential objective interface between a company's management and its independent (outside) auditors to ensure that, at all times, the auditors' opinions and certifications are based on full and accurate information about the company's operations.

SOX Section 301 amended the Securities Exchange Act of 1934 to define the role of the audit committee as follows:

> *The audit committee of each issuer, in its capacity as a committee for the board of directors, shall be directly responsible for the appointment, compensation and oversight of the work of any registered public accounting firm employed by that (including the resolution of disagreements between management and the auditor regarding financial reporting) for the purpose of preparing or issuing an audit report, or related work, and each such registered public accounting firm shall report directly to the audit committee.*

SOX makes audit committee members "directly responsible" for disagreements that crop up regarding specific accounting issues during an audit, including "the resolution of any disagreements between management and the issuer." This provision is intended to keep committee members from capitulating to management when auditors seek to impose policies and adjustments that reflect less favorably on the earnings of the company, and hence management.

Audit committees are responsible for ensuring that a company maintains a work environment that

- ✔ Enables auditors to perform necessary testing.

- ✔ Encourages employees to come forward with issues that may be relevant to the audit process (see "Handling complaints" later in this chapter for more).

Some Stricter NYSE Rules

The audit committees of companies that trade on the NYSE are subject to some requirements that are more stringent than the ones directly imposed by SOX. For example, NYSE rules require that

- ✔ A company's audit committee has a minimum of three members.

- ✔ A company conducts internal audits to assist management and the audit committee in assessing the company's accounting systems and internal control.

  The NYSE listing rules state that a company may "choose to outsource" the internal audit function to "a third party service provider other than its independent auditor."

The NASDAQ listing requirements can be found at www.nasdaq.com/about/listing_information.stm. A copy of the NYSE requirements can be downloaded at www.hlhz.com/main.asp?p=CORP_BDADV_NYSEListingReq.

Membership Requirements

Members of the audit committee are drawn from the corporation's *board of directors.* By law, the board of directors is made up of a majority of members who are financially independent from the company they audit (see Chapter 8 for a detailed explanation of the criteria that must be met for a director to be deemed financially independent). These independent directors may be eligible to serve on the company's audit committee if they also meet the other requirements discussed in this section.

A few independent members

To ensure that audit committees are fair and objective advocates for effective audit procedures, SOX requires that committee members be financially independent from the company in two respects:

- **Compensation:** SOX prohibits a committee member from receiving any type of compensation or fee other than payment for being a director of the company. Audit committee members can be paid for providing accounting, consulting, legal, investment, banking, or financial advisory services to the company or for working for companies that provide these services.

  Compensatory fees don't include payments to an audit committee member serving as a shareholder who doesn't have enough stock in the company to control it.

- **Affiliation:** A member can't be affiliated with the company through family or employment relationships. Unfortunately, SOX Section 302 doesn't define an *affiliated person;* it merely states that if you are one, you're prohibited from serving on an audit committee. However, the legislative history of SOX and past practices of the SEC make it possible to determine who will be deemed an affiliated person and thus ineligible to serve on your company's audit committee.

  The definition of *affiliated person* used in most other sections of securities laws applies to SOX as well. Under this definition, a director is considered an affiliated person if he or she has a direct or indirect influence over the management of the company's business or affairs other than solely by virtue of being a director. Controlling shareholders also are considered affiliated persons and are therefore ineligible to serve. The SEC rules don't specify who's a *controlling shareholder;* the only qualification is that the person directly or indirectly own more than 10 percent of the company's voting stock or equity. However, owning more than 10 percent of the voting stock doesn't automatically make someone an affiliate. In the case of a controlling shareholder, the SEC looks at all relevant facts and circumstances to determine if the individual has enough control to be deemed an affiliate.

SOX gives the SEC the power to make exceptions to the independence requirements; however, few exceptions are anticipated.

Figure in a financial expert

At least one person on a company's audit committee should be a financial expert. Generally, the SEC considers a person a financial expert if he or she has, through education and experience, an understanding of Generally Accepted Accounting Principles (GAAP), financial statements, and internal accounting controls.

The SEC doesn't consider former CEOs to be financial experts.

SEC rules require that a public company disclose in periodic reports whether any of its audit committee members are financial experts. If none are, the SEC requires an explanation as to why not, and the audit committee is expected to hire an outside consultant to provide the committee with the equivalent expertise.

Day-to-Day Committee Responsibilities

NYSE and NASDAQ rules increase the audit committee's authority beyond its former role of simply recruiting and paying the company's auditors. This section summarizes the new role and responsibilities of internal audit committees under SOX.

Monitoring events and policing policies

The audit committee not only must be a corporation's internal moral compass but also must monitor external publicity and events that can impact the audit process and make sure the company responds appropriately.

Under NYSE rules, the audit committee is responsible for reviewing and monitoring the following:

- The annual audited financial statements and quarterly reports filed by the company
- Press releases and financial information provided to the public
- Policies for risk management within the company
- Problems that occur during an audit as well as management's response to such problems

✔ The role and performance of the company's internal auditors

✔ Changes in company accounting policies

✔ Issues regarding internal controls and audit adjustments

✔ The policies and procedures of the committee itself

Interfacing with the auditors

The audit committee, in the broadest sense, is responsible for the appointment and compensation of the company's outside audit firm.

Under SOX, the company's audit firm must report directly to the audit committee. This arrangement is a departure from pre-SOX days, when auditors also reported to management on a variety of issues. Congressional hearings revealed an inherent conflict in the interaction between management and the auditors who were, in effect, evaluating the effectiveness of management's policies.

The audit committee is expected to prevent management from influencing audit outcomes. SOX specifically states that the committee's role includes the resolution of disagreements between management and outside auditors regarding financial reporting. Therefore, the committee must have a full understanding of both events that affect the company and the company's operations to properly understand and resolve these disputes.

Under SOX, auditors are required to report the following information directly to the audit committee:

✔ All critical accounting policies and practices to be used

✔ All alternative treatments of financial information within Generally Accepted Accounting Principles that have been discussed with management, the ramifications of using alternative disclosures and treatments, and the treatment preferred by the auditor

✔ Any other material or written communications between the auditor and management, such as a management letter or schedule of unadjusted differences

Additionally, under NYSE rules, the committee must obtain a report "at least annually" from the independent auditors disclosing:

✔ The audit firm's internal control procedures

✔ Any quality control issues raised about the audit firm by peer reviews (which are reviews by other audit firms) or by government investigations

✔ All relationships between the independent auditors and the company

Preapproving nonaudit services

The audit committee has sign-off authority for audit services, which means it must authorize every accounting service the company's audit firm provides, including confirmation letters and compliance with the financial reporting requirements of regulatory agencies.

In particular, the committee must make sure that the accounting firm performing the company's audit doesn't perform any of the following nonaudit services prohibited under SOX (Chapter 5 explains prohibited nonaudit services in more detail):

- ✔ Bookkeeping or other services related to accounting records or financial statements
- ✔ Financial information systems design and implementation
- ✔ Appraisal or valuation services, fairness opinions, or contribution-in-kind reports
- ✔ Actuarial services
- ✔ Internal audit outsourcing services, management or human resources functions
- ✔ Broker or dealer, investment advisor, or investment banking services
- ✔ Legal services or expert services unrelated to the audit

If a nonaudit service isn't on this list, it's permitted provided that the audit committee approves the service before the audit firm provides it.

With respect to services that aren't specifically prohibited, SOX contains a so-called *de minimus exception.* This exception applies when the services provided aren't significant; a service is considered de minimus if the total amount of nonaudit services in a fiscal year doesn't exceed 5 percent of the total fees to the auditor. If the de minimus exception applies, preapproval isn't required, although the audit committee must approve the service prior to completion of the audit.

A company is required to disclose all nonaudit services its auditors provide in the statements it files with the SEC, including services deemed de minimus. The audit committee is responsible for making sure these disclosures are made.

Handling complaints

Every audit committee must have procedures in place for receiving and handling complaints about the company's accounting, internal accounting controls, or auditing matters, which include maintaining employees' confidentiality and allowing them to anonymously submit information they uncover regarding questionable accounting or auditing actions taken by the company.

The audit committee is responsible for maintaining policies about the disposition of complaints about the company. It's also required to have procedures in place for receiving confidential and anonymous complaints by employees.

The audit committee serves as a resource for employees, management, and the auditors who put themselves on the line to provide essential audit information. With the complaint function, the audit committee complements SOX's whistle-blower provisions, which I discuss in Chapter 16.

Receiving CEO and CFO certifications

Under SOX Section 301, every public company's chief executive officer (CEO) and chief financial officer (CFO) are required to certify in annual and quarterly reports that they have disclosed the following to the auditor and the audit committee:

> *(1) All significant deficiencies and material weaknesses in the design or operation of internal controls that could adversely affect the company's ability to record, process, summarize, and report financial data*

> *(2) Any fraud, whether or not material, that involves management or other employees who have a significant role in the company's internal controls*

The audit committee must make sure that any relevant information gleaned from the certifications is brought to the attention of the audit firm. If appropriate, the audit committee may also be required to bring such information directly to the attention of the SEC.

Monitoring conflicts and cooling-off periods

The audit committee is expected to know which public accounting audit firms are eligible to perform its company's audits and which are not; the committee must be mindful of SOX's provisions that auditors are barred from performing any audit service if the company's CEO, CFO, chief accounting officer, controller, or any person serving in an equivalent position was employed by the auditor and participated in any capacity in an audit of the company during the one-year period preceding the commencement date of the current audit.

Ferreting out improper influence

SOX Section 303 regulates the relationship between the audit committee, the auditors, and management with a catch-all provision to discourage company management from improperly influencing audits and auditors. This section directs the SEC to adopt rules prohibiting officers and directors of public companies or any person acting under the direction of an officer or director from fraudulently influencing, coercing, manipulating, or misleading any outside auditor engaged in an audit for the purpose of making the audited financial statements misleading.

Rotating the audit partners

SOX requires public accounting firms to rotate the following individuals every five years:

- ✔ The audit partner primarily responsible for a company's audit
- ✔ The audit partner responsible for reviewing the audit

The audit committee is responsible for making sure this rotation actually happens.

Engaging advisors

The audit committee may be involved in hiring more than just the auditors. Under SOX, the committee also must have authority to engage independent counsel and other advisors as it deems necessary to carry out its duties. The law requires companies to provide their audit committees with appropriate funding for hiring these advisors.

Providing recognition in annual reports

SOX requires a complex communication matrix: Auditors report to the audit committee, the committee reports to management, management reports back to the committee, the committee reports to the securities exchanges, and everyone reports to the SEC and the shareholders.

Because of this complicated communication trail, SOX requires that the names of all audit committee members be identified in the company's annual reports. If the company doesn't have a separately designated audit committee, it must state that the entire board of directors is acting as the audit committee.

Audit Committee Rules for Private Companies

Companies whose stock isn't available for trade on a public exchange are also affected by Section 301. SOX provides that these "over-the-counter" traded companies must disclose in their proxy statements

- ✔ Whether they have an audit committee.
- ✔ Whether the members of the committee are independent under the rules of the public stock exchanges.

Foreign Company Committee Issues

The NYSE and NASDAQ technically exempt foreign companies from their audit committee requirements. However, SOX doesn't include an exemption from its audit committee requirements for non–U.S. companies, so if these companies want to trade on U.S. markets, they have to convene committees that comply with the requirements imposed by SOX as well as the NYSE and NASDAQ listing requirements.

Chapter 8

Building Boards That Can't Be Bought

In This Chapter

▶ Understanding the function of the board of directors

▶ Recognizing the necessity of director independence

▶ Following procedures for placing directors on the board

▶ Delving into SOX's requirements for boards

▶ Making exceptions to board governance rules

"*B*oard governance" is a buzz phrase circulating throughout corporate America in the wake of Enron, WorldCom, and other scandals. Historically, the term has been used to refer to the policies and procedures that a company's board of directors uses to govern a corporation. However, after the Sarbanes-Oxley Act (SOX), the meaning of the term has expanded to include the selection process for directors and their duty to put the company's interests above their own.

The most shocking aspect of the corporate scandals that seemed to engulf corporate America after Enron was the behavior of the companies' boards. The media revealed that that boards governing the nation's largest corporations routinely strategized to overstate revenues, ignored auditors' proposed adjustments to financial statements, and sold stock during periods of plummeting prices when company employees were prohibited from doing so. Some directors even made loans of corporate funds to themselves to finance their own shaky side ventures. Prior to the passing of the SOX in 2002, these activities were all business-as-usual in corporate America, leaving shareholders and employees holding worthless stock and underfunded retirement plans.

This chapter explores how SOX makes boards more accountable. I provide you with some general information about boards of directors and their functions, and I touch on some examples of board governance gone bad.

Some Background about Boards

Every corporation is run by its board of directors, who in turn answer to the shareholders that elect them. SOX ends an era of autonomy for board directors who, with the consent and consensus of the other board members, were able to embark corporations on ruinous courses.

SOX contains the following provisions to make boards more accountable:

- ✔ Requiring "majority-independent" boards
- ✔ Changing how directors are nominated
- ✔ Regulating how compensation for directors and senior management is set

What does a director do?

Directors manage corporate assets on behalf of the company's shareholders. A corporation's bylaws generally establish the board of directors and specify how many people will sit on it; typically, the number is no less than seven and no more than ten, although there may be more or fewer directors depending on the specific provisions of the bylaws.

The role of the board isn't to manage the day-to-day operations of the corporation but rather to review the company's long-term strategies and make critical decisions.

Typical tasks faced by a board of directors include

- ✔ Identifying the long-term goals of the company
- ✔ Hiring a chief executive officer (CEO) to run the company
- ✔ Receiving reports from the CEO as to the company's doings
- ✔ Making decisions about mergers, acquisitions, and dispositions of corporate assets
- ✔ Deciding what lines of business the company will continue
- ✔ Deciding whether to enter into new lines of business
- ✔ Directing reorganizations of the company structure, including issuing new classes of stock
- ✔ Handling lawsuits and litigation
- ✔ Making major decisions about borrowing on behalf of the company

Off-balance sheet transactions after Enron

The term *off-balance sheet* has recently gotten a bad rap because of Enron. However, not all off-balance sheet transactions are shady. A company can use off-balance sheet transactions for a variety of legitimate purposes; therefore, it's important to distinguish what was off-color about Enron's off-balance sheet transaction from what a legitimate off-balance sheet transaction may be.

Essentially, Enron's board of directors approved deals for banks to loan funds to the special purpose entities (SPEs) owned by chief financial officer Andrew Fastow. A special purpose entity is a company (a partnership or another corporation) formed to achieve a particular purpose or accounting objective for the company.

Enron's board did question Fastow's apparent conflict of interest. The loans to the SPEs weren't shown on Enron's balance sheet because, as the board knew, they were "non-recourse" to Enron, meaning that Enron couldn't be sued if the SPEs defaulted on the debt. The loans to the SPEs were collateralized by shares of appreciating Enron stock. The deal unraveled when Enron's shares began declining in value. Then, to placate the banks, Enron agreed to guarantee the debt. However, because the obligation was never reported to shareholders, it made Enron's publicly filed financial statements fraudulent.

The following are examples of off-balance sheet transactions that boards can legitimately approve:

- ✔ **Operating leases:** Operating leases are popular in industries that use expensive equipment. The leases are disclosed in the footnotes of the company's published balance sheet because the company doesn't own the assets.

- ✔ **Building leases:** A company may enter into an arrangement with a bank in which the bank buys a building and leases it to the company instead of the company borrowing the money to purchase the building. A building lease is a legitimate type of transaction that appears in the footnotes of the company's published balance sheet.

- ✔ **Special assets:** Many companies legitimately create SPEs to segregate special assets they use for collateral or other special purposes from assets the companies intend to keep and use in their businesses.

A board can approve many other types of legitimate off-balance sheet transactions in which there's no conflict of interest and no intent to deceive shareholders. Still, investors must read the footnotes on a balance sheet to identify such transactions.

Looking at some bad, bad boards

Prior to SOX, boards governed companies; seldom did shareholders have the opportunity to delve into their dealings. After Enron and other corporate scandals, many misdirected directors found themselves in the media spotlight. To really understand the kind of conduct SOX's new board governance is intended to preclude in the future, consider SOX's provisions in light of the following scandals:

- ✔ **Enron:** In 2001, during what's referred to as a *blackout period,* Enron employees were prohibited from selling their stock for a period of time while the company that administered their retirement plans was being changed. (The average employee had about 62 percent of his or her stock invested in Enron stock.) Ken Lay, Enron's chairman of the board during this period, enjoyed an exemption for board members that allowed him to sell substantial amounts of his stock as the price plummeted during the blackout from $13.81 to $9.98. Additionally, Enron's board approved the creation of several *special purpose entities,* which the company's chief financial officer, Andrew Fastow, owned. These entities were used to hide corporate losses and get them off Enron's balance sheet so shareholders and employees remained unaware. These off-balance sheet transactions were an important factor in Enron's eventual downfall. (For more on off-balance sheet transactions, see the sidebar "Off-balance sheet transactions after Enron.")

    In what is perhaps one of the biggest understatements of the Enron era, the Senate subcommittee investigating the Enron collapse concluded that the Enron board of directors "failed to safeguard Enron shareholders and contributed to the collapse." Congressional hearings detailed numerous red flags waved in front of the directors and recounted how they repeatedly ignored these warning signs. The subcommittee concluded that the Enron board was hopelessly compromised because of financial ties between the company and certain board members.

- ✔ **Tyco:** In 2002, it came to light that the CEO of Tyco International, Dennis Kozlowski, had paid one director a $10-million fee and contributed $10 million to the director's pet charity. Also, the Tyco board had approved millions of dollars in questionable loans and bonuses to Kozlowski, who was later convicted of conspiracy, securities fraud, falsifying records, and stealing millions of dollars from the manufacturing and service company.

- ✔ **Xerox:** In 2002, Xerox settled a Securities and Exchange Commission (SEC) civil fraud complaint relating to its accounting irregularities. As part of the settlement, Xerox agreed to appoint a committee of outside directors to review its accounting practices and policies.

- ✔ **WorldCom:** In 2002, WorldCom, the second largest long distance carrier in the United States, filed bankruptcy after shocking shareholders with the revelation that the company had overstated cash flows by more than $3.8 billion for the previous five quarters. It came to light that the board had approved over $366 million in loans and loan guarantees to CEO Bernard Ebbers to assist him in concealing losses as stock values declined.

- ✔ **Global Crossing:** In 2002, Global Crossing, one of the nation's largest telecommunications companies, declared bankruptcy amid allegations that the board had sanctioned long-term strategic planning that involved swapping unused fiber-optic capacity with other companies to generate phantom revenues to boost the company's shaky bottom line.

> ✔ **Adelphia:** In 2002, Adelphia Corporation, the world's sixth largest cable television operator, disclosed that it had loaned $2.3 billion to entities controlled by the Rigas family, which founded and controlled Adelphia. When the SEC began looking into these transactions, management came up short on details. The transactions never showed up on the company's balance sheet, so investors in Adelphia's publicly traded stock had no way of knowing about them.

In Search of Independent Directors

There's a historical correlation between corporate fraud and boards of directors dominated by insiders. For example, the Senate subcommittee that investigated Enron concluded that "independence of the Enron board of directors was compromised by financial ties between the company and certain board members." The subcommittee recommended that, first and foremost, Congress require the SEC and stock exchanges to "strengthen the requirements for director independence at publicly traded companies."

Under SOX, stricter board governance requirements are primarily implemented by the listing requirements of stock exchanges such as the New York Stock Exchange and the National Association of Securities Dealers Automated Quotations, better known as NYSE and NASDAQ, respectively. For example, the rules of the NYSE now require that "[l]isted companies must have a majority of independent directors." Companies must also identify which directors are independent and disclose the basis for making that determination.

To be considered independent, directors must meet all the criteria discussed in this section.

No relationships with related companies

According to SOX, an independent director can't serve "either directly or indirectly as a partner, shareholder, or officer of an organization that has a relationship with the company." This provision is intended to apply to the company's affiliates as well as the company itself; for example, the CEO of a company wouldn't be considered an independent director if he or she was an officer of a subsidiary company.

Three-year look-back period

Both the NYSE and NASDAQ want to know what directors have done in the three years prior to joining the board. Under the rules of both exchanges, a director isn't independent if he or a member of his immediate family has been an employee or executive officer of the listed company in the three years prior to joining the board of directors.

Prohibited payments

Prior to SOX, many directors received large payments and bonuses that they were unable to justify to the SEC and company shareholders. Criminal proceedings ensued in many cases, but irreversible damage was done to the companies that directors had treated as their personal trust funds.

In response to the public outrage these large payments inspired, the NYSE and NASDAQ have placed limits on the amount of compensation directors can receive and still be considered independent:

- **Under NYSE rules,** a director isn't independent if he or she has received more than $100,000 in direct compensation from the listed company in the last three years. An exception is made if the compensation is received for serving as a director and on the company's audit committee, which I discuss in Chapter 7. The independent status of a director generally isn't impaired if he or she received a pension or other deferred compensation because of past service.

- **Under NASDAQ rules,** a director isn't independent if he or any family member (as defined in the "Family ties" section) "accepted any payments from the company or any parent or subsidiary of the company in excess of $60,000 during any period of twelve consecutive months within the three years preceding the determination of independence." The NASDAQ rules contain exceptions for board or committee service, compensation paid to family members in a nonexecutive capacity, and benefits paid from retirement plans.

Family ties

Securities exchanges not only look at what directors themselves are doing (or have done) to determine their independence, but also the directors' immediate family members.

NYSE rules provide that a director isn't independent if an immediate family member is employed by the firm (or has been for the last three years) or compensated in any manner that would be directly prohibited for a director. (I discuss these requirements in the previous section.)

SOX defines an immediate family member as any

- ✔ Spouse
- ✔ Minor child or stepchild
- ✔ Adult child or stepchild sharing a home with the director

NYSE rules provide that a director isn't independent if an immediate family member is employed by the firm (or has been within the last three years) or compensated in any manner that would be directly prohibited for a director (see the previous section for details).

When it comes to identifying a director's family members, NASDAQ listing requirements have a broader and therefore stricter definition than the NYSE:

- ✔ A spouse, parent, child, or sibling, whether by blood, marriage, or adoption
- ✔ Anyone residing in such person's home

Mandatory Meetings under SOX

NYSE rules contain a new requirement that distinguishes between board members who are involved in the management of the company and those who are not. The NYSE rules state that "[t]o empower non-management directors to serve as a more effective check on management, the non-management directors of each listed company must meet at regularly scheduled executive sessions without management."

These meetings are intended to promote more open discussion about the effectiveness of a company's management. The company is required to announce the non-management meetings to shareholders and other interested persons and to provide a way for them to communicate concerns they want addressed at the non-management directors' meetings.

Forming Committees for Nominating Directors

The NYSE and NASDAQ take decidedly different approaches when it comes to nominating directors. Although their nominating procedures differ slightly, both exchanges specify publicly disclosed objective criteria for selection.

NYSE nominating procedures

To fill positions on a company's board of directors, the NYSE requires the establishment of a nominating/corporate governance committee that's run pursuant to a written charter displayed on the company's Web site. The NYSE rules recommend that the charter address

- Qualifications of committee members
- How committee members are appointed to the committee and removed from it
- How the committee operates
- The criteria used to select directors
- Policies for paying fees to executive search firms to select director candidates

The nominating/corporate governance committee is permitted to delegate responsibilities to other committees so long as the other committees consist of independent directors and also have written charters.

NASDAQ nominating rules

NASDAQ rules provide for director nominations either by a committee made up of independent directors or by a majority of independent directors. However, "[e]ach issuer must certify that it has adopted a formal written charter or board resolution, as applicable, addressing the nominations process and such related matters as may be required under securities laws."

The NASDAQ rules include a special exception for a nonindependent director to serve on a nominating committee if the board discloses in its proxy why allowing the director in question to serve is in the best interests of the company. A nonindependent director serving on a nominating committee thanks to this exception can't serve more than two years.

Under NASDAQ rules, if a company uses a committee structure to nominate director candidates, evaluation of a candidate can't be delegated to a subcommittee.

Regulating Director Compensation

Under NYSE rules, listed companies must have a compensation committee composed entirely of independent directors to determine the compensation for the entire board of directors and management. The compensation committee is required to post a written charter on the company's Web site that addresses how the committee goes about making recommendations to the CEO and the board. The committee is also required to produce a "compensation committee report on executive officer compensation as required by the SEC to be included in the listed company's annual proxy statement or annual report on Form 10-K filed with the SEC."

NASDAQ allows compensation to be set either by a committee or a majority of independent directors who make recommendations to the board. As with the nominating committee, a special exception is made for a nonindependent director to serve on the compensation committee (for up to two years) if the board discloses in its proxy why allowing the director in question to serve is in the best interests of the company.

Making governance guidelines public

Every corporation listed on the NYSE must post its *corporate governance guidelines* on the company Web site. Governance guidelines need to be tailored to reflect a particular company's operations, but at a minimum, NYSE rules require that the guidelines address the following:

- ✔ Director qualification standards, including procedures for training and continuing education
- ✔ Responsibilities of directors, including obligations to attend meetings
- ✔ Policies for director access to management and independent advisors
- ✔ Procedures for determining director compensation
- ✔ Management succession policies
- ✔ A procedure for the board to conduct an annual self-evaluation (see the following section)

NASDAQ rules don't include any specific requirements for written board governance guidelines. However, most NASDAQ-traded companies are likely to adopt written guidelines.

A sample set of corporate governance guidelines appears in Appendix E.

Evaluating the board's performance

According to the NYSE, an important component of board self-governance is self-evaluation. However, the NYSE guidelines don't specify how boards must go about evaluating themselves. Many boards tackle the self-evaluation requirement by giving board members a questionnaire that asks them to rate how well the board has performed its designated tasks. However, this approach can have unintended consequences: If the board doesn't address problems disclosed by negative feedback on a questionnaire, a perception may arise that the board isn't diligent about fulfilling its responsibility. Thus, the board may feel compelled to follow up on each less-than-perfect rating it receives on the questionnaires.

If a company uses questionnaires for self-evaluation, the questionnaires must be preserved because the company may be required to produce them in the event of future litigation.

For most companies, a more practical approach to self-evaluation is to hold regular meetings for purposes of board discussion and self-evaluation. During such meetings, the board can determine what further action, if any, is necessary as a result of the self-evaluation process. The issues raised in meetings and details about how the issues were handled should be carefully documented.

Some Exempt Boards . . . For the Moment

New board governance initiatives under SOX were primarily introduced as amendments to the Securities Exchange Act of 1934, which I discuss in Chapter 3. The board governance standards are implemented by the requirements of the stock exchanges in which stock is publicly traded. Companies that aren't publicly traded, as discussed in this section, aren't currently subject to SOX.

Nonpublic companies

Although nonpublic corporations aren't currently subject to SOX, they are accountable to their shareholders. Directors have a fiduciary duty to shareholders, which means that they must govern with loyalty to the corporation and not their own self-interest.

SOX ushers in new principles of independence and accountability that are likely to impact the outcome of future lawsuits brought by shareholders who claim that directors haven't acted independently or otherwise in accordance with their fiduciary duties. Accordingly, nonpublic companies are well advised to voluntarily adopt governance standards (such as installing independent board members and establishing audit committees) that reflect those mandated by SOX for public companies.

Nonprofit corporations

Nonprofit corporations aren't currently subject to SOX, but many are eager to comply voluntarily. According to the annual Grant Thornton Board Governance Survey for Not-for-Profit Organizations, 83 percent of nonprofits surveyed said that they're "very" or "somewhat" familiar with SOX.

Nonprofits can't afford to allow a hint of scandal to taint their organizations, and their boards of directors owe a fiduciary duty to the "stakeholders" in their missions. Stakeholders may include organizations that award federal grants, individual and corporate donors, and the intended recipients of services provided by the nonprofit organization.

Other exempt companies

Both the NYSE and NASDAQ exempt certain types of companies whose stocks trade on the exchanges from complying with SOX's stringent board independence and other governance requirements.

Under NYSE rules, the following types of companies are exempt:

- ✔ Companies in which an individual, group, or another company holds more than 50 percent of the voting power
- ✔ Limited partnerships
- ✔ Companies involved in bankruptcy proceedings

NASDAQ exempts the following types of companies:

- ✔ Limited partnerships
- ✔ Issuers who have certain levels of assets to back the stock issuance
- ✔ Certain registered management investment companies

Chapter 9

SOX: Under New Management

In This Chapter

▶ Looking at the duties of chief executive officers after SOX

▶ Singling out the SOX sections that impact management most

▶ Instituting subcertifications to ensure accountability

▶ Practicing practical internal control policy

*T*he Sarbanes-Oxley Act, or SOX, requires managers to do more than just manage; they must now personally sign off on an annual array of financial reports and certifications.

Requiring management to stand behind the public disclosures that the investing public relies upon isn't a new concept. Prior to SOX, management was required to sign off on a representation letter included in the company's annual report. However, the reporting and certification requirements under SOX are more specific as to the representations required. SOX also imposes criminal penalties for CEOs and CFOs that acquiesce to inaccurate reports.

In this chapter, you find a road map of CEO and CFO reporting and certification requirements. It also includes some suggestions as to how managers can comply with SOX requirements in an economically beneficial manner.

Chiefly Responsible: CEOs and CFOs

SOX seems to single out CEOs and CFOs when it comes to corporate ethics and public accountability. Why? The answer lies in their overall job descriptions.

CEO: The chief in charge

The *chief executive officer,* or CEO, is the man or woman primarily responsible (and with the most authority) for carrying out the company's strategic plans and policies as established by the board of directors. The CEO reports to the board of directors and oversees the operations of the company. Because pretty much every employee in the company (except the board members) answers to the CEO, SOX obligates the CEO to take responsibility for maintaining sound financial practices and good control within the company.

Some typical job responsibilities of a CEO include

- **Keeping the board of directors informed:** The CEO advises and informs board members of the company's day-to-day operations and progress with respect to implementation of the board's policies.
- **Making sure the company produces profitable products and services:** Generally, the CEO oversees design, marketing, promotion, and quality of the company's products and services.
- **Budgeting:** The CEO makes budgetary recommendations to the board and manages the company's resources within the budget that the board establishes.
- **Managing tax and regulatory obligations:** CEOs usually are responsible for overseeing tax reporting policies and compliance with industry and government regulations.
- **Managing facilities and human resources:** The CEO is responsible for making recommendations to the board about company personnel and company facilities policies; he or she also implements the policies established by the board in a way that conforms to current laws and regulations.
- **Monitoring community and public relations:** The CEO is generally responsible for making sure that the company maintains a positive public image and a high level of shareholder confidence.

CFO: The financial fact finder

Traditionally, the *chief financial officer,* or CFO, of a company is held accountable for all the financial aspects of the company's operations. He or she is responsible for making sure shareholders, creditors, analysts, employees, and management have accurate information about the company's performance. The CFO must make sure systems are in place to measure how well the company is achieving its financial goals.

Some of the CFO's critical duties include

- ✔ Overseeing the forecasting and budgeting process
- ✔ Maintaining relationships with investment and commercial banks or other sources of capital on which the company may be dependent
- ✔ Supervising control structures within the firm

Because the CFO exercises a great deal of authority over company finances and personnel who carry out financial policy, it makes sense that SOX requires him or her to sign off on reports and personally certify the company's financial structures.

Three SOX sections for the chiefs

Thanks to SOX, life will never be the same for CEOs and CFOs. SOX contains three separate sections that direct top executives to the two tasks they must perform on a regular basis: certifying and reporting.

Sections 302 and 906 require the CEO and CFO to *certify* the accuracy of the company's financial statements. Section 404 (covered in detail in Chapters 11 and 12) further requires management officials to *report* on internal control within their companies and include these reports in the annual and quarterly reports filed with the SEC.

Section 302: Civil certifications

Section 302 requires the CEO and CFO of every publicly traded company to certify the "appropriateness of the financial statements and disclosures contained in the periodic report, and that those financial statements and disclosures fairly present, in all material respects, the operations and financial condition of the issuer." The required contents and mechanics of certifications are discussed in more detail in the section "A Section 302 Certification Checklist" later in this chapter.

Section 906: Criminal penalties

CEOs who willfully certify false financial statements are now subject to criminal penalties. SOX Section 906 adds a provision to the federal criminal code requiring CEOs and CFOs to file additional annual and quarterly reports. This certification is separate and somewhat redundant to the one required in Section 302 (see the preceding section), but it's mandatory. (Applicable penalties are discussed in the section "Viewing Control as a Criminal Matter: Section 906" later in this chapter.)

Overlap with Section 404: Reports

In addition to the certifications described in Sections 302 and 906, SOX Section 404 requires two types of management reports that attest to the accuracy of the financial statements. The reports are

- ✔ **Statement of management's responsibility:** The 404 report must state management's responsibility for establishing and maintaining an adequate internal control structure and procedures for financial reporting.

- ✔ **Assessment of internal control:** Management must include its own assessment of the company's internal control structure and procedures for financial reporting.

The attestations must follow the standards issued by the Public Company Accounting Oversight Board (covered in Chapter 6). For more on Section 404, see the section "More Reporting Responsibilities for Management: Section 404" later in this chapter.

New frequent-filer requirements

SOX requires management to file Section 404 reports once a year, in the company's annual report. However, the certifications mandated by Sections 302 and 906 must be filed both annually and quarterly. SEC rules require companies to perform quarterly evaluations of changes that have materially affected or are reasonably likely to materially affect their internal control over financial reporting.

Companies may also be required to file extra reports between quarters, namely an SEC Form 8-K, if important events affecting their internal control structures occur. For example, an additional 8-K may be required if the company discontinues or outsources sensitive control activity previously done in-house. (I discuss the 8-K form in more detail in Chapter 3.)

A Section 302 Certification Checklist

SOX Section 302 doesn't leave CEOs and CFOs guessing about what their certifications must contain, nor does it give them much wiggle room. In fact, the statute is structured to provide a checklist of what each certification must contain. Each paragraph of Section 302 identifies a particular matter with respect to the company's annual or quarterly report to which management must certify. This section discusses each of these Section 302 paragraphs; I include the text of a sample management certification in Appendix B.

Paragraph 1: Review of periodic report

First and foremost, management must certify that it has actually read the report in which the certification is being included. Paragraph 1 requires the signing officer to certify that he or she has reviewed the report being certified.

Paragraph 2: Material accuracy

Paragraph 2 requires the signing officer to state that based on his or her knowledge, the report doesn't contain any material misstatements or materially misleading statements. The wording in this paragraph is similar to the antifraud section of the Securities and Exchange Act of 1934 (Section 10b-5). (You can find out more about Section 10b-5 in Chapter 3.)

Paragraph 3: Fair presentation of financial information

Paragraph 3 requires management to state that based on the knowledge of the signing officer, the financial statements and other financial information contained in the annual report "fairly presents" in all material respects the company's financial condition, results of operations, and cash flow for the periods being reported.

The SEC clarifies that *financial information* includes any information from which the financial performance of the company can reasonably be construed, including footnotes, financial data included in the report, and discussion and analysis of the financial information.

The SEC also has made clear that it intends, by this paragraph, to hold management to a more stringent standard than the company's accountants. The requirement that the report fairly present financial information isn't limited to Generally Accepted Accounting Principles (GAAP), as discussed in Chapter 5. Rather, management is held to a higher standard of material accuracy.

Paragraph 4: Disclosure controls and procedures

Paragraph 4 of Section 302 is divided into four subparagraphs: A, B, C, and D, each of which imposes a particular duty upon management with respect to evaluating the company's internal control:

- ✔ **Paragraph 4(A)** imposes responsibility on the signing officers "for establishing and maintaining internal controls."

- ✔ **Paragraph 4(B)** addresses the design of the controls, directing management to make sure controls are adequate to ensure that *material,* or significant, information about the company comes to the attention of the officers.

- ✔ **Paragraph 4(C)** imposes a time frame for testing, stating that the relevant signing officers must certify they "have evaluated the effectiveness of the issuer's internal controls as of a date within 90 days prior to the report."

- ✔ **Paragraph 4(D)** requires management to take ownership of the conclusions it has reached, requiring it to represent that it has reached its own conclusions about the effectiveness of the company's internal controls based on an evaluation. This requirement implies that management is directly responsible for the evaluation process and can't delegate this function.

The SEC recommends that management create a *disclosure committee,* which I explain later in this chapter in the section "Establish a disclosure committee," to help it comply with Paragraphs 4(A) and (C).

In addition to the proper disclosure of information, the SEC expects management to develop processes for reviewing and evaluating controls and procedures. Management is also responsible for setting policies for supervising people within the company who implement the internal control procedures.

Paragraph 5: Disclosure to auditors

Paragraph 5 relates to the disclosures that management must make to its auditors and audit committee about the company's internal control environment. Management must certify that the signing officers have disclosed the following:

(A) all significant deficiencies in the design or operation of internal controls which could adversely affect the issuer's ability to record, process, summarize, and report financial data and have identified for the issuer's auditors any material weaknesses in internal controls; and

(B) any fraud, whether or not material, that involves management or other employees who have a significant role in the issuer's internal controls

Subparagraph 5(A) doesn't define *significant deficiencies,* but SEC rules indicate this phrase has the same meaning as under Generally Accepted Auditing Standards (GAAS). GAAS standards state that a significant deficiency is a material weakness that places the company at risk.

Paragraph 5 also doesn't define the phrase *involves management* as it's used in connection with fraud under subparagraph (B). However, Congress intended that it include a failure to supervise and detect fraud as well as an active participation in these activities by management.

Paragraph 6: Changes in internal controls

Paragraph 6 requires management to provide information about any changes in the company's internal controls. The signing officers must certify that they've indicated in the report, in which the certification is included, "whether or not there were significant changes in internal controls or in other factors that could significantly affect internal controls subsequent to the date of their evaluation, including any corrective actions with regard to significant deficiencies and material weaknesses."

Management must make sure that it errs on the side of disclosing *factors* that happen in the company that can affect internal controls. The paragraph also instructs management to let the public know about *corrective actions* that could serve as a signal of ongoing problems to a wary investor. For example, if management discovers discrepancies in reconciling accounts, it may be required to disclose what actions it took to reconcile them.

Clearing Up Common Section 302 Questions

In passing Section 302, Congress was pretty specific about the content and wording of the Section 302 certification (see the sidebar "Cutting and pasting the Section 302 certification" for details). However, some aspects related to whom, when, and how the filing requirements are actually applied can be confusing. This section gives you the skinny on answers to these common questions.

Cutting and pasting the Section 302 certification

The SEC provides a gift to managers every-where in the form of a *standard certification form*. CEOs and CFOs can use the form word-for-word with only a few small changes:

✔ **Switching from plural to singular officers:** The phrase "other certifying officers" in paragraph 4 may be changed if a company has two or fewer certifying officers.

✔ **Adjusting for newly complying companies:** Until the first audit of a company's books are performed, management can omit paragraph 4(B) pertaining to the officers' responsibility for establishing and maintaining internal control systems.

When using the standard certification form, the CEO and CFO must sign separate but identical certifications, and notarization isn't required. After they're signed, the certifications must be filed as exhibits to the report in which they're being included.

I provide a copy of the SEC's general certification form in Appendix B.

What companies are required to file certifications under Section 302?

Section 302 certification requirements apply to all companies defined as *issuers* under SOX. This label generally fits companies that file quarterly and annual reports with the SEC under either Section 13(a) or 15(d) of the Securities Exchange Act of 1934 (see Chapter 3). Specifically, issuers include foreign companies, banks, savings associations, and small business issuers covered by the 1934 Act.

What are the filing deadlines for Section 302?

Most companies, including most smaller public companies (known as *nonaccelerated filers*), must comply with Section 404's internal control over financial reporting requirements for their first fiscal years ending on or after July 15, 2007. (This is a one-year extension from the previously established July 15, 2006 compliance date for nonaccelerated filers.) Section 302 certifications must currently accompany financial statements but may omit the Section 404 language prior to the first year the company is required to comply with that section.

Which reports get certified?

SOX requires CEOs and CFOs to certify liberally; most reports filed with the SEC require management certification. The Section 302 and 906 certification rules apply to

- ✔ Annual reports on Form 10-K
- ✔ Quarterly reports on Form 10-Q
- ✔ Amendments to Form 10-K

Certifications don't have to be included with Form 8-K, which is used to disclose significant corporate events between quarters. (I discuss the 8-K events and reporting requirements in Chapter 3.)

Viewing Control as a Criminal Matter: Section 906

According to SOX Section 906, lack of internal control can be a criminal matter. Chief executive officers can end up in jail if they certify false financial information in an SEC report.

Section 906 requires management to certify "that the periodic report containing the financial statements fully complies with the requirements of section 13(a) or 15(d) of the Securities Exchange Act of 1934 . . . and that information contained in the periodic report fairly presents, in all material respects, the financial condition and results of operations" of the company.

Section 906(c) provides serious criminal penalties for failing to meet these requirements, stating that whoever

> . . . *certifies any statement as set forth in subsections (a) and (b) of this section knowing that the periodic report accompanying the statement does not comport with all the requirements set forth in this section shall be fined not more than $1,000,000, or imprisoned not more than 10 years, or both; or*

> *willfully certifies any statement as set forth in subsections (a) and (b) of this section knowing that the periodic report accompanying the statement does not comport with all the requirements set forth in this section shall be fined not more than $5,000,000, or imprisoned not more than 20 years, or both.*

Famous CEOs and CFOs behind bars

Prior to Enron, sentences for white-collar crimes were minimal. Embezzling executives were viewed as nonviolent and therefore tended to get off more easily than a guy who robbed a convenience store or a repeat shoplifter.

During the big insider trading scandals of the late 1980s, executives received their sentences and were back on the golf course within a matter of months. For example, famous fraudster Ivan Boesky, who amassed a fortune by trading on tips from corporate insiders, got a 10-year sentence but served only 22 months. Boesky cooperated with the SEC and informed on junk bond trader Michael Milken, who also served a mere 22 months of his 10-year sentence.

In contrast, after Enron, judges have begun handing out prison terms of 10 to 30 years they intend to enforce in full. Recent sentences for high-profile CEOs and CFOs include the following:

✔ **Adelphia Communications:** Founder John Rigas got 15 years and his son, Timothy, landed a 20-year prison term after both were ousted from the board of directors. They were convicted on 18 counts each of fraud and conspiracy after Adelphia, the sixth largest cable company in the United States, filed for bankruptcy. During the five-month trial, prosecutors accused the Rigases of conspiring to hide $2.3 billion in corporate debt and stealing $100 million from the company so they could invest in golf courses and other personal assets.

✔ **Dynergy:** Jamie Olis, a former Dynergy executive, is currently serving a sentence of more than 24 years. Olis was found guilty of securities fraud for a gas trading and finance scheme dubbed Project Alpha. The deal inflated Dynergy's cash flow and created bogus tax deductions that overstated the company's revenues to investors by as much as $300 million. When the financials had to be restated, the company's stock plummeted.

✔ **Tyco:** Following their convictions, Tyco CEO Dennis Kozlowski and CFO Mark Swartz received sentences of 8⅓ to 25 years in prison for misappropriating $600 million from the manufacturing conglomerate.

✔ **Enron:** CFO Andrew Fastow received a 10-year sentence after the Enron collapse. Fastow personally profited from partnerships that were used to move debt off the company's books. This tactic caused a $1 billion loss, required Enron to restate $600 million in inflated profits, and cost bout 4,000 workers a job. The partnerships quickly emerged as a leading cause of what was then the largest bankruptcy-protection filing in U.S. history. (As of this writing, it's the second largest, overtaken by WorldCom.) Enron CEO Ken Lay's trial is set for January 2006.

✔ **WorldCom:** Now known as MCI, WorldCom remains the largest bankruptcy in history, surpassing even Enron. Convicted on nine counts of accounting fraud, CEO Bernard Ebbers received 25 years behind bars for his role in the company's collapse.

Ironically, executives involved in these scandals, including Ken Lay, the CEO of Enron, can't be charged with SOX-related crimes because their misdeeds all took place before SOX was passed. It's an odd twist indeed that they can't be tried under the law they inspired. The reasons these execs got such tough sentences has to do with a 1987 change in federal sentencing guidelines linking prison terms to the financial losses caused by the crimes. (The 1987 law also did away with parole.) As of this writing, Richard Scrushy, the former CEO of HealthSouth, is the only defendant to be prosecuted under SOX, and he was exonerated. (You can read more about the Scrushy trial in Chapter 16.)

Most of this section's certification requirements are redundant with those required under Section 302, so some experts think that including the requirement of a separate certification under Section 906 is an SEC oversight.

SOX Section 802 imposes additional criminal penalties for altering documents, including fines and prison time. See the sidebar "Famous CEOs and CFOs behind bars" for details.

More Reporting Responsibilities for Management: Section 404

In addition to certifying several aspects of a company's annual report, management is now required to prepare a key component of the report: Section 404 directs that management and auditors work in tandem to report and assess the company's internal control. This section of SOX assigns specific responsibilities to each party.

What management has to do under Section 404

Under SOX Section 404, in a company's annual report, management is responsible for including an internal control report that

- States the responsibility of management for establishing and maintaining an adequate internal control structure and procedures for financial reporting
- Contains an assessment, as of the end of the company's most recent fiscal year, of the effectiveness of the internal control structure and company procedures for financial reporting

Management has a lot of leeway in choosing what methods to use in fulfilling its Section 404 responsibilities. This flexibility is appropriate considering the management of a company is in the best position to identify control issues and know where financial skeletons lie. Ultimately, management must be confident in signing off on the effectiveness of its company's internal control.

What the auditors need from management

According to Section 404, the independent auditor is responsible for attesting to and reporting on the assessment made by the management of the issuing company. Before signing off on management's internal control report, the independent auditor must make sure management has

✔ Accepted responsibility for the effectiveness of the company's internal control

✔ Evaluated the effectiveness of the company's internal control, using suitable criteria

✔ Supported its (the auditor's) evaluation with sufficient documentation

✔ Presented a written assessment of the effectiveness of the company's internal control

The Benefits of Internal Control from a Management Perspective

CEOs and CFOs have traditionally had a wide range of responsibilities, first and foremost of which has been making their companies profitable. And prior to SOX, assessing internal control may have taken a back seat to activities like developing a global marketing plan or seeking out competitive technologies. Consequently, many CEOs (and even some CFOs) need to get up to speed on the concept of internal control and why it's important to their company. To help you understand this reality, this section takes a look at some of what both the accounting profession and the SEC have to say on the subject of internal control.

Considering the auditor's perspective

According to Generally Accepted Auditing Standard Number 60, a goal of internal control is to "reduce to a relatively low level the risk that errors or irregularities in amounts that would be material in relation to the financial statements . . . may occur and not be detected within a timely period by employees in the normal course of performing their assigned functions." Under SOX, management is required to report on any significant "material weakness" in the company's internal control. Auditing Standard Number 60 states that significant weaknesses (as opposed to material ones) need not be disclosed in management reports, but the aggregate effect of a number of significant deficiencies may amount to a material weakness that does need to be reported.

For more information about Generally Accepted Accounting Standards as they pertain to SOX, turn to Chapter 4.

What the SEC says

SEC rules define internal control over financial reporting as a process designed to provide reasonable assurance regarding the reliability of financial reporting and the preparation of financial statements. The SEC says internal controls must include policies and procedures that address

- **Good recordkeeping:** The maintenance of records that accurately, fairly, and in reasonable detail reflect transactions and dispositions involving company assets

- **Recording and authorization of transactions:** Reasonable assurance that transactions are recorded as needed to permit preparation of financial statements in accordance with Generally Accepted Accounting Principles (GAAP) and that the transactions themselves are authorized by management

- **Fraud detection:** Reasonable assurance regarding prevention or timely detection of unauthorized acquisition, use, or disposition of company assets

Management standards criteria for controls

Although management has a lot of leeway in deciding how to create and enforce internal controls, the criteria it uses must be sensible and well recognized. SEC rules stress that management's evaluation and assessment of internal control must be based on procedures developed by a recognized nongovernmental organization. (The SEC has specifically endorsed the Committee of Sponsoring Organizations of the Treadway Commission's *Internal Control, An Integrated Framework* — better known as the *COSO framework.* I discuss the COSO framework standards in more detail in Chapter 13.)

At a minimum, management's criteria must

- Be unbiased

- Permit consistent measurement of internal control over financial reporting

- Include all factors relevant to evaluating the effectiveness of the company's internal controls

- Be relevant to an evaluation of internal control over financial reporting

Seeking Out Subcertifications

The SEC emphasizes that management must be actively involved in implementing the internal control structures it approves and may not delegate its responsibility for evaluating internal control to the independent auditors.

Nevertheless, in many companies, the CEO and CFO request that people within the organization certify to them that internal control structures and procedures are in working order.

Some of the employees and middle managers within an organization that may have to provide such *subcertifications* include the following:

- ✔ Controller
- ✔ Corporate vice presidents and officers
- ✔ Risk management personnel
- ✔ Managers of information technology departments

CEOs and CFOs are understandably focused on attaining the highest degree of confidence in financial-reporting documentation. It remains to be seen whether the SEC hasn't specifically sanctioned this trickle down accountability approach, and regardless, the SEC is unlikely to shift any liability from management. However, the advantages to the subcertification strategy are clear:

- ✔ It puts employees on notice as to what management's expectations are.
- ✔ It documents management's expectations.
- ✔ It may increase the likelihood of compliance with existing internal control structures.

Some Good Advice for CEOs and CFOs

Most companies already have procedures in place and hold management accountable for gathering and evaluating information to be included in their financial statements, annual reports, and SEC filings. From this standpoint, SOX doesn't really require management or companies to do anything specific. Rather, it directs CEOs and CFOs to take a greater role in these tasks and assume more public responsibility for acting on procedures that safeguard corporate assets.

No two companies have identical business operations, so SOX can't give you a "one-size-fits-all" solution for management. For example, it may not be appropriate for all companies to establish a disclosure committee. The reality is that each CEO and CFO must decide what methods of information gathering and reporting constitute the best internal control for their organization. This section covers three common-sense suggestions that can make the jobs of CEOs and CFOs easier.

Establish a disclosure committee

The SEC suggests that companies consider establishing *disclosure committees* to assist in developing disclosure controls and procedures. The disclosure committee can consist of the company's general counsel, the principal accounting officer, the chief investor relations officer, risk managers, or other people with control-related responsibilities in the company, such as information technology or human resources personnel.

Take an inventory

The first task a disclosure committee may want to undertake (if the company establishes one) is taking inventory of the company's existing practices as well as any known weaknesses. The committee should pay particular attention to any matters raised by the company's independent auditors. This inventory can help management document what policy breaches and material weaknesses happened on their watch as opposed to that of a prior management team.

Woo the whistle-blowers

An important aspect of internal control that receives a lot of publicity is how a company currently handles whistle-blower complaints. (I discuss whistle-blower protections in more detail in Chapter 16.) *Whistle-blowers* are people inside the company who provide information about breaches in internal control, material misstatements, and internal fraud to management or government officials. Management should be familiar with audit committee procedures for handling such complaints and can use the information gleaned to fulfill its own reporting and certification responsibilities.

Chapter 10

More Management Mandates

- -

In This Chapter

▶ Creating a code of ethics

▶ Banning personal loans of corporate funds

▶ Shining a light on blackout trading

▶ Making "mis-managers" pay the penalty

▶ Guarding against audit interference

- -

*T*he Sarbanes-Oxley Act, or SOX, could aptly be renamed the Shareholder Advocacy Act because its primary intent is to make sure that public corporations are managed for the benefit of shareholders, even though corporate health is dependent upon management.

The post-Enron wave of corporate scandals revealed audited financial statements that were fantasy sheets with phantom income on which huge management bonuses were based. Shareholders were left holding the deflated stock when massive accounting adjustments had to be made to reflect the company's true earnings.

This chapter identifies some new tools ushered in by SOX for reigning in management.

Codifying the Corporate Conscience

SOX insists that corporations codify their consciences by requiring

✔ A written code of ethics

✔ Public disclosure of the code and changes to it

✔ Prompt reporting of any potential violations of the code

The Senate Banking Committee, which drafted many management oversight provisions that were ultimately included in SOX, observed that the problems surrounding Enron and other public companies primarily "raised concerns about the ethical standard" of senior management. The report concluded that "investors have a legitimate interest in knowing whether a public company holds its financial officers to certain ethical standards in their financial dealings."

This section takes a look at the practical aspects of requiring companies to write up their ethical standards and communicate them to shareholders.

Explaining the code

SOX Section 406 requires companies to disclose in the periodic 10-K and 10-Q reports they file with the SEC (discussed in Chapter 3) whether the company has a written code of ethics for senior financial officers. If the company hasn't established a written code, an explanation is required.

If a company changes its code of ethics, it must promptly report the changes to the public on the SEC Form 8-K, which the SEC requires for the reporting of special events.

Establishing worthwhile objectives

The SEC Regulation S-K Item 406 explains that a *code of ethics* is a set of standards "reasonably designed to deter wrongdoing." The regulation provides that a written code of ethics should specify the following:

(1) Honest and ethical conduct, including the ethical handling of actual or apparent conflicts of interest between personal and professional relationships;

(2) Full, fair, accurate and timely, and understandable disclosure in reports and documents that a registrant files with, or submits to, the [SEC] and in other public communications made by the registrant;

(3) Compliance with the applicable government rules and regulations;

(4) The prompt internal reporting of violations of the code to an appropriate person or persons identified in the code; and

(5) Accountability and adherence to the code.

Realizing one code doesn't fit all companies

SEC rules provide that companies may have separate codes of ethics governing different types of officers. A company can create a broad code of ethics with special provisions to address additional topics that apply to specific persons within the company.

Disclosing amendments and waivers

SEC regulations require disclosure of any amendment or waiver of the provisions of a company's code of ethics. Amendments can be very telling about corporate culture, particularly if they're made in response to specific events. For example, if a company suddenly implements standards for disclosing off–balance sheet transactions, you may wonder if it has had a problem with this issue in the past.

According to the regulations, the term *waiver* means the approval by the company of "any material departure from a provision of the code of ethics. SEC regulations state that this term includes *implicit waivers,* which refers to the company's failure to take action within a reasonable period of time after management or the board of directors learns of a breach of the written provisions of the code.

Expecting ethics on the exchanges

Stock exchanges, such as the NYSE and NASDAQ, require the companies trading on them to have written codes of ethics. Although the SEC, NYSE, and NASDAQ requirements are similar in many respects, the following are a few significant differences:

- ✔ SOX requires that the code of ethics apply only to senior financial officers. NYSE and NASDAQ rules require that a code be implemented to all directors, officers, and employees.
- ✔ The SEC and NASDAQ require any waivers of code provisions to be disclosed on SEC Form 8-K (discussed in Chapter 3). The NYSE allows waivers to be disclosed by other means, such as in letters to shareholders, press releases, or on the company's Web site.
- ✔ SEC rules require disclosure of amendments to the code of ethics on a Form 8-K, but neither the NYSE nor NASDAQ require the disclosure of amendments.

A checklist of code contents

REMEMBER

Despite their differences (see the preceding section), it's possible to draft a single code of ethics that meets SEC, NYSE, and NASDAQ requirements.

At a minimum, your company's code should do the following:

- ✔ State the objectives of the code, mirroring SEC Rule 406 (check out the section "Establishing worthwhile objectives" earlier in this chapter)

- ✔ Identify the persons to which the code is applicable (for example, "all directors, officers, and employees")

- ✔ List contact people within the company who should be approached when questions about the code of ethics arise

- ✔ Impose an obligation for candid and honest conduct

- ✔ Address how conflicts of interest should be identified and handled

- ✔ Establish policies for full disclosure and representation

- ✔ Identify the obligations of people who become aware of any violations of the code of ethics, and lay out a protocol for notifying persons within the company

- ✔ Establish that people subject to the code of ethics have, at all times, an obligation to advance the company's business interests before their own

- ✔ Impose confidentiality when it's appropriate for achieving the objectives of the code of ethics

- ✔ State that a duty of fair dealing exists at all times

- ✔ Impose on all people who are subject to the code a duty to protect and safeguard the company's assets for the benefit of the shareholders

A sample code of ethics is included in Appendix F.

New Rules for Stock Selling and Telling

Prior to SOX, a huge loophole existed for the sale of company stock back to the company that issued it as opposed to selling it on the open market. Federal securities laws required executive officers and directors to report their ownership interests in the company on SEC Forms 3, 4, and 5. These forms are commonly referred to as *Section 16 reports* because they're required under Sections 16(a) and b-2 of the Securities Exchange Act of 1934. Prior to SOX, the law stated that stock sales were generally reportable 10 days after the end of the month in which the transaction occurred. However, sales of stock back to the company weren't reportable until 45 days after the end of the company's fiscal year.

During its post-Enron hearings, Congress was outraged to learn of the following pre-SOX executive antics:

- ✔ Early in 2001, Enron CEO Ken Lay sold substantial amounts of stock to the company and wasn't required to report the transaction until much later. At that time, SEC Rule 16b-3 required only that a sale to the issuer be reported annually on Form 5 rather than monthly on Form 4, the requirement for sales of stock other than back to the issuing company.

- ✔ Tyco International Ltd.'s CEO and CFO sold more than $100 million of Tyco stock to Tyco in late 2001, just before the company received extensive coverage for corporate mismanagement. The CEO and CFO weren't required to report these sales under the SEC rules in effect at the time because those rules provided that such sales were required to be reported only on an annual basis.

- ✔ Global Crossing founder and chairman Gary Winnick reportedly received $734 million for his stock before it plummeted into worthlessness in January 2002.

These events prompted the Senate to lament that the law should have required stock sales by executives to be brought to the public's attention "not a month or a year later when the damage has already been done."

Because of the numerous crimes and scandals of the past, Section 16 of SOX changes the preexisting requirement for stock-sale reporting by company executives in several ways, which I cover in this section.

Faster disclosure

SEC rules require that stock sales by company executives be reported on SEC Form 4 within two days of the "date of execution." The revised rules also require two-day reporting of certain transactions between employee benefit plans by officers and directors and that transactions involving stock options (such as grants, awards, cancellations, and repricings) be reported in the same time frame.

More disclosure

SEC Forms 3, 4, and 5 have been amended to add columns that show the exact dates that stock was purchased and sold. Under SOX, these forms must be posted on the corporation's Web site so everyone knows what management and directors are up to when it comes to selling their stock.

Owners of more than 10 percent of the common stock of any U.S. company are required to file SEC Forms 3, 4, and 5, regardless of whether they're officers or directors.

Prohibiting Personal Loans

SOX Section 402 prohibits SEC-registered public companies from making or arranging loans to their directors and executive officers. Prior to SOX, this practice was surprisingly commonplace; Enron, WorldCom, Adelphia, Quest, and Global Crossing had all authorized substantial personal loans to their executive officers.

SOX distinguishes between *personal loans* and other *extensions of credit*. Essentially, a loan isn't considered a personal loan or arrangement for a loan if the primary purpose is to advance the business of the company, even though the loan may have the ancillary effect of enhancing the executive's personal credit. For example, some companies have employee benefit programs, such as 401(k)s, under which loans are available on the same basis to all participants. Although the company may have arranged the loan provisions of the benefits plan, the plan isn't a prohibited loan arrangement under SOX.

SOX Section 402 contains a grandfather clause that exempts credit or loan arrangements entered into between the company and its executives prior to its date of enactment (July 30, 2002), so long as the extension of credit hasn't had any material modifications or renewals since its inception.

Banning Blackout Trading

No aspect of the Enron collapse captured more media attention than the infamous management and director stock trades that took place during a blackout period. From October 29 to November 12, 2001, Enron employees were temporarily prohibited from selling the Enron stock in their 401(k) accounts while the company administering the plan was changed. During this period, the price of Enron stock dropped from $13.81 (right before the blackout) to $9.98 (right after the blackout). Enron company executives, most notably CEO Ken Lay, reportedly sold over $1 billion in Enron stock during the blackout period, while employees lost nearly $1 billion from their retirement plans.

Avoiding media images of stricken retirees

During Enron's collapse, the media seized upon images of devastated retirees, and the effect was understandably heartbreaking and enraging. To help reassure members of the public holding stock in their employers as parts of retirement plans that their investments are secure and protected, SOX includes the following points:

- ✔ Section 306(a) contains a general statutory prohibition on stock transactions by directors and executive officers during blackout periods related to employee benefit plans.

- ✔ The Employee Retirement Income Security Act of 1974 (ERISA) is amended to require the administrators of retirement plans to give all plan participants at least 30-days notice before a blackout period is imposed. The company faces a fine of $100 per day for each employee who doesn't receive such notice.

- ✔ ERISA further requires that the public be notified of any impending blackout period; the company must file a Form 8-K within four days of the date that notice of the blackout is provided.

Making some necessary exceptions

The requirements covered in the preceding section are subject to a few notable exceptions. For the most part, these exceptions are intended to strike a compromise between employees' needs for information about blackout periods and the added administrative burden of giving notice of routine and anticipated blackout periods. The exceptions are:

- ✔ Neither ERISA nor SOX require notice of regularly scheduled blackout periods that are disclosed in retirement plan documents distributed to participants and beneficiaries.

- ✔ No notice is required for blackouts that must be imposed in connection with mergers, acquisitions, and divestures.

Making Managers Pay Personally

In 2005, prior to being sentenced to 25 years in prison, WorldCom CEO Bernard Ebbers agreed to pay $5.5 million in cash and turn over his mansion and $40 million in other assets to settle claims filed by WorldCom shareholders who lost billions of dollars when WorldCom collapsed in the largest bankruptcy in history. Prior to the deal, Ebbers had repaid only a small portion of the $408 million in personal loans WorldCom made to him before the board forced him to resign.

SOX now makes it much more difficult for managers to appropriate corporate assets. New laws permit their personal assets to be frozen or recovered under a wide range of circumstances.

The freeze factor

SOX Section 1103 authorizes the SEC to freeze the paychecks of "directors, officers, partners, controlling persons, agents, or employees" that it targets "during the course of a lawful investigation involving possible violations of federal securities laws." The way this deep freeze works is that the SEC requests a federal court to issue a temporary order placing the payments earmarked for these individuals in an interest-bearing escrow account.

The court order is effective for 45 days, during which time the SEC decides whether to file charges against the individuals in question. If the SEC doesn't bring charges and can't convince the court that it has good cause to freeze the assets for another 45 days, the funds are paid out to the individuals who were slated to receive them. In any event, the SEC can't freeze the assets for more than 90 days without bringing charges. If it does bring charges, the freeze remains in effect "until the conclusion of any legal proceedings related thereto."

The danger of disgorgement

Many CEOs and corporate executives are given bonuses and compensation based on the performance of their companies. But what at first blush may seem like a straightforward, merit-based compensation arrangement can become enormously complicated and terribly unfair when the corporate earnings on which the bonuses are based have to be adjusted downward. For this reason, SOX provides that bonuses based on previous (erroneous) earnings also have to be repaid when the restatement is attributable to management's noncompliance.

Under SOX, CEOs must give back their bonuses if the company's financial statements have to be restated due to "material noncompliance" with financial reporting requirements. Specifically, CEOs and CFOs have to give back

✔ Any incentive-based compensation paid during the 12-month period following the initial publication of the financial statements

✔ Any equity in the company received as compensation during the 12-month period following the initial publication of the financial statements

✔ Profits from the sale of the company's securities

Stopping Audit Inference

In 2001, Enron was forced to report that it was required to correct (or *restate*) its 1997 earnings by $96 million, 1998 earnings by $113 million, 1999 earnings by $250 million, and 2000 earnings by $132 million. During investigations, Congress and the public were outraged to learn that its accounting firm, Arthur Anderson, had been pressing for the adjustments for years but had capitulated when management stood firm in refusing to make them.

As a result of this and other events, SOX Section 303 provides that it shall be "unlawful" for any officer or director of an issuer or any other person acting under his or her direction to take any action to fraudulently influence, coerce, manipulate, or mislead any independent public or certified public accountant performing the audit of the issuer's financial statements.

Identifying audit interlopers

SEC rules make it clear that very little leeway is given to managers and directors who attempt to influence the outcome of their company's audits. The following activities aren't tolerated:

✔ Attempting to convince the auditors to issue financial statements that aren't in accordance with Generally Accepted Accounting Principles (GAAP; see Chapter 4)

✔ Attempting to skip or overlook parts of an audit

✔ Failing to communicate required matters to the company's audit committee

✔ Threatening to cancel audit engagements or fire auditors (including undertaking more obvious forms of blackmail threats and intimidation)

✔ Knowingly providing false, misleading, or incomplete information to auditors

Suing audit interlopers

In the aftermath of SOX, if a company was to shred documents, encourage employees to mislead auditors, or skew audit test results, it would find itself defending against a lawsuit by the SEC under a new provision of SOX that specifically authorizes such litigation.

SOX Section 303 and the accompanying SEC Rule 13b2-2 enable the SEC to file civil lawsuits against individuals and public companies that interfere with audits.

Under Section 303, the SEC can make more specific rules to prevent audit interference. Rule 303(b) also provides that in "any civil proceeding," the SEC "shall have the exclusive authority to enforce this section and any rule or regulation issued under this section." This SEC authority means that private individuals usually don't have the right to sue companies for audit interference; they have to wait for the SEC to do so. Similarly, Rule 303(c) states that the anti-interference provisions are enacted "in addition to" and don't supersede any other provisions of the law or rules or regulations that may prohibit the same conduct.

Part III
Surviving Section 404

The 5th Wave   By Rich Tennant

"My favorite pastimes? What do I look for in a man? Are you certain this is a questionnaire for Sarbanes—Oxley compliance?"

In this part . . .

Thanks to its unprecedented documentation requirements, no part of SOX has received more adverse
publicity than Section 404. Section 404 requires companies to document the internal controls that affect the
financial information they distribute to the investing
public. Because it's not quite as simple as it sounds, this
part explains how your company can streamline Section
404 projects and avoid red herrings and tangents. It also
takes a look at potential benefits, cost-savings, and competitive advantages that your company may achieve as a
result of the Section 404 process.

Chapter 11

Clearing Up Confusion About Control

In This Chapter

▶ What Section 404 actually says about internal control

▶ Disclosure controls and procedures under Section 302

▶ Distinguishing internal control under sections 404 and 302

▶ Coping with compliance costs

*B*efore the Securities Act of 1933 was passed, President Roosevelt publicly agreed with Supreme Court Justice Louis Brandies that "sunshine is said to be the best of disinfectants; electric light the most efficient policeman." Like the 1933 Act, SOX attempts to shine a bright light on financial reporting improprieties within corporations by zeroing in on "disclosure controls and procedures" and "internal control over financial reporting." However, in doing so, Congress and the Securities Exchange Commission, or SEC, have also created the inevitable uncertainty that accompanies any new legislation.

This chapter attempts to clarify the concepts of "disclosure controls" and "internal controls" introduced by SOX Sections 302 and 404. It also looks at the costs, dates, criteria, and other threshold issues associated with complying with these sections. I also explain why the term "internal control" has different definitions depending on whether it is used in connection with Section 302 or Section 404.

The Nuts and Bolts of Section 404

Congress included some broad new standards in SOX Section 404, deliberately did not tell companies how to implement them. The section is deliberately short on specifics. Instead, Congress directs the SEC and the Public Company Accounting Oversight Board, or PCAOB, to create more specific rules for companies to follow under SOX. (For more on the PCAOB, turn to Chapter 6.)

What Section 404 says

Section 404 may be only 180 words, but since Section 404 was first introduced, U.S. companies have been busy interpreting every turn of phrase in order to figure out exactly what they must do to comply with the statute. Examining the wording of Section 404 can help you understand the obligations imposed under the SEC and PCAOB rules, which interpret Section 404 and more specifically define companies' obligations.

The following comes directly from Section 404. I've underlined buzzwords and key phrases for you to pay particular attention to:

SEC. 404. MANAGEMENT ASSESSMENT OF INTERNAL CONTROLS.

(a) RULES REQUIRED.—The Commission shall prescribe rules requiring each annual report required by section 13(a) or 15(d) of the Securities Exchange Act of 1934 (15 U.S.C. 78m or 78o(d)) to contain an internal control report, which shall—

    (1) state the responsibility of management for establishing and maintaining an adequate internal control structure and procedures for financial reporting; and

    (2) contain an assessment, as of the end of the most recent fiscal year of the issuer, of the effectiveness of the internal control structure and procedures of the issuer for financial reporting.

(b) INTERNAL CONTROL EVALUATION AND REPORTING.—With respect to the internal control assessment required by subsection (a), each registered public accounting firm that prepares or issues the audit report for the issuer shall attest to, and report on, the assessment made by the management of the issuer. An attestation made under this subsection shall be made in accordance with standards for attestation engagements issued or adopted by the Board. Any such attestation shall not be the subject of a separate engagement.

What Section 404 really does

The concept of internal control really isn't anything new; many companies had excellent controls and procedures in place prior to SOX. But SOX Section 404 accomplishes three objectives:

- ✔ Clarify what's required for a company to maintain adequate internal control

- ✔ Require management and auditors to formally certify that adequate internal controls are in place

- ✔ Specify roles of the SEC and PCAOB in carrying out the objectives of SOX

SEC Rules Under Section 404

In carrying out its mandate to prescribe specific rules for implementing Section 404, the SEC has focused on two critical areas:

- ✔ **Management responsibility:** Annual reports required to be filed with the SEC must state management's responsibility for establishing and maintaining an adequate internal control structure and procedures for financial reporting.

- ✔ **Effectiveness of internal control:** An annual report must contain an assessment of the effectiveness of the company's internal control structure and procedures for financial reporting as of the end of the company's most recent fiscal year.

PCAOB participation in the Section 404 process

SOX 404 requires the PCAOB to create standards specifically for auditors in complying with Section 404. Auditors are responsible, under the Section, for attesting to and reporting on the assessment made by management. They must do so in accordance with standards for attestation engagements adopted by the PCAOB. (The role and duties of the PCOAB in regulating the audit profession are discussed in Chapter 6.)

Audit Standard No. 2 is intended to guide audit firms in complying with Section 404. You can download a copy of Standard No. 2 and the accompanying information release at the PCAOB Standards Web site located at www. pcaobus.org/Standards/index.asp, under the link indicated in Figure 11-1.

Figure 11-1:
The PCAOB
Standards
Web site.

When Do Companies Have to Comply with Section 404?

Most companies have until fiscal years "ending on or after" July 15, 2007, to comply with SOX's internal control reporting and disclosure requirements. Large companies have 60 days after the close of the fiscal year to file their Form 10-k (containing audited financial statements with the SEC). Smaller companies with revenues of less than $75 million in equity (generally its voting and non-voting stock) have 90 days after the close of the fiscal year to file their financial statements.

Since many companies are on a calendar-year fiscal-year basis, their date for 404 compliance will be December 31, 2007. However, many companies use a June 30 or other date for the end of their fiscal year, and they have a longer or shorter period to comply. For example, a company with a June 30 fiscal year would have to comply with Section 404 for its June 30, 2008 fiscal year end.

Accelerated and nonaccelerated filers

If a company is considered an *accelerated filer,* it has a much longer time frame to comply with SOX than a company that is deemed an accelerated filer under SEC rules.

If a company is an accelerated filer, it first meets the following four conditions at the end of its fiscal year:

✔ The market value of the voting and non-voting common equity (stock) of the company is $75 million or more.

✔ The company has been subject to the reporting requirements of requirements of

Section 13(a) or 15(d) of the Exchange Act of 1934 (discussed in Chapter 2) for a period of at least 12 calendar months.

✔ The company has filed at least one annual report under Section 13(a) or 15(d).

✔ The issuer is not eligible to use certain special SEC Forms for small businesses.

If a company does not meet the criteria above, it is deemed a *nonaccelerated filer* and is subject to the recently extended July 15, 2007, compliance date.

As of the writing of the book, the SEC is also considering liberalizing the Section 404 requirements that apply to quarterly and other SEC reports filed during the year. It is also considering liberalizing the requirements to allow more companies to qualify as nonaccelerated, possibly exempting companies with equity of as much as $125 million from having to obtain an independent Section 404 audit. For more discussion which companies are currently required to do what, see the sidebar "Accelerated and nonaccelerated filers."

A "fiscal" year is a year measured for financial reporting purposes, and can end on a date other than December 31, which is the year end date for a calendar year.

Many companies are on a calendar year ending December 31, so their first date for 404 compliance is December 31, 2007, because that is their first fiscal year "on or after July 15, 2007." Another popular date used by companies to end their fiscal year is June 30. These companies would have comply with SOX Section 404 beginning with the June 30, 2008, annual reports.

To keep up with changes and proposals regarding Section 404 compliance deadlines and exemptions, visit my Sarbanes-Oxley update page at www. abtechlaw.com.

Section 302 "Internal Control" versus Section 404 "Internal Control"

One of the biggest sources of confusion under SOX is the term "internal control." It certainly doesn't help that the SEC decided to use the term "internal control" in two different sections of SOX and provide a different meaning for the term under each section.

By using different definitions, the SEC intended to make clear that SOX is aimed at two distinct types of internal controls. Under Section 302, the term internal control means *disclosure controls and procedures*. Under Section 404, the term means *internal control over financial reporting*.

This section attempts to clarify what are considered "disclosure controls and procedures" under SOX Section 302 and what is considered "internal control over financial reporting" under SOX Section 404.

Defining "disclosure controls and procedures" under Section 302

Section 302 of SOX requires each CEO and CFO of a public company to certify that they have designed "internal controls" sufficient to ensure that they know about material information within the company. The certification applies to the period for which each SEC periodic report was prepared (Section 302 is discussed more fully in Chapter 9). The SEC has said that, for purposes of Section 302, references to internal controls mean "disclosure controls and procedures." The SEC has explained disclosure controls and procedures encompass all the controls and procedures a company uses to ensure that information in the 10-K annual reports and 10-Q reports they file with the SEC is accurate.

The scope of the term "disclosure controls and procedures" is broader than the term "internal control over financial reporting." Disclosure controls and procedures includes controls over all information that impacts company resources, not just controls on accounting and financial information.

In addition to complying with the certification requirements discussed in Section 302 to avoid civil liability, management must submit an additional certification containing similar information under Section 906. (I discuss both types of certifications further in Chapter 9.)

Section 302 requirements at the end of every period

SEC rules require management to

✔ Evaluate a company's disclosure controls and procedure as of the end of each period covered by the particular report.

✔ Make conclusions about the effectiveness of the controls and procedures the company has in place.

To comply, most companies begin preliminary testing of internal controls and procedures early in the year being reported and do final testing at the end of the year to make sure management and auditors have submitted a report that is valid as of the end of the year, as required by Section 404.

Minimum Section 302 standards for every company

Disclosure controls and procedures vary according to the industries in which companies operate and the companies' unique corporate structures. However, in every company, certain basic structures need to be present in order for management to prepare its report and for the auditors to indicate that management's report is accurate.

At a minimum, a public company must have the following in place with respect to its disclosure controls and procedures:

✔ **Written procedures:** A company's internal controls and procedures should be written out in enough detail to provide guidance but not in so much detail that they're burdensome and difficult to follow.

Disclosure controls and procedures requiring excessive detail can make the processes rigid and inflexible and create unnecessary compliance issues.

✔ **Systematic management supervision:** Management should be formally involved in supervising internal controls and procedures at a practical level. Companies should put into place a calendar for monitoring controls and procedures and identify milestone dates. Additionally, the SEC recommends they form special disclosure committees, as discussed in Chapter 9.

✔ **A process for reviewing effectiveness:** Internal controls and procedures for U.S. companies should be evaluated on a quarterly basis in order to ensure they continue to be effective.

Interpreting "internal control over financial reporting" under Section 404

Under SOX Section 404, all public companies are required to include in their annual reports a report of management on the company's "internal control over financial reporting." The SEC rules describe a control over financial reporting as a process designed "to provide reasonable assurance regarding the reliability of financial reporting and the preparation of financial statements for external purposes."

This phrase "internal control" as it is used in Section 404 refers to the types of controls a company must have in place in order to prepare its financial statements according to Generally Accepted Accounting Principles (GAAP), which I explain in Chapter 5. Because this term relates only to GAAP, it's narrower in scope than the broader term "disclosure controls and procedures" language used in Section 302, discussed in the preceding section.

Key elements of an internal control over financial reporting

The SEC rules require that an internal control over financial reporting satisfy three key functions:

- ✔ **Recordkeeping:** The process must involve maintaining records that accurately, fairly, and in reasonable detail reflect transactions and dispositions involving the company's assets.

- ✔ **Compliance:** The process must provide reasonable assurance that transactions are actually recorded so as to ensure that receipts and expenditures are made only when authorized by management and are recorded so that financial statements can be prepared in accordance with GAAP.

- ✔ **Prevention and detection:** The process must provide reasonable assurance that unauthorized use or disposition of company assets can and will be detected.

U.S. securities laws have required companies to maintain internal controls since 1977. SOX merely requires management and auditors to formally report on what should already be in place.

Management's evaluation responsibilities under Section 404

Section 404 provides that management's report must establish its responsibilities for maintaining adequate internal accounting controls. The SEC rules warn companies that "inquiry alone will not provide an adequate basis for management's assessment," So management's procedures for testing internal controls must include both:

- ✔ Evaluation of the control's design
- ✔ Testing of the control's effectiveness

In the company's annual report filed with the SEC, management must include its own report on the company's internal control over financial reporting. In addition, the public accounting firm that audits the company's financial statements (the ones that appear in the annual report) must issue an attestation report on management's assessment of internal control; this report gets filed as part of the company's annual report. With respect to quarterly reports, management is required to evaluate any change in the company's internal control occurring during a fiscal quarter that materially affects or is reasonably likely to materially affect the company's internal control.

What evaluation criteria should management use under Section 404?

Management is required to base its assessment of the effectiveness of the company's internal control over financial reporting on a suitable on a set of standards established by recognized experts. The SEC specifically refers to the Committee of Sponsoring Organizations (COSO) of the Treadway Commission as an acceptable framework for management's internal control assessment. The COSO criteria is covered in more detail in Chapter 13, and is the only set of standards specifically recognized by the SEC as of the writing of this book.

The directives in PCAOB's Auditing Standard No. 2 are based on the framework established by COSO. This is because so many public companies are expected to use that framework for their assessments. Other SEC-sanctioned approaches and frameworks may be published in the future; although different frameworks may not contain exactly the same elements as COSO, they probably incorporate most of the same testing concepts and criteria.

The AICPA offers several resources to assist in understanding and complying with the COSO framework, including checklists for internal control testing. You can find these resources at www.cpa2biz.com.

Controlling the Cost of Compliance

Research shows public companies have had to dig deeply into their pockets to comply with SOX. In fact, a survey by Financial Executives International (FEI), the leading professional organization of chief financial officers (CFOs) and other senior financial executives, concluded that in the first year of SOX's enactment, Section 404 cost U.S. companies $3.14 million per company. Much of this initial expense is attributed to costs for consulting, software, and the 58 percent increase in the fees charged by external auditors. (For full coverage of the costs associated with Section 404, check out Chapter 13.)

Although Congress was in a hurry to pass SOX in 2002 as a political response to the Enron crisis, it wasn't totally insensitive to costs of compliance. Section 404(b) provides that the auditor's attestation of management's assessment of internal control shall *not* be the subject of a separate engagement. In other words, Congress carefully conveys its expectation that companies not be forced to pay for duplicative audit services.

Cost-cutting measures by the PCAOB

The Public Company Accounting Oversight Board (PCAOB), which oversees all audit firms, has attempted to make compliance as economical as possible. In an effort to reign in audit costs, the PCAOB has issued *Auditing Standard No. 2*. Under this standard, the audit firm must:

✔ Address the requirements for internal control over financial reporting

✔ Review management's assessment of the effectiveness of the internal control

Standard No. 2 also directs audit firms to perform two tasks required under Section 404 during a single audit engagement, rather than conducting two separate audits (and billing the to do both). This is because the work the objectives and the work involved in performing both audits make them inter-related. For example, the auditor's discovery of misstatements in the financial statements may indicate the existence of weaknesses in the company's internal control over financial reporting.

In addition to issuing Auditing Standard No. 2, the PCAOB has also specially studied the impact Section 404 costs have on companies, particularly small and medium-sized companies. The PCAOB anticipates that most companies regardless of size experience the highest cost of compliance with Section 404 during the first year they're required to comply with the law.

The PCAOB has determined that cost of complying with Section 404 is related to factors such as:

✔ **The adequacy of the company's internal controls in previous years:** Existing control systems, ethical standards, and core values of a senior management group all help determine the costs of compliance with Section 404 and related SEC rules.

✔ **Whether the company does business overseas:** Large, complex, multi-national companies, for example, are likely to need more extensive and sophisticated internal control systems.

✔ **The complexity of the company's corporate structure:** Companies with multiple subsidiaries and related entities may have increased costs of compliance simply because they have more information and locations to track. In contrast, smaller companies and companies with less complex operations may find that compliance is less burdensome than originally anticipated.

Finally, the PCAOB has recognized that audit costs may be impacted by how much the auditor is permitted to rely on the work of internal auditors (which are paid at company salaries rather than expensive hourly rates as the auditors are). Accordingly, PCAOB Auditing Standard No. 2 provides outside auditors lots of discretion and flexibility in using the client company's personnel. The standard does, however, require the audit firm to obtain (through its own auditing procedures) a meaningful portion of the evidence that supports its opinion.

Section 404 sticker shock

A major criticism of SOX has been the huge, unexpected first-year costs of complying with Section 404. These costs are the primary reason the SEC cited for pushing back compliance deadlines for smaller companies to give them an extra year (see the section "When Do Companies Have to Comply with Section 404?" earlier in the chapter).

Decreasing costs in year two

When companies were asked about their anticipated costs in complying with SOX in year two, "85 percent of respondents said they expect nonauditor expenditures to decrease (by an average of 39 percent), and 68 percent said they believe the costs of their primary auditor will also decrease (by an average of 25 percent)," according to a recent study done by Financial Executives International (FEI).

An SEC commissioner's reflections on Section 404 costs

In a September 2005 speech before the Association of State Treasurers, summarized in *Compliance Week Magazine,* SEC Commissioner Paul Atkins blasted the SEC for its poor estimates on the costs of complying with SOX. Atkins charged "Perhaps nothing in recent memory has illustrated the need to perform more probing cost/benefit analysis before requirements take effect than the regulatory regime that has grown under Section 404 of the Sarbanes-Oxley Act." He concluded, "As we enter the second year of the 404 process . . . it is becoming increasingly evident that everyone greatly underestimated the costs."

To support this criticism, Atkins several compelling statistics. He explained "When the SEC first released its implementation rules for Section 404, we estimated aggregate costs of about $1.24 billion or $94,000 per public company." He lamented "Unfortunately our estimates were not just low, they were incredibly low. Surveys have indicated that actual costs incurred for 404 compliance were 20 times higher than what we estimated."

Atkins also warned that year-two compliance costs will not decrease significantly. He predicted "Cost reductions from year one will instead be in the neighborhood of 5 to 20 percent, and I predict that the reduction will be at the low end of this range."

Looking for the sunny side of Section 404

Most businesses (and many politicians) are unhappy with SOX simply because the costs of compliance been so much greater than originally expected. These costs have been viewed as a drain on productivity that puts American businesses at a disadvantage with foreign competitors.

Section 404 is the provision of SOX that businesses complain about most. However, SOX proponents argue there will be less grumbling about Section 404 as businesses move beyond the first year of compliance, when the costs are the highest. After the first year, businesses may also notice benefits from Section 404 audits and increased internal control, such as elimination of fraud and redundancies in internal processes. Companies that have always operated in an ethical, above-board manner consistent with Section 404 may actually enjoy a competitive advantage. These squeaky-clean companies will have an easier time complying with Section 404 and will ultimately have to dedicate less money for compliance than companies that need to substantially scramble and revamp their internal processes in order to get a clean Section 404 opinion from their auditors.

A benefit on the horizon for businesses and investors alike is the increased reliability of financial information and reporting. This is what SOX was passed to accomplish, and it appears that the law is working. According to Financial Executives International (FEI), "55 percent of companies surveyed believe Section 404 gives investors and other external audiences more confidence in a company's financial reports, and 83 percent of large companies (over $25 billion) agree. Significantly, however, 94 percent of all respondents said the costs of compliance exceed the benefits."

Other critics of SOX argue that it has failed to alter the behaviors of boards and management in measurable ways and that this behavior is what ultimately determines the control environment. According to Linda Mertz of Mertz Associates, Inc., a company that specializes in mergers and acquisitions, "SOX has added complexity and cost to a company's economic equation, but has yet to demonstrate the addition of economic value or any measurable change in management's behavior or attitudes." However, changes in board and management "behavior" with respect to internal control may be difficult to measure. How do you measure the costs of lawsuits, frauds, and misstatements of financial information that are avoided?

It's difficult to deny that more qualified, responsible board directors contribute to building better companies. SOX has undeniably raised the bar for board membership (as discussed in Chapter 8), but there is little data on how it has impacted the behavior of board members already ensconced in their positions.

A great way to keep up with what other companies are doing with respect to SOX is to become a member of Financial Executives International. FEI is the "leading advocate for the views of corporate financial management." The organization has more than 15,400 members who hold policymaking positions as chief financial officers, treasurers, and controllers. The organization's Web site is located at www.fei.com.

According to FEI, companies believe they can reduce their SOX compliance costs after the first year by:

- ✔ Focusing on risk areas in the audit
- ✔ Reducing the degree of documentation required in general
- ✔ Being more flexible in remediating control problems uncovered by the Section 404 audit

Chapter 12

Surviving a Section 404 Audit

. . . .

In This Chapter

▶ Defining the role of management in the audit process

▶ Creating a wall between management and the outside auditors

▶ Knowing what auditors test for and ask about

▶ Flunking a 404 audit

. . . .

S OX Section 404 makes it the responsibility of management to assess the company's internal control for financial reporting at the end of each year. Unfortunately, Section 404 and the SEC rules passed to interpret it don't spell out exactly what *internal control* means in all scenarios. Reportedly, this omission has led to extreme scenarios in which auditors insist upon verifying that all restroom keys are accounted for or testing obscure computer code configurations that are unlikely to impact the company's financial statements.

This chapter examines the expanded the role of the audit firm and helps CFOs, compliance officers, and audit committees identify where they can draw the line in a 404 audit.

Dividing Up Responsibilities in a Section 404 Audit

An audit of internal control is, as you might expect, a very controlled process. The 404 audit is a major project to which a company devotes substantial manpower and financial resources to complete. The audit process involves structured communication between management, independent auditors, the company's audit committee, and, on occasion, its board of directors. In a 404 audit, everyone has a specific role to play.

Management's role

Shifting focus from the pursuit of profits to the internal controls within a company is a difficult transition for many managers. Most are still adjusting to their new SOX-related responsibilities.

The major responsibilities of management with respect to the 404 audit are:

- ✔ Learning about the system of internal control that's in place
- ✔ Evaluating the effectiveness of both the design and implementation of internal control structures
- ✔ Preparing a written assessment at the end of the year on the effectiveness of internal control to include in management's report

The independent auditor's role

A Section 404 audit is part of the annual audit of a company's financial statements — it's not a separate process. As part of the overall audit, Section 404 requires the independent audit firm to express an opinion on management's assessment of the effectiveness of internal control. The audit firm must attest that management's assessment of internal control over financial reporting is stated fairly, in all material respects. The auditor must be satisfied that management has performed necessary testing and has formed an accurate basis for its reporting and attestation.

An auditor can't simply take management's word that adequate testing has been done. Auditors are required to form their own opinions about the accuracy of management's reports and attestation and be able to support those opinions with evidence and data from the testing.

Because SOX forecloses audit firms from performing consulting and other nonaudit services (as discussed in Chapter 5), many are hoping to make up the lost revenues on the Section 404 audits.

The outside audit firm can go about getting the evidence it needs in several ways, including:

- ✔ Testing transactions: Performing its own tests on company transactions to see if the internal controls that are supposed to be in place actually kick in
- ✔ Verifying management's assessment process: Retracing the steps taken by management

✔ Evaluating and testing work done by others: Retesting a sampling of transactions on internal control that were tested by the company's own staff (such as internal auditors) to see if their conclusions about the company's internal control can or should be used by the auditors

What the Auditors Are Looking For

What will auditors look at when they're doing a Section 404 audit of your company? They're given guidance in this area by the Public Accounting Oversight Board (PCAOB) (discussed in Chapter 6). The PCAOB issues special standards for public auditors to guide them in complying with SEC rules. Auditing Standard No. 2 is of special importance with respect to Section 404 audits and SOX compliance. This particular standard addresses both the work that is required to audit internal control over financial reporting and also the relationship of the Section 404 audit to the audit of the company's financial statements as a whole.

What Is (and Is Not) Related to the Audit

A Section 404 audit focuses on a company's internal control over financial reporting. Internal controls operate as checks on processes that impact the company's financial statements. However, not everything is within the ambit of the audit. For example, marketing decisions, unrelated administrative procedures, and most personnel policies probably aren't things your auditors should spend time and money digging into.

Examples of internal controls the auditors may be looking for may include:

✔ Policies and procedures for maintaining accounting records: All companies should have controls in place to ensure accurate recording of information and protect against tampering.

✔ Procedures for authorizing receipts and disbursements and safeguarding assets: SEC rules require that all transactions carried out within the company should be appropriately authorized and employees and third parties not be permitted to initiate transactions without appropriate authority to do so.

✔ Tracking systems for use of the company's resources: Transactions involving the company's resources should have controls to ensure that resources (such as labor and inventory) aren't diverted or misused as the transaction progresses.

✔ Verification of balances and transactions: Account balances and transaction amounts should be verified.

✔ Appropriate segregation of responsibilities: Responsibilities should be divided among different persons in a way that makes it harder to perpetrate fraud or error. For example, the employees authorizing payments to vendors shouldn't be the same ones cutting checks.

Taking the broad view, the auditors performing the Section 404 audit are in charge of making sure that the board of directors, management, investors, and others can rely on reported financial information when making decisions.

SOX was passed, in part, because of Congress's concern about cases in which fraudulent reporting on financial statements was initiated by management and resulted from management's ability to exploit weaknesses in internal control. Thus, under SOX, internal controls are now assessed twice: once by management, and once by the auditors.

Complying with Audit Standard No. 2

During congressional hearings on Enron, senior management complained to Congress that at the time, it wasn't aware of the illegal activities taking place at Enron, and the independent auditors didn't bring any problems to management's attention. To remedy this all-too-common scenario, Congress created the Public Company Accounting Oversight Board (PCAOB) as a new arm of the SEC, replacing the system of accounting self-regulation that had previously been in place. Section 404 directs the SEC to create rules for implementation, and the SEC in turn directs the PCAOB to create standards for auditors.

PCAOB Standard No. 2 was approved by the SEC on June 17, 2004, and is effective for audits of internal control over financial reporting required by Section 404(b) of the Sarbanes-Oxley Act of 2002. This section summarizes the key provisions of Auditing Standard No. 2.

Evaluating management's assessment

The starting place for the audit of a company's internal control over financial reporting is management's own assessment of the effectiveness of the company's internal control. The auditor evaluates this assessment with the intent of gaining confidence that management has a basis for its conclusions.

The assessment contains information that helps the auditor understand the company's internal control. It's also a primary source for the evidence the audit firm needs to support its own opinion under Section 404(b).

In preparing its assessment, management generally performs its own testing of the company's internal control. This testing can positively or negatively impact how much work the audit firm must perform because the audit firm is permitted to rely on testing of management that it has independently verified.

Good organization and structure within the company can make it easier for the audit firm to independently test and verify the results of the testing already done by the company. Auditing Standard No. 2 allows the auditor to use, to a reasonable degree, work performed by others, which means that the more extensive and reliable management's assessment is, the less extensive and costly the work of the independent auditor's needs to be. For example, if management has tested controls on a certain type of transaction by giving employees questionnaires, the audit firm may be able to rely on the questionnaires upon verifying their authenticity and scope (the matters surveyed must be appropriate for the particular internal control being tested).

Software can streamline the audit process and substantially reduce the final bill of the independent audit firm. Good SOX software tools that generate specific reports on Section 404 tests performed by management and internal auditors are available. These software tools also maintain user-friendly databases for external auditors to draw upon. Chapters 14 and 15 cover SOX-specific software on the market and look into some examples.

The more clearly management documents its internal control over financial reporting, the easier it is for the auditor to understand the following:

✔ The nature of the internal control being tested

✔ How diligently management performed the testing

✔ Whether management used appropriate criteria in its assessment

Walking through the controls in place

It's the independent auditor's job to make sure that the controls a company has in place are operating as intended. Auditing Standard No. 2 explains that auditors must interview company personnel, but that alone is insufficient. The auditors must perform independent testing to confirm their understanding of how the internal controls work.

Tests the auditors may perform to gain an understanding of the company's internal controls may include the following:

✔ Observing the personnel who actually perform the controls

✔ Reviewing documents that are used in or result from the controls

✔ Comparing supporting documents (for example, sales invoices, contracts, and purchase orders) to the accounting records

✔ Performing walkthroughs of the company's significant processes

Walkthroughs play a major role in helping an auditor gain an understanding of a company's internal controls and are a required method of testing under PCAOB Auditing Standard No. 2. In a walkthrough, the auditor identifies a transaction from each major class of transactions and traces it from origination through the company's accounting systems, information systems, and financial accounting all the way to the reporting of that transaction on the company's financial statements.

Walkthroughs generate evidence for the audit firm to support or refute its understanding of transaction processing and the internal controls in place.

Auditing Standard No. 2 requires walkthroughs at each annual audit of internal control over financial reporting. The PCAOB views walkthroughs as a critical test for confirming the auditor's understanding of the controls as correct and complete. Without actually "walking" transactions through the significant processes each year, there's a high risk that changes to internal control processes could go undetected by the auditor.

When walkthroughs are performed, PCAOB Auditing Standard No. 2 requires the auditor to perform the walkthroughs rather than rely on walkthroughs performed by company personnel. The latter would defeat the purpose of informing the auditor and also would be inappropriate because the audit firm needs to exercise its independent judgment with respect to the information obtained at each stage of the walkthrough.

Auditing Standard No. 2 cautions that walkthroughs should be done by or under the supervision of experienced auditors. Walkthroughs involve a lot of judgment calls as to whether controls are working properly or need to be investigated further. Inexperienced audit personnel who participate in the walkthroughs should be closely supervised by senior audit staff so that what occurs in the walkthrough is correctly interpreted and documented. Inexperienced auditors may not catch subtle omissions or deviations.

Identifying assertions and significant accounts

For independent auditors, an important part of the audit process involves identifying accounts and assertions that should be tested. *Assertions* are facts contained in the financial statements that must be verified in the audit process instead of simply assumed to be true. For example, an auditor may verify that a particular asset actually exists or that a specific transaction occurred.

Auditing Standard No. 2 recognizes that some accounts are more significant than others; it provides criteria for auditors to identify significant accounts for purposes of determining which accounts to test.

Usually, the auditor usually begins by comparing all the company's accounts to determine which are the most significant based on their dollar amounts. The auditor may then look at other factors such as risks that inaccuracies in particular accounts pose to the company. The factors that determine significant accounts vary from company to company.

Some of the questions the auditor asks in evaluating controls relative to significant accounts are:

- ✔ Has the company included all loans outstanding in its loans payable account?

- ✔ Have marketable investments been valued properly?

- ✔ Does the company have the rights to the accounts receivable, and are the loans payable the proper obligation of the company?

- ✔ Are the amounts in the financial statements appropriately presented, and is there adequate disclosure about them?

Answering these questions helps the auditor identify the relevant financial statement assertions for which the company should have controls.

Identifying "relevant" assertions is something that auditors did in audit engagements prior to Section 404's requirements. A *significant assertion* is a line item or statement that would compromise the accuracy of the financial statements if proven incorrect.

Evaluating the design of controls

To be effective, internal controls must be designed properly to catch errors, irregularities, and misstatements that would otherwise show up on a company's financial statements. Poorly designed controls can allow valuable information to slip through the cracks, even if the control procedures are conscientiously implemented.

At some point during the Section 404 audit, the auditor needs to assess the *design effectiveness* of the company's internal controls. The auditor must determine whether the existing controls would be effective if they were used as designed. The auditor must also decide whether all the necessary controls are in place.

The tests the auditor performs to evaluate design effectiveness may include:

- ✔ Interviewing company personnel
- ✔ Observing internal controls
- ✔ Performing walkthroughs (see "Walking through the controls in place" earlier in this chapter)

Taking the "top-down" approach

A PCAOB release issued May 16, 2005, explains that auditors should use a "top-down" approach in testing internal controls, which means that auditors should not start testing every control but should prioritize. The top-down approach means that companies should take an aerial view, and look at the overall control company to identify the high-risk areas.

The controls that keep the highest risks in check are known as key controls. Under the top-down approach, it is the key controls that should be tested. Key controls may include those relating to customer payments, company disbursements, or sensitive financial information. High-risk areas and key controls are different for every company.

Strong internal controls prevent fraud as well as errors. Auditing Standard No. 2 requires the auditor to specifically test controls intended to prevent or detect fraud.

Testing operating effectiveness

The concept of operating effectiveness is closely related to design effectiveness (see the preceding section). Even well-designed controls can fail if unanticipated factors, such as poorly matched information gathering technology, undermine them.

Auditing Standard No. 2 requires the auditor to obtain evidence about the operating effectiveness of controls related to all relevant financial statement assertions for all significant accounts and disclosures. The auditor may perform any of the following tests to obtain evidence:

- ✔ Interviewing appropriate company personnel.
- ✔ Inspecting relevant documentation, such as sales orders and invoices.
- ✔ Observing the controls in operation and performing the controls procedures themselves.

✔ Standard No. 2 encourages "rotating tests of controls" that allow the auditor to vary testing from year to year. Rotating tests have two advantages:

  • They introduce unpredictability into the testing.

  • They make it possible for auditors to respond to changes at the company.

Each year's audit must stand on its own, and auditors can't rely on testing from past audits for assessing operating effectiveness.

Timing the testing

SOX makes specific timing requirements for testing internal control: It requires management's assessment and the auditor's opinion to address whether internal control was effective as of the end of the company's most recent fiscal year.

Obviously, performing all necessary testing on the last day of a company's fiscal year isn't very practical. To address this problem, Auditing Standard No. 2 directs auditors to obtain evidence about operating effectiveness at different times throughout the year. It further requires the auditor to update internal control tests or obtain additional evidence that the controls are effective at the end of the company's fiscal year.

Relying on other peoples' work

PCAOB Auditing Standard No. 2 requires the auditor to understand the results of procedures performed by company personnel (such as internal auditors) and third parties working for the company. The auditor must review all reports issued during the year by company personnel that address internal controls over financial reporting; the auditor also must evaluate any internal control deficiencies identified in those reports.

At a minimum, Auditing Standard No. 2 directs the auditor to consider the results of tests performed by these personnel when

✔ Deciding how to approach the 404 audit.

✔ Forming an opinion on the effectiveness of internal control over financial reporting.

Auditing Standard No. 2 contains an important limitation on using the work of others in an audit of internal control over financial reporting that isn't contained in the Statement on Auditing Standards (SAS) No. 65 (both are based on the same concepts): Auditing Standard No. 2 requires that the auditor's own work provide the principal evidence for the audit opinion.

Identifying control deficiencies

A *control deficiency* exists when an internal control doesn't allow the company's management or employees to prevent or detect misstatements in the financial statements in a timely manner. A control deficiency may be deemed a *significant deficiency* and *material weakness* depending on its magnitude.

An audit firm can generally issue an unqualified opinion on the Section 404 portion of the audit if significant deficiencies are discovered in the audit. However, a material weakness may cause an auditor to issue an unfavorable or qualified opinion on its Section 404 audit. (Companies generally strive to obtain unqualified opinions and avoid unqualified ones, as discussed later in this chapter in the section "Forming an opinion and reporting.")

Auditing Standard No. 2 requires the auditor to evaluate the severity of all control deficiencies identified either by the auditors or by management to determine if they're significant deficiencies or material weaknesses. The auditor is also responsible for making sure that the company's audit committee is aware of control deficiencies that rise to a level of significance determined by the company's audit committee and the auditors.

The SEC and Auditing Standard No. 2 (specifically paragraph 9) offer some guidance as to what makes a significant deficiency and what makes a material weakness:

 ✔ A control deficiency is considered a significant deficiency if, by itself or in combination with other control deficiencies, it results in more than a remote likelihood that a misstatement could occur on the company's financial statements. The misstatement that could potentially occur must be "more than inconsequential."

 ✔ A significant deficiency is classified as a material weakness if, by itself or in combination with other control deficiencies, it results in more than a remote likelihood that a material misstatement in the company's annual or interim financial statements will not be prevented or detected.

Auditing Standard No. 2 requires the auditor to communicate in writing to the company's audit committee and management all significant deficiencies and material weaknesses of which he or she is aware.

Working with the audit committee

Auditing Standard No. 2 identifies circumstances that may indicate the existence of deficiencies or material weaknesses within a company. The most common such scenario is ineffective oversight of the company's financial reporting. Auditing Standard No. 2 explains that effective oversight by the company's board of directors, including its audit committee, is critical to the company's monitoring of its internal control.

SOX requires every public company to have an audit committee that oversees the company's external financial reporting (as discussed in Chapter 7). SOX makes the audit committee a communication portal between management and the auditors.

Because the company's board of directors is responsible for evaluating the performance and effectiveness of the audit committee, Auditing Standard No. 2 requires that the auditor must communicate any significant deficiency or material weakness found directly to the board of directors as well as to the audit committee.

Normally, auditors and audit committees work well together because they have parallel purposes in ensuring that financial statements are fairly represented and that effective internal controls are in place.

When the auditor determines that the company's audit committee (which theoretically oversees it) is ineffective, the auditor must inform the board of directors.

Forming an opinion and reporting

Unqualified opinions are the best type of opinion an auditor can issue to a company. An unqualified opinion means that the auditor believes, without reservation, that the company's financial statements were prepared in accordance with Generally Accepted Accounting Principles (GAAP).

Auditing Standard No. 2 allows auditors to express an unqualified opinion if, after performing all the procedures and tests considered necessary for the Section 404 audit, he or she has identified no material weaknesses in internal control. In the event that the auditor can't perform all the procedures he or she considers necessary, the auditor can qualify or *disclaim* (refuse to issue) an opinion. If the auditor takes either of these actions, Auditing Standard No. 2 requires an explanation of the reasons behind the action.

Additionally, SEC Regulation S-X 2-02(f) provides:

> *The attestation report on management's assessment of internal control over financial reporting shall . . . state the opinion of the accountant as to whether management's assessment of the effectiveness of the registrant's internal control over financial reporting is fairly stated in all material respects, or must include an opinion to the effect that an overall opinion cannot be expressed. If an overall opinion cannot be expressed, explain why.*

The auditor's report is to include two opinions under the Section 404 audit addressing each of the following:

- ✔ Management's assessment of the company's internal control
- ✔ The effectiveness of internal control over financial reporting

The auditor's Section 404 report must follow the same disclosure model as management's assessment, and the SEC's final rules implementing Section 404(a) require management's assessment to disclose only material weaknesses, not significant deficiencies (as discussed in the section "Identifying control deficiencies" earlier in this chapter).

Flunking a 404 Audit

Preliminary research shows that anywhere from 5 to 15 percent of public companies will flunk their Section 404 audits in their initial year of compliance. Despite already spending large amounts to comply with Section 404, these companies may need to invest even more substantial resources to correct the flaws found in the audits they fail.

How to flunk a Section 404 audit

A company essentially flunks its Section 404 audit when it receives either a qualified or an adverse opinion from its auditors with respect to internal control. Either type of opinion reflects material weaknesses in internal control that, in the opinion of the auditor, render it ineffective.

A *qualified opinion* may contain the dreaded phrase, "except for the effect of the material weakness, internal control was effective." An *adverse opinion* more bluntly states "internal control over financial reporting was not effective." Both types of opinions basically mean the company has flunked its 404 audit with respect to the effectiveness of internal control.

If the auditor and the company's management disagree about whether a material weakness exists (that is, the auditor concludes a material weakness exists but management does not), the auditor may render an adverse opinion on management's assessment. This is another way to flunk a 404 audit.

What to do if your company flunks

If your company receives a qualified or adverse audit opinion with respect to its internal control, there's not much you can do to change the opinion. Effectiveness of internal control is measured at year's end, and the 404 audit process is intended to obtain a snapshot as of that date. However, moving forward, the company needs to analyze material weaknesses and deficiencies and take proactive measures to correct the situation before subsequent audits occur. Recommended proactive measures include the following:

- ✔ The audit committee should carefully review the nature of the material weakness identified with the independent auditors.

- ✔ The audit committee should hire appropriate independent consultants (neither affiliated nor related to the company or the audit firm) to decide remedial actions.

- ✔ The company should follow through with the implementation of additional controls recommended by the audit committee and its consultants and document that this action has been taken.

- ✔ Management should work to simplify and update internal control structures where possible (such as getting rid of paper ledgers).

- ✔ Management should use feedback from the prior Section 404 audit and other available information to eliminate redundant processes.

- ✔ The company should implement appropriate software solutions to enhance internal control.

- ✔ Management should elicit feedback from performing and documenting testing.

- ✔ Management should fire or reassign personnel responsible for lapses in implementing internal controls.

- ✔ The company should begin testing well in advance of subsequent Section 404 audits.

- ✔ Management should compare test results to that of the prior year to see if newly implemented controls have achieved a higher level of accuracy and reliability.

These corrective measures will also help prevent fraud or financial loss that could result from ineffective internal control.

A company that receives an adverse or qualified opinion in a Section 404 audit should carefully explore its legal exposure to shareholders who may sue the company alleging they've been damaged by management's failure to implement effective internal control structures.

Chapter 13

Taking the Terror Out of Testing

· ·

In This Chapter

▶ Controlling Section 404 project costs

▶ Streamlining documentation

▶ Figuring out who's running the risks and manning the controls

▶ Getting to know COBIT

· ·

An audit of a company's internal control under Section 404 can turn into a mushroom cloud of resources and manpower that leaves little constructive value when the smoke clears. To avoid this scenario, most companies approach the Section 404 compliance process as a series of projects, with each project having the clear objective of testing a specific type of internal control within the company. Every project in a Section 404 audit must be well-managed, and the information that results from it must fit into the scheme of the Section 404 audit so that management can confidently attest to internal control within the company.

Successful Section 404 compliance under SOX means being able to see the big picture and how a lot of smaller pictures fit into it. This chapter gives you some practical guidelines for managing Section 404 projects and introduces you to the useful COSO framework and auditing standard (SAS 70) developed to help companies in this area.

SOX, in the grand scheme of things, requires companies to study their own internal processes. Under Section 404, people responsible for generating documentation may also be empowered to come up with ideas for improving processes.

The Price of the Project

The major source of criticism of SOX Section 404 is the sheer cost of implementing it. Corporations across the country experience the sticker shock of compliance (as discussed in Chapter 11); actual Section 404 costs exceed projected ones at a staggering rate, and companies everywhere scramble to understand why. This section takes a look at some of the most common costs, both financial and otherwise, associated with a 404 audit.

The six most common Section 404 project costs

Companies are more alike than they are different when it comes to the costs of complying with SOX Section 404. A typical SOX 404 compliance project produces labor costs that fall into the following categories:

- **Documenting the company's processes:** A substantial skilled staff is required to document and chart all the processes that directly impact a company's financial statements and the controls and risks associated with each process.

- **Testing the company's process controls:** Section 404 requires considerable manpower to test controls, such as company policies, cross-checks, records, and internal accounting and audit procedures, associated with all company processes.

- **Documenting information technology controls:** Companies have to test the controls on their information technology systems. Examples of these types of controls include controls on data gathering, computer networks, and the company's computer hardware systems.

- **Reviewing and editing all documentation:** Additional manpower is necessary to review all the documentation collected on the company's processes and controls. (For more on these costs, check out the "Meeting massive manpower requirements" section later in this chapter.)

- **Testing documentation:** After all process-related documentation is compiled and edited, a company needs the staff to test it. Software tools, as discussed in Chapter 14, are particularly useful for helping staff in this area and thus reducing manpower requirements.

- **Audit fees:** Above all, companies must contend with large 404 audit fees from outside CPA firms.

Meeting massive manpower requirements

The most significant cost a company faces in complying with Section 404 comes from the sheer manpower required to document control processes and the results of test on those processes. SOX requires several levels of documentation, some of which may be prepared by the company and some of which must be outsourced. Generally, a company can save a lot of money by using its own employees to compile documentation rather than "outsourcing" the same job to another company. For example, if your company is able to pay employees their usual wages for compiling information about cash disbursements rather than paying a CPA or consulting firm to do it, the savings can be substantial.

To be in a position to realize this type of savings, your company must have capable employees in place to do the tasks and create the documentation required. The personnel on a payroll who are responsible for SOX compliance generally include the following:

✔ **Project managers:** Project managers know a little something about the employees in their departments who are assigned to a Section 404 project, so they can coordinate the employees' work to bring the project to completion. The project manager is responsible for

- Verifying quality control of the work everyone does on the project

- Monitoring all aspects of the project's progress

- Reporting progress to management

- Meeting certain milestone dates in the project's progress

✔ **Internal accounting staff:** Most SOX-compliant companies dedicate significant staff within their accounting departments to test accounts and accounting controls and conduct audits to determine compliance with company policies that affect internal financial controls. The outside independent audit firm may "test the tests" performed by the internal accounting staff by sampling their results.

✔ **Information technology staff:** A critical subject of internal control testing is information technology and how company systems and policies impact the data used to prepare financial statements. Significant staff within the information technology department must be assigned to testing and compiling documentation on these controls.

If your company is of the smaller variety, with common stock valued at less than $75 million, you may be in the process of complying with Section 404. Many larger companies, however, have already complied with Section 404, and you can benefit from their experiences. Industry publications and SEC disclosures filed by these companies (available on the SEC Web site at www.

sec.gov) can yield important information relevant to planning your company's Section 404 projects. (For more information about how to review documents filed by companies with the SEC, take a look at Chapter 4.)

The social challenges of Section 404

Every project in a company needs the support of the people involved in executing it to realize a successful outcome. Your company can save considerable time and money on Section 404 projects by enlisting the support and cooperation of the company's board of directors, the chief executive officers (CEOs), department heads, project managers, and other key personnel.

It's more time efficient to enlist this cooperation at the outset than to contend with internal power struggles along the way. It's unlikely staff will cooperate if their managers responsible are equivocal about the project's benefit or skeptical about the way things are being carried out.

Most human resource experts recommend that department heads and project managers initiating a new Section 404 project call special kick-off meetings to introduce the top-level project management. This meeting offers an opportunity to explain the value of the project as well as its objectives.

Hail to the Documenters

The success or failure of most projects associated with a Section 404 project depends on the quality of the documentation generated. The most skilled people on a project are usually in charge of creating, editing, and approving the documentation before the project is handed off for the next phase of the audit. This section identifies some skills and practices for generating good project documentation.

The right documentation skills

Laws, regulations, and the standards they set are what drive the documentation on a Section 404 project. The documentation must respond to all the relevant standards, answering the questions posed pursuant to those standards. Therefore, documenters must know what information can safely be discarded and what must be scrupulously retained. They also have to present the information so that compliance with the relevant standards is clearly apparent.

Documenters must understand the following standards:

- ✔ Standards issued by the Public Company Accounting Oversight Board (PCAOB) (see Chapter 6)
- ✔ Generally Accepted Accounting Principles (GAAP) and Generally Accepted Auditing Standards (GAAS) (see Chapter 5)
- ✔ SEC rules
- ✔ COSO and COBIT standards (discussed in the sections "Evaluating Control with the COSO Framework" and "A bit about COBIT" later in this chapter, respectively)

Section 404 documenters must also be skilled communicators on both technical and nontechnical levels. Specifically, they must be able to

- ✔ Interview other employees about their day-to-day duties to the extent those duties impact processes covered under Section 404.
- ✔ Prepare flowcharts and reports of business processes.
- ✔ Help identify risks to internal controls and recommend how those risks can be avoided or minimized.

Well-trained documenters save a company a lot of time. Prior to preparing any documentation, the project manager should meet with the documenters to ensure they understand the project scope and how much detail to document.

Getting the documentation down

Before documenters can do their jobs, they need to know *how* they're going to document. Every documenter needs to follow a set of predetermined steps to document each process. The project manager is responsible for spelling out these steps in writing before work begins. Additionally, the project manager needs to assign a budget for each task and let the documenters know how long documentation is expected to take. Documenters should track the actual hours it takes to get the project done for each process and measure their hours against the project manager's estimate (for more on documentation and time, see the following section "Time tracking").

Time tracking

Section 404 project managers have a daunting job in making sure their projects are completed correctly and within the time frames necessary to integrate the project results into the scheme of the entire 404 audit process. Accuracy and timeliness are critical, but an important secondary goal for project managers is ensuring that their projects are accomplished efficiently and inefficiencies in conducting a first-year project aren't repeated in subsequent years.

Tracking the time spent on the project by everyone involved in its execution is a valuable way of identifying inefficiencies in the testing process that may be attributable to some of the following causes:

✔ **Vague scope definition:** If the scope and objectives of the project are poorly defined at the outset, effective time tracking systems can indicate whether staff may be forced to spend inordinate amounts of time clarifying their roles. Staff can also waste time documenting data extraneous to the project goals or omitting data that should have been included in the results of a particular testing project. For more on project scope, jump to the section "Scoping out savings" later in this chapter.

✔ **Untrained staff:** A good project manager knows the skill levels of the people involved in the project and therefore can estimate how long tasks should take. Staff who spend excessive time on a task may be encountering unanticipated issues that require follow-up, or they may be training on the job. Time tracking helps identify skills lacking on a project in a prior year and as well as staff that aren't performing up to project standards.

✔ **Poor budgeting and estimates:** A project may be taking too long because of unexpected glitches and adverse findings, or it may simply be that no one knew how long it was supposed to take. Time tracking can help with 404 project budgets in future years.

Time tracking is so vital to the economics of a Section 404 project that one or more team members may be assigned to the sole task of tracking the time spent by the rest of the project team members.

Scoping out savings

The key to working cost effectively and even saving money when complying with Section 404 is defining the scope of each project.

Clearly defining the scope of the project benefits the company in two ways: It prevents unnecessary work and redundant work, and it ensures that only required data is gathered (so the project can come in on schedule).

Scope definition includes identifying:

- ✔ **The project's objectives:** What controls is the project testing?

- ✔ **What data should be gathered:** What information is being documented to meet the objectives? What's the standard for determining if a particular event is significant enough (material) to be reported in the project results?

- ✔ **Where the data should be gathered from:** Which company locations, departments, and transactions are the subject of the testing?

- ✔ **Acceptable procedures for gathering the data:** What tasks will be performed according to the parameters of the project?

Defining the scope of a project should be a formal, *written* endeavor. Section 404 project managers should take a page from the book of information technology managers, who almost always require a formal written scope statement for any new project. Writing out a formal project scope statement avoids backtracking and second-guessing later on; it also prevents management from attempting to expand the scope of a given project without formally authorizing it.

Taking an inventory of your company processes

A good inventory of processes presents an opportunity for saving time and money on a Section 404 project. In this context, a *process* is a collection of procedures and activities for recording company transactions. Some examples of business processes include:

- ✔ Preparing a requisition to buy inventory

- ✔ Documenting a customer sale

- ✔ Making a bank deposit

- ✔ Processing a credit card transaction

Getting 'em all

Chief executive officers dread nothing more under Section 404 than the possibility of missing a key process in a Section 404 audit because they must personally certify, under fear of both civil and criminal penalties, the effectiveness of their company's internal controls and processes. (For more on management and board certifications, turn to Chapter 9.)

Many large companies (*accelerated filers,* as discussed in Chapter 3) have already completed the Section 404 process. If your company's Section 404 compliance is still underway, you can benefit from the information other companies have already filed with the SEC in their annual and periodic reporting documents. Much of this information is available on the SEC Web site at www.sec.gov.

Identifying the key processes in your company may require the following:

- ✔ **Looking to see what other companies in your industry have already documented:** Outside consultants that have worked with other companies in your industry may have already compiled process lists that you can work from.

- ✔ **Meeting with your own middle managers:** Talking to managers, department heads, project managers, and others familiar with key company processes can help you develop comprehensive process lists.

- ✔ **Capitalizing on "canned" lists:** Many software documentation tools on the market contain their own helpful process lists. For example, the American Institute for Certified Public Accountants (AICPA) sells a COSO Control Environment checklist on its Web site at www.cpa4biz.com. This is a good tool to start with in gathering information about your company's controls. (COSO standards are discussed in more detail in the section "Evaluating Control with the COSO Framework" later in this chapter.)

When documenting processes, it's important for the documenters to understand how financial processes may overlap with company processes that are considered unrelated to the financial statements. Documenters need to gather documentation on processes potentially relevant to financial reporting and be wary of increasing the costs of the project by testing irrelevant controls. For example, aspects of how a company runs its manufacturing plant (operational processes) or legal compliance measures can potentially impact financial statements. Project managers must make a determination as to what reasonably needs to be stated.

Starting with charting

Most companies use flowcharts to help them identify business processes. For example, a company may create a detailed chart of its manufacturing or sales cycle and fill in the processes related to each stage. More flowcharts may be used in the 404 process to document accounting cycles. Ultimately, a final round of flowcharts may be created for the processes themselves, documenting both the steps in the process and how the processes relate to each other.

Looking at the ledger

The company's *general ledger* is likely to be an important source of information for documenting company processes because general ledgers are chronological records of the company's accounting transactions. The general ledger shows the effect of each transaction on the accounts reflected on the financial statements.

Ranking the processes

After processes are inventoried, a company has to figure out which processes are most significant. It's impossible to test them all!

Most companies use some sort of objective system for scoring processes to determine which are the most significant. They identify the factors that determine significance and apply those standards to each individual process in order to produce a rating. The processes that rank the highest receive priority for Section 404 testing.

Some factors that contribute to the significance value of a process include:

- ✔ The dollar amount associated with the process relative to the assets of the company as whole
- ✔ The risk to the company if the process isn't properly controlled
- ✔ The likelihood that the process can be subverted
- ✔ The type and availability of documentation associated with the process and the ease of reviewing that documentation
- ✔ How well employees performing the process are supervised

Creating Section 404 dream teams

Good project teams save their companies money. The first step in creating a good team is deciding what role each team member should play and picking people with the right skills for each role.

Consider the following players when building a winning 404 project team:

- ✔ **Process manager:** The person in the company with management-level responsibility for ensuring the process is correctly carried out.
- ✔ **People who perform the process:** The people who perform the financial process on a daily basis should be consulted when it comes time to test it because they're familiar with the process's intricacies.
- ✔ **Information administrators:** These people are the most familiar with how information about the process is gathered within the organization.

Communicating as colleagues

Team meetings go smoothly if everyone comes prepared, and preparation is most important during a company's initial Section 404 project team meetings.

For these meetings, the project manager should have a clear agenda and information to share with the team about:

✔ The assertions being tested

✔ Possible risks

✔ Controls designed to mitigate the risks

✔ Procedures for documentation

✔ Estimates as to how long the project tasks should take

Walking through the process

One of the best ways to make sure the Section 404 project meets its objectives is to attempt a dry run. Have your team try documenting one process, and review that documentation. Discuss the format and completeness of what the team produces as well as changes the team needs to make before documenting the remaining processes.

Organizing the documentation: Why form is equal to substance

A good set of forms can be a great cost-saver on a Section 404 project. The documentation gathered in all of the company's 404 projects should use a consistent, easy-to-read and ready-to-review format. The document forms should contain information not only about the tests performed but also about who performed the tests. Standardizing forms within the 404 audit helps team members work efficiently and coordinate their efforts. It also makes the forms easier to review and lessens the risks of overlooking important information.

Good Section 404 documentation usually contains the following:

✔ **Information about the process being tested:** A process is commonly explained and illustrated using a flowchart like the one shown in Figure 13-1, which examines an inventory control process.

Visio is an easy-to-use computer program for creating flowcharts for documenting processes. You can download a trial version of this program at www.visio.com.

✔ **A summary of the risk and controls associated with the process:** The procedures for identifying risks are explained in the section "Caveats about Controls" later in this chapter. For the most part, risks and controls usually are identified and tracked using a software program such as SarbOxPro, which I discuss in Chapter 15.

✔ **Identification of the controls used to prevent the risk:** To get a clean bill of health on its 404 audit, the company should have at least one effectively working control for each risk. The project team should identify the controls in place on the standard project form.

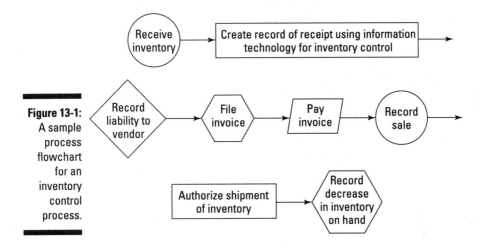

Figure 13-1: A sample process flowchart for an inventory control process.

Caveats about Controls

A *control* is what prevents a risk from happening. There should be at least one control for each risk. If the risk of a flawed control could allow a material error to creep into a company's financial statements, that control needs to be tested. A *material error* is one that is deemed financially significant based on a standard established by the audit committee and independent auditors.

Design your Section 404 tests so a single test covers as many controls as possible.

PCAOB standards state that the independent auditor must

✔ Test each relevant assertion the company makes on the financial statements it files with the SEC

✔ Verify the existence and completeness of the documentation supporting each relevant assertion

As a practical matter, a financial statement assertion can form the basis of a 404 project within the company. For each assertion, the company should determine all the scenarios and situations that could cause it to be inaccurate. Such risks include the possibility that account balances may be understated or overstated or that assets may be undervalued or overvalued. Project managers and auditors must look at all the scenarios that could cause any of these risks to be the case. For example, an employee may be falsifying payable records to a vendor, thus overstating accounts payable; unauthorized disbursements may be lowering other account balances, or assets may be overvalued.

Although testing for all risks is impossible, companies are expected to have a control in place for every identified risk and to test "key" controls. This prioritization is known as the "top-down" approach.

Key controls

A control that prevents a material risk is known as a *key control.* The key controls in every company are different, based on the type of goods and services a company provides and its own peculiar accounting processes. Some questions to ask when identifying key controls at your company are:

- ✔ Does the control prevent fraud or inaccuracy?
- ✔ Does the control safeguard assets?
- ✔ How significant (material) could the impact be if the control failed?

Many controls will be included in the first two categories, so the question of whether a control is a key one will generally hinge on the issue of materiality. *Materiality* is usually (but not always) measured as some sort of dollar amount. Every company must decide on an appropriate level of materiality.

Some common key controls

Although company controls vary and must constantly evolve as new risk factors are identified, some controls are common to most companies. This section examines a few of these standard controls.

Segregation of duties

Segregation of duties exists when responsibility for a financial process is divided among several people so that no one individual can misappropriate company assets. For example, segregation of duties for accounts payable may be accomplished by making sure the same person isn't responsible for more than one of the following tasks:

✔ Authorizing an accounts payable transaction

✔ Entering data for an accounts payable transaction

✔ Having custody of the assets used to pay the transaction

✔ Disbursing assets to pay the vendor

✔ Performing a control to verify the accounts payable transaction

Authorization procedures

An *authorization* control is in place when more than one person in a company has to authorize a decision or action that can impact the company's assets or financial statements. For example, managers' approval may be required for a disbursement.

Reconciliations

Reconciliation is a control process of verifying one account balance by comparing to another account balance that should be affected by the same transaction. If the first account can't be balanced or reconciled using this technique, an error may be present or fraud may be occurring within the company.

Ogling the Outside Vendors: SAS 70 Reports

Almost every company subject to SOX outsources something, but the one thing a company can't outsource is responsibility for matters that impact its financial statements. According to Auditing Standard SAS 70, if a company outsources functions, it must establish that adequate internal control is maintained at the outside vendor.

If outside vendors perform significant financial processes or handle key controls for your company, SOX requires you to vouch for the controls in place at those third-party vendors.

Often, third-party vendors have audit reports prepared by their own auditors and are happy to hand them out to valued customers. If your company chooses to rely on such third-party reports, known as *SAS 70 reports,* keep the following requirements in mind:

✔ **Timing:** The SAS 70 report must be completed close enough to your company's year-end that the third-party controls described in the report can be expected to remain in place at the end of your company's fiscal year.

✔ **Covered controls:** The SAS 70 report must cover all the controls your company relies on given the services the third-party vendor supplies.

✔ **Effectiveness of controls:** Third-party controls must be effective for detecting errors material to your company. Sometimes, a third-party company designates a materiality limit that's much higher than your company would consider appropriate, which means the control in place is less stringent.

The SAS 70 report provided by your third-party vendor doesn't fulfill these requirements; your company needs to perform its own audit of that process. As a practical matter, a competitive vendor will strive to provide its clients with an SAS 70 report on which they can rely. To review a sample SAS 70 report, flip to Appendix G.

Design your Section 404 tests so a single test covers as many controls as possible.

Evaluating Control with the COSO Framework

In 1985, the Committee of Sponsoring Organizations of the Treadway Commission (COSO) was formed to study factors that can lead to fraudulent financial reporting by businesses. In 1992, this commission issued a publication titled *Internal Control — Integrated Framework*. This document is the most widely relied upon framework in the U.S. and set of standards for businesses to evaluate their internal control systems. (The SEC specifically cites the COSO framework as a set of standards management may use permissibly in evaluating internal control.)

Your company is likely to use the COSO framework in conjunction with other standards it has developed.

How COSO breaks down companies' controls

The COSO framework views a company's overall internal control environment as consisting of five components:

✔ **Control environment:** How decisions and policies are made within a business and how authority and responsibly are assigned

✔ **Risk assessment:** How the processes performed within each department may impact the company's financial statements

✔ **Control procedures:** Those that limit risk

✔ **Information and communication:** How polices and control structures are communicated to people within the organization

✔ **Monitoring:** Whether controls are actually operating as expected

The COSO framework takes a very people-oriented approach to the evaluation of internal controls, viewing internal control as "a process, effected by an entity's board of directors, management, and other personnel, designed to provide reasonable assurance" with respect to the following issues that may impact a company's financial statements:

✔ Effectiveness and efficiency of operations

✔ Reliability of financial reporting

✔ Compliance with applicable laws and regulations

The COSO Web site (`www.coso.org`) explains that internal control is "a process. It is a means to an end, not an end in itself. . . . Internal control is effected by people. It's not merely policy manuals and forms, but people at every level of an organization."

COSO guidance for your company

The SEC mandates that your company develop its internal control standards with reference to those developed by COSO or a similar organization.

The COSO framework provides guidance in the following areas:

✔ **Project planning:** COSO provides guidelines and suggested procedures for helping your company determine how to structure project teams and documentation as well as coordinate with internal auditors.

✔ **Identifying control objectives:** COSO contains credible standards that your company can rely upon in identifying which controls are key ones and in determining levels of materiality for testing.

✔ **Documenting controls:** COSO contains documentation guidelines and formats as well as discussion about coordinating your company's internal documentation with that of the independent auditors.

✔ **Testing and evaluating controls:** COSO provides procedural guidelines for conducting tests and standards for evaluating the reliability of particular internal controls.

When you're involved in any SOX 404 project, visit the COSO Web site at `www.coso.org` for great articles and resources on evolving Section 404 audit standards, procedures, and trends.

A Bit about COBIT

COBIT, or Control Objectives for Information and Related Technology, refers to a set of generally applicable and accepted standards for information technology. COBIT standards provide a reference framework specifically for IT control systems as opposed to financial control systems as a whole. The standards relevant to SOX include best practices for each IT process and models to assist in improving internal controls.

The COBIT standards are issued by a not-for-profit organization called the IT Governance Institute (ITGI). In 2003, the ITGI also published *IT Control Objectives for Sarbanes-Oxley,* which specifically addresses the financial reporting aspects of COBIT. Most COBIT information is available for free downloading at www.isaca.org/cobit.htm.

Part IV
Software for SOX Techies

The 5th Wave   By Rich Tennant

"I've got to work this weekend again. There are over 200 games of Torpedo Alley, Click Ball, and Blockbreaker that haven't been tested for Sarbanes-Oxley compliancy yet."

In this part . . .

*I*f you're a software geek at heart, this part's for you. The chapters in this part can guide you through the task of choosing the right software solution for any size company. To illustrate the types of issues SOX-specific software can solve, this part also looks at a couple of simple, economical products on the market.

Chapter 14

Surveying SOX Software

. . . .

In This Chapter

▶ Getting an update on the latest software trends

▶ Revealing what SOX software does for companies

▶ Knowing what questions to ask software vendors

▶ Looking at the standards used for designing software (COSO and COBIT)

▶ Deciding if SOX software is worth the cost

. . . .

*T*horoughly testing your company's internal control under the Sarbanes-Oxley Act's Section 404 is expensive, but the right software tool can soften the blow. Rather than reinvent the wheel, your company can purchase a single software package to prioritize risks, identify key controls for testing, develop standardized forms, and create a system for entering and storing SOX 404 documentation. Many off-the-shelf products are available, which means your company may not have to engage expensive consultants to design a customized solution.

Selecting the right SOX software tool can be a pivotal decision for your company. This chapter addresses some SOX software packages on the market and looks at the ways companies can use them to streamline compliance with the dreaded SOX Section 404 (discussed in excruciating detail in Chapter 11). This chapter also examines the special COSO standards developed for companies to structure the testing of their internal financial control as well as the separately developed COBIT standards developed by information technology professionals. (Most SOX software is designed to comply with the COSO and COBIT standards.)

Some SOX Software Trends

Software vendors are flocking to the SOX software market, offering products for all manner of companies and projects. As of this writing, it's estimated that 85 percent of Fortune 500 companies will be using SOX software products developed outside their companies by the end of 2005.

According to a 2005 estimate in *Business Week Magazine,* the market for Sarbanes-Oxley software could be worth $1 billion to $4 billion by 2008.

This section provides you with some useful background information about the SOX software industry to help you evaluate the viability of the companies from which you may decide to purchase a product. (It is indeed a concern whether or not your software vendor will be around in a year or two when your company is considering a major financial commitment.) Some of the significant economic trends on the SOX software industry include the following:

- **Customized consulting for big firms:** Large accounting and IT consulting firms are being hired to create customized software for many of their clients.

- **Off-the-shelf software for the smaller firms:** Small firms and not-for-profits are optioning for off-the-shelf starter programs, such as SarbOxPro (discussed in Chapter 15), that help them document controls and procedures from scratch.

- **The lack of a dominant market leader:** Currently, no particular vendor has a dominant share of the SOX market. With more than 60 companies offering products, consolidation of some companies and their client bases is inevitable. What this shifting market means is that some companies may go out of business, and their products will no longer be supported, or that you may end up working with a vendor different from the one with whom you originally contracted.

- **No track records:** Because SOX is still relatively new, no company has a track record of multiple releases and a big beta trail. Bugs and flaws are to be expected, and the products will likely be de-bugged and improved based on user feedback and the market data.

- **Costs:** SOX-specific software products range anywhere from $2,500 to millions depending on whether an off-the-shelf solution is selected or the company opts for costly customization from a consulting firm. However, one cost characteristic is assured across the board: In every organization, the cost of the software is very small in relation to the costs of labor and training employees and consultants to use it.

- **Add-ons abound:** Some software vendors, such as Hyperion Solutions Corp, are adding modules and capabilities for SOX compliance to existing financial management programs. Popular add-ons include audit-trail templates and components that document the flow of work within a company to help identify processes that must be monitored for Section 404 compliance.

- **Industry-specific programs find a niche:** Some industries, such as banking, are finding vendors with programs and add-ons designed especially for them. After the first-year crash compliance, many consulting firms are likely to offer specific software for the industries that they most frequently service.

In view of the market trends listed here, your company should carefully negotiate license terms for SOX software. Don't be shy about negotiating for "extras" like longer warranties and clauses that allow you to terminate the contract under circumstances such as disappointing software performance. Intense competition for market share among SOX software vendors should put your company in a strong negotiating position for favorable contract and service terms when purchasing SOX software products.

At this stage of the game, your company should carefully consider what functions software must provide and negotiate software contracts with a clear understanding as to minimum performance standards.

Identifying the Types of Software on the Market

Many different types of SOX-related software products are on the market. They offer different features and have widely different price structures. When shopping for SOX software, make sure you're comparing apples to apples by keeping the following general categories in mind:

- ✔ **One-stop SOX for small companies:** Small companies find programs like SarbOxPro and ProCognis, the interfaces of which are illustrated in Figures 14-1 and 14-2, particularly helpful. For a relatively nominal investment, these programs can help a small company create a centralized database of controls and processes. The programs also track the testing done on key controls as well as several aspects of the company's control environment. Software programs for small companies are designed to gather SOX-related information to document the company's overall compliance with SOX with a single interface. These programs also generate reports on processes, risks, controls, and compliance for management and process owners to assess their effectiveness. For a relatively nominal investment ($1,000–$2,500), these comprehensive off-the-shelf programs provide an overall framework COSO compliance (see "The COSO Standards for Software" later in this chapter).

  SarbOxPro is covered in more detail in Chapter 15.

- ✔ **Monitoring tools:** SOX has created a market for programs that provide enhanced monitoring of company assets or communications. These programs are useful for companies that have SOX-compliant structures in place but need to enhance the monitoring of the controls. An example of this type of program is SpectorSoft (see Figure 14-3), which is available at www.spectorsoft.com.

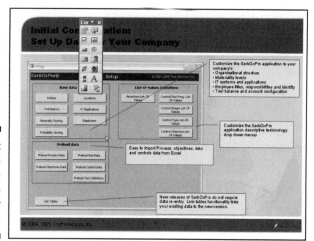

Figure 14-1:
A sample of the SarbOxPro user interface.

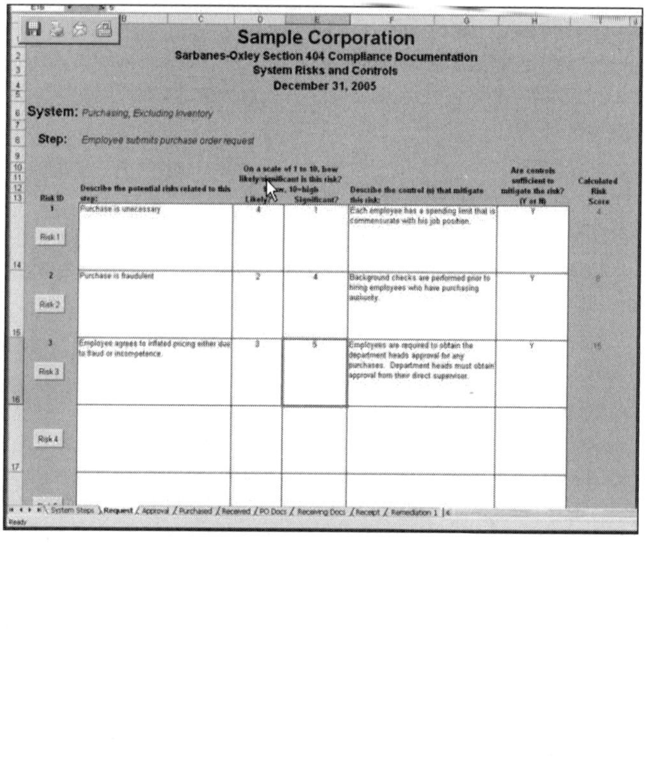

Figure 14-2:
A sample of the ProCognis user interface.

Figure 14-3:
Software tools, such as Spector-Soft, can increase internal control by monitoring employee activity.

✔ **Industry-specific programs:** Many software programs are designed to perform specific SOX-related tasks or are designed for specific industries. For example, some programs monitor receivables and payables. Industries with special overlapping regulatory requirements, such as the mutual fund industry or healthcare industry, may benefit from off-the-shelf software solutions tailored for these niche markets. For example, Physmark (www.physmark.com) is a SOX software compliance product designed especially for the healthcare industry.

✔ **Customized IT solutions:** Large accounting firms, such as KPMG, offer special consulting services to help design and write software for their clients. Generally, companies having gross revenues in excess of $75 million (known as *accelerated filers*) opt for customized solutions.

✔ **Task-specific software:** Some software is designed to perform specific tasks. For example, financial statement certification is designed to provide a process for management to sign off on the accuracy of the financial statements for Section 302. (For more on management certifications and Section 302, turn to Chapter 9.)

Although companies that use SOX software may switch products in subsequent years (or even in the current one), swapping software is likely to raise regulatory issues as well as logistic ones.

Shopping for SOX Software

Although most software vendors have Web sites and online brochures, SOX software products can be very difficult to compare. Product demonstrations generally take several hours, and generally it's hard to get more than an overview of such a complex product during a demo.

The following is list of questions management, IT committees, and process owners should ask vendors when evaluating SOX software products for purchase:

- **How versatile is the software?** Does it fulfill all the functions the company needs for SOX compliance? Does it contain adequate functionality for identifying processes and controls and for document management?

- **What technology does the software require to run?** Exploring technology requirements ahead of time is particularly important for small companies that may run into additional unanticipated outlays as a result of being unprepared for the requirements of new software.

- **Does the product interface well with the company's existing systems?** What kind of customization is necessary for it to do so?

- **How is historical company information imported into the system?** Does this information require special customization or formatting of information?

- **What other companies have used the product?** What have been their experiences?

- **How large is the vendor's current customer base?** Does the vendor currently service a large customer base over which it can spread the costs of support and additional research?

- **What ongoing costs does the software carry?** What's the initial investment, and what are the maintenance fees? What upgrades are expected? Does the vendor have a strategy for upgrading and developing the program?

- **What are the software's security and validation procedures?** How is the system protected from tampering and unauthorized access?

Software maintained by an application service provider and hosted on the company's network should have encrypted data transmission over the Internet and regular backups.

- **What type of training is offered by the vendor?** Do the documenters, auditors, and other personnel perceive the interface as easy to learn?

- **What types of reports can be generated with the product?** What type of data is captured and included in the reports? Can sample reports be viewed?

✔ **Does the vendor have a sample database for demonstration purposes?**
Can company representatives experiment by entering data into a
demonstration version of the program?

✔ **Does the program facilitate document management and workflow?**
How are relevant documents (such as flowcharts, prior reports, and so
on) imported, viewed, and referenced in the program so that those documents can be referenced for documenting processes and controls?

✔ **Does the vendor have adequate staff and funding to support the product?** Is the vendor financially stable and well managed?

✔ **Does the program offer standardized libraries of processes and controls or other embedded content that can save the company time in
the initial years of compliance?**

✔ **Can the software be conveniently accessed from all company locations?** Can it be used by everyone responsible for testing and documenting, or does it require specialized skills?

✔ **Does the software offer any benefits beyond SOX compliance?** Does it
have features that can help the company save money?

SOX Meets Cousin IT

Financial statements filed with the SEC are compiled from data gathered from
dozens, if not hundreds, of financial pulse points within a company. At most
companies, the accuracy and timeliness of financial reporting depend on the
information technology, or IT, environment. SOX Section 404 doesn't explicitly
spell out requirements for corporate IT systems or procedures for gathering
information within a company to document internal control. So if a company
wanted to, it could theoretically document and test all its processes using
pen and paper. However, this method wouldn't be very efficient and probably
wouldn't inspire the confidence of the CEO or CFO forced to flip through
thousands of pages each quarter. For these reasons, IT plays a critical role in
the overall compliance process.

IT and SOX compliance will always go hand-in-hand. In fact, may experts have
indicated that the heads of IT departments (usually called *chief information
officers,* or CIOs) should be required to certify the financials for companies
along with CEOs and CFOs.

SOX requires senior management to include within the company's annual
10-K report filed with the SEC a separate *internal control report* to evaluate
processes for collecting, securing, retaining, and reporting financial information. Companies also have to provide quarterly evaluations of changes that
materially impact internal control over financial reporting or could do so in
the future.

Collecting scattered company data

Most companies already have considerable technology in place for SOX compliance. However, the information gathered is likely to be in lots of places, spread across databases maintained by many departments and locations. Each department is likely to have its own standards and policies for gathering the type of information it needs to conduct its operations and report its results to management.

Many companies rely on SOX software to collect Section 404 data scattered throughout the company. Because everyone uses a single data entry system, the software can standardize Section 404 documentation throughout the company. A software system endorsed by management and used by the company as a whole links the people gathering the documentation in different departments, such as IT, accounting, and operations. The software also connects personnel in different geographical locations and can coordinate the compliance efforts of every subsidiary and division of a single company.

Evaluating your company's existing IT systems: A checklist

Not every company needs to overhaul its existing IT systems to comply with SOX. Some companies that have good internal controls and high levels of standardization for testing and documentation may get by with relatively minimal software upgrades and changes.

SOX-specific tasks

A public company's IT systems must be able to perform certain SOX-related tasks to ensure its ability to comply with Section 404. The following is a checklist of needed capabilities to:

- ✔ **Report transactions and collect data:** Most companies currently collect data on many financial transactions, including receivables, payables, and collections. Thus, IT systems may already be in place to document processes and controls as required by SOX.

- ✔ **Investigate whistle-blower complaints:** If an employee files a complaint under the SOX whistle-blower provision (covered in Chapter 16), the company must be able to locate the necessary data to investigate the basis of the complaint. A company must have IT systems that allow access to records that substantiate a culture of corporate compliance.

✔ **Identify processes and control environments:** Does the company currently document its processes? Does each department document them using relatively uniform tools and output? If not, the company may benefit from a software product that assists in creating a database of processes and documenting workflow. The flowchart in Figure 14-4 illustrates how one such software product from ProCognis (available at www.procognis.com) is structured to document the processes and control environments of a company.

✔ **Document existing controls:** If the company doesn't maintain a centralized database documenting its controls on various processes, a product that offers an existing library of controls and tools for creating this type of database may be a critical component of the company's 404 compliance.

✔ **Identify key controls:** When a company takes an inventory of its internal controls, it needs to be able to determine which are the most significant controls in terms of the risks they're intended to prevent. Software tools can identify the areas in which material risks are likely to occur as well as the key controls for preventing those risks. For example, a software program may identify key controls based on factors such as the dollar amounts involved or the volume of transactions.

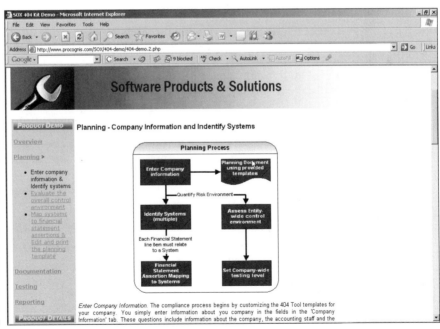

Figure 14-4:
This flowchart illustrates the information users enter into the ProCognis software program to document company processes.

✔ **Create reliable reports:** SOX requires that management know what's happening within the entire company to the extent necessary to certify its internal controls. A company's existing IT systems should have the ability to summarize information in readable report formats that can be reviewed by the process *owners* (the people responsible for ensuring the accurate completion of the process within the company) and by management to fulfill both the requirements of Section 404 and the objectives of Section 302.

✔ **Perform accurate record retention:** Records must be retained and tracked as part of the company's overall internal control and workflow management. Document management software products and modules designed specifically for this purpose are on the market.

✔ **Track costs:** SOX compliance is costly, but companies can save money by planning individual SOX projects and tracking the costs associated with them. If the company currently doesn't have the IT infrastructure to do these tasks, it should investigate software tools on the market for doing so.

✔ **Secure information:** An important aspect of financial control within a company is the ability to secure financial information so that only appropriate persons have access to it, and it can't be improperly altered. Most IT systems have security components in place that can be adapted for an overall SOX-compliant system.

✔ **Report events:** Many software products on the market offer monitoring capabilities to enhance a company's existing internal controls. These products monitor events such as unauthorized transactions or distribution of information and, in some cases, report such events to management in real time.

Software strategies

Although many necessary technology components may be present to some extent in a company's existing IT framework, every company must decide whether to:

✔ Refocus existing IT systems for SOX compliance

✔ Hire independent consultants to design customized systems

✔ Purchase products and modules already designed for SOX compliance and train staff on using them

The COSO Standards for Software

Because SOX is silent as to the types of documentation that satisfy Section 404, the SEC provides some guidance to companies by directing them to a set of standards developed by the Committee of Sponsoring Organizations of the Treadway Commission (COSO). Most SOX software is designed to comply with the COSO standards. (For more on COSO, see the sidebar "Conforming to the COSO standards.")

The COSO standards provide welcome guidance to companies deciding how to organize their documentation. Many software tools have interfaces and formats designed to reflect compliance with COSO, using key terminology from the COSO standards to identify the software functions.

What COSO says

The SEC directs companies to look for established, well-recognized standards to use in documenting internal control and processes. It identifies the COSO Internal Control Framework as its preferred set of standards and has yet to identify any other set of standards.

The COSO framework provides five components that every software program should address:

- **Control environment:** COSO requires every company to establish the foundation for an internal control system by demonstrating that discipline and structure exist within the organization and set the tone for compliance. Having a good software system or well-designed IT components in place can help document the existence of a strong control environment and provide visibility of compliance processes.

- **Risk assessment:** Software applications can help management identify risk factors by assisting in the compilation of data from surveys, comparing practices of the company to a statistical standard, and alerting management to critical events and discrepancies (called *exceptions*).

- **Control activities:** COSO requires that companies evaluate the specific policies and procedures that they have in place to ensure that management's directives are carried out. Companies have to document key processes and identify the controls used to ensure the accuracy of those processes. Software programs can help streamline this COSO component by providing libraries of procedures and controls and user-friendly interfaces that allow people documenting the controls to store the information in a standardized format that can be retrieved by other people in the organization.

Conforming to the COSO standards

COSO was originally formed in 1985 as an independent private-sector initiative to study factors that can lead to fraudulent financial reporting; it developed recommendations for public companies and independent auditors.

The commission was jointly sponsored by five major professional associations: the American Accounting Association, the American Institute of Certified Public Accountants, Financial Executives International, The Institute of Internal Auditors, and the National Association of Accountants (now the Institute of Management Accountants). The commission also had representatives from industry, public accounting, investment firms, and the New York Stock Exchange.

SarbOxPro (available at www.sarboxpro.com) is a program that offers both standard libraries and an interface for adding specific company controls to the standard library. Figure 14-5 shows how controls input into the SarbOxPro program are saved to a standard library. (For more on SarbOxPro, check out Chapter 15.)

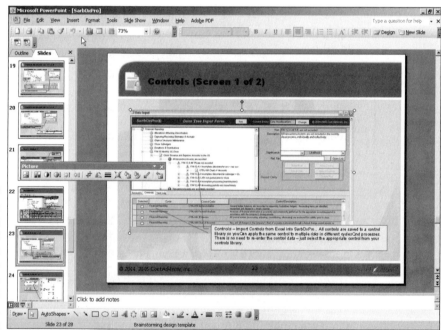

Figure 14-5:
Saving control information to the SarbOxPro control library.

✔ **Information and communication:** An important component of the COSO framework is the premise that internal controls can't be properly implemented unless the company has procedures for communicating the controls to the people who are supposed to carry them out on every level. Usually these procedures are carried out with software and information technology.

✔ **Monitoring:** The quality of the internal controls must be assessed to determine how effectively they detect irregularities. Monitoring also assesses how well people within the organization implement the control. Software programs and IT systems within the company should make data available to assess both of these aspects of the control's effectiveness. Some programs provide continuous monitoring, and others track data that can be analyzed by process owners and management at regular intervals.

Most companies in the United States use the COSO criteria outlined above in designing their IT systems. For example, Figure 14-6 shows the model used by the ProCognis software tool, which is a COSO-based design. (You can find more information on this product at www.procognis.com.)

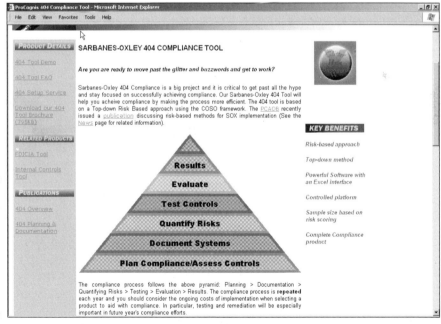

Figure 14-6: A model for ProCognis software, which is based on the COSO framework.

Complying with COBIT

A separate but equally important set of standards with respect to SOX software is the Control Objectives for Information and Related Technology, or COBIT, developed by the IT Governance Institute (ITGI). The purpose of the ITGI (www.isaca.org) is to set standards for measuring performance and risk in information technology professions.

COBIT is a generally applicable and accepted standard for good information technology (IT) security and control practices. These standards are intended to provide "a reference framework for management, users, and IS audit, control and security practitioners."

The COBIT standards can be downloaded for free at www.isaca.org. In 2003, the ITGI published a document called, *IT Control Objectives for Sarbanes-Oxley,* which adapts the COBIT standards specifically for SOX. Of COBIT's usual 34 IT processes and 318 detailed control objectives for IT professionals, the SOX adaptation identifies 27 IT processes and 136 detailed control objectives as critical to SOX compliance.

Will SOX Software Pay for Itself?

SOX requires detailed documentation and analysis of business processes related to financial reporting and disclosures. The right software tools can yield a wealth of data for implanting process improvements. For example, organizations may find duplicate expenditures, redundant processes, and opportunities to standardize processes among divisions and subsidiaries that may offset the cost of complying with SOX.

It's worth noting that in a recent poll by a research organization called the Meta Group, 39 percent of firms surveyed said that SOX will eventually make them more competitive.

Chapter 15

Working with Some Actual SOX Software

. . . .

In This Chapter

▶ Laying the groundwork before you install the software

▶ Deciding what information your SOX software should track

▶ Finding the simplest (and cheapest) software solutions available

. . . .

SOX software can be costly, but if yours is a small business, you have plenty of options that won't strain your petite IT budget. In fact, the three off-the-shelf software solutions programs that I discuss in this chapter are available for only a few thousand dollars. Each of these surprisingly versatile programs offers a comprehensive framework for Section 404 compliance and is designed to minimize training time.

In this chapter, I focus on some simple examples of SOX-compliant software used primarily in smaller companies. As a good representative of the off-the-shelf software solutions available, I've chosen to look at several sample products, including SarbOxPro.

Note: If your company has already worked with costly consultants and implemented a solution, this chapter can still be useful to you as an aerial view of how software and information technology go hand-in-hand with SOX compliance.

Doing Your Research Before a Software Installation

It's never a good idea to throw money at a solution before you analyze the problem. SOX software is a great tool for streamlining documentation — but only if you lay the groundwork for implementing it. This section gives you a sense of how to evaluate the flow of financial information in your company prior to implementing a software solution and introduces you to the important accounting concept of the trial balance.

Cost Advisors, Inc., the makers of SarbOxPro, has put together a terrific report explaining the relationship of SOX and software. You can request a free copy of this report from the SarbOxPro Web site located at www.sarboxpro.com.

Tracking the flow of information in your company

The flow of financial information within every company is unique; it's based on both the structure of the company and its subsidiaries and on the cycles of the company's business. According to Bill Douglas, CEO of Cost Advisors, Inc. "It is important to start with a firm understanding of the big picture (framework) around Sarbanes-Oxley Section 404. . . . There can be many entities within a single consolidated company and many [business] cycles within each entity." The flowchart shown in Figure 15-1 illustrates some of the key terms you'll come across in a Sarbanes-Oxley project that describe the flow of information within a company.

SOX is primarily concerned with risks, controls, and tests — the bottom three boxes to the bottom right of the diagram in Figure 15-1 — but the rest of the information illustrated must be known about the company before risks, controls, and tests can be gathered.

Some of the terms in Figure 15-1 stem from the SOX statute, Securities Exchange Commission (SEC) rules, and COSO and COBIT standards (discussed in Chapter 13), and others are rooted in the vernacular that information technology (IT) professionals have used for years in talking about the flow of information to be documented within a company. Moving from left to right on the diagram, each box represents increasingly specific information about a company. In order to comply with SOX, you must proceed down the hierarchy in this logical manner, generating increasingly specific information about your company.

A documenter must identify a company and all its subsidiaries and locations (entities) before proceeding to collect information about the cycles (sequences of transactions) that occur within the company. After the documenter knows about the business cycles (for example, a sales cycle moving from order to final payment), he can begin to document the processes within that cycle. In turn, after he knows the processes, he can move on to the controls and tests for those processes using a reliable software product. Figure 15-2 illustrates a sample business cycle for a customer sale.

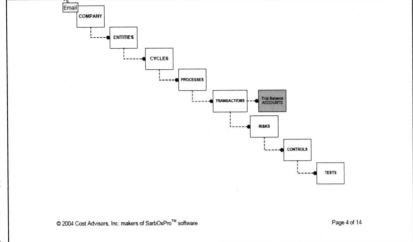

© 2004 Cost Advisors, Inc. makers of SarbOxPro™ software

Page 4 of 14

Figure 15-1:
Some key
SOX
concepts
that impact
a company's
software
solutions.

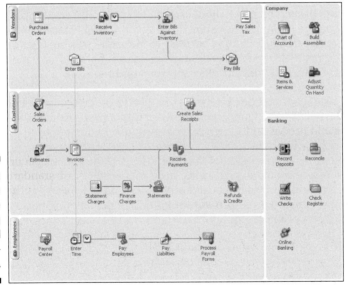

Figure 15-2:
A sample
sales cycle
consisting
of several
trans-
actions.

Following the trial balance trail

Traditionally, a *trial balance* is a document that adds up all the debits and credits for transactions within a company so that mistakes can be traced if debits don't equal credits. (In Figure 15-1, the trial balance appears off to the side and shaded.) Because most of today's accounting software adds correctly, companies create *trial balance reports* as summaries of all the company's individual transactions. Because the trial balance report tracks transactions, it's a valuable cache of information for Section 404 purposes.

The trial balance identifies all the income and asset accounts maintained by the company from the date that the beginning balances were calculated to the date the trial balance was "closed." The trial balance effectively combines the information summarized on both the balance sheet and Income Statement. If all transactions and account adjustments have been recorded properly, the debits and credits balance.

Figure 15-3 illustrates a simple trial balance. By looking at all the accounts in the trial balance, you can identify the most significant ones on a strictly dollars-and-cents basis. The more significant the account, the greater the risk of inaccuracy on the financial statement if the account is misstated. Several SOX software programs, including SarbOxPro, depend upon analysis of a trial balance (or a similar report) as the starting point for statistically identifying a company's most significant risks and key controls.

A trial balance is just one type of report used by a company to document its transactions. (Not all companies will work with a trial balance to identify transactions and processes.) Another type of report commonly used to glean transaction and process data is a *general ledger,* which companies use to record entries of transactions that occur without balancing the debits and credits. In any event, all companies need to start SOX software preparations by documenting transactions and processes, and corporate policies, structures, and individualized software solutions all may dictate how companies go about this preparation.

4:11 PM

12/15/07

Accrual Basis

Rock Castle Construction
Trial Balance
As of November 30, 2007

	Nov 30, 07	
	Debit	Credit
Checking		101,166.95
Savings	49,368.42	
Accounts Receivable	38,446.76	
Tools & Equipment	5,000.00	
Inventory Asset	7,930.29	
Retainage	4,176.80	
Undeposited Funds	52,704.40	
Land	90,000.00	
Buildings	325,000.00	
Trucks	78,352.91	
Trucks:Depreciation	0.00	
Computers	28,501.00	
Furniture	7,325.00	
Accumulated Depreciation		121,887.78
Pre-paid Insurance	1,716.85	
Accounts Payable		70,996.41
QuickBooks Credit Card		70.00
CalOil Card		5,111.80
Payroll Liabilities		7,100.58
Sales Tax Payable		5,596.19
Bank of Anycity Loan		19,932.65
Equipment Loan		3,911.32
Note Payable		18,440.83
Truck Loan		50,662.77
Opening Bal Equity		402,081.82
Owner's Equity:Owner's Contribution		25,000.00
Owner's Equity:Owner's Draw	6,000.00	
Retained Earnings	131,898.50	
Construction:Labor		22,703.25
Construction:Materials		38,341.50
Construction:Miscellaneous		2,328.52
Construction:Subcontractors		35,085.00
Cost of Goods Sold	3,871.59	
Automobile:Insurance	712.56	
Automobile:Fuel	160.08	
Bank Service Charges	37.50	
Freight & Delivery	35.00	
Insurance	297.66	
Insurance:Disability Insurance	150.00	
Insurance:Liability Insurance	1,050.00	
Insurance:Work Comp	825.00	
Interest Expense	619.19	
Interest Expense:Loan Interest	288.05	
Job Expenses:Equipment Rental	300.00	
Job Expenses:Job Materials	35,924.99	
Job Expenses:Permits and Licenses	525.00	
Job Expenses:Subcontractors	38,829.00	
Payroll Expenses	19,764.78	
Rent	0.00	
Repairs:Computer Repairs	45.00	
Repairs:Equipment Repairs	0.00	
Tools and Machinery	350.00	
Utilities:Gas and Electric	154.40	
Utilities:Telephone	100.71	
Utilities:Water	61.85	
Interest Income		93.42
Other Income		12.50
TOTAL	930,523.29	930,523.29

Figure 15-3:
A very simple trial balance for a small company.

Getting to Know SarbOxPro

SarbOxPro is an example of a software program designed to

- ✔ Create a system for documenting internal control.
- ✔ Maintain all the internal control information required for a company's Section 404 compliance in a single repository.

SarbOxPro is a relatively simple software program that uses the information in your company's trial balance to help identify both the greatest risks to your company and the key controls in place to mitigate the most significant risks. As of this writing, SarbOxPro costs under $3,000.

A product like SarbOxPro can really help a company get its arms around an elephant like SOX. If your company meets any of the following characteristics, you may want to consider using SarbOxPro:

- ✔ Small to medium-size public companies
- ✔ Nonpublic companies (including not-for-profit companies) that opt to become SOX-compliant
- ✔ Companies with limited budgets
- ✔ Companies that use Microsoft Office products

The SarbOxPro checklist

Cost Advisors, Inc., the makers of SarbOxPro software, have created a concise checklist for software implementation that you can download at (www.sarboxpro.com). This checklist, shown in Figure 15-4, can be used can be used effectively with many products on the market. It reflects the steps that, according to the SarbOxPro folks, every company has to complete for its SOX software to both save the company money and comply with the law.

Hey, this looks familiar: The SarbOxPro data tree

For anyone familiar with Windows Explorer and its data tree structure of folders and documents, SarbOxPro is an intuitive program. The SarbOxPro data tree looks a lot like Windows Explorer's, as you can see in Figure 15-5; in SarbOxPro, you can directly create or remove elements in the data tree, such as cycles, processes, or controls.

✓ Examine the Costs

✓ Sell the Project Internally

✓ Strategize Documentation Labor

✓ Understand the Documentation Hierarchy

✓ Define the Scope

✓ Establish Process Teams

✓ Structure the Documentation Format and Assessment Techniques

✓ Conduct Process Team Meetings

✓ Evaluate Controls at Third-Party Vendors

✓ Implement Quality Control

✓ Perform Testing

✓ Document the Control Environment

✓ Make Improvements in the Process

✓ Choose a Software Tool

Figure 15-4:
A software implementation checklist from the makers of SarbOxPro software.

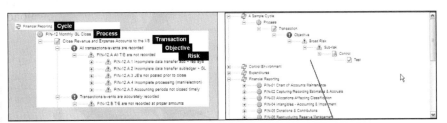

Figure 15-5:
The SarbOxPro data tree structure and the Windows Explorer's data tree structure.

SarbOxPro's data tree breaks down like so:

🖝 A **cycle** can have multiple **processes** under it.

🖝 A **process** usually has only one **transaction** under it, but a **transaction** can have one or more **objectives** listed under it.

✔ An **objective** can have one or more **broad risks.**

✔ A **broad risk** can break down into one or more **subrisks.**

✔ A **risk** can have one or more **controls** under it.

✔ A **control** usually has only one **test** under it.

SarbOxPro stages

The process of documenting Section 404 compliance involves three main task categories, which are represented on the main SarbOxPro screen shown in Figure 15-6. (From this main screen, documenters can access other areas of the program.) The categories are:

✔ **Initial Configuration:** In this area of the program, documenters add information about the company and its accounts. Users input information about the entities being reported upon, import the company's trial balance, and identify processes, employees, and other objectives as well as levels of materiality and other criteria to be used in the testing.

✔ **Data Entry:** In this area, documenters identify specific information about testing and other data gathered during the course of the Section 404 compliance process.

✔ **Reports:** This section of the program allows management and other users to view summaries of data gathered as a result of Section 404 compliance testing and interpret the data to make decisions about certifications and changes in the company's controls.

Each of these task categories is discussed in more detail in the following sections.

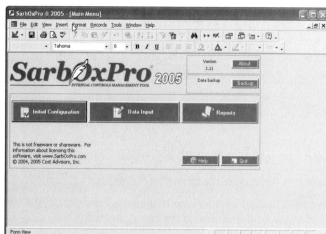

Figure 15-6: This SarbOxPro screen allows you to access the three main areas of the 404 documentation program.

Doing the initial configuration

The makers of SarbOxPro recognize that it's impossible for an organization to test every single process and control and that in order for companies to figure out which processes to test, they need some standard for deciding the importance (materiality) of the processes. At a minimum, software should initially be configured to document the following:

✔ The most significant locations (parents, subsidiaries, branches, and so on) where the company's business is transacted

✔ The processes within each location that cause financial transactions to be recorded in the trial balance

✔ The risks in each process

✔ The controls that prevent the risks from happening

✔ The tests to ensure the controls are in place

Figure 15-7 shows the main screen of the SarbOxPro software program. It's designed to help company employees (rather than costly outside consultants) compile the following data:

✔ **Entities and locations:** SarbOxPro allows users to identify different company entities and locations using the screens like the one shown in Figure 15-8.

SarbOxPro lets you create the equivalent of a standardized template for controls that are constant from location to location. This action simplifies the process of documenting controls at each location.

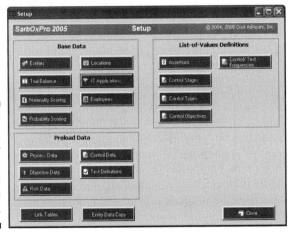

Figure 15-7:
An intuitive interface for aggregating information about the company.

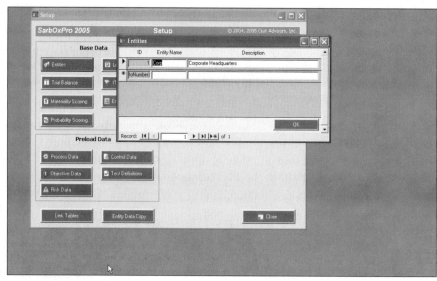

Figure 15-8:
Identifying
entities.

✔ **Trial balance:** Most accounting programs allow you to create documents using an Excel format, so with this part of the program, users can import a trial balance into SarbOxPro from Microsoft Excel.

✔ **IT applications:** Many companies lose track of their IT applications, so SarbOxPro helps users document all the different information technology applications in a company. The program makes it easy to maintain a centralized listing.

✔ **Materiality scoring:** A section of the program allows management and process owners to specify percentages to use to decide whether an account or test result is considered "insignificant," "material," or "critical" (with a few levels in between those criteria).

✔ **Employees:** It's important to know which employees are involved in carrying out process testing in case questions about the testing arise in the future. SarbOxPro maintains a database of employee information as well.

✔ **Processes:** After your company develops a list of its processes, you can begin creating a SarbOxPro database using the screen shown in Figure 15-9. SarbOxPro runs on Microsoft Access and is designed to ensure that processes are named using consistent conventions so that they aren't mistakenly listed and tested more than once or overlooked by all the documenters spread across all the locations in a typical Sox 404 project.

✔ **Controls:** As with processes, SarbOxPro ensures that controls are named using consistent conventions to prevent them from being tested repeatedly or overlooked. The program also has a rich library of identified control types that can be selected and correlated to the company's processes, as shown in Figure 15-10. Users who attempt to add duplicate or nonstandard controls to the library receive a warning message.

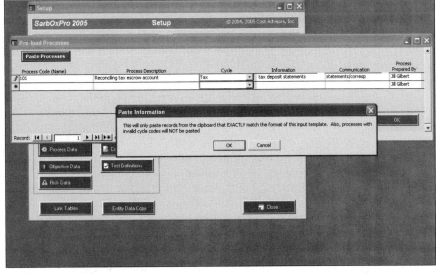

Figure 15-9:
The convenient SarbOxPro screen for documenting processes.

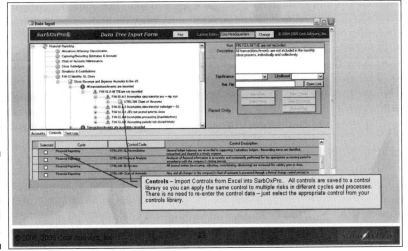

Figure 15-10:
The SarbOxPro control library.

✔ **Assertions:** *Assertions* are representations on the financial statements that must be tested to determine if they're true. SarbOxPro uses a special screen shown to categorize and identify the types of assertions a company makes, each of which must be separately tested.

✔ **Control stages:** Control testing is an ongoing process that's completed in stages. SarbOxPro continuously documents the status of the testing.

✔ **Frequency of controls:** SarbOxPro allows you to document how often your company tests its controls.

Entering all that testing process data

After you enter the initial configuration data discussed in the preceding section, SarbOxPro allows you to enter the data you gather from your Section 404 internal compliance testing. Figure 15-11 illustrates the process of entering test data into SarbOxPro.

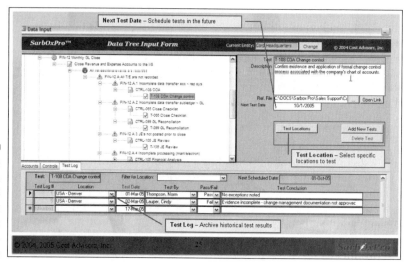

Figure 15-11: Entering the Section 404 test data with SarbOxPro.

Creating reports

The best feature of a program like SarbOxPro is that it allows you to get reports about test results at any time during the Section 404 audit using a variety of filtering criteria, as shown in Figure 15-12. You can export data to Excel to create your own reports or use the preformatted reports offered by the SarbOxPro program. You can also create customized Microsoft Access–based reports to meet specific company requirements.

Reports are a critical management tool because they summarize the data on which management relies on personally certifying the company's financial statements under Sections 302 and 906 (discussed in Chapter 9).

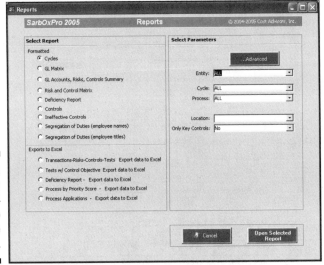

Figure 15-12:
Filtering
Section 404
test data to
create
reports.

Opting for Other Types of Software Solutions

Small companies looking for something even simpler than the popular SarbOxPro program may opt for a general information management system used to gather information other than that which is required by SOX. Web-based solutions are also available. This section explains these types of products and examines a couple representative examples.

Looking at a general information management tool

kManager is an example of a software system that has broad-based IT functionality for managing information within a company. SOX compliance is just one aspect of this program.

You can download a demo of this company's software at www.kmanager.com. A diagram of the program architecture and functions is shown in Figure 15-13, and some of kManager's SOX-specific features are shown in Figure 15-14.

As of this writing, you can implement the kManager system for about $50 a month.

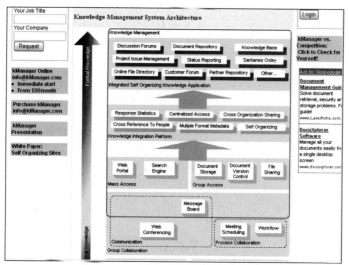

Figure 15-13:
The kManager information management software interface.

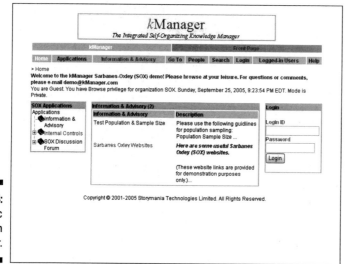

Figure 15-14:
Sox-specific features in kManager.

Using Web-based compliance tools

Web-based SOX products can be a particularly easy-to-implement solution for small companies. An example of such a product is Complyant (www.complyant.com). Complyant provides Web-based templates (such as the one shown in Figure 15-15) for entering information, and content databases. Behind the templates is a relational database that allows the company to create reports on information entered.

Complyant runs on the user's browser software and on a .net framework and SQL server database. All users within must have IDs and passwords in order to access the company's Complyant system.

Web-based SOX solutions like Complyant offer a number of advantages to users:

✔ **Compatibility with existing desktop applications:** Complyant is designed so that everyone in the company can access the tool from their desktops.

✔ **Less paperwork:** With a Web-based tool, employees have fewer documents and databases to manage internally.

✔ **Ease of updating:** These types of systems require no downloads or upgrades; updating is all done by the company offering the Web-based tool.

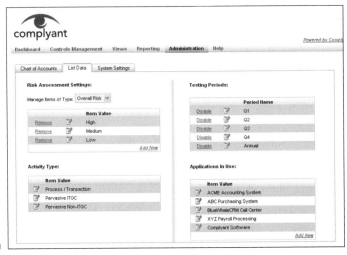

Figure 15-15: A sample Complyant template for SOX Section 404 documentation.

Part V
To SOX-finity and Beyond

The 5th Wave   By Rich Tennant

THE END IS NEAR

"Isn't that our bookkeeper?"

In this part . . .

This section looks at the future of SOX — from who's getting sued under SOX and how you can keep your company (and yourself) clear of the courtroom to how its effects extend beyond large publicly traded companies. After examining the legal side of executive perks and whistle-blowers, this part looks at governance trends for not-for-profit and privately held companies and the compliance requirements for outsourced services.

Chapter 16

Lawsuits Under SOX

. . . .

In This Chapter

▶ Looking at the first major trial after SOX

▶ Examining the ongoing Enron litigation

▶ Understanding how the Arthur Andersen precedent threatens big accounting firms

▶ Explaining why private individuals can't sue under SOX

▶ Avoiding and defending against whistle-blower lawsuits

. . . .

*M*any companies are motivated to comply with SOX out of a sense of social responsibility, but most do it to avoid being sanctioned, sued, or even criminally prosecuted. In the first few years following its enactment, it appears that SOX hasn't been the boon for securities litigators that it has proven to be for auditors. However, it is having an impact on the litigation process. According to the National Economic Research Association (NERA), since the passage of SOX, at least nine settlements of major securities lawsuits have incorporated SOX reforms, including cases involving HCA Inc. and Sprint.

This chapter examines some of the criminal and civil trials played out in the media after SOX. I update you on the aftermath of the Arthur Andersen criminal case and I then explain how recent case law limits the rights of private individuals to bring their own civil suits under SOX. Finally, I look at how SOX's whistle-blower provisions are impacting the nation's workplaces. As of this writing, the big winners in the courtroom and in the media are one high-profile CEO, the big four accounting firms, and a few assorted whistle-blowers.

The Smoking Gun: Knowledge

The most unnerving potential work scenario for any chief executive or financial officers (CEOs and CFOs) of a corporation is the prospect of being sued as an individual. After SOX, we've seen criminal trials against former powerful top management figures as a result of the SOX requirements that they personally certify the accuracy of the company's financial statements. SOX Sections 302 and 906, which contain these requirements, are discussed in detail in Chapter 9.

Enron, WorldCom, and Tyco management have received decades-long prison sentences and massive fines as they attempt to defend their roles in massive corporate collapses. Only one, CEO Richard Scrushy of HealthSouth Corporation, discussed later in this chapter, has been acquitted so far.

SOX Sections 302 and 906 both attempt to create a legal link between chief executive and financial officers (CEOs and CFOs) and the financial statements put out by their companies by requiring that CEOs and CFOs personally certify their companies' financial statements. Both sections impose harsh penalties:

✔ SOX Section 906 authorizes a prison term of up to ten years and a fine of up to $1 million for any executive who "knowingly" certifies a regulatory filing that doesn't "fairly present, in all material respects, the financial condition and results" of the company. Any executive who willfully certifies a false filing faces up to 20 years in prison and a $5 million fine. (*Willfully* is a legal standard predicated on deliberate conduct.)

✔ Section 302 contains civil penalties for signing false reports. It provides that the signing officer must certify that he or she has reviewed the report and that, based on his or her knowledge, the financial statements fairly represent the company's operations.

Harsh as the requirement that CEOs and CFOs personally certify their company's financial statements may have sounded when the law was first passed, liability under both sections is predicated on what the CEOs and CFOs actually know. This legal standard means that at least one CEO (Richard Scrushy, as discussed later) was able to successfully defend against criminal charges by claiming that his subordinates pulled the wool over his eyes.

It is a demoralizing prospect to prosecutors that high-level management may walk out of criminal courtrooms as free men and women while employees who claimed to have taken direction from them are convicted. Accordingly, the prosecutors are likely to revamp their strategies and attempt to shift the courtroom focus from what CEOs and CFOs actually knew to what they *should* have known.

The First Big SOX Trial: Richard Scrushy

Top executives across the country were riveted in 2005 by coverage of the trial of Richard Scrushy, one of the first CEOs to be prosecuted under SOX. Under SOX Section 906, the prosecution had to prove that Scrushy acted willfully in order to convict him. Legal analysts are still debating exactly what *willfully* means under Section 906, but most lawyers seem to concur that it requires clearly knowing what was happening and either participating or deliberately not preventing it.

The squishy Scrushy facts

In early 2005, Richard Scrushy, the former CEO of HealthSouth Corporation, was prosecuted for SOX-related violations tied to HealthSouth's downfall. Scrushy was indicted on 36 criminal counts, including charges of criminal conspiracy, securities fraud, wire and mail fraud, false statements, false certification under SOX Section 906, and money laundering.

Scrushy was a former respiratory therapist who cofounded HealthSouth in 1984 and built it into a national chain of rehabilitation and outpatient surgery hospitals. At issue in the lawsuit was an alleged scheme to inflate HealthSouth's earnings by $2.7 billion from 1996 to 2002. Prosecutors contended Scrushy personally amassed more than $200 million as the price of HealthSouth's stock rose based on fraudulent financial reports. They argued that HealthSouth was precisely an Enron-type scenario that SOX was created to prevent.

The prosecution had persuasive evidence against Scrushy as compared to the cases against former top executives at WorldCom, Adelphia Communications, and Tyco International. The case was viewed as strong for the following reasons:

- ✔ Five former company CFOs pleaded guilty to fraud and implicated their former boss.

- ✔ The jury heard recorded conversations between Mr. Scrushy and a CFO in which they discussed balance-sheet problems. (During the conversation, Scrushy asked, "You're not wired, are you?")

- ✔ Aaron Beam, the former CFO at HealthSouth, claimed Scrushy had direct knowledge of accounting fraud at the company.

The Scrushy trial lasted four months and centered on testimony of the five former CFOs who cooperated with the government by pointing fingers at Scrushy and pled guilty to various charges. As in other CEO trials, lawyers argued Scrushy was a victim of a conspiracy by his subordinates and unaware that fraud was perpetuated by those beneath him.

The judge in the case carefully instructed the jury not to assume that Scrushy was responsible for the fraud just because he was the CEO. However, she also instructed the jury they could find Scrushy guilty if he "deliberately closed his eyes" to wrongdoing. Ultimately, on July 1, 2005, Scrushy was acquitted on all 36 charges that he signed false financial filings. One juror observed after the trial, "As for evidence, I wanted something in black and white, something like fingerprints. That wasn't there."

The Scrushy post-game recap

Congress intended, after Enron and the wave of corporate scandals that followed it, that the certification requirement would make it easier to prosecute white-collar crimes. Even if other elements of a fraud weren't linked to the executive, the signing of a false affidavit would serve as a smoking gun. But that's not quite how things have worked out. However, as the Scrushy trial indicates, convicting an executive of knowingly violating the certification requirement involves proving the same facts necessary to support other criminal charges that were on the books long before SOX. In the end, all that appears certain is that SOX increases possible prison time.

The crucial element of SOX Section 906 is knowledge. Proving what an executive knew or didn't know of a fraud in a large, publicly traded company with thousands of employees is a huge prosecutorial undertaking.

In addition to charging Richard Scrushy under SOX Section 906, prosecutors brought charges against him for securities fraud and conspiracy. In post-trial interviews, jurors revealed that after they failed to find Scrushy guilty of the non-SOX charges, the SOX-related counts fell like dominoes. A prominent securities attorney quoted in *The New York Times* surmised, "I can't imagine a case where you couldn't prove that the person had engaged in fraud, so you found them not guilty on that count, but then found him guilty" for certifying false filings [under SOX]."

Of the failure to get a conviction against Scrushy, the lead prosecutor in the case said, "I don't think it says anything on the strength of the Sarbanes-Oxley Act." She observed that SOX "was just one of several federal statutes that was used. It will be tested again."

Questions raised by the Scrushy trial regarding executives' behavior include:

- ✔ Is recklessly disregarding information the same as "knowing"?
- ✔ Do company executives have a duty to inquire about all ongoing financial matters?
- ✔ To what extent do executives have a duty to supervise subordinates and verify their actions?

In the end, many lawyers have concluded that the liability that top executives face under SOX may not be all that different from that which they faced under criminal and securities laws prior to SOX.

What's next: Scrushy civil suits

Although he was acquitted on all 36 criminal charges, Scrushy still faces civil suits from HealthSouth's shareholders. (The shares reached a high of just above $30 in April 1998 only to plummet to 10 cents a share after the fraud became public in March 2003.)

Mister Scrushy remains one of HealthSouth's biggest shareholders. However, the company has predictably sought to distance itself from its embattled CEO. "The new board and new management team remain appalled by the multibillion-dollar fraud that took place under Mr. Scrushy's management and environment under which such fraud could occur," HealthSouth officials said in a public statement. "Under no circumstances will Mr. Scrushy be offered any position within the company by this management team or by this board of directors."

The "Ignorance" Defense of Kenneth Lay

In the fall of 2005, the Justice Department and Securities Exchange Commission (SEC) finally brought charges against Enron's former CEO, Kenneth Lay. Many Enron officials (and even Lea Fastow, one official's wife) were already tried, sentenced, and had begun serving time for their roles in Enron's collapse. Still, government agencies continued to ponder whether to indict Mister Lay. The delay, it appears, was attributable to that tricky issue of knowledge: What did Mister Lay know — or not know — about the fraud being perpetrated at Enron while he was at the helm? The Justice Department, after consternating for years, finally opted to indict Lay for covering up Enron's fraud (beginning in 2001). The SEC filed a corresponding civil suit.

Both government agencies appeared convinced. Lay didn't initially know of the fraud that brought his company down. Neither agency indicted Lay for organizing the fraud or even knowing that the books were being cooked in 1999 and 2000.

These are the factors that persuaded the Justice Department to finally indict Lay:

- ✔ **As he was reassuring Enron employees that the company would be saved, he was secretly selling off his own shares of company stock.** He used what's now known as the _Lay loophole_ in federal securities, which provided that stock transactions between an executive and the company itself didn't have to be disclosed until the following year.

   SOX slams the Lay loophole closed by requiring that all insider transactions be disclosed within days of taking place.

- ✔ **He repeatedly borrowed $4 million from the company and then satisfied the loan by tendering stock to the company.**

   SOX now prohibits corporations from making loans to their executives.

Oh Kenny Boy . . .

The following ballad is sung to the tune of "Danny Boy":

Oh Kenny Boy, the jails, the jails are calling,
From state to state, and through the world so wide.
The money's gone, and all the chips are falling,
'Tis you, 'tis you must go and you must hide.

But come ye back when lawmen stop their yam'ring,
Or when Congress is hushed and Dems are eating crow.
'Tis I'll be there in office or in Crawford,
Oh Kenny Boy, oh Kenny Boy, I love you so.

But if you're jailed, and I am in the Oval,
If I'm still Prez, as Prez I expect to be,

Don't come and ask for favors or a pardon,
Don't kneel and say a rescue plea to me.

For I shan't hear, tho' loud you beg before me,
Though all I craved you gladly gave to me.
You'll have to fend without me if you love me,
And you will keep your peace, so I stay Prez and free

I found this tune on the Web site of humorist Madeline Begun Kane, located a www.madkane.com/bushkennyboy.html. Ms. Kane sings and writes poetic tributes to Bush, DeLay, and Supreme Court nominees and justices, and she pokes fun at the legal profession and even at feminism. Check out her latest: *Ode to Tom DeLay*.

In the civil suit filed by the SEC, the agency alleged Lay violated insider-trading laws by selling stock when he knew of the fraud in 2001, but not prior to that. In fact, the only crime that Lay's alleged to have committed prior to 2001 is failing to disclose to lending banks that money he was borrowing would be used to purchase Enron shares.

Some observers have speculated that the delay in indicting Lay signaled a weak case. They infer that because Lay was the face of Enron, the prosecutors' goal was to get any indictment.

President Bush once publicly called Kenneth Lay "Kenny Boy." The media seized upon this to assert Lay's supposed connections to the Bush administration, inspiring political jibes like the ballad *Oh Kenny Boy,* reprinted in the sidebar.

In late August 2001, Lay deflected a reporter's question about the partnerships used to shelter Enron losses, and these off–balance sheet losses became symbolic of Enron's fraud. "You're getting way over my head," Lay told the reporter, despite the fact that he held a PhD in economics.

As of this writing, the public has professed shock that Lay may walk free even though those Enron officers under his direction went to prison. The inescapable conclusion of this case is that it's difficult to prove what a CEO knew and didn't know at the time fraud occurred. The question of knowledge will continue to be the critical burden of proof under SOX Sections 302 and 906. These sections (discussed in Chapter 9) now require CEOs and CFOs to personally sign off on their companies' financial statements, something Mr. Lay wasn't required to do prior to SOX.

Timing Is Everything: Andersen, Ernst, and KPMG Litigation Outcomes

In 2001, Arthur Andersen was the largest accounting firm in the world with 28,000 employees in the U.S. alone. By 2002, it had collapsed under a criminal indictment.

Prior to Anderson's demise, there were only five major firms (the "Big Five") with the capability to audit the largest U.S. firms. The availability of sophisticated audit service providers for large firms was suddenly constricted. Concerns surfaced about the future quality of accounting professionals in the workplace since Arthur Andersen had been the training ground for the CPA profession. Thousands lost their jobs.

In 2005, KPMG, one of the remaining the "Big Four" firms, came very close to suffering the same fate as Andersen for peddling illegal tax shelters. However, with KPMG, the Justice Department proceeded carefully; it didn't want its indictment to put the KPMG under and shrink the number of major accounting firms to the "Big Three."

William McDonough, head of the Public Company Accounting Oversight Board (PCAOB), publicly expressed relief in September 2005 that the Department of Justice had reached a settlement with KPMG over its past sales of tax avoidance schemes to clients. As of this writing, the remaining Big Four firms are Deloitte & Touche, Ernst & Young, KPMG, and PricewaterhouseCoopers. The public has a sense that all of the Big Four remain vulnerable in the marketplace to scandal and litigation at any time.

PCAOB Chairman McDonough has warned that the solution to the problem of audit concentration can't be solved by a merger of smaller accounting firms. Even if the firms ranked five through eight were all merged into one, the resulting company would still be far smaller and less capable of doing large-scale audits than any of the Big Four.

"None of us has a clue what to do if one of the big four failed," McDonough told the press in 2005. He explained that if even one of the big four accounting firms was to collapse, the best accountants would likely flee from the profession to seek better opportunities in other fields. Other experts point out that competition in the industry would be severely diminished, and fees for public companies already socked by SOX compliance costs would skyrocket.

Moreover, the possibility of losing a major accounting firm raises a question of whether enough high-quality, experienced firms would be available to perform the complex public company audits that the U.S. economy and the investing public depend upon.

Andersen's victory: Three years too late

In June 2002, Andersen was convicted of a single count of obstruction of justice, which was enough to precipitate the accounting giant's downfall. The count alleged Anderson deliberately shredded Enron documents in order to thwart a pending investigation.

This was only one of the many misdeeds that came to light after the collapse of Enron, as discussed in Chapter 2.

A member of the firm sent a memo allegedly advocating shredding as part of the firm's "document retention policy." Those involved in the Enron audit were all too eager to comply. The company defended its document retention policy as necessary financial housekeeping and denied the shredding was intended to block a future investigation.

On May 31, 2005, the U.S. Supreme Court overturned Arthur Andersen's conviction; in a unanimous opinion, the nine justices on the high court concluded the "jury instructions at issue simply failed to convey the requisite consciousness of wrongdoing." Chief Justice William Rehnquist admonished, "Indeed, it is striking how little culpability the instructions required."

Unfortunately, at the time that the Supreme Court overturned its conviction, Andersen was nearly defunct, with only about 200 employees left (most of whom handled its ongoing legal matters). Its downfall had an economic ripple effect. Not only were about 28,000 Andersen employees thrown out of work, but substantial jobs were lost in companies that provided goods and services to Andersen. The Andersen downfall also served to restrict competition and drive up audit fees just as most public companies were experiencing the initial sticker shock of SOX compliance.

An Ernst error

In the fall of 2005, the SEC chief administrative law judge Brenda Murray ruled that accounting firm Ernst & Young acted improperly by auditing PeopleSoft Inc., a huge public company with which the firm had a profitable relationship in other business areas. Because of the SEC's contention that Ernst had violated rules on auditor independence, Judge Murray entered an unusual order barring Ernst from accepting new audit clients in the United States for six months. She also fined the firm $1.7 million.

The SEC contended Ernst had violated rules on auditor independence because of its profitable relationship with PeopleSoft Inc. in other business areas.

Ernst's consulting and tax practices used PeopleSoft software in their business, and the two companies collaborated in promoting some of their joint business activities. The evidence in the SEC's case revealed that

- ✔ Ernst had billed itself in marketing materials as an "implementation partner" of PeopleSoft.
- ✔ Ernst had earned $500 million over five years from installing PeopleSoft programs at other companies.

SEC officials said the decision against Ernst & Young would send a message to other firms that, "auditor independence is one of the centerpieces of ensuring the integrity of the audit process."

 Ernst ties with its competitor, KPMG, for receiving the longest suspension of signing new clients ever imposed by the SEC. In 1975, Peat Marwick, a predecessor of KPMG, received a similar six-month suspension for failing to audit five companies, one of which was Penn Central, a railroad that subsequently went bankrupt.

Kid gloves for KPMG?

In 2005, in a case described as the largest tax evasion scheme in U.S. history, the Justice Department criminally charged eight former executives of the major accounting firm KPMG with conspiracy to sell fraudulent tax shelters that shorted the IRS at least $2.5 billion.

According to prosecutors, the firm earned around $115 million in fees for selling illegal tax shelters over a seven-year period. Court documents described the shelters "as a means for wealthy individuals with taxable income or gains generally in excess of $10 million in 1996 and of $20 million in 1998–2000 fraudulently to eliminate or reduce the tax paid to the IRS on that income or gain." KPMG received a $456 million fine to settle the federal investigation of its marketing of the illegal tax shelters.

Although KPMG as an entity was charged with conspiracy in a criminal complaint, the firm was granted something referred to as *deferred prosecution*. Basically, deferred prosecution means that the Justice Department made a decision not to prosecute the firm; it allowed KPMG to avoid a grand jury criminal indictment by paying the penalty, submitting to some independent monitoring, and continuing to cooperate with the Justice Department investigation.

Attorney General Alberto Gonzales defended the government's decision to defer prosecution, but in the minds of many, the decision sent a message that prosecution is risky because there are simply too few big accounting firms, and the Justice Department didn't want to set in motion an Andersen-esque demise for KMPG. Gonzalez publicly stated: "I want to be clear. No company is too big to be prosecuted. We have zero tolerance for corporate fraud, but we also recognize the importance of avoiding collateral consequences whenever possible." Gonzales also pointed out the range of potential economic victims from the possible fallout of a KPMG downfall; Gonzalez explained that the Justice Department's decision reflected "the reality that the conviction of an organization can affect innocent workers and others associated with the organization, and can even have an impact on the national economy."

While deferring to prosecute KPMG, federal prosecutors had no such reservations indicting individuals associated with the scandal. In August 2005, the Justice Department indicted eight former KPMG LLP officials and a lawyer accused of helping wealthy clients evade billions of dollars in taxes. It's the largest criminal tax fraud case in history.

The Gemstar Case: Interpreting Section 1103

SOX Section 1103 is a provision directed at recouping big bonuses paid to fraudulent executives. The statute kicks into effect if a company is being investigated for a possible violation of federal securities laws and it appears to the SEC "likely" that the company will make "extraordinary payments (whether compensation or otherwise)." Under the statute, the SEC may ask a federal district court for a temporary order requiring the issuer to hold the fund in a special interest-bearing account (called an *escrow account*) for 45 days. If the individual slated to receive the supposed "extraordinary payments" actually is charged with a securities violation in a civil proceeding, a court can withhold the payments until the end of the trial.

Because neither SOX Section 1103 nor any SEC rule defines an "extraordinary payment," courts have begun to look at this issue. For example, in May 2005, a three-judge panel ruled that multimillion dollar termination fees to be paid to two executives of Gemstar after the company discovered that it had overstated its revenue by millions of dollars were not extraordinary. The panel in this case noted the lack of "evidence as to what would be an ordinary payment under comparable circumstances."

In the Gemstar case, the district court had placed the funds in escrow, but its logic was vague in that it had relied, in part, on the fact that the payments at issue had been negotiated over a long period of time by many different people in the company. The district court called this process extraordinary, but the appeals court said the circumstances didn't constitute that label and complained it hadn't received enough evidence from the lower (district) court to review the case on appeal and had no choice but to reverse the district court's ruling.

Suing Under SOX Section 304

SOX Section 304 calls for *disgorgement* of profits and bonuses from top corporate executives in the wake of an alleged accounting scandal. (Disgorgement is an odd word choice that simply means they have to give it back.)

Who can sue officers and directors to disgorge their bonuses? According to a recent federal district court case, only the SEC can. In Neer v. Pelino, the court held that SOX doesn't provide a private right of action for shareholders to file a suit on their own behalf. (This type of lawsuit is known as a *shareholders' derivative suit.*)

The Court held that Congress intended for Section 304 to be enforced only by the SEC, and not by shareholders in private lawsuits. The judge reasoned that Congress "explicitly created a private right of action in only one place, and that is in Section 306" — a provision that prohibits corporate officers from buying or selling securities during a pension fund blackout period. (Blackout periods are covered in Chapter 10.)

Suing Under Section 806: The Whistle-Blower Provision

Section 806 of the Sarbanes-Oxley Act of 2002 confers public company employees who report suspected violations of a range of federal offenses the right to sue both the company and its employees and agents for reinstatement and back pay.

Blowing the whistle before and after SOX

Whistle-blowers, employees who lawfully disclose private employer information, have been the heart and soul of many federal fraud cases against many well-known companies. Prior to SOX, most of these types of complaints were brought under the False Claims Act, which encourages whistle-blowers to come forward by promising them up to 25 percent of the money recovered by the government as a result of the shared information. The act was first passed during the Civil War but was resurrected and amended in 1985. Since then, it has generated $12 billion for the federal treasury (and more than $1 billion for hundreds of whistle-blowers).

The decades-old False Claims Act gives whistle-blowers a reward of up to 25 percent of the funds recovered. SOX offers additional whistle-blower protections to those who help uncover fraud against publicly traded companies.

Specifically, SOX

- ✔ Protects whistle-blowers from being fired.
- ✔ Provides remedies for whistle-blower reinstatement.

What happens when the whistle blows?

Under SOX, a whistle-blower is an employee who provides information to a federal regulatory or law enforcement agency, to a member or committee of Congress, or to a person with supervisory authority over the employee about conduct that the employee reasonably believes constitutes a violation of:

- ✔ Any rule or regulation of the SEC
- ✔ Federal criminal provisions relating to securities
- ✔ Bank, mail, or wire fraud
- ✔ Any other federal law relating to fraud against company's shareholders

SOX Section 806, which is enforced by the federal Occupational Health and Safety Administration (OSHA), declares that officers, employees, contractors, subcontractors, and agents of the company are forbidden to engage in any retaliation against a whistle-blower.

According to OSHA, the protection of Section 806 extends not only to employees, but also to the employees of contractors, subcontractors, and agents of public companies.

Windfalls for whistle-blowers

Several years before SOX, hospital CFO Jim Alderson refused to go along with his employer's phony billing practices and was let go. Alderson sued for wrongful discharge and alerted the government to the fact that it was being cheated out of $1.7 billion in Medicare funds by the nation's largest commercial hospital chain. Under the False Claims Act, Mr. Alderson received a 10-percent share of the money recovered by the government.

Filing the complaint

If an employee believes he or she has been fired, demoted, suspended, threatened, harassed, coerced, or put on any sort of blacklist because of whistle-blowing, he or she can file a complaint with OSHA within 90 days of the alleged discriminatory treatment. After OSHA receives the complaint, the agency notifies the employer of the allegations and evidence and gives it an opportunity to respond. The Secretary of Labor issues its decision within 180 days of the filing of the complaint.

OSHA's review of the complaint

OSHA conducts an initial review of each SOX-related whistle-blower complaint and decides whether the employee filing the complaint makes the required basic case (called a *prima facie case*) against the employer. The required elements for a prima facie case are:

- ✓ **Protected activity:** The employee engaged in conduct or an activity that was protected by SOX or another law.

- ✓ **Employer knowledge:** Either actually or constructively, the employer knew or suspected that the employee engaged in the protected activity.

- ✓ **Unfavorable action by employer:** The employee suffered an unfavorable personnel action, such as termination, demotion, or suspension.

- ✓ **Sufficient circumstances:** The circumstances must raise the inference that the protected activity was a contributing factor in the unfavorable action.

Whether the employer actually violated the specified SOX laws and regulations isn't important. All that's required for a valid Section 806 complaint is that the employee have an objectively reasonable belief that the employer's conduct constitutes such a violation for the employee to be protected under Section 806.

OSHA's investigation

If OSHA finds that the complainant has the elements for a prima facie case (as explained in the preceding section), the employer is given 20 days to respond after it receives notice of the complaint filing. The employer can respond in writing or request a personal meeting with OSHA; it's required to demonstrate by clear and convincing evidence that it would have taken the same personnel action even in the absence of the employee's whistle-blowing activity. If OSHA finds that the employer has met this burden, it dismisses the complaint. Otherwise, OSHA must conduct a formal investigation into the merits of the complaint.

OSHA takes the position that an employer's company counsel doesn't have the right to be present during interviews of nonmanagement and nonsupervisory personnel. In fact, as a matter of practice, OSHA often doesn't notify the company or its lawyers when such employees are contacted in the course of an investigation. OSHA also redacts witness statements or summarizes them to protect employees who ask to remain anonymous.

After OSHA finishes its investigation, it decides whether there's reasonable cause to believe the company violated Section 806 by discriminating against the whistle-blower. If it sides with the employee, OSHA's order may include reinstatement or coverage of lost pay. The employer has an opportunity to submit a written response or to meet with the investigators to interview more witnesses and submit evidence within ten business days of OSHA's notification to the employer.

Dealing with appeals

If either party disagrees with OSHA's findings, it may file an appeal with the Chief Administrative Law Judge in the Department of Labor. If neither party appeals within 30 days of receiving OSHA's findings, the preliminary order becomes the final decision of the Secretary of Labor, and no further judicial review is allowed.

If an appeal crops up within 30 days, an administrative law judge conducts a new hearing on the complaint. The administrative law judge's order may be appealed to the Department of Labor's Administrative Review Board. A petition for review must be filed within ten business days of the administrative law judge's decision, and review by the board is discretionary. Unless the board accepts the case within 30 days of the filing of the petition for review, the administrative law judge's decision becomes final. It may be appealed to the United States Court of Appeals.

As of this writing, the Department of Labor has reported approximately five dozen cases that have been appealed or considered by administrative law judges. Most have been dismissed for untimely filing or withdrawn, signaling settlement without reaching a decision on the legal merits of the case.

Tips for defending against whistle-blower suits

Whistle-blower complaints in the post-SOX era require more attention and certainly more paperwork than before. No matter how unfounded the complaint may seem, your company can practice safe SOX by doing the following:

- ✔ **Take all complaints seriously.** Make sure that all complaints brought by employees are fully investigated and documented. Employees should be instructed on procedures for processing complaints and directed never to make a determination that the complaint is trivial or frivolous.

- ✔ **Track the timing.** If an employee is contentious and requires discipline, try to delay taking any action until his or her complaint is investigated. The mere coincidence of timing may lead to an inference that the company fired the employee in retaliation for the whistle-blower complaint.

- ✔ **Document every phase of the investigation.** Document the complaint itself, everyone who is made aware of it, information gathered that's relevant to the outcome of the complaint, action taken in response to the complaint (if any), and how the matter is concluded.

Chapter 17

The Surprising Scope of SOX

In This Chapter

▶ Meeting SOX Section 404 standards for outsourced work

▶ Considering how SOX impacts not-for-profit companies

▶ Looking at how foreign companies are responding to SOX

*T*his chapter explores the outer limits of SOX, taking a look at its surprisingly broad scope. Congress probably didn't consider the impact passing SOX would have on outsourced services, not-for-profit organizations, and foreign corporations. Nevertheless, these types of entities are being impacted by the pervasive standards introduced by SOX.

In this chapter, I examine a company's obligations with respect to the work it sends out beyond its four walls. I also look at the guidance SOX offers to not-for-profits as they struggle with their own governance issues. Finally, I take you across the ocean to understand how SOX impacts European companies that list their stock on U.S. exchanges.

Outsourcing Under SOX

SOX Section 404 requires companies to assess and audit the effectiveness of their internal control and how they impact the companies' financial statements. (Internal control is discussed in Chapter 11.) This requirement extends to *all* aspects of a company's financial operations — even if some of them happen to occur outside the company.

If your company relies on outside companies to process financial information, it must make sure adequate internal controls are in place just as if the company had done the work in-house. SOX requires companies to monitor control conditions at facilities where they outsource services and at hosting sites where they may store sensitive company data.

The responsibility for monitoring internal control for outsourced services arises from *SAS 70*, an auditing standard developed by the American Institute of Certified Public Accountants (discussed in Chapter 5). This document contains audit requirements for the control activities a company puts in place at a service organization or outsourcing firm.

Summarizing SAS 70

Under SAS 70, an audit of internal control for outsourced services can be performed by the service provider's auditors or by the company relying on its work. SAS 70 identifies two types of audit approaches:

- **Type 1 audit:** Focuses on general controls at one point in time. This type of audit is a "snapshot" approach that doesn't involve audit testing.

- **Type 2 audit:** Looks at control conditions over a designated period of time. Auditors conduct tests that span this time period and perform testing to verify the effectiveness of controls at service organizations.

Regardless of the type of audit approach chosen by the audit firm, the company's audit committee must work with the audit committee to make sure that the SAS 70 report generated is adequate to address the requirements of Section 404 (discussed in Chapter 11). The issues that must be addressed include the following:

- **Scope:** It's up to the company and the service provider to determine the scope of the audit and what will be tested. Ultimately, the company's outside auditors are required to include an evaluation of this testing within their overall Section 404 audit of the company.

- **Lead time:** Many service providers are just getting up to speed with SOX. Smaller service providers who have until July 15, 2007, to comply with SOX may need extra lead time to comply with SAS 70 requests. (For details on the SEC compliance deadlines, turn to Chapter 11.)

- **Standardized certifications:** Companies that provide outsourced service may be able to save money and better service their clients by asking their own outside audit firms to develop SAS 70 certifications that they can provide to companies. Doing so meets the needs of their customers in a proactive manner and helps the service provider avoid having to reinvent the wheel each time a customer requests an SAS 70 certification. (A sample SAS certification report is included in Appendix E.)

- **Additional testing:** After the SAS audit results come back, additional testing may be required. Ultimately, the customer is responsible for the testing.

Sidestepping SAS 70

Not all outsourced functions require SAS audits. Sensitive services, such as payroll, may require your company to secure an SAS 70 audit. However, your company may *not* need an SAS 70 from the following types of services providers:

- ✔ **Staffing:** If you use a temporary agency to help staff your company's IT or accounting departments, you probably don't need an SAS audit because the sensitive services are performed internally.

- ✔ **Software development:** You probably don't need an SAS 70 from a company to which you outsource application development activities if controls are already in place within your company to monitor the quality of the work.

- ✔ **Law firms and other outside consultants:** As with software development, the quality of these services is monitored within your company, so an SAS 70 certification probably isn't required.

Extending SOX Principles to Not-for-Profits

Although SOX applies to publicly traded companies, *not-for-profit companies* (NFPs) are becoming increasingly concerned about being sued and held to judicially created standards akin to those found in SOX. For this reason, SOX considerations are starting to surface in some unexpected places — school boards, charities, and other tax-exempt organizations are seeking some level of reform and accountability.

Altruism is not enough

Not-for-profits must be prepared to demonstrate a commitment to good governance and internal control. Not-for-profits, as a rule, depend on public good will and their reputations to attract funds. Despite the most altruistic motives, a financial scandal can permanently undermine an organization's ability to attract contributions. Thus, words such as "accountability," "ethics," "transparency," "duty," "full-disclosure," and "social responsibility" have always been part of the vernacular of NFP governance — from the smallest NFPs to the largest.

Legislators are looking at nonprofit governance standards

In September 2004, Senate Finance Committee Chairman Charles Grassley contacted the president of a group called the Independent Sector and asked it to convene an independent national panel to make recommendations on issues of governance, ethical practice, and accountability for the nonprofit sector. As a result, the national Panel on the Nonprofit Sector was named.

The panel made recommendations in 15 major areas for actions to be taken by the nonprofits themselves, by the IRS, and by Congress. At a minimum, the panel recommended that all nonprofit organizations voluntarily:

✔ Adopt and implement a policy regulating conflicts of interest.

✔ Include on their boards of directors individuals with financial literacy skills (that is, with experience reading and interpreting financial statements and information).

✔ Develop policies regarding whistle-blowers (which are people who report fraud and mismanagement within an organization. The whistle-blower provisions of SOX are discussed in Chapter 16.

The panel also recommended the Congress and the IRS take the following actions:

✔ Create rules to suspend the tax-exempt status of any organization that fails to file required annual Form 990 series returns with the IRS for two or more consecutive years after notice from the IRS.

✔ Require that CEOs (or other top management) certify that their IRS Form 990 returns are correct and complete.

✔ Require charitable organizations to conduct an independent audit of their finances if they must file a Form 990 return with the IRS each year and have total annual revenues of $2 million or more.

✔ Require that charities with $25,000 in annual revenues complete an annual notice supplying basic information.

You can locate the full text of the panel's final report and recommendations at www. nonprofitpanel.org/final/.

Although the SOX doesn't legally apply to NFPs, the statute has increased public awareness as to how companies of all types govern themselves. NFPs are likely to look to SOX for guidance in developing their own governance standards. Audit committees, compensation committees, written codes of ethics, and governance guidelines are all likely to find their way into NFPs.

Since SOX was proposed, several bills have been introduced in both federal and state legislatures to make nonprofit corporations, municipal agencies, and charitable groups more accountable. While this type of legislation is still years away, SOX-type standards for NFPs are inevitable.

Proponents of holding not-for-profits to SOX standards cite scandals in school districts, public colleges, and charities across the country. The IRS has already contacted 2,000 tax-exempt organizations across the country to inquire about their executive compensation.

NFPs aren't immune to lawsuits, and it's likely no NFP will want to risk being sued without certain safeguards in place. Many SOX-sensitive attorneys and accountants working for NFPs recommend that every NFP adopt most, if not all, of the following SOX-type standards:

- ✔ **Audit committee:** The NFP should create an audit committee and separate the function of that committee from the finance committee. As in the private sector, the NFP's audit committee should be composed of board members who aren't compensated for serving on the committee and don't have a financial interest or other conflict of interest with any company or person doing business with the NFP.

- ✔ **Outside consultants for the audit committee:** Most nonprofit organizations have volunteer board members who may or may not be trained in business and accounting principles. Therefore, it's important that independent, outside consultants, or other advisors be available to work with the audit committee. (SOX mandates that audit committees be permitted to hire outside consultants and that their companies be required to pay for the consulting services.)

- ✔ **Procedures for adopting the auditor's report:** The NFP audit committee should meet with the outside audit firm and recommend to the full board of directors whether the audit report should be approved or modified. The full board should formally accept or reject the committee's report.

- ✔ **Auditor independence:** SOX contains a number of requirements to ensure the independence of outside auditors. For example, SOX requires that audit firms rotate the lead partner every five years.

- ✔ **Prohibited services:** SOX prohibits the audit firm from providing certain nonaudit services. Prohibited services include bookkeeping, financial information systems, and other services (see Chapter 5 for a more complete list). NFPs may be used to receiving these services from audit firms. Consistent with the standards in SOX, an NFP's audit committee may, however, preapprove certain types nonaudit services outside these categories, such as tax preparation. Additionally, auditors may be allowed to prepare Form 990 or 990-PF (for private foundations) if such services are preapproved.

- ✔ **CEO/CFO certification:** Like their counterparts in the private sector, the NFP should consider having CEOs and CFOs certify both the appropriateness of financial statements and the officers' fair presentations of the financial conditions and operations of their companies.

SOX and Foreign Companies

Under current law a company that wants to sell securities to the public in the United States, listing those securities either on the New York Stock Exchange (NYSE) or the NASDAQ, must reconcile its financial statements to U.S. accounting rules and comply with American securities laws, including SOX.

European companies that do business in the U.S. are becoming increasingly worried about the costs and restrictions of complying with SOX. Like U.S. companies, European companies have found the Section 404 provisions requiring attestation of internal controls to be the most burdensome, driving up their costs and audit fees. The European companies also express concern about SOX's ban on company loans to executives. As a result, they're mounting overseas efforts to make it easier for them to flat out quit complying with U.S. securities laws. Among these efforts, in 2005, 11 organizations representing 100,000 European companies sent a letter to the SEC chairman asking for changes that would allow them to simply stop registering with the SEC.

A European company can *delist* from the U.S. exchanges, meaning that its stock is no longer traded on the exchange (as discussed in Chapter 3). However, the company is still subject to securities laws unless it proves it has fewer than 300 American investors. If the company is able to do this, it may have to resume compliance with U.S. rules in the future if its American investor count passes the 300 mark.

According to a December 2004 article, which appeared in BusinessWeek Online, "the London Stock Exchange (LSE) is in discussions with a number of companies from China and Russia seeking refuge from U.S. regulation." The BusinessWeek Online article also reported that the "British online-travel group Lastminute and German software company Lion Bioscience already have initiated the process to withdraw from U.S. stock exchanges."

European companies have proposed that they be exempted from SEC registration if they delist and show that less than 5 percent of their total share volumes are in the U.S. This proposal is likely to run into some opposition from the SEC, however, for the following reasons:

- ✔ The arrangement could be considered akin to accepting lower international standards in lieu of SOX.

- ✔ Foregoing SOX requirements for foreign companies could place U.S. companies at a competitive disadvantage because of their relatively higher compliance costs.

- ✔ Many American institutional investors would likely buy shares of companies that aren't listed on U.S. exchanges from overseas exchanges.

Part VI
The Part of Tens

The 5th Wave   By Rich Tennant

"This is classic voodoo economics, Bernice, right down to the chicken blood it's written in."

In this part . . .

In the grand *For Dummies* tradition, this part provides you with useful reminders and tips to help keep you from getting bogged down in the details of SOX. It provides you with bare-bones information about how to avoid getting sued, how your audit committee should proceed, how management can meet new obligations, and how auditors can and can't help your company. Finally, this part concludes with a list of resources for finding more information about SOX.

Chapter 18

Ten Ways to Avoid Getting Sued or Criminally Prosecuted Under SOX

● ●

In This Chapter

▶ Avoiding litigation and SEC investigations after SOX

▶ Implementing safe SOX practices and defensive measures

▶ Understanding why management delegation is alright, but insulation is not

● ●

*W*ho is the SEC going to be looking at after Enron, WorldCom, Global TelLink, and HealthSouth? Why did Tyco's Dennis Koslowski get 20 years under the old SEC rules while James Scrushy, the first CEO to face prosecution under SOX, left the court room a free man? How could Scrushy walk while five of his subordinates pleaded guilty? How do you keep yourself, your department, and your company out of the SOX spotlight? Can you spend your bonus, or will you have to give it back if the company has a bad year?

You aren't the only one asking these questions and many more. In this chapter, I provide you with a few tips for keeping the litigators off your doorstep and sleeping soundly after SOX.

Maintain an Active and Visible Audit Committee

Under SOX, every public company is required to have an audit committee that interfaces with the company's outside auditors. Many not-for-profit and private companies are opting to establish audit committees as well because they provide additional credibility for the audit process. The audit committee is responsible for giving good information to the auditors and communicating audit issues to management, so this is one committee you want to make active, visible, and well funded in your company. (Flip to Chapter 7 for full audit committee details.)

Communicate About How to Communicate

In the first major case to go to trial after SOX, James Scrushy, the CEO of the teetering HealthSouth Corporation, was acquitted in July 2005 of 36 counts of signing false financial filings. Scrushy claimed he didn't know of the fraudulent activity that sent the five HealthSouth subordinates who reported to him to jail. (The Scrushy trial is recounted in Chapter 16.) As this lawsuit makes clear, documented communication channels and visible networks can help you and your company maintain credibility in a SOX-related investigation. Documentation can help buttress testimony and jog memories.

 Put policies in place to document how delegated work is supervised and how results and conclusions are communicated. Policies will vary for every company and may even be different within particular departments. An employee titles don't always convey the actual level of supervisory responsibility a position entails.

Combat Policy Paranoia and Section 404 Audit-Chondria

Communication is key under SOX (see the preceding section), but too much of it can also be a bad thing. Policies that micromanage workflow and audit minutiae can create their own red flags. For example, cynical attorneys may raise questions about why trivial policies were flexibly applied, or future auditors may demand discussion about why nonmaterial discrepancies weren't further investigated or why items from last year's audit were dropped from this year's agenda. (For more information on surviving a Section 404 audit, turn to Chapter 12.)

Under SOX, a company's audit committee has the authority to hire independent advisors, such as attorneys, to help write good policies and determine how to handle audit issues. SOX-savvy attorneys can help the committee adopt policies that contain an appropriate level of detail. Attorneys also can act as good advocates when auditors propose resources reviewing potentially irrelevant or nonmaterial issues or when issues arise about the scope of sensitive SOX-related projects under Section 404.

Policies that have ill-conceived phrasing or extraneous detail create the risk that the employees cannot literally comply with them and leave insufficient room for employees to exercise appropriate discretion in unforeseen circumstances.

Keep Bonuses Within Bounds

During Enron, WorldCom, and other corporate scandals, the media had a field day reporting on huge, questionable bonuses paid to executives of these failing corporations. In the post-SOX era, executive compensation has become a politically sensitive issue.

Document how and why executive bonuses were awarded. Your company's compensation committee should have a market analysis on hand to support that bonus amounts are in line in the event that they are later challenged. For instance, questions may be raised in a lean year as to why big bonuses were paid in a prior profitable one. (For a more detailed discussion of executive compensation, turn to Chapter 10.)

Separate the Whistle-blowers from the Whiners

Whistle-blowers are employees who raise questions of fraud or noncompliance with accounting or governmental regulations in the workplace. So that a serious and valid complaint doesn't get glossed over and later return to cause major lawsuit trouble for the company, every whistle-blower complaint should be fully investigated and its disposition documented. Make sure that levels of review are afforded to complaints based upon their seriousness and credibility and that compliance with company policy is documented at every level to determine which complaints may have hidden merit. (Chapter 16 provides detailed information on avoiding and handling whistle-blower complaints.)

Invest in IT Tools

Buying and using a sensible SOX software product is a good way to demonstrate that your company is committed to strong internal controls and is being systematic in its compliance. (Software solutions for companies of all sizes are discussed in Chapters 14 and 15.)

If the software tool generates good reports and summaries, it's easier to document what people in the company knew for certification purposes (which I discuss in Chapter 9).

Do Something with All That Data

Data gathered during a Section 404 audit should be evaluated according to a stated policy and also should be shared with the audit committee, management, and board of directors as appropriate.

It's logical that many companies, having spent considerable resources to comply with Section 404, don't want to dedicate *more* resources to analyze the data. Understandably, companies want to get back on track developing core services and products. However, taking extra steps to parcel out the data to relevant decision makers can provide valuable databases of company-specific and current information on which to base future decisions affecting their departments.

Be Attuned to Triggering Events

Within four days of their occurrence (and sometimes less), SOX requires companies to disclose to the public (on Form 8-K) certain triggering events, such as the termination of major contracts, new financial obligations, write-offs, and financial restatements. Companies that don't disclose these events in a timely manner (as discussed in Chapter 3) risk both public sanctions and private litigation.

Document What's Delegated

Litigation under SOX has an increased focus on what management knew and what it was supposed to know. Under SOX, management is allowed to delegate authority and even outsource certain types of decisions. It is not, however, acceptable for management to take measures to insulate itself from information as to how that authority is being carried out.

Delegation of authority was a key issue in the HealthSouth scandal, when CEO Richard Scrushy walked free while five of his subordinates were convicted of fraud (as discussed in Chapter 16). Prosecutors and the public were aghast and determined not to let many more slippery CEOs escape liability under SOX by claiming they didn't know what their subordinates were doing.

Focus on Product and Service Delivery

SOX is legislation aimed at protecting the public from false financial reporting. If your company's credo is to focus on product and service delivery that generates real growth, rather than on plumping up paper profits, your company will meet the objectives of SOX.

Chapter 19

Ten Tips for an Effective Audit Committee

In This Chapter

▶ Identifying the right size for an audit committee

▶ Delegating to subcommittees

▶ Communicating with auditors and auditees

▶ Finding and funding financial experts

▶ Keeping qualified members

The Sarbanes-Oxley Act (SOX) arms your company's audit committee with an arsenal of authority, including the ability to hire its own legal and accounting advisors. This critical committee is the linchpin of corporate accountability, serving as an essential interface between your company's management, auditors, employees, and board of directors.

Because the audit committee is so important, this chapter offers ten tips on how to structure it to function most effectively.

Pick the Right Number of Members

Your company has plenty of leeway in deciding how many people should sit on its audit committee. The New York Stock Exchange (NYSE) rules provide that a committee must have a minimum of three members, but it doesn't place a limit on how large the committee can be. In fact, you can invite the entire board of directors to join (provided they meet the financial independence and other requirements discussed in Chapter 8).

Each member of the audit committee must also sit on the company's board of directors.

As a practical matter, putting your entire board of directors on the audit committee probably isn't a good idea, nor is it a good idea to routinely limit membership to three members. A large audit committee can become bureaucratic and inefficient with respect to decision-making and review functions. On the other hand, a three-person committee can quickly become overwhelmed managing an audit and several employee complaints simultaneously.

When determining the optimum number of audit committee members (which may depend on who's up to the task), ask the following questions:

- ✔ Is it more practical for a small committee to keep all board members informed of its activities or for all board members to be directly involved?

- ✔ Does the board believe that a larger committee will give shareholders a greater sense of accountability?

- ✔ How much responsibility are committee members willing to assume?

- ✔ To what extent are board members willing and able to devote the time necessary to serve on the committee, and will this commitment cause them to be diverted from other essential board functions?

- ✔ Will the logistics of coordinating a large committee make it inherently bureaucratic?

Set Up Subcommittees

SOX and Securities Exchange Commission (SEC) regulations permit an audit committee to delegate responsibility for matters under its direction to specific committee members. These *subcommittees* report back to the committee as a whole.

Subcommittees can be used effectively with regards to:

- ✔ **Handling specific complaints:** The audit committee can assign a subcommittee member to investigate specific complaints it receives or issues that are brought to its attention; in most cases, the subcommittee member then makes informed recommendations to the entire committee. The committee can take advantage of particular members' areas of expertise in assigning matters for investigation.

- ✔ **Addressing specific reporting issues:** Issues may arise during the course of an audit that warrant additional research and analysis as to their treatment. These tasks can be delegated to a subcommittee for further recommendations.

- ✔ **Hiring and communicating with consultants:** SOX provides that audit committees must be permitted to hire consultants to assist in performing committee functions. A subcommittee can be assigned to select consultants and obtain and evaluate their recommendations.

✔ **Communication and report drafting:** Subcommittees can be used to prepare initial drafts of reports and communications for approval by the audit committee as a whole.

✔ **Dealing with certain segments of company operations:** Some committee members may be more familiar with particular operations or sectors of the company's operations and therefore can effectively make recommendations to the committee on related matters.

Find Your Financial Expert

SOX provides that at least *one* member of the audit committee must be a *financial expert.* According to SEC regulations, a financial expert has expertise in Generally Accepted Accounting Principles (GAAP), audit procedures, and internal control.

Unfortunately, not every board of directors includes a former auditor, banker, or other financial expert who's willing to serve on the company's audit committee. However, because the NYSE and other major stock exchanges require an audit committee with a financial expert, you must find the requisite financial expertise to meet listing standards.

Your company can pursue several options when it finds itself without a financial expert. One option is to recruit another director for your board, one who qualifies as a financial expert. This approach, however, has at least one major drawback: The company may feel compelled to compromise on its usual criteria and standards for selecting directors because it's under pressure to locate a specific type of person to serve a specific purpose.

Another solution is to hire an outside consultant to advise the audit committee (SOX authorizes the audit committee to hire experts to assist in carrying out its functions). Hiring a financial expert rather than electing one to the board of directors is a strategy that offers the following advantages:

✔ An outside expert can be chosen solely on the basis of his or her expertise without regard to any other consideration.

✔ The board of directors may be more willing to defer to the judgment of an outside expert than to the audit committee (which, as you recall, is made up of board members).

✔ Most state and federal laws and corporate bylaws permit directors to rely in good faith on advice given by an outside expert.

✔ Differentiating the roles and responsibilities of audit committee members based on the fact that one or more members are financial experts is unnecessary.

When selecting an expert, inquire as to whether his or her professional liability insurance covers advising your committee. As a safeguard, your company should be able to recover from the expert's malpractice insurance carrier in the event that the expert provides incorrect advice that damages the company.

Create Questionnaires

SOX strives to ensure that both external audit firms and internal committee members have conflict-free consciences in every respect. To that end, auditors must be rotated after five years with a particular company and be stacked two per audit. In addition, committee members and their immediate families must relinquish any financial ties to the company and its affiliates (other than receiving their directors' fees and ordinary dividends on stock). (For more information about the requirements that now apply to audit firms, see Chapter 5.)

Unexpected conflicts, however, creep into many scenarios For example, a director may not realize that his adult child has taken a position with an affiliate; or an auditor may change jobs, and the new audit firm may not realize that she audited the new company two years ago while in the employ of the prior company.

To avoid unpleasant surprises, audit committees should compile routine questionnaires designed to elicit all relevant information regarding potential conflicts of interest from potential committee members, consultants, and experts.

Adopt a Smart Charter

No company can trade on the NYSE or NASDAQ without a written audit committee charter. The exchanges each specify in their listing requirements what the charter must contain, but generally, contents include the committee's purpose, role within the company, and policies.

For more on audit committee charters, check out Chapter 7. Also, you can find a sample charter that meets the requirements of both exchanges in Appendix C.

Keep Track of Complaints

Congress and the SEC are serious about creating a safe environment for employees, accounting staff, and auditors to come forward with information that can impact audited financial statements. In this type of regulatory environment, no company can afford for its audit committee to treat any complaint as frivolous.

SOX requires an audit committee to have procedures in place for receiving and handling complaints about the company's "accounting, internal accounting controls or auditing matters, including procedures for submission of anonymous complaints by employees."

Your company should keep careful records of how complaints are handled. The audit committee should make sure that these records are complete, reasonably detailed, and consistent. Your committee should make sure that the records reflect that every complaint was handled without any bias or predisposition as to its merits.

Communicate Liberally

A recurring theme of the congressional hearings preceding SOX was the need for more communication among audit committees, internal and external auditors, employees, management, and directors.

The audit committee, in the spirit of the law, should always communicate issues that need to be aired rather than sweep such issues under the rug. In particular, the committee should demonstrate a consistent pattern of communication with management with respect to the following:

- The annual audited financial statements and quarterly reports filed by the company
- Press releases and financial information provided to the public
- Policies for risk management within the company
- Problems that occur during an audit and management's response
- The role and performance of the company's internal auditors
- Changes in company accounting polices
- Issues regarding internal controls and audit adjustments
- Committee policies and procedures

Report Annually

Corporations are required to hold annual meetings, but because shareholders may be located anywhere in the world, not everyone can attend the meetings and exercise their votes directly. Some of the shareholders may do so by proxy. (The process of voting by proxy is described in more detail in Chapter 3.)

The audit committee is required to make a report in the annual company's annual proxy statement, which is sent to shareholders just prior to an annual meeting. The timing is critical because the annual meeting is when members of the board of directors are elected. An unfavorable audit committee report can make it harder for directors to hold onto their seats, and because of the timing, directors may have little time to respond to the committee report before they're voted out.

Identify Conflicts . . . and Nonconflicts

Good audit committee members may be hard to come by, so you may not want to disqualify them unnecessarily. Some situations that seem to involve a conflict of interest for a committee member actually may not be a problem, so it's important to be able to draw the line between conflict and nonconflict.

For example, it's *not* a conflict for an audit committee member to also serve on the audit committee of an affiliated company. Both companies benefit from the financial expertise of a single member, and both committees benefit from the added experience the member gains by serving in both positions.

SOX expressly prohibits an executive officer, general partner, manager, or employee who holds any sort of policymaking position in the company or any affiliated company from serving on the audit committee.

Give Notice When Needed

What if an audit committee member ceases to be independent because of a merger or acquisition? What if the sole financial expert on the committee resigns for health reasons? If your company acts promptly and provides the required notice to the exchanges on which its stock is listed, the shortcomings may not be fatal.

Under SOX, stock exchanges must establish procedures for companies to remedy conditions that result in an audit committee's noncompliance. For example, the NYSE and NASDAQ generally allow a committee member who ceases to be independent for reasons outside his or her reasonable control to continue serving until either the next shareholders' meeting or one year passes from the event that caused the member to lose independence. In a case such as this, the company must give prompt notice of the change to the applicable stock exchange.

Chapter 20

Ten Smart Management Moves

In This Chapter

▶ Forming a disclosure committee

▶ Holding meaningful meetings

▶ Maintaining constructive communication with the audit committee

▶ Seeking out subcertifications

▶ Being diligent about compliance deadlines

A good manager is hard to find, which is why the Sarbanes-Oxley Act (SOX) contains several provisions for top executives who fail to implement mandated internal controls. Chief executive officers (CEOs) and chief financial officers (CFOs) are expected to keep their companies profitable against an unprecedented backdrop of jittery boards, stringent certification requirements, and threats of personal liability for decisions made in the corporate context.

This section contains a few sensible practices that can serve as defensive tactics for management caught in the tightly regulated and politically charged post-SOX environment.

Form a Disclosure Committee

Although it's not required, the SEC recommends that every company form a *disclosure committee* to assist senior management by communicating and reporting material events. Disclosure committees also can be given responsibility for evaluating the significance (materiality) of information and deciding how and when to disclose it to the public.

Candidates for your company's disclosure committee may include:

✔ Senior management

✔ Middle management responsible for financial control processes, risk management, information technology, or human resources

> ✔ Controller
>
> ✔ General counsel
>
> ✔ Investor relations officer

The committee should review the company's existing practices and make recommendations for providing control in areas of perceived weaknesses.

Set Reporting Schedules

CEOs and CFOs who establish disclosure committees (see the preceding section) likely will want to work with the committees to schedule and manage the preparation of annual and quarterly reports. SOX's increased reporting, assessment, and certification requirements mean that CEOs must allocate more lead time than ever before for reviewing and communicating report contents.

The disclosure committee can determine a schedule that takes into account:

> ✔ The time needed to collect information about the company's disclosure controls and processes
>
> ✔ The time needed to evaluate the effectiveness of the company's disclosure controls and procedures
>
> ✔ The time needed for independent auditors to sign off on management's assessment under Section 404 (as discussed in more detail in Chapter 12)

Have More Meetings

One face-to-face meeting may be worth a million memos in the world of corporate compliance. CEOs and CFOs should be sure to schedule regular discussions with the following groups and individuals:

> ✔ **Disclosure committee:** At least 90 days prior to the filing of the annual report, the CEO and CFO should meet with the disclosure committee to confirm that company procedures were carefully followed in generating report data and to discuss the results of the committee's evaluation of the effectiveness of disclosure controls and procedures.

✔ **Department heads and senior managers:** The CEO and CFO should meet with senior management in accounting, technology, financial reporting, and other relevant areas to discuss:

- Any problems or issues that have arisen with the company's internal financial controls

- Any changes that have been made to the internal controls

✔ **Independent auditor:** The CEO and CFO should meet with the lead audit partner of the company's independent audit firm to discuss:

- Changes in the accountant-recommended financial statements

- Any alternative treatments that the company should consider in preparing its financial statements

Challenge Dated and Overly Detailed Policies

Management shouldn't be shy about bringing ambiguous, overly detailed, or dated financial reporting policies to the attention of the board of directors or the audit committee. Management at all levels should be proactive in promoting policies and internal control procedures that are clearly worded and practical to follow.

Overly detailed policies can be particularly perilous for CEOs and CFOs who are required to personally certify that company financial statements are accurate or provide assessments of internal control (as discussed in Chapter 9). When procedures are outdated or are too detailed, there's an increased risk that the policy can't be followed, and deviations from policies may be red flags to auditors that internal control issues exist.

Review Reports with Their Preparers

Before signing off on and certifying the company's report, the CEO and CFO should thoroughly review specific sections, including the financial statements, with the employees who prepared the section. It's critical that the CEO and CFO understand how people within the company are making decisions about financial reporting and how these choices impact the report.

Management should directly communicate with employees who generate key reports to ferret out errors and incorrect assumptions that impact financial reporting.

Keep Up with Current Certification Requirements

SOX Sections 302 and 906 (see Chapter 9) require CEOs and CFOs to personally certify that periodic reports filed with the SEC are accurate. Section 302 imposes civil liability for false certifications, and Section 906 imposes criminal liability under SOX. The fact that two separate certifications are required for essentially the same conduct has caused some confusion among public companies. The form of the certifications is slightly different, as is the liability to which CEOs and CFOs are subject under them.

Section 302 certifications by the CEO and CFO are required for quarterly reports on Form 10-Q and annual reports on Form 10-K. SOX also requires a separate certification under the Section 906 criminal provisions.

On June 5, 2003, the SEC released its final rules interpreting the Section 302 and 906 requirements. The following are a few key points to keep in mind when filing Section 302 and 906 certifications:

- **All certifications should be included as exhibits.** The final rules issued by the SEC require companies to include the Section 302 and Section 906 certifications as *exhibits* to the reports, which means that they're documents submitted at the end of each report. (Prior to these rules companies simply added special language to the signature pages of their SEC reports.)

- **Certifications may not yet need to include internal control statements.** The SEC has delayed implementation of the internal control rules under Section 404 for nonaccelerated filers until July 15, 2007. In the meantime, if Section 404 doesn't yet apply to a company, its certifying officers may modify the Section 302 certification to eliminate references to internal control over financial reporting.

- **The language of the certifications is different.** Although Section 302 imposing civil penalties and Section 906 imposing criminal penalties under SOX are directed at the same objective, the language required for each type of certification is different. Appendix B contains a sample Section 302 certification and a sample Section 906 certification.

Avoid Animosity with the Audit Committee

Management should never fall into an adversarial relationship with the audit committee and should generally err on the side of over-communicating events to the committee.

It's important for the CEO and CFO to discuss and fully understand any deficiencies detected in the company's internal controls identified by independent auditors and to work with the audit committee in developing a plan of action to correct them.

In the event that management has a disagreement with the audit committee, it can ask the committee to hire an independent consultant (such as an attorney) to advise the audit committee on how to resolve the issue. If the issue remains unresolved, the CEO and CFO may consider bringing the issue before the company's board of directors.

Don't Confuse Certification with Control

CEOs and CFOs aren't required to certify every form filed with the SEC under SOX Sections 302 and 906 (for the skinny on certifications, flip to Chapter 9). However, every form must be prepared using control procedures and standards that ensure the accuracy of the reporting.

Reports that only cover current events, such as reports on Form 8-K, need not be accompanied by Section 302 and 906 certifications.

Consider Getting Subcertifications

It's becoming a trend in corporate America for CEOs and CFOs to ask senior management to provide them with certifications on matters that they (the CEOs and CFOs) must certify. Requiring principal persons within the organization to certify their work can set an important tone for compliance within the organization. However, subcertifications don't have the actual legal effect of shifting any legal liability from the CEO or CFO. Chapter 9 discusses subcertifications more fully, and you can see a sample subcertification in Appendix B.

Track All the Timelines

SOX accelerates a number of SEC filing deadlines for standard types of forms. For example, the timelines for filing quarterly report Form 10-Q and annual report Form 10-K are shortened to 35 days and 60 days, respectively, after the end of the related fiscal period. (For more on these forms, check out Chapter 3.) In addition, SOX has increased substantially the number of events that require current reporting on Form 8-K within four days or less. (The SEC filing requirements are discussed in more detail in Chapter 3.)

Chapter 21

Ten Things You Can't Ask an Auditor to Do After SOX

In This Chapter

▶ Banning auditors from bookkeeping

▶ Considering whether auditors can still be consultants

▶ Avoiding appraisals and other services by auditors

▶ Keeping auditors from serving as lawyers, experts, or consultants

*I*n order to comply with the Sarbanes-Oxley Act (SOX), your company is required to retain several firms simultaneously to do the work that one firm previously performed, and that extra manpower may mean higher accounting costs, both internally and externally. For auditors to maintain the required independence from audit clients, SOX Section 201 as well as SEC and PCAOB regulations tell CPAs what services they can no longer offer to clients to whom they provide audit services.

Prior to passing SOX, Congress concluded that large audit firms and the companies they audited were becoming way too chummy. Auditors who rendered unfavorable opinions risked losing lucrative consulting deals for other services they performed for the company. Also, auditors were sometimes involved in preparing the financial information and statements they would later audit. Management was free to negotiate with auditors about the adjustments the auditors recommended making to the financial statements.

SOX is intended to ensure that auditors remain objective and firm in their commitment to the accuracy of the financial statements on which the investing public relies. This chapter lists ten tasks you can no longer ask a CPA firm to perform if it's auditing your company.

Keep Your Books

During the congressional hearings following the Enron debacle, it came to light that accounting firm Arthur Andersen had received $25 million in audit fees and $27 million in consulting fees from Enron in the years prior to its bankruptcy filing. This revelation led Congress to conclude that auditors shouldn't be auditing their own work. The CPAs who keep the books for a company should be different from the ones auditing the company's books.

SOX Section 201(a) states that it's unlawful for a CPA firm to provide accounting and related services "contemporaneously" with any audit. Specifically, Section 201 forbids firms from performing "bookkeeping or other financial services related to the accounting records or the financial statements of the audit client."

The SEC rule further broadens the prohibition, going beyond simply banning services that are contemporaneously provided. SEC regulations ban CPAs from providing bookkeeping services at any point in time if it's reasonable to conclude that such services will become subject to audit by the same CPA firm at any time in the future. The SEC rule also makes clear that there are no "emergency" exceptions to these regulations.

Fix Your Financial Information Systems

Prior to SOX, most large accounting firms had management information systems departments or similarly designated divisions that helped design and implement software systems for their clients.

According to SOX Section 201, your audit firm can no longer help you design or implement financial information systems. The auditors ultimately may be called upon to evaluate the same systems they put into place or helped you maintain.

The SEC rules further broaden this SOX prohibition: The SEC directs auditors to steer clear of any system in your company that compiles source data that may end up on your financial statements in one form or another. In some situations, your auditors may not even be able to help you out with software systems *unrelated* to your financial statements.

Subsequent to SOX, many accounting firms, such as PricewaterhouseCoopers, have sold off their computer consulting and information management divisions.

Appraise Company Property

Appraisal and valuation issues directly impact your financial statements, so it's not surprising that auditors are prohibited from getting involved in them under SOX Section 201. In the course of the audit, your company's auditors may be asked to assess the value of assets reported on your balance sheet. Valuation also involves determinations of fairness and reasonableness of transactions affecting the appraised assets.

Consistent with SOX, auditors can no longer issue opinions as to the fairness of *like-kind exchanges*. Like-kind exchanges are common transactions in which businesses exchange one type of property for another asset of the same type. For example, your company may exchange one factory building for another that meets its current needs. The transaction then qualifies for tax treatment as an exchange rather than a sale, and the company may defer some tax liability. But the whole transaction still has to be evaluated from the standpoint of whether it was conducted in an arms-length manner, which means that the amounts paid or received should be consistent with similar deals in the marketplace. The overall transaction must be fair to company shareholders.

The SEC rule also prohibits auditors from rendering an opinion on your company's pension liabilities. This service falls within the ambit of appraisal and valuation.

Act as an Actuary

Actuarial services are the kind of number-crunching services many people envision accountants performing. SOX Section 201 now prohibits a company's auditors from providing them because actuarial services involve a determination of amounts recorded in the financial statements. Making this determination can lead to a conflict of interest if the actuarially determined amounts are questioned later in an audit.

Perform Internal Audit Services for Your Company

SOX Section 201 provides a special limitation in the situation where a company hires its auditors to assist its own accounting staff in checking out the company's books. This is known as an *internal audit,* as distinct from the *independent audit* that outside CPA firms are engaged to perform.

Under SOX, the firm that audits your company can't participate in creating or maintaining your company's internal accounting controls because the auditor may ultimately be reviewing and rendering an opinion on the controls.

Internal audits are performed primarily for the purpose of assisting the company's management in running the company profitably. In contrast, the outside audit firm is usually engaged to render opinions on a company's financial statements.

SEC rules don't prohibit your auditor from performing services related to your company's internal audit if those services aren't related to the internal accounting controls, financial systems, or financial statements.

Fill In for Your Management Team

Sox Section 201 says that your auditor can't provide management services to your company. Doing so would be an inherent conflict of interest under SOX because auditors are engaged in large part to evaluate management and to certify management's reports regarding the company's internal controls.

SEC Regulation S-X Rule 210.2-01(c)(4)(vi) explains that auditors are prohibited from "acting, temporarily or permanently, as a director, officer, or employee of an audit client, or performing any decision-making, supervisory, or ongoing monitoring function for the audit client."

Be a Headhunter

SOX seeks to keep auditors from forming the chummy relationships with management that characterized the relationships that Enron, WorldCom, and other large firms developed prior to SOX. Helping a management candidate get a job with the company could lead to a scenario in which the grateful manager recommends a specific audit firm, and, in turn, the audit firm is ingratiated to management. Such events can compromise the objectivity of the audit process.

Auditors can't act as headhunters for your company or recommend a specific candidate for a job under any circumstances. As SEC Regulation S-X Rule 210.2-01 (c)(4)(vii) spells out, they can't help your company find "prospective candidates for managerial, executive, or director positions."

Auditors also can't help your company evaluate prospective management candidates by

- ✔ Performing psychological testing.
- ✔ Conducting reference checks.
- ✔ Negotiating employment or compensation contracts.

Advise You on Investments

Some provisions of SOX simply reiterate what previously has been the law. Such is the case with Section 201's prohibition of auditors from providing "broker or dealer, investment adviser, or investment banking services." Were such a prohibition not in place, auditors would likely tend to uncritically rely on investment performance data they had prepared themselves.

Auditors also can't act as promoters or underwriters on behalf of the clients they audit.

Dispense Legal Advice

Attorneys have always carefully guarded their professional turf against accountants and other potentially competing professional service providers, which explains why most states have specific legal prohibitions on practicing law without a law license.

SOX prohibits auditors from providing services to audit clients. However, most CPA firms already are well aware of the restrictions imposed by state statutes prohibiting the unauthorized practice of law and don't have a sense that this particular SOX provision further restricts their activities.

The provision of tax services has always been an area of overlap and controversy between lawyers and accountants. Accountants render tax advice even though it's impossible to do so without interpreting the applicable tax laws and advising clients on the way the tax laws should be applied.

Give You an Expert Opinion

Auditors can't give their clients expert opinions on specific issues that must be addressed during the course of an audit. For example, your auditor can't write you a memo giving his or her opinion about a regulatory issue, a lawsuit, or an administrative proceeding in which your company may be involved.

The reasoning for this rule is that your auditor may become a witness in such a proceeding or may be subpoenaed to give information in a related investigation in which your company may become embroiled. In a legal proceeding, auditors may be called as witnesses to explain an accounting position your company has taken based on an expert opinion. In that event, you're likely to be thankful for their unimpaired and credible testimony.

Because SOX doesn't define *expert services,* the accounting profession has no real way of knowing how broadly the PCAOB or SEC will define them. CPAs also worry that SOX's limitations in this area could inspire parallel state legislation or rule changes that directly affect both nonpublic companies and CPAs who provide services to them.

Chapter 22

Top Ten Places to Get Smart About SOX

In This Chapter

▶ Finding the most prestigious SOX publications

▶ Frequenting the funniest SOX sites

▶ Keeping up with current SOX events and regulatory actions

*T*he Sarbanes-Oxley Act (SOX) was Congress's attempt to head off a public revolt at the polls after the wave of corporate scandals that kicked off with Enron and peaked with WorldCom (as I recount in Chapter 2). The legislature and the Justice Department directed their wrath at the accounting profession and corporate management, resulting in the criminal conviction of the nation's largest accounting firm, Arthur Andersen, LLP, and decades-long prison sentences for some of the most powerful figures in corporate America (and even one executive's wife).

Now, the media frenzy seems to be subsiding, and even the Justice Department has lost its momentum, as symbolized by the acquittal of Richard Scrushy, the CEO of the embattled HealthSouth Corporation, in the first criminal trial after SOX's passage. (Check out Chapter 16 for the Scrushy story.)

In the aftermath of the major scandals and trials, the SEC is still issuing regulations, the Public Company Accounting Oversight Board (PCAOB) is still spewing standards, and courts continue to make case law. Numerous publications and books (like this one) have been spawned, and Web sites hawk every conceivable SOX service and product from software systems to t-shirts.

In an era of information overload, this chapter directs you to the ten best online and print resources for staying in synch with SOX developments.

Spring for a Subscription to Compliance Week

If you're pulling down a six-figure salary in a job that depends on you being smart about SOX, you should invest in a subscription to *Compliance Week*. It's the kind of publication that gives you status just by having a copy on your desk (unlike this book).

For a few thousand dollars a year, your company gets:

✔ A weekly newsletter authored by SOX-perts such as former SEC chairman Harvey Pitt

✔ Access to a companion Web site that contains sample documents, databases, and resources

✔ A glossy print magazine with pictures of all your favorite SOX stars and articles on topics such as reducing compliance costs, cutting-edge governance strategies, perspectives on new rulings, and gossip about turnover and policy changes at the PCAOB and SEC

The publishers of *Compliance Week* boast that the magazine and Web site have over 4,000 corporate subscribers and are "widely recognized as a critical tool for senior corporate executives to carry out their duties in this heavily regulated business environment."

The single-user price for *Compliance Week* is $999. Firm-wide subscriptions for an unlimited number of users at one company cost $2,999. (It may seem pricey, but it's much cheaper than defending an indictment or weathering an SEC investigation.)

To get a 30-day trial subscription and for more information, visit www. complianceweek.com.

Sample SOX-online

SOX-online (www.sox-online.com) is definitely the hippest SOX site on the Web. It dubs itself "the vendor-neutral site," and as far as I can tell, it really is. SOX-online doesn't seem to be selling anything other than advertising. The site is updated daily and links to hundreds of articles on compliance topics and SOX developments. It also has really cool links, including the following:

✔ **Dear Ms. Sarbox:** An advice column for the SOX-ually frustrated (see the sidebar "Dear Ms. Sarbox")

✔ **Accountant jokes:** How many accountants does it take to screw in a light bulb? . . .

✔ **SOX jokes and games:** Bound to amuse you for hours

✔ **Sing-along with Sarbox:** Features hits like "The Ballad of Kenny-boy"

The Special SOX for Dummies Update Page

New SOX proposals are popping up and new standards are spewing forth faster than I can write this book. Late in 2005, an SEC advisory panel voted to recommend to the SEC that it exempt public companies having less than $125 million in equity from the requirement that they obtain a independent Section 404 audit. The recommendation requires full committee and SEC approval to become effective, so the outcome is anyone's guess.

For breaking updates on the status of this proposal and other changes that come about after the publication of this book, visit the SOX for Dummies update link at my law firm website located at `www.abtechlaw.com`.

Visit the SEC Web Site

In response to popular demand, the Securities and Exchange Commission (SEC) has created a Web site at `www.sec.gov/spotlight/sarbanes-oxley.htm` with links to press releases, rules, proposed rules, and FAQs about SOX. Unfortunately, there are no good jokes on this site. This Web site is discussed in more detail in Chapter 4.

Peruse the PCAOB Web Site

On the Public Company Accounting Oversight Board's Web site, located at `www.pcaobus.org`, you can link to audit standards, press releases on PCAOB actions, and information about inspections of registered public accounting firms. This Web site is discussed in more detail in Chapter 6.

Get Inside Sarbanes-Oxley Trenches

The Inside Sarbanes-Oxley Web site (www.insidesarbanesoxley.com) is a comprehensive site with current articles, blogs, discussion groups, and book lists. Another up-and-coming site is the Candela Solutions site located at www.candelasolutions.com. Candela Solutions is an accounting firm that

---

Dear Ms. Sarbox

The following is some expert advice from Ms. Sarbox, whose column can be found at www.sox-online.com/ms_sarbox.html. Each letter links you to useful articles about SOX found elsewhere on the SOX-online site. (In the examples below, the links appear in parentheses.)

↳ Dear Ms. Sarbox: Early in my career, the managers of my company actually specified the super extreme (professional) dress code — to the level of "underwear required." I'd like to know if the requirements for SOX are a little less confining.... Or is "al a natural" a little more acceptable in this age? *Becca from Kentucky*

Dear BFK: The key principle behind Sarbanes-Oxley is forced transparency. Now cloaked only in translucent veils of commerce, corporate leaders' little ... inadequacies ... are there for all of Wall Street to see. But a nice girl like you can still take comfort in the modesty provided by proper foundation garments. (Governance Articles)

↳ Dear Ms. Sarbox: The SEC estimates that it will cost $91,000 annually in order to be in compliance with just Sec. 404. Is it really worth it? *Cheap in Charleston*

Dear Cheap: Try looking at it from another angle. Cost of compliance: $91,000. Not being a convicted felon: Priceless. (Costs Articles)

↳ Dear Ms. Sarbox: How will I know if my company practices are ethical? *Clueless in Cleveland*

Dear Clueless: Have you tried changing the batteries twice a year in your ethics detector? (Ethics Articles)

↳ Dear Ms. Sarbox: There is so much advice from vendors about how to prepare. Are they just after my money? *Distrustful in Detroit*

Dear Distrustful: I'm sure they like you for your personality, too. (Press Releases from Vendors)

↳ Dear Ms. Sarbox: The janitor told me that shredders are now illegal. Is this true? *Gullible in Greensboro*

Dear Gullible: Is your janitor a former Arthur Andersen partner? Shredding is now a tricky process, and proper data retention is imperative. (Record Retention Articles)

↳ Dear Ms. Sarbox: I'm having trouble getting my software up. Will this keep me from satisfying Sarbanes-Oxley? *Helpless in Houston*

[Ms. Sarbox to Editor: Are you sure these are all real letters?] (Tools Articles)

↳ Dear Ms. Sarbox: What if I have a small or private company? How does this affect me? *Ignorant in Iowa*

Dear Ignorant: Are you small or private or both? Be honest, we won't judge. (Small/Private/Nonprofit Company Articles)

✔ Dear Ms. Sarbox: Do I need a big tool in order to comply with Sec. 404? *Worried in Wisconsin*

Dear Worried: Why are you readers always worried about the size of your tools? If you know how to use the tool you have, you might not need anything else. (Governance Articles)

✔ Dear Ms. Sarbox: What about the Children? *Concerned in Columbia*

Dear Concerned: If you'd like them to serve as financial experts on Audit Committees, you can sign them up with the Financial Expert Registry at www.fei.org.

---

focuses on working directly with Boards and Management. SOX practitioners can also access a page containing information on internal auditing, technology, and governance.

Link to the AICPA Web Site

The American Institute of Certified Public Accountants (AICPA) has been a very good sport about sharing its oversight authority with the PCAOB, and has handled the shift from self-regulation of the accounting profession rather graciously. (See Chapter 6.) The organization has magnanimously added a page to its site, aggregating useful links and resources related to SOX as it pertains to the accounting profession. Visit www.aicpa.org/sarbanes/index-old.aspccess for this information.

Frequent the Forum

The Sarbanes-Oxley Act forum at www.sarbanes-oxley-forum.com is "an interactive community portal designed to facilitate the exchange of information" about SOX. It has a FAQ section and "fully functional online forum" for visitors to share SOX experiences.

Click On the COSO Web Site

COSO, or the Committee of Sponsoring Organizations of the Treadway Commission, is a voluntary organization that has developed the only set of internal control standards recognized by the SEC (as discussed in Chapter 13). At www.coso.org, you can download a free set of COSO standards and other resources to help you interpret them.

Find the FEI Web Site

Financial Executives International is an organization made up of 15,000 peers — CFOs, VPs of finance, treasurers, controllers, tax executives, academics, and audit committee members. Its Web site is located at www.fei.org and contains a copy of the current issue of the organization's magazine, which is heavily loaded with SOX articles.

Part VII
Appendixes

The 5th Wave   By Rich Tennant

"I like the numbers on this company. They show a very impressive acquittal to conviction ratio."

In this part . . .

This part begins with the entire Sarbanes-Oxley Act, which you're sure to find a rip-roaring read. Then I provide sample certifications, a sample audit committee charter, a sample audit committee report, and much more to illustrate real-life applications of SOX and its requirements.

Appendix A

The Entire Sarbanes-Oxley Act

. . . .

*H*ere is what is likely the world's smallest copy of the Sarbanes-Oxley Act. I wanted you to have a print copy of the entire Act in this book just in case you need to check something I say and don't have Internet access. (Sorry about you having to turn the book sideways, but we wanted to save a few trees.) However, if you can get on the Web, you can view the searchable, downloadable version of this statute located at news.findlaw.com/hdocs/docs/gwbush/sarbanesoxley072302.pdf or on the SEC Web site at www.sec.gov/about/laws/soa2002.pdf. The Internet versions are a lot easier to read; SOX gives people enough headaches.

H.R. 3763—2

Sec. 404. Management assessment of internal controls.
Sec. 405. Exemption.
Sec. 406. Code of ethics for senior financial officers.
Sec. 407. Disclosure of audit committee financial expert.
Sec. 408. Enhanced review of periodic disclosures by issuers.
Sec. 409. Real time issuer disclosures.

TITLE V—ANALYST CONFLICTS OF INTEREST

Sec. 501. Treatment of securities analysts by registered securities associations and national securities exchanges.

TITLE VI—COMMISSION RESOURCES AND AUTHORITY

Sec. 601. Authorization of appropriations.
Sec. 602. Appearance and practice before the Commission.
Sec. 603. Federal court authority to impose penny stock bars.
Sec. 604. Qualifications of associated persons of brokers and dealers.

TITLE VII—STUDIES AND REPORTS

Sec. 701. GAO study and report regarding consolidation of public accounting firms.
Sec. 702. Commission study and report regarding credit rating agencies.
Sec. 703. Study and report on violators and violations
Sec. 704. Study of enforcement actions.
Sec. 705. Study of investment banks.

TITLE VIII—CORPORATE AND CRIMINAL FRAUD ACCOUNTABILITY

Sec. 801. Short title.
Sec. 802. Criminal penalties for altering documents.
Sec. 803. Debts nondischargeable if incurred in violation of securities fraud laws.
Sec. 804. Statute of limitations for securities fraud.
Sec. 805. Review of Federal Sentencing Guidelines for obstruction of justice and extensive criminal fraud.
Sec. 806. Protection for employees of publicly traded companies who provide evidence of fraud.
Sec. 807. Criminal penalties for defrauding shareholders of publicly traded companies.

TITLE IX—WHITE-COLLAR CRIME PENALTY ENHANCEMENTS

Sec. 901. Short title.
Sec. 902. Attempts and conspiracies to commit criminal fraud offenses.
Sec. 903. Criminal penalties for mail and wire fraud.
Sec. 904. Criminal penalties for violations of the Employee Retirement Income Security Act of 1974.
Sec. 905. Amendment to sentencing guidelines relating to certain white-collar offenses.
Sec. 906. Corporate responsibility for financial reports.

TITLE X—CORPORATE TAX RETURNS

Sec. 1001. Sense of the Senate regarding the signing of corporate tax returns by chief executive officers.

TITLE XI—CORPORATE FRAUD AND ACCOUNTABILITY

Sec. 1101. Short title.
Sec. 1102. Tampering with a record or otherwise impeding an official proceeding.
Sec. 1103. Temporary freeze authority for the Securities and Exchange Commission.
Sec. 1104. Amendment to the Federal Sentencing Guidelines.
Sec. 1105. Authority of the Commission to prohibit persons from serving as officers or directors.
Sec. 1106. Increased criminal penalties under Securities Exchange Act of 1934.
Sec. 1107. Retaliation against informants.

SEC. 2. DEFINITIONS.

(a) IN GENERAL.—In this Act, the following definitions shall apply:

(1) APPROPRIATE STATE REGULATORY AUTHORITY.—The term "appropriate State regulatory authority" means the State agency or other authority responsible for the licensure or other regulation of the practice of accounting in the State or States

---

One Hundred Seventh Congress
of the
United States of America

AT THE SECOND SESSION

Begun and held at the City of Washington on Wednesday, the twenty-third day of January, two thousand and two

An Act

To protect investors by improving the accuracy and reliability of corporate disclosures made pursuant to the securities laws, and for other purposes.

Be it enacted by the Senate and House of Representatives of the United States of America in Congress assembled,

SECTION 1. SHORT TITLE; TABLE OF CONTENTS.

(a) SHORT TITLE.—This Act may be cited as the "Sarbanes-Oxley Act of 2002".

(b) TABLE OF CONTENTS.—The table of contents for this Act is as follows:

Sec. 1. Short title; table of contents.
Sec. 2. Definitions.
Sec. 3. Commission rules and enforcement.

TITLE I—PUBLIC COMPANY ACCOUNTING OVERSIGHT BOARD

Sec. 101. Establishment; administrative provisions.
Sec. 102. Registration with the Board.
Sec. 103. Auditing, quality control, and independence standards and rules.
Sec. 104. Inspections of registered public accounting firms.
Sec. 105. Investigations and disciplinary proceedings.
Sec. 106. Foreign public accounting firms.
Sec. 107. Commission oversight of the Board.
Sec. 108. Accounting standards.
Sec. 109. Funding.

TITLE II—AUDITOR INDEPENDENCE

Sec. 201. Services outside the scope of practice of auditors.
Sec. 202. Preapproval requirements.
Sec. 203. Audit partner rotation.
Sec. 204. Auditor reports to audit committees.
Sec. 205. Conforming amendments.
Sec. 206. Conflicts of interest.
Sec. 207. Study of mandatory rotation of registered public accounting firms.
Sec. 208. Commission authority.
Sec. 209. Considerations by appropriate State regulatory authorities.

TITLE III—CORPORATE RESPONSIBILITY

Sec. 301. Public company audit committees.
Sec. 302. Corporate responsibility for financial reports.
Sec. 303. Improper influence on conduct of audits.
Sec. 304. Forfeiture of certain bonuses and profits.
Sec. 305. Officer and director bars and penalties.
Sec. 306. Insider trades during pension fund blackout periods.
Sec. 307. Rules of professional responsibility for attorneys.
Sec. 308. Fair funds for investors.

TITLE IV—ENHANCED FINANCIAL DISCLOSURES

Sec. 401. Disclosures in periodic reports.
Sec. 402. Enhanced conflict of interest provisions.
Sec. 403. Disclosures of transactions involving management and principal stockholders.

H.R. 3763

H.R. 3763—3

having jurisdiction over a registered public accounting firm or associated person thereof, with respect to the matter in question.

(2) AUDIT.—The term "audit" means an examination of the financial statements of any issuer by an independent public accounting firm in accordance with the rules of the Board or the Commission (or, for the period preceding the adoption of applicable rules of the Board under section 103, in accordance with then-applicable generally accepted auditing and related standards for such purposes), for the purpose of expressing an opinion on such statements.

(3) AUDIT COMMITTEE.—The term "audit committee" means—

(A) a committee (or equivalent body) established by and amongst the board of directors of an issuer for the purpose of overseeing the accounting and financial reporting processes of the issuer and audits of the financial statements of the issuer; and

(B) if no such committee exists with respect to an issuer, the entire board of directors of the issuer.

(4) AUDIT REPORT.—The term "audit report" means a document or other record—

(A) prepared following an audit performed for purposes of compliance by an issuer with the requirements of the securities laws; and

(B) in which a public accounting firm either—

(i) sets forth the opinion of that firm regarding a financial statement, report, or other document; or

(ii) asserts that no such opinion can be expressed.

(5) BOARD.—The term "Board" means the Public Company Accounting Oversight Board established under section 101.

(6) COMMISSION.—The term "Commission" means the Securities and Exchange Commission.

(7) ISSUER.—The term "issuer" means an issuer (as defined in section 3 of the Securities Exchange Act of 1934 (15 U.S.C. 78c)), the securities of which are registered under section 12 of that Act (15 U.S.C. 78l), or that is required to file reports under section 15(d) (15 U.S.C. 78o(d)), or that files or has filed a registration statement that has not yet become effective under the Securities Act of 1933 (15 U.S.C. 77a et seq.), and that it has not withdrawn.

(8) NON-AUDIT SERVICES.—The term "non-audit services" means any professional services provided to an issuer by a registered public accounting firm, other than those provided to an issuer in connection with an audit or a review of the financial statements of an issuer.

(9) PERSON ASSOCIATED WITH A PUBLIC ACCOUNTING FIRM.—

(A) IN GENERAL.—The terms "person associated with a public accounting firm" (or with a "registered public accounting firm") and "associated person of a public accounting firm" (or of a "registered public accounting firm") mean any individual proprietor, partner, shareholder, principal, accountant, or other professional employee of a public accounting firm, or any other individual independent contractor or entity that, in connection with the preparation or issuance of any audit report—

H.R. 3763—4

(i) shares in the profits of, or receives compensation in any other form from, that firm; or

(ii) participates as agent or otherwise on behalf of such accounting firm in any activity of that firm.

(B) EXEMPTION AUTHORITY.—The Board may, by rule, exempt persons engaged only in ministerial tasks from the definition in subparagraph (A), to the extent that the Board determines that any such exemption is consistent with the purposes of this Act, the public interest, or the protection of investors.

(10) PROFESSIONAL STANDARDS.—The term "professional standards" means—

(A) accounting principles that are—

(i) established by the standard setting body described in section 19(b) of the Securities Act of 1933, as amended by section 108, or prescribed by the Commission under section 19(a) of that Act (15 U.S.C. 17a(s)) or section 13(b) of the Securities Exchange Act of 1934 (15 U.S.C. 78a(m)); and

(ii) relevant to audit reports for particular issuers, or dealt with in the quality control system of a particular registered public accounting firm; and

(B) auditing standards, standards for attestation engagements, quality control policies and procedures, ethical and competency standards, and independence standards (including rules implementing title II) that the Board or the Commission determines—

(i) relate to the preparation or issuance of audit reports for issuers; and

(ii) are established or adopted by the Board under section 103(a), or are promulgated as rules of the Commission.

(11) PUBLIC ACCOUNTING FIRM.—The term "public accounting firm" means—

(A) a proprietorship, partnership, incorporated association, corporation, limited liability company, limited liability partnership, or other legal entity that is engaged in the practice of public accounting or preparing or issuing audit reports; and

(B) to the extent so designated by the rules of the Board, any associated person of any entity described in subparagraph (A).

(12) REGISTERED PUBLIC ACCOUNTING FIRM.—The term "registered public accounting firm" means a public accounting firm registered with the Board in accordance with this Act.

(13) RULES OF THE BOARD.—The term "rules of the Board" means the bylaws and rules of the Board (as submitted to, and approved, modified, or amended by the Commission, in accordance with section 107), and those stated policies, practices, and interpretations of the Board that the Commission, by rule, may deem to be rules of the Board, as necessary or appropriate in the public interest or for the protection of investors.

(14) SECURITY.—The term "security" has the same meaning as in section 3(a) of the Securities Exchange Act of 1934 (15 U.S.C. 78c(a)).

H. R. 3763—6

(B) striking "and 16," each place it appears and inserting "and 16 of this Act, and sections 302, 303, 304, 306, 401(b), 404, 406, and 407 of the Sarbanes-Oxley Act of 2002,".

(c) EFFECT ON COMMISSION AUTHORITY.—Nothing in this Act or the rules of the Board shall be construed to impair or limit—

(1) the authority of the Commission to regulate the accounting profession, accounting firms, or persons associated with such firms for purposes of enforcement of the securities laws;

(2) the authority of the Commission to set standards for accounting or auditing practices or auditor independence, derived from other provisions of the securities laws or the rules or regulations thereunder, for purposes of the preparation and issuance of any audit report, or otherwise under applicable law; or

(3) the ability of the Commission to take, on the initiative of the Commission, legal, administrative, or disciplinary action against any registered public accounting firm or any associated person thereof.

TITLE I—PUBLIC COMPANY ACCOUNTING OVERSIGHT BOARD

SEC. 101. ESTABLISHMENT; ADMINISTRATIVE PROVISIONS.

(a) ESTABLISHMENT OF BOARD.—There is established the Public Company Accounting Oversight Board, to oversee the audit of public companies that are subject to the securities laws, and related matters, in order to protect the interests of investors and further the public interest in the preparation of informative, accurate, and independent audit reports for companies the securities of which are sold to, and held by and for, public investors. The Board shall be a body corporate, operate as a nonprofit corporation, and have succession until dissolved by an Act of Congress.

(b) STATUS.—The Board shall not be an agency or establishment of the United States Government, and, except as otherwise provided in this Act, shall be subject to, and have all the powers conferred upon a nonprofit corporation by, the District of Columbia Nonprofit Corporation Act. No member or person employed by, or agent for, the Board shall be deemed to be an officer or employee of or agent for the Federal Government by reason of such service.

(c) DUTIES OF THE BOARD.—The Board shall, subject to action by the Commission under section 107, and once a determination is made by the Commission under subsection (d) of this section—

(1) register public accounting firms that prepare audit reports for issuers, in accordance with section 102;

(2) establish or adopt, or both, by rule, auditing, quality control, ethics, independence, and other standards relating to the preparation of audit reports for issuers, in accordance with section 103;

(3) conduct inspections of registered public accounting firms, in accordance with section 104 and the rules of the Board;

(4) conduct investigations and disciplinary proceedings concerning, and impose appropriate sanctions where justified upon,

---

H. R. 3763—5

(15) SECURITIES LAWS.—The term "securities laws" means the provisions of law referred to in section 3(a)(47) of the Securities Exchange Act of 1934 (15 U.S.C. 78c(a)(47)), as amended by this Act, and includes the rules, regulations, and orders issued by the Commission thereunder.

(16) STATE.—The term "State" means any State of the United States, the District of Columbia, Puerto Rico, the Virgin Islands, or any other territory or possession of the United States.

(b) CONFORMING AMENDMENT.—Section 3(a)(47) of the Securities Exchange Act of 1934 (15 U.S.C. 78c(a)(47)) is amended by inserting "the Sarbanes-Oxley Act of 2002," before "the Public".

SEC. 3. COMMISSION RULES AND ENFORCEMENT.

(a) REGULATORY ACTION.—The Commission shall promulgate such rules and regulations, as may be necessary or appropriate in the public interest or for the protection of investors, and in furtherance of this Act.

(b) ENFORCEMENT.—

(1) IN GENERAL.—A violation by any person of this Act, any rule or regulation of the Commission issued under this Act, or any rule of the Board shall be treated for all purposes in the same manner as a violation of the Securities Exchange Act of 1934 (15 U.S.C. 78a et seq.) or the rules and regulations issued thereunder, consistent with the provisions of this Act, and any such person shall be subject to the same penalties, and to the same extent, as for a violation of that Act or such rules or regulations.

(2) INVESTIGATIONS, INJUNCTIONS, AND PROSECUTION OF OFFENSES.—Section 21 of the Securities Exchange Act of 1934 (15 U.S.C. 78u) is amended—

(A) in subsection (a)(1), by inserting "the rules of the Public Company Accounting Oversight Board, of which such person is a registered public accounting firm or a person associated with such a firm," after "is a participant,";

(B) in subsection (d)(1), by inserting "the rules of the Public Company Accounting Oversight Board, of which such person is a registered public accounting firm or a person associated with such a firm," after "is a participant,";

(C) in subsection (e), by inserting "the rules of the Public Company Accounting Oversight Board, of which such person is a registered public accounting firm or a person associated with such a firm," after "is a participant,"; and

(D) in subsection (f), by inserting "or the Public Company Accounting Oversight Board" after "self-regulatory organization" each place that term appears.

(3) CEASE-AND-DESIST PROCEEDINGS.—Section 21C(c)(2) of the Securities Exchange Act of 1934 (15 U.S.C. 78u–3(c)(2)) is amended by inserting "registered public accounting firm (as defined in section 2 of the Sarbanes-Oxley Act of 2002)," after "government securities dealer,".

(4) ENFORCEMENT BY FEDERAL BANKING AGENCIES.—Section 12(i) of the Securities Exchange Act of 1934 (15 U.S.C. 78l(i)) is amended by—

(A) striking "sections 12," each place it appears and inserting "sections 10A(m), 12,"; and

H.R. 3763—7

registered public accounting firms and associated persons of such firms, in accordance with section 105;

(5) perform such other duties or functions as the Board (or the Commission, by rule or order) determines are necessary or appropriate to promote high professional standards among, and improve the quality of audit services offered by, registered public accounting firms and associated persons thereof, or otherwise to carry out this Act, in order to protect investors, or to further the public interest;

(6) enforce compliance with this Act, the rules of the Board, professional standards, and the securities laws relating to the preparation and issuance of audit reports and the obligations and liabilities of accountants with respect thereto, by registered public accounting firms and associated persons thereof, and

(7) set the budget and manage the operations of the Board and the staff of the Board.

(d) COMMISSION DETERMINATION.—The members of the Board shall take such action (including hiring of staff, proposal of rules, and adoption of initial and transitional auditing and other professional standards) as may be necessary or appropriate to enable the Commission to determine, not later than 270 days after the date of enactment of this Act, that the Board is so organized and has the capacity to carry out the requirements of this title, and to enforce compliance with this title by registered public accounting firms and associated persons thereof. The Commission shall be responsible, prior to the appointment of the Board, for the planning for the establishment and administrative transition to the Board's operation.

(e) BOARD MEMBERSHIP.—

(1) COMPOSITION.—The Board shall have 5 members, appointed from among prominent individuals of integrity and reputation who have a demonstrated commitment to the interests of investors and the public, and an understanding of the responsibilities for and nature of the financial disclosures required of issuers under the securities laws and the obligations of accountants with respect to the preparation and issuance of audit reports with respect to such disclosures.

(2) LIMITATION.—Two members, and only 2 members, of the Board shall be or have been certified public accountants pursuant to the laws of 1 or more States, provided that, if 1 of those 2 members is the chairperson, he or she may not have been a practicing certified public accountant for at least 5 years prior to his or her appointment to the Board.

(3) FULL-TIME INDEPENDENT SERVICE.—Each member of the Board shall serve on a full-time basis, and may not, concurrent with service on the Board, be employed by any other person or engage in any other professional or business activity. No member of the Board may share in any of the profits of, or receive payments from, a public accounting firm (or any other person, as determined by rule of the Commission), other than fixed continuing payments, subject to such conditions as the Commission may impose, under standard arrangements for the retirement of members of public accounting firms.

(4) APPOINTMENT OF BOARD MEMBERS.—

(A) INITIAL BOARD.—Not later than 90 days after the date of enactment of this Act, the Commission, after consultation with the Chairman of the Board of Governors

H.R. 3763—8

of the Federal Reserve System and the Secretary of the Treasury, shall appoint the chairperson and other initial members of the Board, and shall designate a term of service for each.

(B) VACANCIES.—A vacancy on the Board shall not affect the powers of the Board, but shall be filled in the same manner as provided for appointments under this section.

(5) TERM OF SERVICE.—

(A) IN GENERAL.—The term of service of each Board member shall be 5 years, and until a successor is appointed, except that—

(i) the terms of office of the initial Board members (other than the chairperson) shall expire in annual increments, 1 on each of the first 4 anniversaries of the initial date of appointment; and

(ii) any Board member appointed to fill a vacancy occurring before the expiration of the term for which the predecessor was appointed shall be appointed only for the remainder of that term.

(B) TERM LIMITATION.—No person may serve as a member of the Board, or as chairperson of the Board, for more than 2 terms, whether or not such terms of service are consecutive.

(6) REMOVAL FROM OFFICE.—A member of the Board may be removed by the Commission from office, in accordance with section 107(d)(3), for good cause shown before the expiration of the term of that member.

(f) POWERS OF THE BOARD.—In addition to any authority granted to the Board otherwise in this Act, the Board shall have the power, subject to section 107—

(1) to sue and be sued, complain and defend, in its corporate name and through its own counsel, with the approval of the Commission, in any Federal, State, or other court;

(2) to conduct its operations and maintain offices, and to exercise all other rights and powers authorized by this Act, in any State, without regard to any qualification, licensing, or other provision of law in effect in such State (or a political subdivision thereof);

(3) to lease, purchase, accept gifts or donations of or otherwise acquire, improve, use, sell, exchange, or convey, all of or an interest in any property, wherever situated;

(4) to appoint such employees, accountants, attorneys, and other agents as may be necessary or appropriate, and to determine their qualifications, define their duties, and fix their salaries or other compensation (at a level that is comparable to private sector self-regulatory, accounting, technical, supervisory, or other staff or management positions);

(5) to allocate, assess, and collect accounting support fees established pursuant to section 109, for the Board, and other fees and charges imposed under this title; and

(6) to enter into contracts, execute instruments, incur liabilities, and do any and all other acts and things necessary, appropriate, or incidental to the conduct of its operations and the exercise of its obligations, rights, and powers imposed or granted by this title.

H.R. 3763—9

(g) RULES OF THE BOARD.—The rules of the Board shall, subject to the approval of the Commission—

(1) provide for the operation and administration of the Board, the exercise of its authority, and the performance of its responsibilities under this Act;

(2) permit, as the Board determines necessary or appropriate, delegation by the Board of any of its functions to an individual member or employee of the Board, or to a division of the Board, including functions with respect to hearing, determining, ordering, certifying, reporting, or otherwise acting as to any matter, except that—

(A) the Board shall retain a discretionary right to review any action pursuant to any such delegated function, upon its own motion;

(B) a person shall be entitled to a review by the Board with respect to any matter so delegated, and the decision of the Board upon such review shall be deemed to be the action of the Board for all purposes (including appeal or review thereof); and

(C) if the right to exercise a review described in subparagraph (A) is declined, or if no such review is sought within the time stated in the rules of the Board, then the action taken by the holder of such delegation shall for all purposes, including appeal or review thereof, be deemed to be the action of the Board;

(3) establish ethics rules and standards of conduct for Board members and staff, including a bar on practice before the Board (and the Commission, with respect to Board-related matters) of 1 year for former members of the Board, and appropriate periods (not to exceed 1 year) for former staff of the Board; and

(4) provide as otherwise required by this Act.

(h) ANNUAL REPORT TO THE COMMISSION.—The Board shall submit an annual report (including its audited financial statements) to the Commission, and the Commission shall transmit a copy of that report to the Committee on Banking, Housing, and Urban Affairs of the Senate, and the Committee on Financial Services of the House of Representatives, not later than 30 days after the date of receipt of that report by the Commission.

SEC. 102. REGISTRATION WITH THE BOARD.

(a) MANDATORY REGISTRATION.—Beginning 180 days after the date of the determination of the Commission under section 101(d), it shall be unlawful for any person that is not a registered public accounting firm to prepare or issue, or to participate in the preparation or issuance of, any audit report with respect to any issuer.

(b) APPLICATIONS FOR REGISTRATION.—

(1) FORM OF APPLICATION.—A public accounting firm shall use such form as the Board may prescribe, by rule, to apply for registration under this section.

(2) CONTENTS OF APPLICATIONS.—Each public accounting firm shall submit, as part of its application for registration, in such detail as the Board shall specify—

(A) the names of all issuers for which the firm prepared or issued audit reports during the immediately preceding calendar year, and for which the firm expects to prepare or issue audit reports during the current calendar year;

H.R. 3763—10

(B) the annual fees received by the firm from each such issuer for audit services, other accounting services, and non-audit services, respectively;

(C) such other current financial information for the most recently completed fiscal year of the firm as the Board may reasonably request;

(D) a statement of the quality control policies of the firm for its accounting and auditing practices;

(E) a list of all accountants associated with the firm who participate in or contribute to the preparation of audit reports, stating the license or certification number of each such person, as well as the State license numbers of the firm itself;

(F) information relating to criminal, civil, or administrative actions or disciplinary proceedings pending against the firm or any associated person of the firm in connection with any audit report;

(G) copies of any periodic or annual disclosure filed by an issuer with the Commission during the immediately preceding calendar year which discloses accounting disagreements between such issuer and the firm in connection with an audit report furnished or prepared by the firm for such issuer; and

(H) such other information as the rules of the Board or the Commission shall specify as necessary or appropriate in the public interest or for the protection of investors.

(3) CONSENTS.—Each application for registration under this subsection shall include—

(A) a consent executed by the public accounting firm to cooperation in and compliance with any request for testimony or the production of documents made by the Board in the furtherance of its authority and responsibilities under this title (and an agreement to secure and enforce similar consents from each of the associated persons of the public accounting firm as a condition of their continued employment by or other association with such firm); and

(B) a statement that such firm understands and agrees that cooperation and compliance, as described in the consent required by subparagraph (A), and the securing and enforcement of consents from its associated persons, in accordance with the rules of the Board, shall be a condition to the continuing effectiveness of the registration of the firm with the Board.

(c) ACTION ON APPLICATIONS.—

(1) TIMING.—The Board shall approve a completed application for registration not later than 45 days after the date of receipt of the application, in accordance with the rules of the Board, unless the Board, prior to such date, issues a written notice of disapproval to, or requests more information from, the prospective registrant.

(2) TREATMENT.—A written notice of disapproval of a completed application under paragraph (1) for registration shall be treated as a disciplinary sanction for purposes of sections 105(d) and 107(c).

(d) PERIODIC REPORTS.—Each registered public accounting firm shall submit an annual report to the Board, and may be required

H.R. 3763—11

to report more frequently, as necessary to update the information contained in its application for registration under this section, and to provide to the Board such additional information as the Board or the Commission may specify, in accordance with subsection (b)(2).

(e) PUBLIC AVAILABILITY.—Registration applications and annual reports required by this subsection, or such portions of such applications or reports as may be designated under rules of the Board, shall be made available for public inspection, subject to rules of the Board or the Commission, and to applicable laws relating to the confidentiality of proprietary, personal, or other information contained in such applications or reports, provided that, in all events, the Board shall protect from public disclosure information reasonably identified by the subject accounting firm as proprietary information.

(f) REGISTRATION AND ANNUAL FEES.—The Board shall assess and collect a registration fee and an annual fee from each registered public accounting firm, in amounts that are sufficient to recover the costs of processing and reviewing applications and annual reports.

SEC. 103. AUDITING, QUALITY CONTROL, AND INDEPENDENCE STANDARDS AND RULES.

(a) AUDITING, QUALITY CONTROL, AND ETHICS STANDARDS.—
(1) IN GENERAL.—The Board shall, by rule, establish, including, to the extent it determines appropriate, through adoption of standards proposed by 1 or more professional groups of accountants designated pursuant to paragraph (3)(A) or advisory groups convened pursuant to paragraph (4), and amend or otherwise modify or alter, such auditing and related attestation standards, such quality control standards, and such ethics standards to be used by registered public accounting firms in the preparation and issuance of audit reports, as required by this Act or the rules of the Commission, or as may be necessary or appropriate in the public interest or for the protection of investors.

(2) RULE REQUIREMENTS.—In carrying out paragraph (1), the Board—
(A) shall include in the auditing standards that it adopts, requirements that each registered public accounting firm shall—
(i) prepare, and maintain for a period of not less than 7 years, audit work papers, and other information related to any audit report, in sufficient detail to support the conclusions reached in such report;
(ii) provide a concurring or second partner review and approval of such audit report (and other related information), and concurring approval in its issuance, by a qualified person (as prescribed by the Board) associated with the public accounting firm, other than the person in charge of the audit, by an independent reviewer (as prescribed by the Board); and
(iii) describe in each audit report the scope of the auditor's testing of the internal control structure and procedures of the issuer, required by section 404(b), and present (in such report or in a separate report)—

H.R. 3763—12

(I) the findings of the auditor from such testing;
(II) an evaluation of whether such internal control structure and procedures—
(aa) include maintenance of records that in reasonable detail accurately and fairly reflect the transactions and dispositions of the assets of the issuer;
(bb) provide reasonable assurance that transactions are recorded as necessary to permit preparation of financial statements in accordance with generally accepted accounting principles, and that receipts and expenditures of the issuer are being made only in accordance with authorizations of management and directors of the issuer; and
(III) a description, at a minimum, of material weaknesses in such internal controls, and of any material noncompliance found on the basis of such testing.
(B) shall include, in the quality control standards that it adopts with respect to the issuance of audit reports, requirements for every registered public accounting firm relating to—
(i) monitoring of professional ethics and independence from issuers on behalf of which the firm issues audit reports;
(ii) consultation within such firm on accounting and auditing questions;
(iii) supervision of audit work;
(iv) hiring, professional development, and advancement of personnel;
(v) the acceptance and continuation of engagements;
(vi) internal inspection; and
(vii) such other requirements as the Board may prescribe, subject to subsection (a)(1).
(3) AUTHORITY TO ADOPT OTHER STANDARDS.—
(A) IN GENERAL.—In carrying out this subsection, the Board—
(i) may adopt as its rules, subject to the terms of section 107, any portion of any statement of auditing standards or other professional standards that the Board determines satisfy the requirements of paragraph (1), and that were proposed by 1 or more professional groups of accountants that shall be designated or recognized by the Board, by rule, for such purpose, pursuant to this paragraph or 1 or more advisory groups convened pursuant to paragraph (4); and
(ii) notwithstanding clause (i), shall retain full authority to modify, supplement, revise, or subsequently amend, modify, or repeal, in whole or in part, any portion of any statement described in clause (i).
(B) INITIAL AND TRANSITIONAL STANDARDS.—The Board shall adopt standards described in subparagraph (A)(i) as initial or transitional standards, to the extent the Board determines necessary, prior to a determination of the

H.R.3763—13

Commission under section 101(d), and such standards shall be separately approved by the Commission at the time of that determination, without regard to the procedures required by section 107 that otherwise would apply to the approval of rules of the Board.

(4) ADVISORY GROUPS.—The Board shall convene, or authorize its staff to convene, such expert advisory groups as may be appropriate, which may include practicing accountants and other experts, as well as representatives of other interested groups, subject to such rules as the Board may prescribe to prevent conflicts of interest, to make recommendations concerning the content (including proposed drafts) of auditing, quality control, ethics, independence, or other standards required to be established under this section.

(b) INDEPENDENCE STANDARDS AND RULES.—The Board shall establish such rules as may be necessary or appropriate in the public interest or for the protection of investors, to implement, or as authorized under, title II of this Act.

(c) COOPERATION WITH DESIGNATED PROFESSIONAL GROUPS OF ACCOUNTANTS AND ADVISORY GROUPS.—

(1) IN GENERAL.—The Board shall cooperate on an ongoing basis with professional groups of accountants designated under subsection (a)(3)(A) and advisory groups convened under subsection (a)(4) in the examination of the need for changes in any standards subject to its authority under subsection (a), recommend issues for inclusion on the agendas of such designated professional groups of accountants or advisory groups, and take such other steps as it deems appropriate to increase the effectiveness of the standard setting process.

(2) BOARD RESPONSES.—The Board shall respond in a timely fashion to requests from designated professional groups of accountants and advisory groups referred to in paragraph (1) for any changes in standards over which the Board has authority.

(d) EVALUATION OF STANDARD SETTING PROCESS.—The Board shall include in the annual report required by section 101(h) the results of its standard setting responsibilities during the period to which the report relates, including a discussion of the work of the Board with any designated professional groups of accountants and advisory groups described in paragraphs (3)(A) and (4) of subsection (a), and its pending issues agenda for future standard setting projects.

SEC. 104. INSPECTIONS OF REGISTERED PUBLIC ACCOUNTING FIRMS.

(a) IN GENERAL.—The Board shall conduct a continuing program of inspections to assess the degree of compliance of each registered public accounting firm and associated persons of that firm with this Act, the rules of the Board, the rules of the Commission, or professional standards, in connection with its performance of audits, issuance of audit reports, and related matters involving issuers.

(b) INSPECTION FREQUENCY.—

(1) IN GENERAL.—Subject to paragraph (2), inspections required by this section shall be conducted—

(A) annually with respect to each registered public accounting firm that regularly provides audit reports for more than 100 issuers; and

H.R.3763—14

(B) not less frequently than once every 3 years with respect to each registered public accounting firm that regularly provides audit reports for 100 or fewer issuers.

(2) ADJUSTMENTS TO SCHEDULES.—The Board may, by rule, adjust the inspection schedules set under paragraph (1) if the Board finds that different inspection schedules are consistent with the purposes of this Act, the public interest, and the protection of investors. The Board may conduct special inspections at the request of the Commission or upon its own motion.

c) PROCEDURES.—The Board shall, in each inspection under this section, and in accordance with its rules for such inspections—

(1) identify any act or practice or omission to act by the registered public accounting firm, or by any associated person thereof, revealed by such inspection that may be in violation of this Act, the rules of the Board, the rules of the Commission, the firm's own quality control policies, or professional standards;

(2) report any such act, practice, or omission, if appropriate, to the Commission and each appropriate State regulatory authority; and

(3) begin a formal investigation or take disciplinary action, if appropriate, with respect to any such violation, in accordance with this Act and the rules of the Board.

(d) CONDUCT OF INSPECTIONS.—In conducting an inspection of a registered public accounting firm under this section, the Board shall—

(1) inspect and review selected audit and review engagements of the firm which may include audit engagements that are the subject of ongoing litigation or other controversy between the firm and 1 or more third parties), performed at various offices and by various associated persons of the firm, as selected by the Board;

(2) evaluate the sufficiency of the quality control system of the firm, and the manner of the documentation and communication of that system by the firm; and

(3) perform such other testing of the audit, supervisory, and quality control procedures of the firm as are necessary or appropriate in light of the purpose of the inspection and the responsibilities of the Board.

(e) RECORD RETENTION.—The rules of the Board may require the retention by registered public accounting firms for inspection purposes of records whose retention is not otherwise required by section 103 or the rules issued thereunder.

(f) PROCEDURES FOR REVIEW.—The rules of the Board shall provide a procedure for the review of and response to a draft inspection report by the registered public accounting firm under inspection. The Board shall take such action with respect to such response as it considers appropriate (including revising the draft report or continuing or supplementing its inspection activities before issuing a final report), but the text of any such response, appropriately redacted to protect information reasonably identified by the accounting firm as confidential, shall be attached to and made part of the inspection report.

(g) REPORT.—A written report of the findings of the Board for each inspection under this section, subject to subsection (h), shall be—

H.R. 3763—16

(2) TESTIMONY AND DOCUMENT PRODUCTION.—In addition to such other actions as the Board determines to be necessary or appropriate, the rules of the Board may—

(A) require the testimony of the firm or of any person associated with a registered public accounting firm, with respect to any matter that the Board considers relevant or material to an investigation;

(B) require the production of audit work papers and any other document or information in the possession of a registered public accounting firm or any associated person thereof, wherever domiciled, that the Board considers relevant or material to the investigation, and may inspect the books and records of such firm or associated person to verify the accuracy of any documents or information supplied;

(C) request the testimony of, and production of any document in the possession of, any other person, including any client of a registered public accounting firm, that the Board considers relevant or material to an investigation under this section, with appropriate notice, subject to the needs of the investigation, as permitted under the rules of the Board; and

(D) provide for procedures to seek issuance by the Commission, in a manner established by the Commission, of a subpoena to require the testimony of, and production of any document in the possession of, any person, including any client of a registered public accounting firm, that the Board considers relevant or material to an investigation under this section.

(3) NONCOOPERATION WITH INVESTIGATIONS.—

(A) IN GENERAL.—If a registered public accounting firm or any associated person thereof refuses to testify, produce documents, or otherwise cooperate with the Board in connection with an investigation under this section, the Board may—

(i) suspend or bar such person from being associated with a registered public accounting firm, or require the registered public accounting firm to end such association;

(ii) suspend or revoke the registration of the public accounting firm; and

(iii) invoke such other lesser sanctions as the Board considers appropriate, and as specified by rule of the Board.

(B) PROCEDURE.—Any action taken by the Board under this paragraph shall be subject to the terms of section 107(c).

(4) COORDINATION AND REFERRAL OF INVESTIGATIONS.—

(A) COORDINATION.—The Board shall notify the Commission of any pending Board investigation involving a potential violation of the securities laws, and thereafter coordinate its work with the work of the Commission's Division of Enforcement, as necessary to protect an ongoing Commission investigation.

(B) REFERRAL.—The Board may refer an investigation under this section—

(i) to the Commission;

H.R. 3763—15

(1) transmitted, in appropriate detail, to the Commission and each appropriate State regulatory authority, accompanied by any letter or comments by the Board or the inspector, and any letter or response from the registered public accounting firm; and

(2) made available in appropriate detail to the public (subject to section 105(b)(5)(A), and to the protection of such confidential and proprietary information as the Board may determine to be appropriate, or as may be required by law), except that no portions of the inspection report that deal with criticisms of or potential defects in the quality control systems of the firm under inspection shall be made public if those criticisms or defects are addressed by the firm, to the satisfaction of the Board, not later than 12 months after the date of the inspection report.

(h) INTERIM COMMISSION REVIEW.—

(1) REVIEWABLE MATTERS.—A registered public accounting firm may seek review by the Commission, pursuant to such rules as the Commission shall promulgate, if the firm—

(A) has provided the Board with a response, pursuant to rules issued by the Board under subsection (f), to the substance of particular items in a draft inspection report, and disagrees with the assessments contained in any final report prepared by the Board following such response; or

(B) disagrees with the determination of the Board that criticisms or defects identified in an inspection report have not been addressed to the satisfaction of the Board within 12 months of the date of the inspection report, for purposes of subsection (g)(2).

(2) TREATMENT OF REVIEW.—Any decision of the Commission with respect to a review under paragraph (1) shall not be reviewable under section 25 of the Securities Exchange Act of 1934 (15 U.S.C. 78y), or deemed to be "final agency action" for purposes of section 704 of title 5, United States Code.

(3) TIMING.—Review under paragraph (1) may be sought during the 30-day period following the date of the event giving rise to the review under subparagraph (A) or (B) of paragraph (1).

SEC. 105. INVESTIGATIONS AND DISCIPLINARY PROCEEDINGS.

(a) IN GENERAL.—The Board shall establish, by rule, subject to the requirements of this section, fair procedures for the investigation and disciplining of registered public accounting firms and associated persons of such firms.

(b) INVESTIGATIONS.—

(1) AUTHORITY.—In accordance with the rules of the Board, the Board may conduct an investigation of any act or practice, or omission to act, by a registered public accounting firm, any associated person of such firm, or both, that may violate any provision of this Act, the rules of the Board, the provisions of the securities laws relating to the preparation and issuance of audit reports and the obligations and liabilities of accountants with respect thereto, including the rules of the Commission issued under this Act, or professional standards, regardless of how the act, practice, or omission is brought to the attention of the Board.

H.R. 3763—17

(ii) to any other Federal functional regulator (as defined in section 509 of the Gramm-Leach-Bliley Act (15 U.S.C. 6809)), in the case of an investigation that concerns an audit report for an institution that is subject to the jurisdiction of such regulator; and

(iii) at the direction of the Commission, to—

(I) the Attorney General of the United States;

(II) the attorney general of 1 or more States; and

(III) the appropriate State regulatory authority.

(5) USE OF DOCUMENTS.—

(A) CONFIDENTIALITY.—Except as provided in subparagraph (B), all documents and information prepared or received by or specifically for the Board, and deliberations of the Board and its employees and agents, in connection with an inspection under section 104 or with an investigation under this section, shall be confidential and privileged as an evidentiary matter (and shall not be subject to civil discovery or other legal process) in any proceeding in any Federal or State court or administrative agency, and shall be exempt from disclosure, in the hands of an agency or establishment of the Federal Government, under the Freedom of Information Act (5 U.S.C. 552a), or otherwise, unless and until presented in connection with a public proceeding or released in accordance with subsection (c).

(B) AVAILABILITY TO GOVERNMENT AGENCIES.—Without the loss of its status as confidential and privileged in the hands of the Board, all information referred to in subparagraph (A) may—

(i) be made available to the Commission; and

(ii) in the discretion of the Board, when determined by the Board to be necessary to accomplish the purposes of this Act or to protect investors, be made available to—

(I) the Attorney General of the United States;

(II) the appropriate Federal functional regulator (as defined in section 509 of the Gramm-Leach-Bliley Act (15 U.S.C. 6809)), other than the Commission, with respect to an audit report for an institution subject to the jurisdiction of such regulator;

(III) State attorneys general in connection with any criminal investigation; and

(IV) any appropriate State regulatory authority,

each of which shall maintain such information as confidential and privileged.

(6) IMMUNITY.—Any employee of the Board engaged in carrying out an investigation under this Act shall be immune from any civil liability arising out of such investigation in the same manner and to the same extent as an employee of the Federal Government in similar circumstances.

(c) DISCIPLINARY PROCEDURES.—

(1) NOTIFICATION; RECORDKEEPING.—The rules of the Board shall provide that in any proceeding by the Board to determine

H.R. 3763—18

whether a registered public accounting firm, or an associated person thereof, should be disciplined, the Board shall—

(A) bring specific charges with respect to the firm or associated person;

(B) notify such firm or associated person of, and provide to the firm or associated person an opportunity to defend against, such charges; and

(C) keep a record of the proceedings.

(2) PUBLIC HEARINGS.—Hearings under this section shall not be public, unless otherwise ordered by the Board for good cause shown, with the consent of the parties to such hearing.

(3) SUPPORTING STATEMENT.—A determination by the Board to impose a sanction under this subsection shall be supported by a statement setting forth—

(A) each act or practice in which the registered public accounting firm, or associated person, has engaged (or omitted to engage), or that forms a basis for all or a part of such sanction;

(B) the specific provision of this Act, the securities laws, the rules of the Board, or professional standards which the Board determines has been violated; and

(C) the sanction imposed, including a justification for that sanction.

(4) SANCTIONS.—If the Board finds, based on all of the facts and circumstances, that a registered public accounting firm or associated person thereof has engaged in any act or practice, or omitted to act, in violation of this Act, the rules of the Board, the provisions of the securities laws relating to the preparation and issuance of audit reports and the obligations and liabilities of accountants with respect thereto, including the rules of the Commission issued under this Act, or professional standards, the Board may impose such disciplinary or remedial sanctions as it determines appropriate, subject to applicable limitations under paragraph (6), including—

(A) temporary suspension or permanent revocation of registration under this title;

(B) temporary or permanent suspension or bar of a person from further association with any registered public accounting firm;

(C) temporary or permanent limitation on the activities, functions, or operations of such firm or person (other than in connection with required additional professional education or training);

(D) a civil money penalty for each such violation, in an amount equal to—

(i) not more than $100,000 for a natural person or $2,000,000 for any other person; and

(ii) in any case to which paragraph (5) applies, not more than $750,000 for a natural person or $15,000,000 for any other person;

(E) censure;

(F) required additional professional education or training; or

(G) any other appropriate sanction provided for in the rules of the Board.

H. R. 3763—19

(5) INTENTIONAL OR OTHER KNOWING CONDUCT.—The sanctions and penalties described in subparagraphs (A) through (C) and (D)(ii) of paragraph (4) shall only apply to—

(A) intentional or knowing conduct, including reckless conduct, that results in violation of the applicable statutory, regulatory, or professional standard; or

(B) repeated instances of negligent conduct, each resulting in a violation of the applicable statutory, regulatory, or professional standard.

(6) FAILURE TO SUPERVISE.—

(A) IN GENERAL.—The Board may impose sanctions under this section on a registered accounting firm or upon the supervisory personnel of such firm, if the Board finds that—

(i) the firm has failed reasonably to supervise an associated person, either as required by the rules of the Board relating to auditing or quality control standards, or otherwise, with a view to preventing violations of this Act, the rules of the Board, the provisions of the securities laws relating to the preparation and issuance of audit reports and the obligations and liabilities of accountants with respect thereto, including the rules of the Commission under this Act, or professional standards; and

(ii) such associated person commits a violation of this Act, or any of such rules, laws, or standards.

(B) RULE OF CONSTRUCTION.—No associated person of a registered public accounting firm shall be deemed to have failed reasonably to supervise any other person for purposes of subparagraph (A), if—

(i) there have been established in and for that firm procedures, and a system for applying such procedures, that comply with applicable rules of the Board and that would reasonably be expected to prevent and detect any such violation by such associated person; and

(ii) such person has reasonably discharged the duties and obligations incumbent upon that person by reason of such procedures and system, and had no reasonable cause to believe that such procedures and system were not being complied with.

(7) EFFECT OF SUSPENSION.—

(A) ASSOCIATION WITH A PUBLIC ACCOUNTING FIRM.—It shall be unlawful for any person that is suspended or barred from being associated with a registered public accounting firm under this subsection willfully to become or remain associated with any registered public accounting firm, or for any registered public accounting firm that knew, or, in the exercise of reasonable care should have known, of the suspension or bar, to permit such an association, without the consent of the Board or the Commission.

(B) ASSOCIATION WITH AN ISSUER.—It shall be unlawful for any person that is suspended or barred from being associated with an issuer under this subsection willfully to become or remain associated with any issuer in an accountancy or a financial management capacity, and for any issuer that knew, or in the exercise of reasonable

H. R. 3763—19

(5) INTENTIONAL OR OTHER KNOWING CONDUCT.—The sanctions and penalties described in subparagraphs (A) through (C) and (D)(ii) of paragraph (4) shall only apply to—

(A) intentional or knowing conduct, including reckless conduct, that results in violation of the applicable statutory, regulatory, or professional standard; or

(B) repeated instances of negligent conduct, each resulting in a violation of the applicable statutory, regulatory, or professional standard.

(6) FAILURE TO SUPERVISE.—

(A) IN GENERAL.—The Board may impose sanctions under this section on a registered accounting firm or upon the supervisory personnel of such firm, if the Board finds that—

(i) the firm has failed reasonably to supervise an associated person, either as required by the rules of the Board relating to auditing or quality control standards, or otherwise, with a view to preventing violations of this Act, the rules of the Board, the provisions of the securities laws relating to the preparation and issuance of audit reports and the obligations and liabilities of accountants with respect thereto, including the rules of the Commission under this Act, or professional standards; and

(ii) such associated person commits a violation of this Act, or any of such rules, laws, or standards.

(B) RULE OF CONSTRUCTION.—No associated person of a registered public accounting firm shall be deemed to have failed reasonably to supervise any other person for purposes of subparagraph (A), if—

(i) there have been established in and for that firm procedures, and a system for applying such procedures, that comply with applicable rules of the Board and that would reasonably be expected to prevent and detect any such violation by such associated person; and

(ii) such person has reasonably discharged the duties and obligations incumbent upon that person by reason of such procedures and system, and had no reasonable cause to believe that such procedures and system were not being complied with.

(7) EFFECT OF SUSPENSION.—

(A) ASSOCIATION WITH A PUBLIC ACCOUNTING FIRM.—It shall be unlawful for any person that is suspended or barred from being associated with a registered public accounting firm under this subsection willfully to become or remain associated with any registered public accounting firm, or for any registered public accounting firm that knew, or, in the exercise of reasonable care should have known, of the suspension or bar, to permit such an association, without the consent of the Board or the Commission.

(B) ASSOCIATION WITH AN ISSUER.—It shall be unlawful for any person that is suspended or barred from being associated with an issuer under this subsection willfully to become or remain associated with any issuer in an accountancy or a financial management capacity, and for any issuer that knew, or in the exercise of reasonable

H.R. 3763—21

(or firms) for purposes of registration under, and oversight by the Board in accordance with, this title.

(b) PRODUCTION OF AUDIT WORKPAPERS.—

(1) CONSENT BY FOREIGN FIRMS.—If a foreign public accounting firm issues an opinion or otherwise performs material services upon which a registered public accounting firm relies in issuing all or part of any audit report or any opinion contained in an audit report, that foreign public accounting firm shall be deemed to have consented—

(A) to produce its audit workpapers for the Board or the Commission in connection with any investigation by either body with respect to that audit report; and

(B) to be subject to the jurisdiction of the courts of the United States for purposes of enforcement of any request for production of such workpapers.

(2) CONSENT BY DOMESTIC FIRMS.—A registered public accounting firm that relies upon the opinion of a foreign public accounting firm, as described in paragraph (1), shall be deemed—

(A) to have consented to supplying the audit workpapers of that foreign public accounting firm in response to a request for production by the Board or the Commission; and

(B) to have secured the agreement of that foreign public accounting firm to such production, as a condition of its reliance on the opinion of that foreign public accounting firm.

(c) EXEMPTION AUTHORITY.—The Commission, and the Board, subject to the approval of the Commission, may, by rule, regulation, or order, and as the Commission (or Board) determines necessary or appropriate in the public interest or for the protection of investors, either unconditionally or upon specified terms and conditions exempt any foreign public accounting firm, or any class of such firms, from any provision of this Act, or the rules of the Board or the Commission issued under this Act.

(d) DEFINITION.—In this section, the term "foreign public accounting firm" means a public accounting firm that is organized and operates under the laws of a foreign government or political subdivision thereof.

SEC. 107. COMMISSION OVERSIGHT OF THE BOARD.

(a) GENERAL OVERSIGHT RESPONSIBILITY.—The Commission shall have oversight and enforcement authority over the Board, as provided in this Act. The provisions of section 17(a)(1) of the Securities Exchange Act of 1934 (15 U.S.C. 78q(a)(1)), and of section 17(b)(1) of the Securities Exchange Act of 1934 (15 U.S.C. 78q(b)(1)) shall apply to the Board as fully as if the Board were a "registered securities association" for purposes of those sections 17(a)(1) and 17(b)(1).

(b) RULES OF THE BOARD.—

(1) DEFINITION.—In this section, the term "proposed rule" means any proposed rule of the Board, and any modification of any such rule.

(2) PRIOR APPROVAL REQUIRED.—No rule of the Board shall become effective without prior approval of the Commission in accordance with this section, other than as provided in section 103(a)(3)(B) with respect to initial or transitional standards.

H.R. 3763—22

(3) APPROVAL CRITERIA.—The Commission shall approve a proposed rule, if it finds that the rule is consistent with the requirements of this Act and the securities laws, or is necessary or appropriate in the public interest or for the protection of investors.

(4) PROPOSED RULE PROCEDURES.—The provisions of paragraphs (1) through (3) of section 19(b) of the Securities Exchange Act of 1934 (15 U.S.C. 78s(b)) shall govern the proposed rules of the Board, as fully as if the Board were a "registered securities association" for purposes of that section 19(b), except that, for purposes of this paragraph—

(A) the phrase "consistent with the requirements of this title and the rules and regulations thereunder applicable to such organization" in section 19(b)(2) of that Act shall be deemed to read "consistent with the requirements of title I of the Sarbanes-Oxley Act of 2002, and the rules and regulations issued thereunder applicable to such organization, or as necessary or appropriate in the public interest or for the protection of investors"; and

(B) the phrase "otherwise in furtherance of the purposes of this title", in section 19(b)(3)(C) of that Act shall be deemed to read "otherwise in furtherance of the purposes of title I of the Sarbanes-Oxley Act of 2002".

(5) COMMISSION AUTHORITY TO AMEND RULES OF THE BOARD.—The provisions of section 19(c) of the Securities Exchange Act of 1934 (15 U.S.C. 78s(c)) shall govern the abrogation, deletion, or addition to portions of the rules of the Board by the Commission as fully as if the Board were a "registered securities association" for purposes of that section 19(c), except that the phrase "to conform its rules to the requirements of this title and the rules and regulations thereunder applicable to such organization, or otherwise in furtherance of the purposes of this title" in section 19(c) of that Act shall, for purposes of this paragraph, be deemed to read "to assure the fair administration of the Public Company Accounting Oversight Board, conform the rules promulgated by that Board to the requirements of title I of the Sarbanes-Oxley Act of 2002, or otherwise further the purposes of that Act, the securities laws, and the rules and regulations thereunder applicable to that Board".

(c) COMMISSION REVIEW OF DISCIPLINARY ACTION TAKEN BY THE BOARD.—

(1) NOTICE OF SANCTION.—The Board shall promptly file notice with the Commission of any final sanction on any registered public accounting firm or on any associated person thereof, in such form and containing such information as the Commission, by rule, may prescribe.

(2) REVIEW OF SANCTIONS.—The provisions of sections 19(d)(2) and 19(e)(1) of the Securities Exchange Act of 1934 (15 U.S.C. 78s (d)(2) and (e)(1)) shall govern the review by the Commission of final disciplinary sanctions imposed by the Board (including sanctions imposed under section 105(b)(3) of this Act) as fully as if the Board were a self-regulatory organization and the Commission were the appropriate regulatory agency for such organization for purposes of those sections 19(d)(2) and 19(e)(1), except that, for purposes of this paragraph—

H.R. 3763—23

(A) section 105(e) of this Act (rather than that section 19(d)(2)) shall govern the extent to which application for, or institution by the Commission on its own motion of, review of any disciplinary action of the Board operates as a stay of such action;

(B) references in that section 19(e)(1) to "members" of such an organization shall be deemed to be references to registered public accounting firms;

(C) the phrase "consistent with the purposes of this title" in that section 19(e)(1) shall be deemed to read "consistent with the purposes of this title and title I of the Sarbanes-Oxley Act of 2002";

(D) references to rules of the Municipal Securities Rulemaking Board in that section 19(e)(1) shall not apply; and

(E) the reference to section 19(e)(2) of the Securities Exchange Act of 1934 shall refer instead to section 107(c)(3) of this Act.

(3) COMMISSION MODIFICATION AUTHORITY.—The Commission may enhance, modify, cancel, reduce, or require the remission of a sanction imposed by the Board upon a registered public accounting firm or associated person thereof, if the Commission, having due regard for the public interest and the protection of investors, finds, after a proceeding in accordance with this subsection, that the sanction—

(A) is not necessary or appropriate in furtherance of this Act or the securities laws; or

(B) is excessive, oppressive, inadequate, or otherwise not appropriate to the finding or the basis on which the sanction was imposed.

(d) CENSURE OF THE BOARD; OTHER SANCTIONS.—

(1) RESCISSION OF BOARD AUTHORITY.—The Commission, by rule, consistent with the public interest, the protection of investors, and the other purposes of this Act and the securities laws, may relieve the Board of any responsibility to enforce compliance with any provision of this Act, the securities laws, the rules of the Board, or professional standards.

(2) CENSURE OF THE BOARD; LIMITATIONS.—The Commission may, by order, as it determines necessary or appropriate in the public interest, for the protection of investors, or otherwise in furtherance of the purposes of this Act or the securities laws, censure or impose limitations upon the activities, functions, and operations of the Board, if the Commission finds, on the record, after notice and opportunity for a hearing, that the Board—

(A) has violated or is unable to comply with any provision of this Act, the rules of the Board, or the securities laws; or

(B) without reasonable justification or excuse, has failed to enforce compliance with any such provision or rule, or any professional standard by a registered public accounting firm or an associated person thereof.

(3) CENSURE OF BOARD MEMBERS; REMOVAL FROM OFFICE.—The Commission may, as necessary or appropriate in the public interest, for the protection of investors, or otherwise in furtherance of the purposes of this Act or the securities laws, remove

H.R. 3763—24

from office or censure any member of the Board, if the Commission finds, on the record, after notice and opportunity for a hearing, that such member—

(A) has willfully violated any provision of this Act, the rules of the Board, or the securities laws;

(B) has willfully abused the authority of that member; or

(C) without reasonable justification or excuse, has failed to enforce compliance with any such provision or rule, or any professional standard by any registered public accounting firm or any associated person thereof.

SEC. 108. ACCOUNTING STANDARDS.

(a) AMENDMENT TO SECURITIES ACT OF 1933.—Section 19 of the Securities Act of 1933 (15 U.S.C. 77s) is amended—

(1) by redesignating subsections (b) and (c) as subsections (c) and (d), respectively; and

(2) by inserting after subsection (a) the following:

"(b) RECOGNITION OF ACCOUNTING STANDARDS.—

"(1) IN GENERAL.—In carrying out its authority under subsection (a) and under section 13(b) of the Securities Exchange Act of 1934, the Commission may recognize, as 'generally accepted' for purposes of the securities laws, any accounting principles established by a standard setting body—

"(A) that—

"(i) is organized as a private entity;

"(ii) has, for administrative and operational purposes, a board of trustees (or equivalent body) serving in the public interest, the majority of whom are not, concurrent with their service on such board, and have not been during the 2-year period preceding such service, associated persons of any registered public accounting firm;

"(iii) is funded as provided in section 109 of the Sarbanes-Oxley Act of 2002;

"(iv) has adopted procedures to ensure prompt consideration, by majority vote of its members, of changes to accounting principles necessary to reflect emerging accounting issues and changing business practices; and

"(v) considers, in adopting accounting principles, the need to keep standards current in order to reflect changes in the business environment, the extent to which international convergence on high quality accounting standards is necessary or appropriate in the public interest and for the protection of investors; and

"(B) that the Commission determines has the capacity to assist the Commission in fulfilling the requirements of subsection (a) and section 13(b) of the Securities Exchange Act of 1934, because, at a minimum, the standard setting body is capable of improving the accuracy and effectiveness of financial reporting and the protection of investors under the securities laws.

"(2) ANNUAL REPORT.—A standard setting body described in paragraph (1) shall submit an annual report to the Commission and the public, containing audited financial statements of that standard setting body."

(b) COMMISSION AUTHORITY.—The Commission shall promulgate such rules and regulations to carry out section 19(b) of the Securities Act of 1933, as added by this section, as it deems necessary or appropriate in the public interest or for the protection of investors.

(c) NO EFFECT ON COMMISSION POWERS.—Nothing in this Act, including this section and the amendment made by this section, shall be construed to impair or limit the authority of the Commission to establish accounting principles or standards for purposes of enforcement of the securities laws.

(d) STUDY AND REPORT ON ADOPTING PRINCIPLES-BASED ACCOUNTING.—

(1) STUDY.—

(A) IN GENERAL.—The Commission shall conduct a study on the adoption by the United States financial reporting system of a principles-based accounting system.

(B) STUDY TOPICS.—The study required by subparagraph (A) shall include an examination of—

(i) the extent to which principles-based accounting and financial reporting exists in the United States;

(ii) the length of time required for change from a rules-based to a principles-based financial reporting system;

(iii) the feasibility of and proposed methods by which a principles-based system may be implemented; and

(iv) a thorough economic analysis of the implementation of a principles-based system.

(2) REPORT.—Not later than 1 year after the date of enactment of this Act, the Commission shall submit a report on the results of the study required by paragraph (1) to the Committee on Banking, Housing, and Urban Affairs of the Senate and the Committee on Financial Services of the House of Representatives.

SEC. 109. FUNDING.

(a) IN GENERAL.—The Board, and the standard setting body designated pursuant to section 19(b) of the Securities Act of 1933, as amended by section 108, shall be funded as provided in this section.

(b) ANNUAL BUDGETS.—The Board and the standard setting body referred to in subsection (a) shall each establish a budget for each fiscal year, which shall be reviewed and approved according to their respective internal procedures not less than 1 month prior to the commencement of the fiscal year to which the budget pertains (or at the beginning of the Board's first fiscal year, which may be a short fiscal year). The budget of the Board shall be subject to approval by the Commission. The budget for the first fiscal year of the Board shall be prepared and approved promptly following the appointment of the initial five Board members, to permit action by the Board of the organizational tasks contemplated by section 1011(d).

(c) SOURCES AND USES OF FUNDS.—

(1) RECOVERABLE BUDGET EXPENSES.—The budget of the Board (reduced by any registration or annual fees received under section 102(e) for the year preceding the year for which the budget is being computed), and all of the budget of the standard setting body referred to in subsection (a), for each fiscal year of each of those 2 entities, shall be payable from annual accounting support fees, in accordance with subsections (c) and (e). Accounting support fees and other receipts of the Board and of such standard-setting body shall not be considered public monies of the United States.

(2) FUNDS GENERATED FROM THE COLLECTION OF MONETARY PENALTIES.—Subject to the availability in advance in an appropriations Act, and notwithstanding subsection (i), all funds collected by the Board as a result of the assessment of monetary penalties shall be used to fund a merit scholarship program for undergraduate and graduate students enrolled in accredited accounting degree programs, which program is to be administered by the Board or by an entity or agent identified by the Board.

(d) ANNUAL ACCOUNTING SUPPORT FEE FOR THE BOARD.—

(1) ESTABLISHMENT OF FEE.—The Board shall establish, with the approval of the Commission, a reasonable annual accounting support fee (or a formula for the computation thereof), as may be necessary or appropriate to establish and maintain the Board. Such fee may also cover costs incurred in the Board's first fiscal year (which may be a short fiscal year), or may be levied separately with respect to such short fiscal year.

(2) ASSESSMENTS.—The rules of the Board under paragraph (1) shall provide for the equitable allocation, assessment, and collection by the Board (or an agent appointed by the Board) of the fee established under paragraph (1), among issuers, in accordance with subsection (g), allowing for differentiation among classes of issuers, as appropriate.

(e) ANNUAL ACCOUNTING SUPPORT FEE FOR STANDARD SETTING BODY.—The annual accounting support for the standard setting body referred to in subsection (a)—

(1) shall be allocated in accordance with subsection (g), and assessed and collected against each issuer, on behalf of the standard setting body, by 1 or more appropriate designated collection agents, as may be necessary or appropriate to pay for the budget and provide for the expenses of that standard setting body, and to provide for an independent, stable source of funding for such body, subject to review by the Commission; and

(2) may differentiate among different classes of issuers.

(f) LIMITATION ON FEE.—The amount of fees collected under this section for a fiscal year on behalf of the Board or the standards setting body, as the case may be, shall not exceed the recoverable budget expenses of the Board or body, respectively (which may include operating, capital, and accrued items), referred to in subsection (c)(1).

(g) ALLOCATION OF ACCOUNTING SUPPORT FEES AMONG ISSUERS.—Any amount due from issuers (or a particular class of issuers) under this section to fund the budget of the Board or the standard setting body referred to in subsection (a) shall be allocated among and payable by each issuer (or each issuer in

H. R. 3763—27

a particular class, as applicable) in an amount equal to the total of such amount, multiplied by a fraction—

"(1) the numerator of which is the average monthly equity market capitalization of the issuer for the 12-month period immediately preceding the beginning of the fiscal year to which such budget relates; and

"(2) the denominator of which is the average monthly equity market capitalization of all such issuers for such 12-month period.

"(h) CONFORMING AMENDMENTS.—Section 13(b)(2) of the Securities Exchange Act of 1934 (15 U.S.C. 78m(b)(2)) is amended—

"(1) in subparagraph (A), by striking "and" at the end; and

"(2) in subparagraph (B), by striking the period at the end and inserting the following: "; and

"(C) notwithstanding any other provision of law, pay the allocable share of such issuer of a reasonable annual accounting support fee or fees, determined in accordance with section 109 of the Sarbanes-Oxley Act of 2002.".

"(i) RULE OF CONSTRUCTION.—Nothing in this section shall be construed to render either the Board, the standard setting body referred to in subsection (a), or both, subject to procedures in Congress to authorize or appropriate public funds, or to prevent such organization from utilizing additional sources of revenue for its activities, such as earnings from publication sales, provided that each additional source of revenue shall not jeopardize, in the judgment of the Commission, the actual and perceived independence of such organization.

"(j) START-UP EXPENSES OF THE BOARD.—From the unexpended balances of the appropriations to the Commission for fiscal year 2003, the Secretary of the Treasury is authorized to advance to the Board not to exceed the amount necessary to cover the expenses of the Board during its first fiscal year (which may be a short fiscal year).

TITLE II—AUDITOR INDEPENDENCE

SEC. 201. SERVICES OUTSIDE THE SCOPE OF PRACTICE OF AUDITORS.

(a) PROHIBITED ACTIVITIES.—Section 10A of the Securities Exchange Act of 1934 (15 U.S.C. 78j–1) is amended by adding at the end the following:

"(g) PROHIBITED ACTIVITIES.—Except as provided in subsection (h), it shall be unlawful for a registered public accounting firm (and any associated person of that firm, to the extent determined appropriate by the Commission) that performs for any issuer any audit required by this title or the rules of the Commission under this title or, beginning 180 days after the date of commencement of the operations of the Public Company Accounting Oversight Board established under section 101 of the Sarbanes-Oxley Act of 2002 (in this section referred to as the 'Board'), the rules of the Board, to provide to that issuer, contemporaneously with the audit, any non-audit service, including—

"(1) bookkeeping or other services related to the accounting records or financial statements of the audit client;

"(2) financial information systems design and implementation;

H. R. 3763—28

"(3) appraisal or valuation services, fairness opinions, or contribution-in-kind reports;

"(4) actuarial services;

"(5) internal audit outsourcing services;

"(6) management functions or human resources;

"(7) broker or dealer, investment adviser, or investment banking services;

"(8) legal services and expert services unrelated to the audit; and

"(9) any other service that the Board determines, by regulation, is impermissible.

"(h) PREAPPROVAL REQUIRED FOR NON-AUDIT SERVICES.—A registered public accounting firm may engage in any non-audit service, including tax services, that is not described in any of paragraphs (1) through (9) of subsection (g) for an audit client, only if the activity is approved in advance by the audit committee of the issuer, in accordance with subsection (i).".

"(b) EXEMPTION AUTHORITY.—The Board may, on a case by case basis, exempt any person, issuer, public accounting firm, or transaction from the prohibition on the provision of services under section 10A(g) of the Securities Exchange Act of 1934 (as added by this section), to the extent that such exemption is necessary or appropriate in the public interest and is consistent with the protection of investors, and subject to review by the Commission in the same manner as for rules of the Board under section 107.

SEC. 202. PREAPPROVAL REQUIREMENTS.

Section 10A of the Securities Exchange Act of 1934 (15 U.S.C. 78j–1), as amended by this Act, is amended by adding at the end the following:

"(i) PREAPPROVAL REQUIREMENTS.—

"(1) IN GENERAL.—

"(A) AUDIT COMMITTEE ACTION.—All auditing services (which may entail providing comfort letters in connection with securities underwritings or statutory audits required for insurance companies for purposes of State law) and non-audit services, other than as provided in subparagraph (B), provided to an issuer by the auditor of the issuer shall be preapproved by the audit committee of the issuer.

"(B) DE MINIMUS EXCEPTION.—The preapproval requirement under subparagraph (A) is waived with respect to the provision of non-audit services for an issuer, if—

"(i) the aggregate amount of all such non-audit services provided to the issuer constitutes not more than 5 percent of the total amount of revenues paid by the issuer to its auditor during the fiscal year in which the nonaudit services are provided;

"(ii) such services were not recognized by the issuer at the time of the engagement to be non-audit services; and

"(iii) such services are promptly brought to the attention of the audit committee of the issuer and approved prior to the completion of the audit by the audit committee or by 1 or more members of the audit committee who are members of the board of directors to whom authority to grant such approvals has been delegated by the audit committee.

H.R. 3763—30

purpose of overseeing the accounting and financial reporting processes of the issuer and audits of the financial statements of the issuer; and

"(B) if no such committee exists with respect to an issuer, the entire board of directors of the issuer.

"(69) REGISTERED PUBLIC ACCOUNTING FIRM.—The term 'registered public accounting firm' has the same meaning as in section 2 of the Sarbanes-Oxley Act of 2002.".

(b) AUDITOR REQUIREMENTS.—Section 10A of the Securities Exchange Act of 1934 (15 U.S.C. 78j—1) is amended—

(1) by striking "an independent public accountant" each place that term appears and inserting "a registered public accounting firm";

(2) by striking "the independent public accountant" each place that term appears and inserting "the registered public accounting firm";

(3) in subsection (c), by striking "No independent public accountant" and inserting "No registered public accounting firm"; and

(4) in subsection (b)—

(A) by striking "the accountant" each place that term appears and inserting "the firm";

(B) by striking "such accountant" each place that term appears and inserting "such firm'; and

(C) in paragraph (4), by striking "the accountant's report" and inserting "the report of the firm.".

(c) OTHER REFERENCES.—The Securities Exchange Act of 1934 (15 U.S.C. 78a et seq.) is amended—

(1) in section 12(b)(1) (15 U.S.C. 78l(b)(1)), by striking "independent public accountants" each place that term appears and inserting "a registered public accounting firm"; and

(2) in subsections (e) and (i) of section 17 (15 U.S.C. 78q), by striking "an independent public accountant" each place that term appears and inserting "a registered public accounting firm".

(d) CONFORMING AMENDMENT.—Section 10A(f) of the Securities Exchange Act of 1934 (15 U.S.C. 78k(f)) is amended—

(1) by striking "DEFINITION" and inserting "DEFINITIONS"; and

(2) by adding at the end the following: "As used in this section, the term 'issuer' means an issuer (as defined in section 3), the securities of which are registered under section 12, or that is required to file reports pursuant to section 15(d), or that files or has filed a registration statement that has not yet become effective under the Securities Act of 1933 (15 U.S.C. 77a et seq.), and that it has not withdrawn.".

SEC. 206. CONFLICTS OF INTEREST.

Section 10A of the Securities Exchange Act of 1934 (15 U.S.C. 78j—1), as amended by this Act, is amended by adding at the end the following:

"(l) CONFLICTS OF INTEREST.—It shall be unlawful for a registered public accounting firm to perform for an issuer any audit service required by this title, if a chief executive officer, controller, chief financial officer, chief accounting officer, or any person serving in an equivalent position for the issuer, was employed by that registered independent public accounting firm and participated in

H.R. 3763—29

"(2) DISCLOSURE TO INVESTORS.—Approval by an audit committee of an issuer under this subsection of a non-audit service to be performed by the auditor of the issuer shall be disclosed to investors in periodic reports required by section 13(a).

"(3) DELEGATION AUTHORITY.—The audit committee of an issuer may delegate to 1 or more designated members of the audit committee who are independent directors of the board of directors, the authority to grant preapprovals required by this subsection. The decisions of any member to whom authority is delegated under this paragraph to preapprove an activity under this subsection shall be presented to the full audit committee at each of its scheduled meetings.

"(4) APPROVAL OF AUDIT SERVICES FOR OTHER PURPOSES.— In carrying out its duties under subsection (m)(2), if the audit committee of an issuer approves an audit service within the scope of the engagement of the auditor, such audit service shall be deemed to have been preapproved for purposes of this subsection.".

SEC. 203. AUDIT PARTNER ROTATION.

Section 10A of the Securities Exchange Act of 1934 (15 U.S.C. 78j—1), as amended by this Act, is amended by adding at the end the following:

"(j) AUDIT PARTNER ROTATION.—It shall be unlawful for a registered public accounting firm to provide audit services to an issuer if the lead (or coordinating) audit partner (having primary responsibility for the audit), or the audit partner responsible for reviewing the audit, has performed audit services for that issuer in each of the 5 previous fiscal years of that issuer.".

SEC. 204. AUDITOR REPORTS TO AUDIT COMMITTEES.

Section 10A of the Securities Exchange Act of 1934 (15 U.S.C. 78j—1), as amended by this Act, is amended by adding at the end the following:

"(k) REPORTS TO AUDIT COMMITTEES.—Each registered public accounting firm that performs for any issuer any audit required by this title shall timely report to the audit committee of the issuer—

"(1) all critical accounting policies and practices to be used;

"(2) all alternative treatments of financial information within generally accepted accounting principles that have been discussed with management officials of the issuer, ramifications of the use of such alternative disclosures and treatments, and the treatment preferred by the registered public accounting firm; and

"(3) other material written communications between the registered public accounting firm and the management of the issuer, such as any management letter or schedule of unadjusted differences.".

SEC. 205. CONFORMING AMENDMENTS.

(a) DEFINITIONS.—Section 3(a) of the Securities Exchange Act of 1934 (15 U.S.C. 78c(a)) is amended by adding at the end the following:

"(58) AUDIT COMMITTEE.—The term 'audit committee' means—

"(A) a committee (or equivalent body) established by and amongst the board of directors of an issuer for the

H.R. 3763—31

any capacity in the audit of that issuer during the 1-year period preceding the date of the initiation of the audit."

SEC. 207. STUDY OF MANDATORY ROTATION OF REGISTERED PUBLIC ACCOUNTING FIRMS.

(a) STUDY AND REVIEW REQUIRED.—The Comptroller General of the United States shall conduct a study and review of the potential effects of requiring the mandatory rotation of registered public accounting firms.

(b) REPORT REQUIRED.—Not later than 1 year after the date of enactment of this Act, the Comptroller General shall submit a report to the Committee on Banking, Housing, and Urban Affairs of the Senate and the Committee on Financial Services of the House of Representatives on the results of the study and review required by this section.

(c) DEFINITION.—For purposes of this section, the term "mandatory rotation" refers to the imposition of a limit on the period of years in which a particular registered public accounting firm may be the auditor of record for a particular issuer.

SEC. 208. COMMISSION AUTHORITY.

(a) COMMISSION REGULATIONS.—Not later than 180 days after the date of enactment of this Act, the Commission shall issue final regulations to carry out each of subsections (g) through (l) of section 10A of the Securities Exchange Act of 1934, as added by this title.

(b) AUDITOR INDEPENDENCE.—It shall be unlawful for any registered public accounting firm (or an associated person thereof, as applicable) to prepare or issue any audit report with respect to any issuer, if the firm or associated person engages in any activity with respect to that issuer prohibited by any of subsections (g) through (l) of section 10A of the Securities Exchange Act of 1934, as added by this title, or any rule or regulation of the Commission or of the Board issued thereunder.

SEC. 209. CONSIDERATIONS BY APPROPRIATE STATE REGULATORY AUTHORITIES.

In supervising nonregistered public accounting firms and their associated persons, appropriate State regulatory authorities should make an independent determination of the proper standards applicable, particularly taking into consideration the size and nature of the business of the accounting firms they supervise and the size and nature of the business of the clients of those firms. The standards applied by the Board under this Act should not be presumed to be applicable for purposes of this section for small and medium sized nonregistered public accounting firms.

TITLE III—CORPORATE RESPONSIBILITY

SEC. 301. PUBLIC COMPANY AUDIT COMMITTEES.

Section 10A of the Securities Exchange Act of 1934 (15 U.S.C. 78f) is amended by adding at the end the following:

"(m) STANDARDS RELATING TO AUDIT COMMITTEES.—

"(1) COMMISSION RULES.—

H.R. 3763—32

"(A) IN GENERAL.—Effective not later than 270 days after the date of enactment of this subsection, the Commission shall, by rule, direct the national securities exchanges and national securities associations to prohibit the listing of any security of an issuer that is not in compliance with the requirements of any portion of paragraphs (2) through (6).

"(B) OPPORTUNITY TO CURE DEFECTS.—The rules of the Commission under subparagraph (A) shall provide for appropriate procedures for an issuer to have an opportunity to cure any defects that would be the basis for a prohibition under subparagraph (A), before the imposition of such prohibition.

"(2) RESPONSIBILITIES RELATING TO REGISTERED PUBLIC ACCOUNTING FIRMS.—The audit committee of each issuer, in its capacity as a committee of the board of directors, shall be directly responsible for the appointment, compensation, and oversight of the work of any registered public accounting firm employed by that issuer (including resolution of disagreements between management and the auditor regarding financial reporting) for the purpose of preparing or issuing an audit report or related work, and each such registered public accounting firm shall report directly to the audit committee.

"(3) INDEPENDENCE.—

"(A) IN GENERAL.—Each member of the audit committee of the issuer shall be a member of the board of directors of the issuer, and shall otherwise be independent.

"(B) CRITERIA.—In order to be considered to be independent for purposes of this paragraph, a member of an audit committee of an issuer may not, other than in his or her capacity as a member of the audit committee, the board of directors, or any other board committee—

"(i) accept any consulting, advisory, or other compensatory fee from the issuer; or

"(ii) be an affiliated person of the issuer or any subsidiary thereof.

"(C) EXEMPTION AUTHORITY.—The Commission may exempt from the requirements of subparagraph (B) a particular relationship with respect to audit committee members, as the Commission determines appropriate in light of the circumstances.

"(4) COMPLAINTS.—Each audit committee shall establish procedures for—

"(A) the receipt, retention, and treatment of complaints received by the issuer regarding accounting, internal accounting controls, or auditing matters; and

"(B) the confidential, anonymous submission by employees of the issuer of concerns regarding questionable accounting or auditing matters.

"(5) AUTHORITY TO ENGAGE ADVISERS.—Each audit committee shall have the authority to engage independent counsel and other advisers, as it determines necessary to carry out its duties.

"(6) FUNDING.—Each issuer shall provide for appropriate funding, as determined by the audit committee, in its capacity as a committee of the board of directors, for payment of compensation—

H.R. 3763—33

"(A) to the registered public accounting firm employed by the issuer for the purpose of rendering or issuing an audit report; and

"(B) to any advisers employed by the audit committee under paragraph (5).".

SEC. 302. CORPORATE RESPONSIBILITY FOR FINANCIAL REPORTS.

(a) REGULATIONS REQUIRED.—The Commission shall, by rule, require, for each company filing periodic reports under section 13(a) or 15(d) of the Securities Exchange Act of 1934 (15 U.S.C. 78m, 78o(d)), that the principal executive officer or officers and the principal financial officer or officers, or persons performing similar functions, certify in each annual or quarterly report filed or submitted under either such section of such Act that—

(1) the signing officer has reviewed the report;

(2) based on the officer's knowledge, the report does not contain any untrue statement of a material fact or omit to state a material fact necessary in order to make the statements made, in light of the circumstances under which such statements were made, not misleading;

(3) based on such officer's knowledge, the financial statements, and other financial information included in the report, fairly present in all material respects the financial condition and results of operations of the issuer as of, and for, the periods presented in the report;

(4) the signing officers—

(A) are responsible for establishing and maintaining internal controls;

(B) have designed such internal controls to ensure that material information relating to the issuer and its consolidated subsidiaries is made known to such officers by others within those entities, particularly during the period in which the periodic reports are being prepared;

(C) have evaluated the effectiveness of the issuer's internal controls as of a date within 90 days prior to the report; and

(D) have presented in the report their conclusions about the effectiveness of their internal controls based on their evaluation as of that date;

(5) the signing officers have disclosed to the issuer's auditors and the audit committee of the board of directors (or persons fulfilling the equivalent function)—

(A) all significant deficiencies in the design or operation of internal controls which could adversely affect the issuer's ability to record, process, summarize, and report financial data and have identified for the issuer's auditors any material weaknesses in internal controls; and

(B) any fraud, whether or not material, that involves management or other employees who have a significant role in the issuer's internal controls; and

(6) the signing officers have indicated in the report whether or not there were significant changes in internal controls or in other factors that could significantly affect internal controls subsequent to the date of their evaluation, including any corrective actions with regard to significant deficiencies and material weaknesses.

H.R. 3763—34

(b) FOREIGN REINCORPORATIONS HAVE NO EFFECT.—Nothing in this section 302 shall be interpreted or applied in any way to allow any issuer to lessen the legal force of the statement required under this section 302, by an issuer having reincorporated or having engaged in any other transaction that resulted in the transfer of the corporate domicile or offices of the issuer from inside the United States to outside of the United States.

(c) DEADLINE.—The rules required by subsection (a) shall be effective not later than 30 days after the date of enactment of this Act.

SEC. 303. IMPROPER INFLUENCE ON CONDUCT OF AUDITS.

(a) RULES TO PROHIBIT.—It shall be unlawful, in contravention of such rules or regulations as the Commission shall prescribe as necessary and appropriate in the public interest or for the protection of investors, for any officer or director of an issuer, or any other person acting under the direction thereof, to take any action to fraudulently influence, coerce, manipulate, or mislead any independent public or certified accountant engaged in the performance of an audit of the financial statements of that issuer for the purpose of rendering such financial statements materially misleading.

(b) ENFORCEMENT.—In any civil proceeding, the Commission shall have exclusive authority to enforce this section and any rule or regulation issued under this section.

(c) NO PREEMPTION OF OTHER LAW.—The provisions of subsection (a) shall be in addition to, and shall not supersede or preempt, any other provision of law or any rule or regulation issued thereunder.

(d) DEADLINE FOR RULEMAKING.—The Commission shall—

(1) propose the rules or regulations required by this section, not later than 90 days after the date of enactment of this Act; and

(2) issue final rules or regulations required by this section, not later than 270 days after that date of enactment.

SEC. 304. FORFEITURE OF CERTAIN BONUSES AND PROFITS.

(a) ADDITIONAL COMPENSATION PRIOR TO NONCOMPLIANCE WITH COMMISSION FINANCIAL REPORTING REQUIREMENTS.—If an issuer is required to prepare an accounting restatement due to the material noncompliance of the issuer, as a result of misconduct, with any financial reporting requirement under the securities laws, the chief executive officer and chief financial officer of the issuer shall reimburse the issuer for—

(1) any bonus or other incentive-based or equity-based compensation received by that person from the issuer during the 12-month period following the first public issuance or filing with the Commission (whichever first occurs) of the financial document embodying such financial reporting requirement; and

(2) any profits realized from the sale of securities of the issuer during that 12-month period.

(b) COMMISSION EXEMPTION AUTHORITY.—The Commission may exempt any person from the application of subsection (a), as it deems necessary and appropriate.

SEC. 305. OFFICER AND DIRECTOR BARS AND PENALTIES.

(a) UNFITNESS STANDARD.—

H.R. 3763—35

(1) SECURITIES EXCHANGE ACT OF 1934.—Section 21(d)(2) of the Securities Exchange Act of 1934 (15 U.S.C. 78u(d)(2)) is amended by striking "substantial unfitness" and inserting "unfitness".

(2) SECURITIES ACT OF 1933.—Section 20(e) of the Securities Act of 1933 (15 U.S.C. 77t(e)) is amended by striking "substantial unfitness" and inserting "unfitness".

(b) EQUITABLE RELIEF.—Section 21(d) of the Securities Exchange Act of 1934 (15 U.S.C. 78u(d)) is amended by adding at the end the following:

"(5) EQUITABLE RELIEF.—In any action or proceeding brought or instituted by the Commission under any provision of the securities laws, the Commission may seek, and any Federal court may grant, any equitable relief that may be appropriate or necessary for the benefit of investors."

SEC. 306. INSIDER TRADES DURING PENSION FUND BLACKOUT PERIODS.

(a) PROHIBITION OF INSIDER TRADING DURING PENSION FUND BLACKOUT PERIODS.—

(1) IN GENERAL.—Except to the extent otherwise provided by rule of the Commission pursuant to paragraph (3), it shall be unlawful for any director or executive officer of an issuer of any equity security (other than an exempted security), directly or indirectly, to purchase, sell, or otherwise acquire or transfer any equity security of the issuer (other than an exempted security) during any blackout period with respect to such equity security if such director or officer acquires such equity security in connection with his or her service or employment as a director or executive officer.

(2) REMEDY.—

(A) IN GENERAL.—Any profit realized by a director or executive officer referred to in paragraph (1) from any purchase, sale, or other acquisition or transfer in violation of this subsection shall inure to and be recoverable by the issuer, irrespective of any intention on the part of such director or executive officer in entering into the transaction.

(B) ACTIONS TO RECOVER PROFITS.—An action to recover profits in accordance with this subsection may be instituted at law or in equity in any court of competent jurisdiction by the issuer, or by the owner of any security of the issuer in the name and in behalf of the issuer if the issuer fails or refuses to bring such action within 60 days after the date of request, or fails diligently to prosecute the action thereafter, except that no such suit shall be brought more than 2 years after the date on which such profit was realized.

(3) RULEMAKING AUTHORIZED.—The Commission shall, in consultation with the Secretary of Labor, issue rules to clarify the application of this subsection and to prevent evasion thereof. Such rules shall provide for the application of the requirements of paragraph (1) with respect to entities treated as a single employer with respect to an issuer under section 414(b), (c), (m), or (o) of the Internal Revenue Code of 1986 to the extent necessary to clarify the application of such requirements and to prevent evasion thereof. Such rules may also provide for

H.R. 3763—36

appropriate exceptions from the requirements of this subsection, including exceptions for purchases pursuant to an automatic dividend reinvestment program or purchases or sales made pursuant to an advance election.

(4) BLACKOUT PERIOD.—For purposes of this subsection, the term "blackout period", with respect to the equity securities of any issuer—

(A) means any period of more than 3 consecutive business days during which the ability of not fewer than 50 percent of the participants or beneficiaries under all individual account plans maintained by the issuer to purchase, sell, or otherwise acquire or transfer an interest in any equity of such issuer held in such an individual account plan is temporarily suspended by the issuer or by a fiduciary of the plan; and

(B) does not include, under regulations which shall be prescribed by the Commission—

(i) a regularly scheduled period in which the participants and beneficiaries may not purchase, sell, or otherwise acquire or transfer an interest in any equity of such issuer, if such period is—

(I) incorporated into the individual account plan; and

(II) timely disclosed to employees before becoming participants under the individual account plan or as a subsequent amendment to the plan; or

(ii) any suspension described in subparagraph (A) that is imposed solely in connection with persons becoming participants or beneficiaries, or ceasing to be participants or beneficiaries, in an individual account plan by reason of a corporate merger, acquisition, divestiture, or similar transaction involving the plan or plan sponsor.

(5) INDIVIDUAL ACCOUNT PLAN.—For purposes of this subsection, the term "individual account plan" has the meaning provided in section 3(34) of the Employee Retirement Income Security Act of 1974 (29 U.S.C. 1002(34), except that such term shall not include a one-participant retirement plan (within the meaning of section 101(i)(8)(B) of such Act (29 U.S.C. 1021(i)(8)(B))).

(6) NOTICE TO DIRECTORS, EXECUTIVE OFFICERS, AND THE COMMISSION.—In any case in which a director or executive officer is subject to the requirements of this subsection in connection with a blackout period (as defined in paragraph (4)) with respect to any equity securities, the issuer of such equity securities shall timely notify such director or officer and the Securities and Exchange Commission of such blackout period.

(b) NOTICE REQUIREMENTS TO PARTICIPANTS AND BENEFICIARIES UNDER ERISA.—

(1) IN GENERAL.—Section 101 of the Employee Retirement Income Security Act of 1974 (29 U.S.C. 1021) is amended by redesignating the second subsection (h) as subsection (j), and by inserting after the first subsection (h) the following new subsection:

H.R. 3763—37

"(i) NOTICE OF BLACKOUT PERIODS TO PARTICIPANT OR BENEFICIARY UNDER INDIVIDUAL ACCOUNT PLAN.—

"(1) DUTIES OF PLAN ADMINISTRATOR.—In advance of the commencement of any blackout period with respect to an individual account plan, the plan administrator shall notify the plan participants and beneficiaries who are affected by such action in accordance with this subsection.

"(2) NOTICE REQUIREMENTS.—

"(A) IN GENERAL.—The notices described in paragraph (1) shall be written in a manner calculated to be understood by the average plan participant and shall include—

"(i) the reasons for the blackout period,

"(ii) an identification of the investments and other rights affected,

"(iii) the expected beginning date and length of the blackout period,

"(iv) in the case of investments affected, a statement that the participant or beneficiary should evaluate the appropriateness of their current investment decisions in light of their inability to direct or diversify assets credited to their accounts during the blackout period, and

"(v) such other matters as the Secretary may require by regulation.

"(B) NOTICE TO PARTICIPANTS AND BENEFICIARIES.—Except as otherwise provided in this subsection, notices described in paragraph (1) shall be furnished to all participants and beneficiaries under the plan to whom the blackout period applies at least 30 days in advance of the blackout period.

"(C) EXCEPTION TO 30-DAY NOTICE REQUIREMENT.—In any case in which—

"(i) a deferral of the blackout period would violate the requirements of subparagraph (A) or (B) of section 404(a)(1), and a fiduciary of the plan reasonably so determines in writing, or

"(ii) the inability to provide the 30-day advance notice is due to events that were unforeseeable or circumstances beyond the reasonable control of the plan administrator, and a fiduciary of the plan reasonably so determines in writing,

subparagraph (B) shall not apply, and the notice shall be furnished to all participants and beneficiaries under the plan to whom the blackout period applies as soon as reasonably possible under the circumstances unless such a notice in advance of the termination of the blackout period is impracticable.

"(D) WRITTEN NOTICE.—The notice required to be provided under this subsection shall be in writing, except that such notice may be in electronic or other form to the extent that such form is reasonably accessible to the recipient.

"(E) NOTICE TO ISSUERS OF EMPLOYER SECURITIES SUBJECT TO BLACKOUT PERIOD.—In the case of any blackout period in connection with an individual account plan, the plan administrator shall provide timely notice of such

H.R. 3763—38

blackout period to the issuer of any employer securities subject to such blackout period.

"(3) EXCEPTION FOR BLACKOUT PERIODS WITH LIMITED APPLICABILITY.—In any case in which the blackout period applies only to 1 or more participants or beneficiaries in connection with a merger, acquisition, divestiture, or similar transaction involving the plan or plan sponsor and occurs solely in connection with becoming or ceasing to be a participant or beneficiary under the plan by reason of such merger, acquisition, divestiture, or transaction, the requirement of this subsection that the notice be provided to all participants and beneficiaries shall be treated as met if the notice required under paragraph (1) is provided to such participants or beneficiaries to whom the blackout period applies as soon as reasonably practicable.

"(4) CHANGES IN LENGTH OF BLACKOUT PERIOD.—If, following the furnishing of the notice pursuant to this subsection, there is a change in the beginning date or length of the blackout period (specified in such notice pursuant to paragraph (2)(A)(iii)), the administrator shall provide affected participants and beneficiaries notice of the change as soon as reasonably practicable. In relation to the extended blackout period, such notice shall meet the requirements of paragraph (2)(D) and shall specify any material change in the matters referred to in clauses (i) through (v) of paragraph (2)(A).

"(5) REGULATORY EXCEPTIONS.—The Secretary may provide by regulation for additional exceptions to the requirements of this subsection which the Secretary determines are in the interests of participants and beneficiaries.

"(6) GUIDANCE AND MODEL NOTICES.—The Secretary shall issue guidance and model notices which meet the requirements of this subsection.

"(7) BLACKOUT PERIOD.—For purposes of this subsection—

"(A) IN GENERAL.—The term 'blackout period' means, in connection with an individual account plan, any period for which any ability of participants or beneficiaries under the plan, which is otherwise available under the terms of such plan, to direct or diversify assets credited to their accounts, to obtain loans from the plan, or to obtain distributions from the plan is temporarily suspended, limited, or restricted, if such suspension, limitation, or restriction is for any period of more than 3 consecutive business days.

"(B) EXCLUSIONS.—The term 'blackout period' does not include a suspension, limitation, or restriction—

"(i) which occurs by reason of the application of the securities laws (as defined in section 3(a)(47) of the Securities Exchange Act of 1934),

"(ii) which is a change to the plan which provides for a regularly scheduled suspension, limitation, or restriction through any summary of material modifications, any materials describing specific investment alternatives under the plan, or any changes thereto, or

"(iii) which applies only to 1 or more individuals, each of whom is the participant, an alternate payee

H.R. 3763—39

(as defined in section 206(d)(3)(K)), or any other beneficiary pursuant to a qualified domestic relations order (as defined in section 206(d)(3)(B)(i)).

"(8) INDIVIDUAL ACCOUNT PLAN.—

"(A) IN GENERAL.—For purposes of this subsection, the term 'individual account plan' shall have the meaning provided such term in section 3(34), except that such term shall not include a one-participant retirement plan.

"(B) ONE-PARTICIPANT RETIREMENT PLAN.—For purposes of subparagraph (A), the term 'one-participant retirement plan' means a retirement plan that—

"(i) on the first day of the plan year—

"(I) covered only the employer (and the employer's spouse) and the employer owned the entire business (whether or not incorporated), or

"(II) covered only one or more partners (and their spouses) in a business partnership (including partners in an S or C corporation (as defined in section 1361(a) of the Internal Revenue Code of 1986)),

"(ii) meets the minimum coverage requirements of section 410(b) of the Internal Revenue Code of 1986 (as in effect on the date of the enactment of this paragraph) without being combined with any other plan of the business that covers the employees of the business,

"(iii) does not provide benefits to anyone except the employer (and the employer's spouse) or the partners (and their spouses),

"(iv) does not cover a business that is a member of an affiliated service group, a controlled group of corporations, or a group of businesses under common control, and

"(v) does not cover a business that leases employees.'.

(2) ISSUANCE OF INITIAL GUIDANCE AND MODEL NOTICE.— The Secretary of Labor shall issue initial guidance and a model notice pursuant to section 101(i)(6) of the Employee Retirement Income Security Act of 1974 (as added by this subsection) not later than January 1, 2003. Not later than 75 days after the date of the enactment of this Act, the Secretary shall promulgate interim final rules necessary to carry out the amendments made by this subsection.

(3) CIVIL PENALTIES FOR FAILURE TO PROVIDE NOTICE.— Section 502 of such Act (29 U.S.C. 1132) is amended—

(A) in subsection (a)(6), by striking "(5), or (6)" and inserting "(5), (6), or (7)";

(B) by redesignating paragraph (7) of subsection (c) as paragraph (8); and

(C) by inserting after paragraph (6) of subsection (c) the following new paragraph:

"(7) The Secretary may assess a civil penalty against a plan administrator of up to $100 a day from the date of the plan administrator's failure or refusal to provide notice to participants and beneficiaries in accordance with section 101(i). For purposes of this paragraph, each violation with respect to any single participant or beneficiary shall be treated as a separate violation.'.".

H.R. 3763—40

(3) PLAN AMENDMENTS.—If any amendment made by this subsection requires an amendment to any plan, such plan amendment shall not be required to be made before the first plan year beginning on or after the effective date of this section, if—

(A) during the period after such amendment made by this subsection takes effect and before such first plan year, the plan is operated in good faith compliance with the requirements of such amendment made by this subsection, and

(B) such plan amendment applies retroactively to the period after such amendment made by this subsection takes effect and before such first plan year.

(c) EFFECTIVE DATE.—The provisions of this section (including the amendments made thereby) shall take effect 180 days after the date of the enactment of this Act. Good faith compliance with the requirements of such provisions in advance of the issuance of applicable regulations thereunder shall be treated as compliance with such provisions.

SEC. 307. RULES OF PROFESSIONAL RESPONSIBILITY FOR ATTORNEYS.

Not later than 180 days after the date of enactment of this Act, the Commission shall issue rules, in the public interest and for the protection of investors, setting forth minimum standards of professional conduct for attorneys appearing and practicing before the Commission in any way in the representation of issuers, including a rule—

(1) requiring an attorney to report evidence of a material violation of securities law or breach of fiduciary duty or similar violation by the company or any agent thereof, to the chief legal counsel or the chief executive officer of the company (or the equivalent thereof); and

(2) if the counsel or officer does not appropriately respond to the evidence (adopting, as necessary, appropriate remedial measures or sanctions with respect to the violation), requiring the attorney to report the evidence to the audit committee of the board of directors of the issuer or to another committee of the board of directors comprised solely of directors not employed directly or indirectly by the issuer, or to the board of directors.

SEC. 308. FAIR FUNDS FOR INVESTORS.

(a) CIVIL PENALTIES ADDED TO DISGORGEMENT FUNDS FOR THE RELIEF OF VICTIMS.—If in any judicial or administrative action brought by the Commission under the securities laws (as such term is defined in section 3(a)(47) of the Securities Exchange Act of 1934 (15 U.S.C. 78c(a)(47)) the Commission obtains an order requiring disgorgement against any person for a violation of such laws or the rules or regulations thereunder, or such person agrees in settlement of any such action to such disgorgement, and the Commission also obtains pursuant to such laws a civil penalty against such person, the amount of such civil penalty shall, on the motion or at the direction of the Commission, be added to and become part of the disgorgement fund for the benefit of the victims of such violation.

(b) ACCEPTANCE OF ADDITIONAL DONATIONS.—The Commission is authorized to accept, hold, administer, and utilize gifts, bequests and devises of property, both real and personal, to the United

H.R. 3763—41

States for a disgorgement fund described in subsection (a). Such gifts, bequests, and devises of money and proceeds from sales of other property received as gifts, bequests, or devises shall be deposited in the disgorgement fund and shall be available for allocation in accordance with subsection (a).

(c) STUDY REQUIRED.—

(1) SUBJECT OF STUDY.—The Commission shall review and analyze—

(A) enforcement actions by the Commission over the five years preceding the date of the enactment of this Act that have included proceedings to obtain civil penalties or disgorgements to identify areas where such proceedings may be utilized to efficiently, effectively, and fairly provide restitution for injured investors; and

(B) other methods to more efficiently, effectively, and fairly provide restitution to injured investors, including methods to improve the collection rates for civil penalties and disgorgements.

(2) REPORT REQUIRED.—The Commission shall report its findings to the Committee on Financial Services of the House of Representatives and the Committee on Banking, Housing, and Urban Affairs of the Senate within 180 days after of the date of the enactment of this Act, and shall use such findings to revise its rules and regulations, as necessary. The report shall include a discussion of regulatory or legislative actions that are recommended or that may be necessary to address concerns identified in the study.

(d) CONFORMING AMENDMENTS.—Each of the following provisions is amended by inserting ", except as otherwise provided in section 308 of the Sarbanes-Oxley Act of 2002" after "Treasury of the United States":

(1) Section 21(d)(3)(C)(i) of the Securities Exchange Act of 1934 (15 U.S.C. 78u(d)(3)(C)(i)).

(2) Section 21A(d)(1) of such Act (15 U.S.C. 78u-1(d)(1)).

(3) Section 20(d)(3)(A) of the Securities Act of 1933 (15 U.S.C. 77t(d)(3)(A)).

(4) Section 42(e)(3)(A) of the Investment Company Act of 1940 (15 U.S.C. 80a-41(e)(3)(A)).

(5) Section 209(e)(3)(A) of the Investment Advisers Act of 1940 (15 U.S.C. 80b-9(e)(3)(A)).

(e) DEFINITION.—As used in this section, the term "disgorgement fund" means a fund established in any administrative or judicial proceeding described in subsection (a).

TITLE IV—ENHANCED FINANCIAL DISCLOSURES

SEC. 401. DISCLOSURES IN PERIODIC REPORTS.

(a) DISCLOSURES REQUIRED.—Section 13 of the Securities Exchange Act of 1934 (15 U.S.C. 78m) is amended by adding at the end the following:

"(i) ACCURACY OF FINANCIAL REPORTS.—Each financial report that contains financial statements, and that is required to be prepared in accordance with (or reconciled to) generally accepted accounting principles under this title and filed with the Commission shall reflect all material correcting adjustments that have been

H.R. 3763—42

identified by a registered public accounting firm in accordance with generally accepted accounting principles and the rules and regulations of the Commission.

"(j) OFF-BALANCE SHEET TRANSACTIONS.—Not later than 180 days after the date of enactment of the Sarbanes-Oxley Act of 2002, the Commission shall issue final rules providing that each annual and quarterly financial report required to be filed with the Commission shall disclose all material off-balance sheet transactions, arrangements, obligations (including contingent obligations), and other relationships of the issuer with unconsolidated entities or other persons, that may have a material current or future effect on financial condition, changes in financial condition, results of operations, liquidity, capital expenditures, capital resources, or significant components of revenues or expenses.".

(b) COMMISSION RULES ON PRO FORMA FIGURES.—Not later than 180 days after the date of enactment of the Sarbanes-Oxley Act fo 2002, the Commission shall issue final rules providing that pro forma financial information included in any periodic or other report filed with the Commission pursuant to the securities laws, or in any public disclosure or press or other release, shall be presented in a manner that—

(1) does not contain an untrue statement of a material fact or omit to state a material fact necessary in order to make the pro forma financial information, in light of the circumstances under which it is presented, not misleading; and

(2) reconciles it with the financial condition and results of operations of the issuer under generally accepted accounting principles.

(c) STUDY AND REPORT ON SPECIAL PURPOSE ENTITIES.—

(1) STUDY REQUIRED.—The Commission shall, not later than 1 year after the effective date of adoption of off-balance sheet disclosure rules required by section 13(j) of the Securities Exchange Act of 1934, as added by this section, complete a study of filings by issuers and their disclosures to determine—

(A) the extent of off-balance sheet transactions, including assets, liabilities, leases, losses, and the use of special purpose entities; and

(B) whether generally accepted accounting rules result in financial statements of issuers reflecting the economics of such off-balance sheet transactions to investors in a transparent fashion.

(2) REPORT AND RECOMMENDATIONS.—Not later than 6 months after the date of completion of the study required by paragraph (1), the Commission shall submit a report to the President, the Committee on Banking, Housing, and Urban Affairs of the Senate, and the Committee on Financial Services of the House of Representatives, setting forth—

(A) the amount or an estimate of the amount of off-balance sheet transactions, including assets, liabilities, leases, and losses of, and the use of special purpose entities by, issuers filing periodic reports pursuant to section 13 or 15 of the Securities Exchange Act of 1934;

(B) the extent to which special purpose entities are used to facilitate off-balance sheet transactions;

H.R. 3763—43

"(C) whether generally accepted accounting principles or the rules of the Commission result in financial statements of issuers reflecting the economics of such transactions to investors in a transparent fashion;

"(D) whether generally accepted accounting principles specifically result in the consolidation of special purpose entities sponsored by an issuer in cases in which the issuer has the majority of the risks and rewards of the special purpose entity; and

"(E) any recommendations of the Commission for improving the transparency and quality of reporting off-balance sheet transactions in the financial statements and disclosures required to be filed by an issuer with the Commission.

SEC. 402. ENHANCED CONFLICT OF INTEREST PROVISIONS.

(a) PROHIBITION ON PERSONAL LOANS TO EXECUTIVES.—Section 13 of the Securities Exchange Act of 1934 (15 U.S.C. 78m), as amended by this Act, is amended by adding at the end the following:

"(k) PROHIBITION ON PERSONAL LOANS TO EXECUTIVES.—

"(1) IN GENERAL.—It shall be unlawful for any issuer (as defined in section 2 of the Sarbanes-Oxley Act of 2002), directly or indirectly, including through any subsidiary, to extend or maintain credit, to arrange for the extension of credit, or to renew an extension of credit, in the form of a personal loan to or for any director or executive officer (or equivalent thereof) of that issuer. An extension of credit maintained by the issuer on the date of enactment of this subsection shall not be subject to the provisions of this subsection, provided that there is no material modification to any term of any such extension of credit or any renewal of any such extension of credit on or after that date of enactment.

"(2) LIMITATION.—Paragraph (1) does not preclude any home improvement and manufactured home loans (as that term is defined in section 5 of the Home Owners' Loan Act (12 U.S.C. 1464)), consumer credit (as defined in section 103 of the Truth in Lending Act (15 U.S.C. 1602)), or any extension of credit under an open end credit plan (as defined in section 103 of the Truth in Lending Act (15 U.S.C. 1602)), or a charge card (as defined in section 127(c)(4)(e) of the Truth in Lending Act (15 U.S.C. 1637(c)(4)(e)), or any extension of credit by a broker or dealer registered under section 15 of this title to an employee of that broker or dealer to buy, trade, or carry securities, that is permitted under rules or regulations of the Board of Governors of the Federal Reserve System pursuant to section 7 of this title (other than an extension of credit that would be used to purchase the stock of that issuer), that is—

"(A) made or provided in the ordinary course of the consumer credit business of such issuer;

"(B) of a type that is generally made available by such issuer to the public; and

"(C) made by such issuer on market terms, or terms that are no more favorable than those offered by the issuer to the general public for such extensions of credit.

"(3) RULE OF CONSTRUCTION FOR CERTAIN LOANS.—Paragraph (1) does not apply to any loan made or maintained

---

H.R. 3763—44

by an insured depository institution (as defined in section 3 of the Federal Deposit Insurance Act (12 U.S.C. 1813)), if the loan is subject to the insider lending restrictions of section 22(h) of the Federal Reserve Act (12 U.S.C. 375b).".

SEC. 403. DISCLOSURES OF TRANSACTIONS INVOLVING MANAGEMENT AND PRINCIPAL STOCKHOLDERS.

(a) AMENDMENT.—Section 16 of the Securities Exchange Act of 1934 (15 U.S.C. 78p) is amended by striking the heading of such section and subsection (a) and inserting the following:

"SEC. 16. DIRECTORS, OFFICERS, AND PRINCIPAL STOCKHOLDERS.

"(a) DISCLOSURES REQUIRED.—

"(1) DIRECTORS, OFFICERS, AND PRINCIPAL STOCKHOLDERS REQUIRED TO FILE.—Every person who is directly or indirectly the beneficial owner of more than 10 percent of any class of any equity security (other than an exempted security) which is registered pursuant to section 12, or who is a director or an officer of the issuer of such security, shall file the statements required by this subsection with the Commission (and, if such security is registered on a national securities exchange, also with the exchange).

"(2) TIME OF FILING.—The statements required by this subsection shall be filed—

"(A) at the time of the registration of such security on a national securities exchange or by the effective date of a registration statement filed pursuant to section 12(g);

"(B) within 10 days after he or she becomes such beneficial owner, director, or officer;

"(C) if there has been a change in such ownership, or if such person shall have purchased or sold a security-based swap agreement (as defined in section 206(b) of the Gramm-Leach-Bliley Act (15 U.S.C. 78c note)) involving such equity security, before the end of the second business day following the day on which the subject transaction has been executed, or at such other time as the Commission shall establish, by rule, in any case in which the Commission determines that such 2-day period is not feasible.

"(3) CONTENTS OF STATEMENTS.—A statement filed—

"(A) under subparagraph (A) or (B) of paragraph (2) shall contain a statement of the amount of all equity securities of such issuer of which the filing person is the beneficial owner; and

"(B) under subparagraph (C) of such paragraph shall indicate ownership by the filing person at the date of filing, any such changes in such ownership, and such purchases and sales of the security-based swap agreements as have occurred since the most recent such filing under such subparagraph.

"(4) ELECTRONIC FILING AND AVAILABILITY.—Beginning not later than 1 year after the date of enactment of the Sarbanes-Oxley Act of 2002—

"(A) a statement filed under subparagraph (C) of paragraph (2) shall be filed electronically;

"(B) the Commission shall provide each such statement on a publicly accessible Internet site not later than the end of the business day following that filing; and

H. R. 3763—45

"(C) the issuer (if the issuer maintains a corporate website) shall provide that statement on that corporate website, not later than the end of the business day following that filing.".

(b) EFFECTIVE DATE.—The amendment made by this section shall be effective 30 days after the date of the enactment of this Act.

SEC. 404. MANAGEMENT ASSESSMENT OF INTERNAL CONTROLS.

(a) RULES REQUIRED.—The Commission shall prescribe rules requiring each annual report required by section 13(a) or 15(d) of the Securities Exchange Act of 1934 (15 U.S.C. 78m or 78o(d)) to contain an internal control report, which shall—

(1) state the responsibility of management for establishing and maintaining an adequate internal control structure and procedures for financial reporting; and

(2) contain an assessment, as of the end of the most recent fiscal year of the issuer, of the effectiveness of the internal control structure and procedures of the issuer for financial reporting.

(b) INTERNAL CONTROL EVALUATION AND REPORTING.—With respect to the internal control assessment required by subsection (a), each registered public accounting firm that prepares or issues the audit report for the issuer shall attest to, and report on, the assessment made by the management of the issuer. An attestation made under this subsection shall be made in accordance with standards for attestation engagements issued or adopted by the Board. Any such attestation shall not be the subject of a separate engagement.

SEC. 405. EXEMPTION.

Nothing in section 401, 402, or 404, the amendments made by those sections, or the rules of the Commission under those sections shall apply to any investment company registered under section 8 of the Investment Company Act of 1940 (15 U.S.C. 80a-8).

SEC. 406. CODE OF ETHICS FOR SENIOR FINANCIAL OFFICERS.

(a) CODE OF ETHICS DISCLOSURE.—The Commission shall issue rules to require each issuer, together with periodic reports required pursuant to section 13(a) or 15(d) of the Securities Exchange Act of 1934, to disclose whether or not, and if not, the reason therefor, such issuer has adopted a code of ethics for senior financial officers, applicable to its principal financial officer and comptroller or principal accounting officer, or persons performing similar functions.

(b) CHANGES IN CODES OF ETHICS.—The Commission shall revise its regulations concerning matters requiring prompt disclosure on Form 8-K (or any successor thereto) to require the immediate disclosure, by means of the filing of such forms, dissemination by the Internet or by other electronic means, by any issuer of any change in or waiver of the code of ethics for senior financial officers.

(c) DEFINITION.—In this section, the term "code of ethics" means such standards as are reasonably necessary to promote—

(1) honest and ethical conduct, including the ethical handling of actual or apparent conflicts of interest between personal and professional relationships;

H. R. 3763—46

(2) full, fair, accurate, timely, and understandable disclosure in the periodic reports required to be filed by the issuer; and

(3) compliance with applicable governmental rules and regulations.

(d) DEADLINE FOR RULEMAKING.—The Commission shall—

(1) propose rules to implement this section, not later than 30 days after the date of enactment of this Act; and

(2) issue final rules to implement this section, not later than 180 days after that date of enactment.

SEC. 407. DISCLOSURE OF AUDIT COMMITTEE FINANCIAL EXPERT.

(a) RULES DEFINING "FINANCIAL EXPERT".—The Commission shall issue rules, as necessary or appropriate in the public interest and consistent with the protection of investors, to require each issuer, together with periodic reports required pursuant to sections 13(a) and 15(d) of the Securities Exchange Act of 1934, to disclose whether or not, and if not, the reasons therefor, the audit committee of that issuer is comprised of at least 1 member who is a financial expert, as such term is defined by the Commission.

(b) CONSIDERATIONS.—In defining the term "financial expert" for purposes of subsection (a), the Commission shall consider whether a person has, through education and experience as a public accountant or auditor or a principal financial officer, comptroller, or principal accounting officer of an issuer, or from a position involving the performance of similar functions—

(1) an understanding of generally accepted accounting principles and financial statements;

(2) experience in—

(A) the preparation or auditing of financial statements of generally comparable issuers; and

(B) the application of such principles in connection with the accounting for estimates, accruals, and reserves;

(3) experience with internal accounting controls; and

(4) an understanding of audit committee functions.

(c) DEADLINE FOR RULEMAKING.—The Commission shall—

(1) propose rules to implement this section, not later than 90 days after the date of enactment of this Act; and

(2) issue final rules to implement this section, not later than 180 days after that date of enactment.

SEC. 408. ENHANCED REVIEW OF PERIODIC DISCLOSURES BY ISSUERS.

(a) REGULAR AND SYSTEMATIC REVIEW.—The Commission shall review disclosures made by issuers reporting under section 13(a) of the Securities Exchange Act of 1934 (including reports filed on Form 10-K), and which have a class of securities listed on a national securities exchange or traded on an automated quotation facility of a national securities association, on a regular and systematic basis for the protection of investors. Such review shall include a review of an issuer's financial statement.

(b) REVIEW CRITERIA.—For purposes of scheduling the reviews required by subsection (a), the Commission shall consider, among other factors—

(1) issuers that have issued material restatements of financial results;

(2) issuers that experience significant volatility in their stock price as compared to other issuers;

(3) issuers with the largest market capitalization;

(4) emerging companies with disparities in price to earning ratios;

(5) issuers whose operations significantly affect any material sector of the economy; and

(6) any other factors that the Commission may consider relevant.

(c) MINIMUM REVIEW PERIOD.—In no event shall an issuer required to file reports under section 13(a) or 15(d) of the Securities Exchange Act of 1934 be reviewed under this section less frequently than once every 3 years.

SEC. 409. REAL TIME ISSUER DISCLOSURES.

Section 13 of the Securities Exchange Act of 1934 (15 U.S.C. 78m), as amended by this Act, is amended by adding at the end the following:

"(l) REAL TIME ISSUER DISCLOSURES.—Each issuer reporting under section 13(a) or 15(d) shall disclose to the public on a rapid and current basis such additional information concerning the issuer, in plain English, which may include trend and qualitative information and graphic presentations, as the Commission determines, by rule, is necessary or useful for the protection of investors and in the public interest."

TITLE V—ANALYST CONFLICTS OF INTEREST

SEC. 501. TREATMENT OF SECURITIES ANALYSTS BY REGISTERED SECURITIES ASSOCIATIONS AND NATIONAL SECURITIES EXCHANGES.

(a) RULES REGARDING SECURITIES ANALYSTS.—The Securities Exchange Act of 1934 (15 U.S.C. 78a et seq.) is amended by inserting after section 15C the following new section:

"SEC. 15D. SECURITIES ANALYSTS AND RESEARCH REPORTS.

"(a) ANALYST PROTECTIONS.—The Commission, or upon the authorization and direction of the Commission, a registered securities association or national securities exchange, shall have adopted, not later than 1 year after the date of enactment of this section, rules reasonably designed to address conflicts of interest that can arise when securities analysts recommend equity securities in research reports and public appearances, in order to improve the objectivity of research and provide investors with more useful and reliable information, including rules designed—

"(1) to foster greater public confidence in securities research, and to protect the objectivity and independence of securities analysts, by—

"(A) restricting the prepublication clearance or approval of research reports by persons employed by the broker or dealer who are engaged in investment banking activities, or persons not directly responsible for investment research, other than legal or compliance staff;

"(B) limiting the supervision and compensatory evaluation of securities analysts to officials employed by the broker or dealer who are not engaged in investment banking activities; and

"(C) requiring that a broker or dealer and persons employed by a broker or dealer who are involved with investment banking activities may not, directly or indirectly, retaliate against or threaten to retaliate against any securities analyst employed by that broker or dealer or its affiliates as a result of an adverse, negative, or otherwise unfavorable research report that may adversely affect the present or prospective investment banking relationship of the broker or dealer with the issuer that is the subject of the research report, except that such rules may not limit the authority of a broker or dealer to discipline a securities analyst for causes other than such research report in accordance with the policies and procedures of the firm;

"(2) to define periods during which brokers or dealers who have participated, or are to participate, in a public offering of securities as underwriters or dealers should not publish or otherwise distribute research reports relating to such securities or to the issuer of such securities;

"(3) to establish structural and institutional safeguards within registered brokers or dealers to assure that securities analysts are separated by appropriate informational partitions within the firm from the review, pressure, or oversight of those whose involvement in investment banking activities might potentially bias their judgment or supervision; and

"(4) to address such other issues as the Commission, or such association or exchange, determines appropriate.

"(b) DISCLOSURE.—The Commission, or upon the authorization and direction of the Commission, a registered securities association or national securities exchange, shall have adopted, not later than 1 year after the date of enactment of this section, rules reasonably designed to require each securities analyst to disclose in public appearances, and each registered broker or dealer to disclose in each research report, as applicable, conflicts of interest that are known or should have been known by the securities analyst or the broker or dealer, to exist at the time of the appearance or the date of distribution of the report, including—

"(1) the extent to which the securities analyst has debt or equity investments in the issuer that is the subject of the appearance or research report;

"(2) whether any compensation has been received by the registered broker or dealer, or any affiliate thereof, including the securities analyst, from the issuer that is the subject of the appearance or research report, subject to such exemptions as the Commission may determine appropriate and necessary to prevent disclosure by virtue of this paragraph of material non-public information regarding specific potential future investment banking transactions of such issuer, as is appropriate in the public interest and consistent with the protection of investors;

"(3) whether an issuer, the securities of which are recommended in the appearance or research report, currently is, or during the 1-year period preceding the date of the appearance or date of distribution of the report has been, a client of the registered broker or dealer, and if so, stating the types of services provided to the issuer;

"(4) whether the securities analyst received compensation with respect to a research report, based upon (among any other factors) the investment banking revenues (either generally or specifically earned from the issuer being analyzed) of the registered broker or dealer; and

"(5) such other disclosures of conflicts of interest that are material to investors, research analysts, or the broker or dealer as the Commission, or such association or exchange, determines appropriate.

"(c) DEFINITIONS.—In this section—

"(1) the term 'securities analyst' means any associated person of a registered broker or dealer that is principally responsible for, and any associated person who reports directly or indirectly to a securities analyst in connection with, the preparation of a research report, whether or not any such person has the job title of 'securities analyst'; and

"(2) the term 'research report' means a written or electronic communication that includes an analysis of equity securities of individual companies or industries, and that provides information reasonably sufficient upon which to base an investment decision.".

(b) ENFORCEMENT.—Section 21B(a) of the Securities Exchange Act of 1934 (15 U.S.C. 78u-2(a)) is amended by inserting "15D," before "15B".

(c) COMMISSION AUTHORITY.—The Commission may promulgate and amend its regulations, or direct a registered securities association or national securities exchange to promulgate and amend its rules, to carry out section 15D of the Securities Exchange Act of 1934, as added by this section, as is necessary for the protection of investors and in the public interest.

TITLE VI—COMMISSION RESOURCES AND AUTHORITY

SEC. 601. AUTHORIZATION OF APPROPRIATIONS.

Section 35 of the Securities Exchange Act of 1934 (15 U.S.C. 78kk) is amended to read as follows:

"SEC. 35. AUTHORIZATION OF APPROPRIATIONS.

"In addition to any other funds authorized to be appropriated to the Commission, there are authorized to be appropriated to carry out the functions, powers, and duties of the Commission, $776,000,000 for fiscal year 2003, of which—

"(1) $102,700,000 shall be available to fund additional compensation, including salaries and benefits, as authorized in the Investor and Capital Markets Fee Relief Act (Public Law 107–123; 115 Stat. 2390 et seq.);

"(2) $108,400,000 shall be available for information technology, security enhancements, and recovery and mitigation activities in light of the terrorist attacks of September 11, 2001; and

"(3) $98,000,000 shall be available to add not fewer than an additional 200 qualified professionals to provide enhanced oversight of auditors and audit services required by the Federal securities laws, and to improve Commission investigative and

ciplinary efforts with respect to such auditors and services, as well as for additional professional support staff necessary to strengthen the programs of the Commission involving Full Disclosure and Prevention and Suppression of Fraud, risk management, industry technology review, compliance, inspections, examinations, market regulation, and investment management.".

SEC. 602. APPEARANCE AND PRACTICE BEFORE THE COMMISSION.

The Securities Exchange Act of 1934 (15 U.S.C. 78a et seq.) is amended by inserting after section 4B the following:

"SEC. 4C. APPEARANCE AND PRACTICE BEFORE THE COMMISSION.

"(a) AUTHORITY TO CENSURE.—The Commission may censure any person, or deny, temporarily or permanently, to any person the privilege of appearing or practicing before the Commission in any way, if that person is found by the Commission, after notice and opportunity for hearing in the matter—

"(1) not to possess the requisite qualifications to represent others;

"(2) to be lacking in character or integrity, or to have engaged in unethical or improper professional conduct; or

"(3) to have willfully violated, or willfully aided and abetted the violation of, any provision of the securities laws or the rules and regulations issued thereunder.

"(b) DEFINITION.—With respect to any registered public accounting firm or associated person, for purposes of this section, the term 'improper professional conduct' means—

"(1) intentional or knowing conduct, including reckless conduct, that results in a violation of applicable professional standards; and

"(2) negligent conduct in the form of—

"(A) a single instance of highly unreasonable conduct that results in a violation of applicable professional standards in circumstances in which the registered public accounting firm or associated person knows, or should know, that heightened scrutiny is warranted; or

"(B) repeated instances of unreasonable conduct, each resulting in a violation of applicable professional standards, that indicate a lack of competence to practice before the Commission.".

SEC. 603. FEDERAL COURT AUTHORITY TO IMPOSE PENNY STOCK BARS.

(a) SECURITIES EXCHANGE ACT OF 1934.—Section 21(d) of the Securities Exchange Act of 1934 (15 U.S.C. 78u(d)), as amended by this Act, is amended by adding at the end the following:

"(6) AUTHORITY OF A COURT TO PROHIBIT PERSONS FROM PARTICIPATING IN AN OFFERING OF PENNY STOCK.—

"(A) IN GENERAL.—In any proceeding under paragraph (1) against any person participating in, or, at the time of the alleged misconduct who was participating in, an offering of penny stock, the court may prohibit that person from participating in an offering of penny stock, conditionally or unconditionally, and permanently or for such period of time as the court shall determine.

"(B) DEFINITION.—For purposes of this paragraph, the term 'person participating in an offering of penny stock' includes

H.R. 3763—51

any person engaging in activities with a broker, dealer, or issuer for purposes of issuing, trading, or inducing or attempting to induce the purchase or sale of, any penny stock. The Commission may, by rule or regulation, define such term to include other activities, and may, by rule, regulation, or order, exempt any person or class of persons, in whole or in part, conditionally or unconditionally, from inclusion in such term.''

(b) SECURITIES ACT OF 1933.—Section 20 of the Securities Act of 1933 (15 U.S.C. 77t) is amended by adding at the end the following:

''(g) AUTHORITY OF A COURT TO PROHIBIT PERSONS FROM PARTICIPATING IN AN OFFERING OF PENNY STOCK.—

''(1) IN GENERAL.—In any proceeding under subsection (a) against any person participating in, or, at the time of the alleged misconduct, who was participating in, an offering of penny stock, the court may prohibit that person from participating in an offering of penny stock, conditionally or unconditionally, and permanently or for such period of time as the court shall determine.

''(2) DEFINITION.—For purposes of this subsection, the term 'person participating in an offering of penny stock' includes any person engaging in activities with a broker, dealer, or issuer for purposes of issuing, trading, or inducing or attempting to induce the purchase or sale of, any penny stock. The Commission may, by rule or regulation, define such term to include other activities, and may, by rule, regulation, or order, exempt any person or class of persons, in whole or in part, conditionally or unconditionally, from inclusion in such term.''

SEC. 604. QUALIFICATIONS OF ASSOCIATED PERSONS OF BROKERS AND DEALERS.

(a) BROKERS AND DEALERS.—Section 15(b)(4) of the Securities Exchange Act of 1934 (15 U.S.C. 78o) is amended—

(1) by striking subparagraph (F) and inserting the following:

''(F) is subject to any order of the Commission barring or suspending the right of the person to be associated with a broker or dealer''; and

(2) in subparagraph (G), by striking the period at the end and inserting the following: ''; or

''(H) is subject to any final order of a State securities commission (or any agency or officer performing like functions), State authority that supervises or examines banks, savings associations, or credit unions, State insurance commission (or any agency or office performing like functions), an appropriate Federal banking agency (as defined in section 3 of the Federal Deposit Insurance Act (12 U.S.C. 1813(q))), or the National Credit Union Administration, that—

''(i) bars such person from association with an entity regulated by such commission, authority, agency, or officer, or from engaging in the business of securities, insurance, banking, savings association activities, or credit union activities; or

H.R. 3763—52

''(ii) constitutes a final order based on violations of any laws or regulations that prohibit fraudulent, manipulative, or deceptive conduct.''

(b) INVESTMENT ADVISERS.—Section 203(e) of the Investment Advisers Act of 1940 (15 U.S.C. 80b–3(e)) is amended—

(1) by striking paragraph (7) and inserting the following:

''(7) is subject to any order of the Commission barring or suspending the right of the person to be associated with an investment adviser;'';

(2) in paragraph (8), by striking the period at the end and inserting ''; or''; and

(3) by adding at the end the following:

''(9) is subject to any final order of a State securities commission (or any agency or officer performing like functions), State authority that supervises or examines banks, savings associations, or credit unions, State insurance commission (or any agency or office performing like functions), an appropriate Federal banking agency (as defined in section 3 of the Federal Deposit Insurance Act (12 U.S.C. 1813(q))), or the National Credit Union Administration, that—

''(A) bars such person from association with an entity regulated by such commission, authority, agency, or officer, or from engaging in the business of securities, insurance, banking, savings association activities, or credit union activities, or

''(B) constitutes a final order based on violations of any laws or regulations that prohibit fraudulent, manipulative, or deceptive conduct.''

(c) CONFORMING AMENDMENTS.—

(1) SECURITIES EXCHANGE ACT OF 1934.—The Securities Exchange Act of 1934 (15 U.S.C. 78a et seq.) is amended—

(A) in section 3(a)(39)(F) (15 U.S.C. 78c(a)(39)(F))—

(i) by striking ''or (G)'' and inserting ''(H), or (G)'', and

(ii) by inserting '', or is subject to an order or finding,'' before ''enumerated'';

(B) in each of section 15(b)(6)(A)(i) (15 U.S.C. 78o(b)(6)(A)(i)), paragraphs (2) and (4) of section 15B(c) (15 U.S.C. 78o–4(c)), and subparagraphs (A) and (C) of section 15C(c)(1) (15 U.S.C. 78o–5(c)(1))—

(i) by striking ''or (G)'' each place that term appears and inserting ''(H), or (G)'', and

(ii) by striking ''or omission'' each place that term appears, and inserting '', or is subject to an order or finding,'', and

(C) in each of paragraphs (3)(A) and (4)(C) of section 17A(c) (15 U.S.C. 78q–1(c))—

(i) by striking ''or (G)'' each place that term appears and inserting ''(H), or (G)'', and

(ii) by inserting '', or is subject to an order or finding,'' before ''enumerated'' each place that term appears.

(2) INVESTMENT ADVISERS ACT OF 1940.—Section 203(f) of the Investment Advisers Act of 1940 (15 U.S.C. 80b–3(f)) is amended—

(A) by striking ''or (8)'' and inserting ''(8), or (9)'', and

(B) by inserting ''or (3)'' after ''paragraph (2)''.

H. R. 3763—53

TITLE VII—STUDIES AND REPORTS

SEC. 701. GAO STUDY AND REPORT REGARDING CONSOLIDATION OF PUBLIC ACCOUNTING FIRMS.

(a) STUDY REQUIRED.—The Comptroller General of the United States shall conduct a study—

(1) to identify—

(A) the factors that have led to the consolidation of public accounting firms since 1989 and the consequent reduction in the number of firms capable of providing audit services to large national and multi-national business organizations that are subject to the securities laws;

(B) the present and future impact of the condition described in subparagraph (A) on capital formation and securities markets, both domestic and international; and

(C) solutions to any problems identified under subparagraph (B), including ways to increase competition and the number of firms capable of providing audit services to large national and multinational business organizations that are subject to the securities laws;

(2) of the problems, if any, faced by business organizations that have resulted from limited competition among public accounting firms, including—

(A) higher costs;

(B) lower quality of services;

(C) impairment of auditor independence; or

(D) lack of choice; and

(3) whether and to what extent Federal or State regulations impede competition among public accounting firms.

(b) CONSULTATION.—In planning and conducting the study under this section, the Comptroller General shall consult with—

(1) the Commission;

(2) the regulatory agencies that perform functions similar to the Commission within the other member countries of the Group of Seven Industrialized Nations;

(3) the Department of Justice; and

(4) any other public or private sector organization that the Comptroller General considers appropriate.

(c) REPORT REQUIRED.—Not later than 1 year after the date of enactment of this Act, the Comptroller General shall submit a report on the results of the study required by this section to the Committee on Banking, Housing, and Urban Affairs of the Senate and the Committee on Financial Services of the House of Representatives.

SEC. 702. COMMISSION STUDY AND REPORT REGARDING CREDIT RATING AGENCIES.

(a) STUDY REQUIRED.—

(1) IN GENERAL.—The Commission shall conduct a study of the role and function of credit rating agencies in the operation of the securities market.

(2) AREAS OF CONSIDERATION.—The study required by this subsection shall examine—

(A) the role of credit rating agencies in the evaluation of issuers of securities;

H. R. 3763—54

(B) the importance of that role to investors and the functioning of the securities markets;

(C) any impediments to the accurate appraisal by credit rating agencies of the financial resources and risks of issuers of securities;

(D) any barriers to entry into the business of acting as a credit rating agency, and any measures needed to remove such barriers;

(E) any measures which may be required to improve the dissemination of information concerning such resources and risks when credit rating agencies announce credit ratings; and

(F) any conflicts of interest in the operation of credit rating agencies and measures to prevent such conflicts or ameliorate the consequences of such conflicts.

(b) REPORT REQUIRED.—The Commission shall submit a report or the study required by subsection (a) to the President, the Committee on Financial Services of the House of Representatives, and the Committee on Banking, Housing, and Urban Affairs of the Senate not later than 180 days after the date of enactment of this Act.

SEC. 703. STUDY AND REPORT ON VIOLATORS AND VIOLATIONS.

(a) STUDY.—The Commission shall conduct a study to determine, based upon information for the period from January 1, 1998, to December 31, 2001—

(1) the number of securities professionals, defined as public accountants, public accounting firms, investment bankers, investment advisers, brokers, dealers, attorneys, and other securities professionals practicing before the Commission—

(A) who have been found to have aided and abetted a violation of the Federal securities laws, including rules or regulations promulgated thereunder (collectively referred to in this section as "Federal securities laws"), but who have not been sanctioned, disciplined, or otherwise penalized as a primary violator in any administrative action or civil proceeding, including in any settlement of such an action or proceeding (referred to in this section as "aiders and abettors"); and

(B) who have been found to have been primary violators of the Federal securities laws;

(2) a description of the Federal securities laws violations committed by aiders and abettors and by primary violators, including—

(A) the specific provision of the Federal securities laws violated;

(B) the specific sanctions and penalties imposed upon such aiders and abettors and primary violators, including the amount of any monetary penalties assessed upon and collected from such persons;

(C) the occurrence of multiple violations by the same person or persons, either as an aider or abettor or as a primary violator; and

(D) whether, as to each such violator, disciplinary sanctions have been imposed, including any censure, suspension, temporary bar, or permanent bar to practice before the Commission; and

H.R. 3763—55

(3) the amount of disgorgement, restitution, or any other fines or payments that the Commission has assessed upon and collected from, aiders and abettors and from primary violators.

(b) REPORT.—A report based upon the study conducted pursuant to subsection (a) shall be submitted to the Committee on Banking, Housing, and Urban Affairs of the Senate, and the Committee on Financial Services of the House of Representatives not later than 6 months after the date of enactment of this Act.

SEC. 704. STUDY OF ENFORCEMENT ACTIONS.

(a) STUDY REQUIRED.—The Commission shall review and analyze all enforcement actions by the Commission involving violations of reporting requirements imposed under the securities laws, and restatements of financial statements, over the 5-year period preceding the date of enactment of this Act, to identify areas of reporting that are most susceptible to fraud, inappropriate manipulation, or inappropriate earnings management, such as revenue recognition and the accounting treatment of off-balance sheet special purpose entities.

(b) REPORT REQUIRED.—The Commission shall report its findings to the Committee on Financial Services of the House of Representatives and the Committee on Banking, Housing, and Urban Affairs of the Senate, not later than 180 days after the date of enactment of this Act, and shall use such findings to revise its rules and regulations, as necessary. The report shall include a discussion of regulatory or legislative steps that are recommended or that may be necessary to address concerns identified in the study.

SEC. 705. STUDY OF INVESTMENT BANKS.

(a) GAO STUDY.—The Comptroller General of the United States shall conduct a study on whether investment banks and financial advisers assisted public companies in manipulating their earnings and obfuscating their true financial condition. The study should address the rule of investment banks and financial advisers—

(1) in the collapse of the Enron Corporation, including with respect to the design and implementation of derivatives transactions, transactions involving special purpose vehicles, and other financial arrangements that may have had the effect of altering the company's reported financial statements in ways that obscured the true financial picture of the company;

(2) in the failure of Global Crossing, including with respect to transactions involving swaps of fiberoptic cable capacity, in the designing transactions that may have had the effect of altering the company's reported financial statements in ways that obscured the true financial picture of the company; and

(3) generally, in creating and marketing transactions which may have been designed solely to enable companies to manipulate revenue streams, obtain loans, or move liabilities off balance sheets without altering the economic and business risks faced by the companies or any other mechanism to obscure a company's financial picture.

(b) REPORT.—The Comptroller General shall report to Congress not later than 180 days after the date of enactment of this Act on the results of the study required by this section. The report shall include a discussion of regulatory or legislative steps that

H.R. 3763—56

are recommended or that may be necessary to address concerns identified in the study.

TITLE VIII—CORPORATE AND CRIMINAL FRAUD ACCOUNTABILITY

SEC. 801. SHORT TITLE.

This title may be cited as the "Corporate and Criminal Fraud Accountability Act of 2002".

SEC. 802. CRIMINAL PENALTIES FOR ALTERING DOCUMENTS.

(a) IN GENERAL.—Chapter 73 of title 18, United States Code, is amended by adding at the end the following:

"§ 1519. Destruction, alteration, or falsification of records in Federal investigations and bankruptcy

"Whoever knowingly alters, destroys, mutilates, conceals, covers up, falsifies, or makes a false entry in any record, document, or tangible object with the intent to impede, obstruct, or influence the investigation or proper administration of any matter within the jurisdiction of any department or agency of the United States or any case filed under title 11, or in relation to or contemplation of any such matter or case, shall be fined under this title, imprisoned not more than 20 years, or both.

"§ 1520. Destruction of corporate audit records

"(a)(1) Any accountant who conducts an audit of an issuer of securities to which section 10A(a) of the Securities Exchange Act of 1934 (15 U.S.C. 78j–1(a)) applies, shall maintain all audit or review workpapers for a period of 5 years from the end of the fiscal period in which the audit or review was concluded.

"(2) The Securities and Exchange Commission shall promulgate, within 180 days, after adequate notice and an opportunity for comment, such rules and regulations, as are reasonably necessary, relating to the retention of relevant records such as workpapers, documents that form the basis of an audit or review, memoranda, correspondence, communications, other documents, and records (including electronic records) which are created, sent, or received in connection with an audit or review and contain conclusions, opinions, analyses, or financial data relating to such an audit or review, which is conducted by any accountant who conducts an audit of an issuer of securities to which section 10A(a) of the Securities Exchange Act of 1934 (15 U.S.C. 78j–1(a)) applies. The Commission may, from time to time, amend or supplement the rules and regulations that it is required to promulgate under this section, after adequate notice and an opportunity for comment, in order to ensure that, such rules and regulations adequately comport with the purposes of this section.

"(b) Whoever knowingly and willfully violates subsection (a)(1), or any rule or regulation promulgated by the Securities and Exchange Commission under subsection (a)(2), shall be fined under this title, imprisoned not more than 10 years, or both.

"(c) Nothing in this section shall be deemed to diminish or relieve any person of any other duty or obligation imposed by Federal or State law or regulation to maintain, or refrain from destroying, any document.".

H.R. 3763—57

(b) CLERICAL AMENDMENT.—The table of sections at the beginning of chapter 73 of title 18, United States Code, is amended by adding at the end the following new items:

"1519. Destruction, alteration, or falsification of records in Federal investigations and bankruptcy.

"1520. Destruction of corporate audit records."

SEC. 803. DEBTS NONDISCHARGEABLE IF INCURRED IN VIOLATION OF SECURITIES FRAUD LAWS.

Section 523(a) of title 11, United States Code, is amended—
(1) in paragraph (17), by striking "or" after the semicolon;
(2) in paragraph (18), by striking the period at the end and inserting "; or"; and
(3) by adding at the end, the following:
"(19) that—
"(A) is for—
"(i) the violation of any of the Federal securities laws (as that term is defined in section 3(a)(47) of the Securities Exchange Act of 1934), any of the State securities laws, or any regulation or order issued under such Federal or State securities laws; or
"(ii) common law fraud, deceit, or manipulation in connection with the purchase or sale of any security; and
"(B) results from—
"(i) any judgment, order, consent order, or decree entered in any Federal or State judicial or administrative proceeding;
"(ii) any settlement agreement entered into by the debtor; or
"(iii) any court or administrative order for any damages, fine, penalty, citation, restitutionary payment, disgorgement payment, attorney fee, cost, or other payment owed by the debtor."

SEC. 804. STATUTE OF LIMITATIONS FOR SECURITIES FRAUD.

(a) IN GENERAL.—Section 1658 of title 28, United States Code, is amended—
(1) by inserting "(a)" before "Except"; and
(2) by adding at the end the following:
"(b) Notwithstanding subsection (a), a private right of action that involves a claim of fraud, deceit, manipulation, or contrivance in contravention of a regulatory requirement concerning the securities laws, as defined in section 3(a)(47) of the Securities Exchange Act of 1934 (15 U.S.C. 78c(a)(47)), may be brought not later than the earlier of—
"(1) 2 years after the discovery of the facts constituting the violation; or
"(2) 5 years after such violation.".

(b) EFFECTIVE DATE.—The limitations period provided by section 1658(b) of title 28, United States Code, as added by this section, shall apply to all proceedings addressed by this section that are commenced on or after the date of enactment of this Act.

(c) NO CREATION OF ACTIONS.—Nothing in this section shall create a new, private right of action.

H.R. 3763—58

SEC. 805. REVIEW OF FEDERAL SENTENCING GUIDELINES FOR OBSTRUCTION OF JUSTICE AND EXTENSIVE CRIMINAL FRAUD.

(a) ENHANCEMENT OF FRAUD AND OBSTRUCTION OF JUSTICE SENTENCES.—Pursuant to section 994 of title 28, United States Code, and in accordance with this section, the United States Sentencing Commission shall review and amend, as appropriate, the Federal Sentencing Guidelines and related policy statements to ensure that—
(1) the base offense level and existing enhancements contained in United States Sentencing Guideline 2J1.2 relating to obstruction of justice are sufficient to deter and punish that activity;
(2) the enhancements and specific offense characteristics relating to obstruction of justice are adequate in cases where—
(A) the destruction, alteration, or fabrication of evidence involves—
(i) a large amount of evidence, a large number of participants, or is otherwise extensive;
(ii) the selection of evidence that is particularly probative or essential to the investigation; or
(iii) more than minimal planning; or
(B) the offense involved abuse of a special skill or a position of trust;
(3) the guideline offense levels and enhancements for violations of section 1519 or 1520 of title 18, United States Code, as added by this title, are sufficient to deter and punish that activity;
(4) a specific offense characteristic enhancing sentencing is provided under United States Sentencing Guideline 2B1.1 (as in effect on the date of enactment of this Act) for a fraud offense that endangers the solvency or financial security of a substantial number of victims; and
(5) the guidelines that apply to organizations in United States Sentencing Guidelines, chapter 8, are sufficient to deter and punish organizational criminal misconduct.

(b) EMERGENCY AUTHORITY AND DEADLINE FOR COMMISSION ACTION.—The United States Sentencing Commission is requested to promulgate the guidelines or amendments provided for under this section as soon as practicable, and in any event not later than 180 days after the date of enactment of this Act, in accordance with the procedures set forth in section 219(a) of the Sentencing Reform Act of 1987, as though the authority under that Act had not expired.

SEC. 806. PROTECTION FOR EMPLOYEES OF PUBLICLY TRADED COMPANIES WHO PROVIDE EVIDENCE OF FRAUD.

(a) IN GENERAL.—Chapter 73 of title 18, United States Code, is amended by inserting after section 1514 the following:

"§ 1514A. Civil action to protect against retaliation in fraud cases

"(a) WHISTLEBLOWER PROTECTION FOR EMPLOYEES OF PUBLICLY TRADED COMPANIES.—No company with a class of securities registered under section 12 of the Securities Exchange Act of 1934 (15 U.S.C. 78l), or that is required to file reports under section 15(d) of the Securities Exchange Act of 1934 (15 U.S.C. 78o(d)),

H. R. 3763—59

or any officer, employee, contractor, subcontractor, or agent of such company, may discharge, demote, suspend, threaten, harass, or in any other manner discriminate against an employee in the terms and conditions of employment because of any lawful act done by the employee—

"(1) to provide information, cause information to be provided, or otherwise assist in an investigation regarding any conduct which the employee reasonably believes constitutes a violation of section 1341, 1343, 1344, or 1348, any rule or regulation of the Securities and Exchange Commission, or any provision of Federal law relating to fraud against shareholders, when the information or assistance is provided to or the investigation is conducted by—

"(A) a Federal regulatory or law enforcement agency;

"(B) any Member of Congress or any committee of Congress; or

"(C) a person with supervisory authority over the employee (or such other person working for the employer who has the authority to investigate, discover, or terminate misconduct); or

"(2) to file, cause to be filed, testify, participate in, or otherwise assist in a proceeding filed or about to be filed (with any knowledge of the employer) relating to an alleged violation of section 1341, 1343, 1344, or 1348, any rule or regulation of the Securities and Exchange Commission, or any provision of Federal law relating to fraud against shareholders.

"(b) ENFORCEMENT ACTION.—

"(1) IN GENERAL.—A person who alleges discharge or other discrimination by any person in violation of subsection (a) may seek relief under subsection (c), by—

"(A) filing a complaint with the Secretary of Labor; or

"(B) if the Secretary has not issued a final decision within 180 days of the filing of the complaint and there is no showing that such delay is due to the bad faith of the claimant, bringing an action at law or equity for de novo review in the appropriate district court of the United States, which shall have jurisdiction over such an action without regard to the amount in controversy.

"(2) PROCEDURE.—

"(A) IN GENERAL.—An action under paragraph (1)(A) shall be governed under the rules and procedures set forth in section 42121(b) of title 49, United States Code.

"(B) EXCEPTION.—Notification made under section 42121(b)(1) of title 49, United States Code, shall be made to the person named in the complaint and to the employer.

"(C) BURDENS OF PROOF.—An action brought under paragraph (1)(B) shall be governed by the legal burdens of proof set forth in section 42121(b) of title 49, United States Code.

"(D) STATUTE OF LIMITATIONS.—An action under paragraph (1) shall be commenced not later than 90 days after the date on which the violation occurs.

"(c) REMEDIES.—

"(1) IN GENERAL.—An employee prevailing in any action under subsection (b)(1) shall be entitled to all relief necessary to make the employee whole.

H. R. 3763—60

"(2) COMPENSATORY DAMAGES.—Relief for any action under paragraph (1) shall include—

"(A) reinstatement with the same seniority status that the employee would have had, but for the discrimination;

"(B) the amount of back pay, with interest; and

"(C) compensation for any special damages sustained as a result of the discrimination, including litigation costs, expert witness fees, and reasonable attorney fees.

"(d) RIGHTS RETAINED BY EMPLOYEE.—Nothing in this section shall be deemed to diminish the rights, privileges, or remedies of any employee under any Federal or State law, or under any collective bargaining agreement."

"(b) CLERICAL AMENDMENT.—The table of sections at the beginning of chapter 73 of title 18, United States Code, is amended by inserting after the item relating to section 1514 the following new item:

"1514A. Civil action to protect against retaliation in fraud cases."

SEC. 807. CRIMINAL PENALTIES FOR DEFRAUDING SHAREHOLDERS OF PUBLICLY TRADED COMPANIES.

(a) IN GENERAL.—Chapter 63 of title 18, United States Code, is amended by adding at the end the following:

"§ 1348. Securities fraud

"Whoever knowingly executes, or attempts to execute, a scheme or artifice—

"(1) to defraud any person in connection with any security of an issuer with a class of securities registered under section 12 of the Securities Exchange Act of 1934 (15 U.S.C. 78l) or that is required to file reports under section 15(d) of the Securities Exchange Act of 1934 (15 U.S.C. 78o(d)); or

"(2) to obtain, by means of false or fraudulent pretenses, representations, or promises, any money or property in connection with the purchase or sale of any security of an issuer with a class of securities registered under section 12 of the Securities Exchange Act of 1934 (15 U.S.C. 78l) or that is required to file reports under section 15(d) of the Securities Exchange Act of 1934 (15 U.S.C. 78o(d));

shall be fined under this title, or imprisoned not more than 25 years, or both.".

(b) CLERICAL AMENDMENT.—The table of sections at the beginning of chapter 63 of title 18, United States Code, is amended by adding at the end the following new item:

"1348. Securities fraud.".

TITLE IX—WHITE-COLLAR CRIME PENALTY ENHANCEMENTS

SEC. 901. SHORT TITLE.

This title may be cited as the "White-Collar Crime Penalty Enhancement Act of 2002".

H.R. 3763—61

SEC. 902. ATTEMPTS AND CONSPIRACIES TO COMMIT CRIMINAL FRAUD OFFENSES.

(a) IN GENERAL.—Chapter 63 of title 18, United States Code, is amended by inserting after section 1348 as added by this Act the following:

"§ 1349. Attempt and conspiracy

"Any person who attempts or conspires to commit any offense under this chapter shall be subject to the same penalties as those prescribed for the offense, the commission of which was the object of the attempt or conspiracy.

(b) CLERICAL AMENDMENT.—The table of sections at the beginning of chapter 63 of title 18, United States Code, is amended by adding at the end the following new item:

"1349. Attempt and conspiracy.".

SEC. 903. CRIMINAL PENALTIES FOR MAIL AND WIRE FRAUD.

(a) MAIL FRAUD.—Section 1341 of title 18, United States Code, is amended by striking "five" and inserting "20".

(b) WIRE FRAUD.—Section 1343 of title 18, United States Code, is amended by striking "five" and inserting "20".

SEC. 904. CRIMINAL PENALTIES FOR VIOLATIONS OF THE EMPLOYEE RETIREMENT INCOME SECURITY ACT OF 1974.

Section 501 of the Employee Retirement Income Security Act of 1974 (29 U.S.C. 1131) is amended—

(1) by striking "$5,000" and inserting "$100,000";

(2) by striking "one year" and inserting "10 years"; and

(3) by striking "$100,000" and inserting "$500,000".

SEC. 905. AMENDMENT TO SENTENCING GUIDELINES RELATING TO CERTAIN WHITE-COLLAR OFFENSES.

(a) DIRECTIVE TO THE UNITED STATES SENTENCING COMMISSION.—Pursuant to its authority under section 994(p) of title 18, United States Code, and in accordance with this section, the United States Sentencing Commission shall review and, as appropriate, amend the Federal Sentencing Guidelines and related policy statements to implement the provisions of this Act.

(b) REQUIREMENTS.—In carrying out this section, the Sentencing Commission shall—

(1) ensure that the sentencing guidelines and policy statements reflect the serious nature of the offenses and the penalties set forth in this Act, the growing incidence of serious fraud offenses which are identified above, and the need to modify the sentencing guidelines and policy statements to deter, prevent, and punish such offenses;

(2) consider the extent to which the guidelines and policy statements adequately address whether the guideline offense levels and enhancements for violations of the sections amended by this Act are sufficient to deter and punish such offenses, and specifically, are adequate in view of the statutory increases in penalties contained in this Act;

(3) assure reasonable consistency with other relevant directives and sentencing guidelines;

(4) account for any additional aggravating or mitigating circumstances that might justify exceptions to the generally applicable sentencing ranges;

H.R. 3763—62

(5) make any necessary conforming changes to the sentencing guidelines; and

(6) assure that the guidelines adequately meet the purposes of sentencing, as set forth in section 3553(a)(2) of title 18, United States Code.

(c) EMERGENCY AUTHORITY AND DEADLINE FOR COMMISSION ACTION.—The United States Sentencing Commission is requested to promulgate the guidelines or amendments provided for under this section as soon as practicable, and in any event not later than 180 days after the date of enactment of this Act, in accordance with the procedures set forth in section 219(a) of the Sentencing Reform Act of 1987, as though the authority under that Act had not expired.

SEC. 906. CORPORATE RESPONSIBILITY FOR FINANCIAL REPORTS.

(a) IN GENERAL.—Chapter 63 of title 18, United States Code, is amended by inserting after section 1349, as created by this Act, the following:

"§ 350. Failure of corporate officers to certify financial reports

"(a) CERTIFICATION OF PERIODIC FINANCIAL REPORTS.—Each periodic report containing financial statements filed by an issuer with the Securities Exchange Commission pursuant to section 13(a) or 15(d) of the Securities Exchange Act of 1934 (15 U.S.C. 78m(a) or 78o(d)) shall be accompanied by a written statement by the chief executive officer and chief financial officer (or equivalent thereof) of the issuer.

"(b) CONTENT.—The statement required under subsection (a) shall certify that the periodic report containing the financial statements fully complies with the requirements of section 13(a) or 15(d) of the Securities Exchange Act of 1934 (15 U.S.C. 78m or 78o(d)) and that information contained in the periodic report fairly presents, in all material respects, the financial condition and results of operations of the issuer.

"(c) CRIMINAL PENALTIES.—Whoever—

"(1) certifies any statement as set forth in subsections (a) and (b) of this section knowing that the periodic report accompanying the statement does not comport with all the requirements set forth in this section shall be fined not more than $1,000,000 or imprisoned not more than 10 years, or both; or

"(2) willfully certifies any statement as set forth in subsections (a) and (b) of this section knowing that the periodic report accompanying the statement does not comport with all the requirements set forth in this section shall be fined not more than $5,000,000, or imprisoned not more than 20 years, or both.".

(b) CLERICAL AMENDMENT.—The table of sections at the beginning of chapter 63 of title 18, United States Code, is amended by adding at the end the following:

"1350. Failure of corporate officers to certify financial reports.".

TITLE X—CORPORATE TAX RETURNS

SEC. 1001. SENSE OF THE SENATE REGARDING THE SIGNING OF CORPORATE TAX RETURNS BY CHIEF EXECUTIVE OFFICERS.

It is the sense of the Senate that the Federal income tax return of a corporation should be signed by the chief executive officer of such corporation.

TITLE XI—CORPORATE FRAUD ACCOUNTABILITY

SEC. 1101. SHORT TITLE.

This title may be cited as the "Corporate Fraud Accountability Act of 2002".

SEC. 1102. TAMPERING WITH A RECORD OR OTHERWISE IMPEDING AN OFFICIAL PROCEEDING.

Section 1512 of title 18, United States Code, is amended—

(1) by redesignating subsections (c) through (i) as subsections (d) through (j), respectively; and

(2) by inserting after subsection (b) the following new subsection:

"(c) Whoever corruptly—

"(1) alters, destroys, mutilates, or conceals a record, document, or other object, or attempts to do so, with the intent to impair the object's integrity or availability for use in an official proceeding; or

"(2) otherwise obstructs, influences, or impedes any official proceeding, or attempts to do so,

shall be fined under this title or imprisoned not more than 20 years, or both.".

SEC. 1103. TEMPORARY FREEZE AUTHORITY FOR THE SECURITIES AND EXCHANGE COMMISSION.

(a) IN GENERAL.—Section 21C(c) of the Securities Exchange Act of 1934 (15 U.S.C. 78u–3(c)) is amended by adding at the end the following:

"(3) TEMPORARY FREEZE.—

"(A) IN GENERAL.—

"(i) ISSUANCE OF TEMPORARY ORDER.—Whenever, during the course of a lawful investigation involving possible violations of the Federal securities laws by an issuer of publicly traded securities or any of its directors, officers, partners, controlling persons, agents, or employees, it shall appear to the Commission that it is likely that the issuer will make extraordinary payments (whether compensation or otherwise) to any of the foregoing persons, the Commission may petition a Federal district court for a temporary order requiring the issuer to escrow, subject to court supervision, those payments in an interest-bearing account for 45 days.

"(ii) STANDARD.—A temporary order shall be entered under clause (i), only after notice and opportunity for a hearing, unless the court determines that

notice and hearing prior to entry of the order would be impracticable or contrary to the public interest.

"(iii) EFFECTIVE PERIOD.—A temporary order issued under clause (i) shall—

"(I) become effective immediately;

"(II) be served upon the parties subject to it; and

"(III) unless set aside, limited or suspended by a court of competent jurisdiction, shall remain effective and enforceable for 45 days.

"(iv) EXTENSIONS AUTHORIZED.—The effective period of an order under this subparagraph may be extended by the court upon good cause shown for not longer than 45 additional days, provided that the combined period of the order shall not exceed 90 days.

"(B) PROCESS ON DETERMINATION OF VIOLATIONS.—

"(i) VIOLATIONS CHARGED.—If the issuer or other person described in subparagraph (A) is charged with any violation of the Federal securities laws before the expiration of the effective period of a temporary order under subparagraph (A) (including any applicable extension period), the order shall remain in effect, subject to court approval, until the conclusion of any legal proceedings related thereto, and the affected issuer or other person, shall have the right to petition the court for review of the order.

"(ii) VIOLATIONS NOT CHARGED.—If the issuer or other person described in subparagraph (A) is not charged with any violation of the Federal securities laws before the expiration of the effective period of a temporary order under subparagraph (A) (including any applicable extension period), the escrow shall terminate at the expiration of the 45-day effective period (or the expiration of any extension period, as applicable), and the disputed payments (with accrued interest) shall be returned to the issuer or other affected person.".

(b) TECHNICAL AMENDMENT.—Section 21C(c)(2) of the Securities Exchange Act of 1934 (15 U.S.C. 78u–3(c)(2)) is amended by striking "This" and inserting "paragraph (1)".

SEC. 1104. AMENDMENT TO THE FEDERAL SENTENCING GUIDELINES.

(a) REQUEST FOR IMMEDIATE CONSIDERATION BY THE UNITED STATES SENTENCING COMMISSION.—Pursuant to its authority under section 994(p) of title 28, United States Code, and in accordance with this section, the United States Sentencing Commission is requested to—

(1) promptly review the sentencing guidelines applicable to securities and accounting fraud and related offenses;

(2) expeditiously consider the promulgation of new sentencing guidelines or amendments to existing sentencing guidelines to provide an enhancement for officers or directors of publicly traded corporations who commit fraud and related offenses; and

(3) submit to Congress an explanation of actions taken by the Sentencing Commission pursuant to paragraph (2) and

H.R. 3763—65

any additional policy recommendations the Sentencing Commission may have for combating offenses described in paragraph (1).

(b) CONSIDERATIONS IN REVIEW.—In carrying out this section, the Sentencing Commission is requested to—

(1) ensure that the sentencing guidelines and policy statements reflect the serious nature of securities, pension, and accounting fraud and the need for aggressive and appropriate law enforcement action to prevent such offenses;

(2) assure reasonable consistency with other relevant directives and with other guidelines;

(3) account for any aggravating or mitigating circumstances that might justify exceptions, including circumstances for which the sentencing guidelines currently provide sentencing enhancements;

(4) ensure that guideline offense levels and enhancements for an obstruction of justice offense are adequate in cases where documents or other physical evidence are actually destroyed or fabricated;

(5) ensure that the guideline offense levels and enhancements under United States Sentencing Guideline 2B1.1 (as in effect on the date of enactment of this Act) are sufficient for a fraud offense when the number of victims adversely involved is significantly greater than 50;

(6) make any necessary conforming changes to the sentencing guidelines; and

(7) assure that the guidelines adequately meet the purposes of sentencing as set forth in section 3553 (a)(2) of title 18, United States Code.

(c) EMERGENCY AUTHORITY AND DEADLINE FOR COMMISSION ACTION.—The United States Sentencing Commission is requested to promulgate the guidelines or amendments provided for under this section as soon as practicable, and in any event not later than the 180 days after the date of enactment of this Act, in accordance with the procedures set forth in section 21(a) of the Sentencing Reform Act of 1987, as though the authority under that Act had not expired.

SEC. 1105. AUTHORITY OF THE COMMISSION TO PROHIBIT PERSONS FROM SERVING AS OFFICERS OR DIRECTORS.

(a) SECURITIES EXCHANGE ACT OF 1934.—Section 21C of the Securities Exchange Act of 1934 (15 U.S.C. 78u-3) is amended by adding at the end the following:

"(f) AUTHORITY OF THE COMMISSION TO PROHIBIT PERSONS FROM SERVING AS OFFICERS OR DIRECTORS.—In any cease-and-desist proceeding under subsection (a), the Commission may issue an order to prohibit, conditionally or unconditionally, and permanently or for such period of time as it shall determine, any person who has violated section 10(b) or the rules or regulations thereunder, from acting as an officer or director of any issuer that has a class of securities registered pursuant to section 12, or that is required to file reports pursuant to section 15(d), if the conduct of that person demonstrates unfitness to serve as an officer or director of any such issuer."

(b) SECURITIES ACT OF 1933.—Section 8A of the Securities Act of 1933 (15 U.S.C. 77h-1) is amended by adding at the end of the following:

H.R. 3763—66

"(f) AUTHORITY OF THE COMMISSION TO PROHIBIT PERSONS FROM SERVING AS OFFICERS OR DIRECTORS.—In any cease-and-desist proceeding under subsection (a), the Commission may issue an order to prohibit, conditionally or unconditionally, and permanently or for such period of time as it shall determine, any person who has violated section 17(a)(1) or the rules or regulations thereunder, from acting as an officer or director of any issuer that has a class of securities registered pursuant to section 12 of the Securities Exchange Act of 1934, or that is required to file reports pursuant to section 15(d) of that Act, if the conduct of that person demonstrates unfitness to serve as an officer or director of any such issuer."

SEC. 1106. INCREASED CRIMINAL PENALTIES UNDER SECURITIES EXCHANGE ACT OF 1934.

Section 32(a) of the Securities Exchange Act of 1934 (15 U.S.C. 78ff(a)) is amended—

(1) by striking "$1,000,000, or imprisoned not more than 10 years" and inserting "$5,000,000, or imprisoned not more than 20 years"; and

(2) by striking "$2,500,000" and inserting "$25,000,000".

SEC. 1107. RETALIATION AGAINST INFORMANTS.

(a) IN GENERAL.—Section 1513 of title 18, United States Code, is amended by adding at the end the following:

"(e) Whoever knowingly, with the intent to retaliate, takes any action harmful to any person, including interference with the lawful employment or livelihood of any person, for providing to a law enforcement officer any truthful information relating to the commission or possible commission of any Federal offense, shall be fined under this title or imprisoned not more than 10 years, or both.".

Speaker of the House of Representatives.

Vice President of the United States and President of the Senate.

Appendix B

Sample Certifications

· ·

SOX Sections 302 and 906 require chief executive officers and financial officers to certify as to the accuracy of the company's financial statements in filings and periodic reports with the Securities and Exchange Commission (SEC). A misleading or inaccurate Section 302 certification may result in civil penalties, and criminal penalties may follow for failure to execute an accurate Section 906 certification (discussed in Chapter 9). The substance of both certifications is somewhat redundant, and experts have questioned whether the requirement of separate certifications was an error.

Although SOX does not require chief information officers and other management to sign Section 302 and 906 certifications, it is the practice of many companies to require them to sign employee subcertifications. A sample form for an employee subcertification is included at the end of this appendix.

Sample General Section 302 Certification

Note: Text printed in bold may be omitted until the registrant is required to comply with the reporting requirements concerning internal control over financial reporting (that is, July 15, 2007, for non-accelerated filers, as discussed in Chapter 9).

I, [identify the certifying individual], certify that:

1. I have reviewed this [specify report] of [identify registrant];
2. Based on my knowledge, this report does not contain any untrue statement of a material fact or omit to state a material fact necessary to make the statements made, in light of the circumstances under which such statements were made, not misleading with respect to the period covered by this report;
3. Based on my knowledge, the financial statements, and other financial information included in this report, fairly present in all material respects the financial condition, results of operations and cash flows of the registrant as of, and for, the periods presented in this report;

4. The registrant's other certifying officer(s) and I are responsible for establishing and maintaining disclosure controls and procedures (as defined in Exchange Act Rules 13a-15(e) and 15d-15(e)) **and internal control over financial reporting (as defined in Exchange Act Rules 13a-15(f) and 15d-15(f))** for the registrant and have:

   (a) Designed such disclosure controls and procedures, or caused such disclosure controls and procedures to be designed under our supervision, to ensure that material information relating to the registrant, including its consolidated subsidiaries, is made known to us by others within those entities, particularly during the period in which this report is being prepared;

   (b) **Designed such internal control over financial reporting, or caused such internal control over financial reporting to be designed under our supervision, to provide reasonable assurance regarding the reliability of financial reporting and the preparation of financial statements for external purposes in accordance with generally accepted accounting principles;**

   (c) Evaluated the effectiveness of the registrant's disclosure controls and procedures and presented in this report our conclusions about the effectiveness of the disclosure controls and procedures, as of the end of the period covered by this report based on such evaluation; and

   (d) Disclosed in this report any change in the registrant's internal control over financial reporting that occurred during the registrant's most recent fiscal quarter (the registrant's fourth fiscal quarter in the case of an annual report) that has materially affected, or is reasonably likely to materially affect, the registrant's internal control over financial reporting; and

5. The registrant's other certifying officer(s) and I have disclosed, based on our most recent evaluation of internal control over financial reporting, to the registrant's auditors and the audit committee of the registrant's board of directors (or persons performing the equivalent functions):

   (a) All significant deficiencies and material weaknesses in the design or operation of internal control over financial reporting which are reasonably likely to adversely affect the registrant's ability to record, process, summarize and report financial information; and

   (b) Any fraud, whether or not material, that involves management or other employees who have a significant role in the registrant's internal control over financial reporting.

Date: _____

Signature: _____

Title: _____

Sample Section 906 Certification

The undersigned officer of _____ (the "Company") hereby certifies [to my knowledge][1] that the Company's quarterly report on Form 10-Q for the quarterly period ended June 30, 2002 [Modify Name of Report as Appropriate] (the "Report"), as filed with the Securities and Exchange Commission on the date hereof, fully complies with the requirements of Section 13(a) or 15(d), as applicable, of the Securities Exchange Act of 1934, as amended, and that the information contained in the Report fairly presents, in all material respects, the financial condition and results of operations of the Company. This certification is provided solely pursuant to 18 U.S.C. Section 1350, as adopted pursuant to Section 906 of the Sarbanes-Oxley Act of 2002 [*, and shall not be deemed to be a part of the Report or "filed" for any purpose whatsoever]*[2].

Date: _____

Signature: _____

Title: _____

The bracketed language should be used if the certification is delivered as separate correspondence.

Sample Subcertification of Employee

Certificate of Employee Regarding SEC Filings Of _____ Company ("the Company")

I am aware that in connection with _____ Company's (the "Company") quarterly report on Form 10-K for the year ended _____ (as the Chief Executive Officer and Chief Financial Officer of the Company) file certifications with the Securities and Exchange Commission (the "SEC"), as to the best of their knowledge, regarding the accuracy and completeness of the covered filing.

I understand that I have been asked to file this Certificate to help ensure that the Certifications that the Chief Executive Officer and Chief Financial Officer will file with the SEC are complete and accurate. A substantially final draft of the SEC filing accompanies this Certificate.

In executing this Certificate, I have considered information that I believe would be important to a reasonable investor, including (without limitation) significant business developments and trends, the Company's cash flow situation, capital resources, critical accounting policies, executive compensation and related party transactions.

I understand the Chief Executive Office and Chief Financial Office of the Company rely upon these statements, and I hereby certify, represent, and warrant to the Company the following:

1. I have read the portions of the accompanying draft SEC filing that relate directly to the scope of my employment responsibilities, and am in a position to certify the information relevant to my employment responsibilities (the certified information). Based on my knowledge:

2. The certified information, as of the end of the period covered by such filing, does not contain any untrue statement of a material fact or omit to state a material fact necessary to make the statements accurate and not misleading.

3. The certified information fairly presents, in all material respects, the financial condition, results of operations and cash flows of the Company for the period covered by the accompanying draft filing.

4. Sales transactions have been fully documented and recorded in a manner sufficient to allow accurate representation of such sales in financial documents for the appropriate period.

5. All agreements relating to future periods have been fully documented and recorded in a manner sufficient to allow accurate representation in financial documents.

6. All costs related to production and inventory have been completely incorporated in financial documents.

7. No significant undisclosed expenses or liabilities exist for the covered filing period that have not been invoiced or otherwise communicated to the Finance department.

8. I am not aware of any deficiencies in the effectiveness of the Company's disclosure controls and procedures that could adversely affect the Company's ability to record, process, summarize, and report information required to be disclosed.

9. I am not aware of any significant deficiencies or material weaknesses in the design or operation of the Company's internal controls that could adversely affect the Company's ability to record, process, summarize and report financial data.

10. I am not aware of any fraud, whether or not material, that involves the Company's management or other employees who have a significant role in the company's internal controls.

11. I understand that Chief Financial Officer and Chief Executive Officer will be filing their certifications with the SEC for the material contained in the attached draft filing. If, at any time before such filing date, if I become aware that this Certificate is incorrect for any reason, I will immediately notify the Chief Financial Office and Chief Executive Officer of the Company.

Dated this _____ day of _____, 200_.

Signature: _____

Printed name: _____

Title: _____

Appendix C

Sample Audit Committee Charter

Endorsed by the Association of Public Pension Fund Auditors (APPFA)

*T*he following Example Audit Committee Charter, reproduced with permission from the APPFA, captures many of the best practices used at the time of its writing, July of 2003. Of course, no example charter encompasses all activities that might be appropriate to a particular audit committee, nor will all activities identified in an example charter be relevant to every committee. Accordingly, this example charter may be tailored to each committee's needs and governing rules. Moreover, as applicable laws, rules, and customs change, the audit committee charter should be updated.

This sample charter was developed for use in connection with public pension systems, but is an excellent example to which you can refer in creating your company's own audit committee charter.

Audit Committee Charter

Purpose

The purpose of this "Example Audit Committee Charter" is to assist the Board of Directors in fulfilling its fiduciary oversight responsibilities for the:

1. Financial Reporting Process
2. System of Risk Management
3. System of Internal Control
4. Internal Audit Process
5. External Audit of the Financial Statements
6. Engagements with Other External Audit Firms

7. Organization's Processes for Monitoring Compliance with Laws and Regulations and the Ethics Policy, Code of Conduct and Fraud Policy

8. Special Investigations and Whistleblower Mechanism

9. Audit Committee Management and Reporting Responsibilities

Authority

The audit committee has authority to conduct or authorize investigations into any matters within its scope of responsibility. It is empowered to perform the following functions, which are numbered according to the purposes listed above:

(1) Financial Reporting Process

- ✔ Oversee the reporting of all financial information.

- ✔ Resolve any disagreements between management, the external auditor, and/or the internal auditor regarding financial reporting.

(2) System of Risk Management

- ✔ Provide the policy and framework for an effective system of risk management, and provide the mechanisms for periodic assessment of the system of risk management, including risks of the information systems, and risks of business relationships with significant vendors and consultants.

- ✔ Oversee all consultants and experts that make recommendations concerning the risk management structure and internal control structure.

(3) System of Internal Control

- ✔ Provide the policy and framework for an effective system of internal controls, and provide the mechanisms for periodic assessment of the system of internal controls, including information systems, and internal control over purchases from significant vendors and consultants.

- ✔ Ensure that contracts with external service providers contain appropriate record-keeping and audit language.

- ✔ Seek any information it requires from employees-all of whom are directed to cooperate with the committee's requests, or the requests of internal or external parties working for the audit committee. These parties include the internal auditors, all external auditors, consultants, investigators, and any other specialists working for the audit committee.

(4) Internal Audit Process

- ✔ Appoint, compensate, and oversee the work of the Chief Audit Executive and oversee the work of the internal audit unit.

- ✔ Serve as the primary liaison and provide the appropriate forum for handling all matters related to audits, examinations, investigations, or inquiries of the State Auditor and other appropriate State or Federal agencies.

(5) External Audit of the Financial Statements

- ✔ Appoint, compensate, and oversee the work of the certified public accounting firm employed by the organization to audit the financial statements.

- ✔ Pre-approve all auditing, other attest and non-audit services performed by the external financial statement audit firm.

(6) Engagements with Other External Audit Firms

- ✔ Appoint, compensate, and oversee the work of any other certified public accounting firm employed by the organization to perform any audits or agreed-upon-procedures other than the audit of the financial statements.

(7) Organization's Processes for Monitoring Compliance with Laws and Regulations and the Ethics Policy, Code of Conduct and Fraud Policy

- ✔ Provide the policy and framework for compliance with laws and regulations, and provide the mechanisms for periodic assessment of compliance, including compliance by significant vendors and consultants.

- ✔ Communicate with the Board regarding the organization's policy on ethics, code of conduct and fraud policy as it relates to internal control, financial reporting, and all auditing activities.

(8) Special Investigations and Whistleblower Mechanism

- ✔ Retain independent counsel, accountants, or other specialists to advise the committee or assist in the conduct of an investigation.

- ✔ Ensure creation of and maintenance of an appropriate whistleblower mechanism for reporting of financial statement fraud and other fraud and inappropriate activities.

(9) Audit Committee Management and Reporting Responsibilities

- ✔ Receive and review reports on all public disclosures related to the purpose, authority, and responsibilities of the Audit Committee. Consider having a Disclosure Subcommittee for this purpose.

- ✔ Report to the Board on the activities, findings, and recommendations of the Audit Committee.

(1 – 9) Comprehensive Communication Responsibility

Meet with the organization's officers, external auditors, internal auditors, outside counsel and/or specialists, as necessary.

Composition

The audit committee will consist of at least three and no more than seven members of the Board of Directors. The Board or its nominating committee will appoint committee members and the committee chair.

Each committee member will be both independent and financially literate. At least one member shall be designated as the "financial expert," as defined by applicable legislation and regulation.

Meetings

The committee will meet at least four times a year, with authority to convene additional meetings, as circumstances require. All committee members are expected to attend each meeting, in person or via tele- or video-conference. Meeting notices will be provided to interested parties in conformance with applicable laws, regulations, customs, and practices. The committee will invite members of management, external auditors, internal auditors and/or others to attend meetings and provide pertinent information, as necessary. It will hold private meetings with auditors {Subject to open meeting laws} and executive sessions as provided by law. Meeting agendas will be prepared and provided in advance to members, along with appropriate briefing materials. Minutes will be prepared.

Responsibilities

The committee will carry out the following responsibilities:

(1) Financial Reporting Process

✔ Obtain information and training to enhance the committee members' expertise in financial reporting standards and processes so that the committee may adequately oversee financial reporting.

✔ Review significant accounting and reporting issues, including complex or unusual transactions and highly judgmental areas, and recent professional and regulatory pronouncements, and understand their impact on the financial statements.

- ✔ Review with management, the external auditors, and the internal auditors the results of the audit, including any difficulties encountered.

- ✔ Review all significant adjustments proposed by the external financial statement auditor and by the internal auditor.

- ✔ Review all significant suggestions for improved financial reporting made by the external financial statement auditor and by the internal auditor.

- ✔ Review with the General Counsel the status of legal matters that may have an effect on the financial statements.

- ✔ Review the annual financial statements, and consider whether they are complete, consistent with information known to committee members, and reflect appropriate accounting principles.

- ✔ Review other sections of the annual report and related regulatory filings before release and consider the accuracy and completeness of the information.

- ✔ Review with management and the external auditors all matters required to be communicated to the committee under generally accepted auditing *Standards*.

- ✔ Understand how management develops interim financial information, and the nature and extent of internal and external auditor involvement.

- ✔ Review interim financial reports with management and the external auditors before filing with regulators, and consider whether they are complete and consistent with the information known to committee members.

- ✔ Review the statement of management responsibility for and the assessment of the effectiveness of the internal control structure and procedures of the organization for financial reporting. Review the attestation on this management assertion by the financial statement auditor as part of the financial statement audit engagement.

(2) System of Risk Management

- ✔ Obtain information about, training in and an understanding of risk management in order to acquire the knowledge necessary to adequately oversee the risk management process.

- ✔ Ensure that the organization has a comprehensive policy on risk management.

- ✔ Consider the effectiveness of the organization's risk management system, including risks of information technology systems.

- ✔ Consider the risks of business relationships with significant vendors and consultants.

- ✔ Reviews management's reports on management's self-assessment of risks and the mitigations of these risks.

✔ Understand the scope of internal auditor's and external auditor's review of risk management over financial reporting.

✔ Understand the scope of internal auditor's review of risk management over all other processes, and obtain reports on significant findings and recommendations, together with management's responses.

✔ Understand the scope of any other external auditor's or consultant's review of risk management.

✔ Hire outside experts and consultants in risk management as necessary.

(3) System of Internal Control

✔ Obtain information about, training in, and an understanding of internal control in order to acquire the knowledge necessary to adequately oversee the internal control process.

✔ Ensure that the organization has a comprehensive policy on internal control and compliance.

✔ Review periodically the policy on ethics, code of conduct, and fraud policy.

✔ Consider the effectiveness of the organization's internal control system, including information technology security and control.

✔ Consider any internal controls required because of business relationships with significant vendors and consultants.

✔ Understand the scope of internal auditor's and external auditor's review of internal control over financial reporting, and obtain reports on significant findings and recommendations, together with management's responses.

✔ Understand the scope of internal auditor's review of internal control over all other processes, and obtain reports on significant findings and recommendations, together with management's responses.

✔ Review the role of the internal auditor's involvement in the corporate governance process, including corporate governance documentation and training.

✔ Ensure that contracts with external service providers contain appropriate record-keeping and audit language.

✔ Direct employees to cooperate with the committee's requests, or the requests of internal or external parties working for the audit committee. These parties include the internal auditors, all external auditors, consultants, investigators, and any other specialists working for the audit committee.

(4) Internal Audit Process

- ✔ Obtain the information and training needed to enhance the committee members' understanding of the role of internal audits so that the committee may adequately oversee the internal audit function.

- ✔ Oversee the selection process for the chief audit executive.

- ✔ Assure and maintain, through the organizational structure of the organization and by other means, the independence of the internal audit process.

- ✔ Ensure that internal auditors have access to all documents, information, and systems in the organization.

- ✔ Ensure there are no unjustified restrictions or limitations placed on the Chief Audit Executive and internal audit staff.

- ✔ Review with management and the Chief Audit Executive the charter, objectives, plans, activities, staffing, budget, qualifications, and organizational structure of the internal audit function.

- ✔ Receive and review all internal audit reports and management letters.

- ✔ Review the responsiveness and timeliness of management's follow-up activities pertaining to any reported findings and recommendations.

- ✔ Receive periodic notices of advisory and consulting activities by internal auditors.

- ✔ Review and concur in the appointment, replacement, or dismissal of the Chief Audit Executive, if allowed by state law.

- ✔ Review the performance of the Chief Audit Executive periodically.

- ✔ Review the effectiveness of the internal audit function, including compliance with The Institute of Internal Auditors' *Standards for the Professional Practice of Internal Auditing.*

- ✔ On a regular basis, meet separately with the Chief Audit Executive to discuss any matters that the committee or internal audit believes should be discussed privately {Subject to open meeting laws}.

- ✔ Delegate to the Chief Audit Executive the management of the contract for the external financial statement auditor, and the management of the contracts for any other certified public accountants.

- ✔ Designate the Chief Audit Executive as the primary point of contact for handling all matters related to audits, examinations, investigations, or inquiries of the State Auditor and other appropriate State or Federal agencies.

(5) External Audit of the Financial Statements

✔ Obtain the information and training needed to enhance the committee members' understanding of the purpose of the financial statements audit and the role of external financial statement auditor so that the committee may adequately oversee the financial statement audit function.

✔ Review the external auditor's proposed audit scope and approach, including coordination of audit effort with internal audit.

✔ Review the performance of the external financial statement audit firm, and exercise final approval on the request for proposal for, and the appointment, retention or discharge of the audit firm. Obtain input from the Chief Audit Executive, management, and other parties as appropriate.

✔ Define the services that the external financial statement auditor is allowed to perform and the services that are prohibited.

✔ Pre-approve all services to be performed by the external financial statement auditor.

✔ Review the independence of the external financial statement audit firm by obtaining statements from the auditors on relationships between the audit firm and the organization, including any non-audit services, and discussing these relationships with the audit firm. Obtain from management a listing of all services provided by the external audit firm. Obtain information from the Chief Audit Executive and other sources as necessary.

✔ Review and approve the audited financial statements, associated management letter, attestation on the effectiveness of the internal control structure, and procedures for financial reporting, other required auditor communications, and all other auditor reports and communications relating to the financial statements.

✔ Review and approve all other reports and communications made by the external financial statement auditor.

✔ Review the responsiveness and timeliness of management's follow-up activities pertaining to any reported findings and recommendations.

✔ On a regular basis, meet separately with the external financial statement audit firm to discuss any matters that the committee or auditors believe should be discussed privately {Subject to open meeting laws}.

✔ Provide guidelines and mechanisms so that no member of the audit committee or organization staff shall improperly influence the auditors or the firm engaged to perform audit services.

✔ Ensure production of a report of all costs of and payments to the external financial statement auditor. The listing should separately disclose the costs of the financial statement audit, other attest projects, agreed-upon-procedures, and any non-audit services provided.

(6) Engagements with Other External Audit Firms

✔ Obtain the information and training needed to enhance the committee members' understanding of the role of the other external audit firm(s) so that the committee may adequately oversee their function(s).

✔ Review the other external audit firm's (firms') proposed audit or agreed-upon-procedures scope and approach, including coordination of effort with internal audit.

✔ Review the performance of the other external audit firm(s), and exercise final approval on the request for proposal for, and the appointment, retention, or discharge of these audit firm(s).

✔ Pre-approve the scope of all services to be performed by the other external auditor.

✔ Review the independence of the other external audit firm(s) by obtaining statements from the audit firm(s) on relationships between these audit firm(s) and the organization, including any non-audit or non-attest services, and discussing the relationships with the audit firm(s). Obtain from management a listing of all services provided by the other external audit firm(s). Obtain information from the Chief Audit Executive and other sources as necessary.

✔ Review and approve the reports of the audits and/or agreed-upon-procedures.

✔ Provide a forum for follow up of findings from the audit reports or agreed-upon-procedures.

✔ Meet separately with the other external audit firm(s) on a regular basis to discuss any matters that the committee or staff of the audit firm(s) believes should be discussed privately {Subject to open meeting laws}.

✔ Ensure production of a report of all costs of and payments to other external audit firm(s). The listing should separately disclose the costs of any audit, other attest projects, agreed-upon-procedures, and any non-audit services provided.

(7) Organization's Processes for Monitoring Compliance

✔ Review the effectiveness of the system for monitoring compliance with laws and regulations and the results of management's investigation and follow-up (including disciplinary action) of any instances of noncompliance.

✔ Review the findings of any examinations by regulatory agencies, and any auditor observations, including investigations of misconduct and fraud.

✔ Review the process for communicating to all affected parties the ethics policy, code of conduct and fraud policy to organization personnel, and for monitoring compliance therewith.

> ✔ Obtain regular updates from management and organization legal counsel regarding compliance matters.

> ✔ Monitor changes and proposed changes in laws, regulations, and rules affecting the organization.

(8) Special Investigations and Whistleblower Mechanism

> ✔ Institute and oversee special investigations as needed.

> ✔ Provide an appropriate confidential mechanism for whistleblowers to provide information on potentially fraudulent financial reporting or breaches of internal control to the audit committee.

(9) Audit Committee Management and Reporting Responsibilities

> ✔ Regularly report to the Board of Directors about all committee activities, issues, and related recommendations.

> ✔ Perform other activities related to this charter as requested by the Board of Directors, and report to the Board.

> ✔ Provide an open avenue of communication between internal audit, the external financial statement auditors, other external auditors, management, and the Board of Directors.

> ✔ Review any other reports that the organization issues that relate to audit committee responsibilities.

> ✔ Confirm annually that all responsibilities outlined in this charter have been carried out. Report annually to the Board, members, retirees, and beneficiaries, describing the committee's composition, responsibilities, and how they were discharged, and any other information required by rule, including approval of non-audit services.

> ✔ Evaluate the committee's and individual member's performance on a regular basis, and report to the Board.

> ✔ Review and assess the adequacy of the committee charter annually, requesting Board approval for proposed changes, and ensure appropriate disclosure as may be required by law or regulation.

Appendix D

Sample Audit Committee Report

· ·

*A*n audit committee's report can be its most significant means of communicating with management and with regard to how effectively the committee has fulfilled its responsibilities. The audit committee report should go above and beyond the SEC's minimum disclosure requirements and communicate any matters of importance to stockholders. The following is a simplified example of an audit committee report that may form a starting point for the specific disclosures required within your company.

XYZ Corporation Audit Committee Report

The Audit Committee (the "Committee") of the **XYZ Corporation** Board of Directors (the "Board") consists of (number _____) of independent Directors pursuant to the requirements of the New York Stock Exchange, NASDAQ and the Securities and Exchange Commission (the "Commission").

The Committee has a written charter that is publicly available for review at (Web site _____).

The Board has determined that the following directors are financial experts as defined by the rules of the Securities and Exchange Commission:

(name _____)

(name _____)

(Web site _____)

The following Committee members serve on other public company audit committees as indicated below:

(name _____) (Board _____)

(name _____) (Board _____)

(name _____) (Board _____)

The Committee has determined that the simultaneous service on these public company audit committees does not impair the ability of the Directors.

The Committee had _____ meetings during 20__. Of these meetings, ____ included sessions of the Committee with the independent auditors ____ included sessions with the internal auditor. ____ included sessions with management.

The company also had _____ conference calls with _____ related to the company's earnings and financial statements.

Responsibility for the financial statements of XYZ company is delegated as follows:

- Board of Directors: This Committee oversees the Company's financial reporting process on behalf of the Board of Directors.
- Management: Management has primary responsibility for the financial statements of XYZ company and the reporting process.
- Independent audit firm: The independent audit firm of _____ is responsible for expressing an opinion on the conformity of the Company's consolidated audited financial statements with Generally Accepted Accounting Principles.

The Committee has reviewed and discussed with management and the independent auditors the audited financial statements of XYZ company and all matters pertinent to the preparation of the financial statements.

The Committee has pre-approved the following with respect to the services of the independent auditors:

- All audit services
- Permitted non-audit services
- The related fees for such services provided by the independent auditors

The Committee's charter allows delegation of the following authority, which has been assigned to subcommittees: [describe authority].

The Committee recommended to the Board of Directors, and the Board approved, that the audited financial statements be included in the Company's Annual Report on Form 10-K for the year ended December 31, 20__, for filing with the Securities and Exchange Commission.

Audit Committee Signatures:

_____

_____

_____

_____

Appendix E

Sample Corporate Governance Principles

Every company is a unique animal with its own products or services, management structures, and board personas. However, all companies in this era of post-SOX scrutiny must adopt principles and practices that fulfill its commitment to creating a top-down control environment and atmosphere of accountability. The following is sample set of governance principals adopted by the company that publishes this book, John Wiley & Sons, Inc.

Corporate Governance Principles

To promote the best corporate governance practices, John Wiley & Sons, Inc. adheres to the Corporate Governance Principles ("Principles"), many of which have been in effect for more than a decade. The Board of Directors (the "Board") and management believe that these Principles, which are consistent with the requirements of the Securities and Exchange Commission and the New York Stock Exchange, are in the best interests of the Company, its shareholders and other stakeholders, including employees, authors, customers and suppliers. The Board is responsible for ensuring that the Company has a management team capable of representing these interests and of achieving superior business performance.

1. Primary Duties

The Board, which is elected annually by the shareholders, exercises oversight and has final authority and responsibility with respect to the Company's affairs, except with respect to those matters reserved to shareholders. All major decisions are considered by the Board as a whole.

The Board elects the Chief Executive Officer ("CEO") and other corporate officers, acts as an advisor to and resource for management, and monitors management's performance. The Board plans for the succession of the CEO. The Compensation Committee annually evaluates the CEO's performance, approves the CEO's compensation, and informs the Board of its decision. The Board also oversees the succession process for certain other management positions, and the CEO reviews with the Board annually his assessment of key management incumbents and their professional growth and development plans. The Board also:

   a. reviews the Company's business and strategic plans and actual operating performance;

   b. reviews and approves the Company's financial objectives, investment plans and programs; and

   c. provides oversight of internal and external audit processes and financial reporting.

11. Director Independence

The Board has long held that it is in the best interests of the Company for the Board to consist of a substantial majority of independent Directors. The Board determines that a Director is independent if he or she has no material relationship, either directly or indirectly, with the Company, defined as follows:

   a. is not and has not been within the three years immediately prior to the annual meeting at which the nominees of the Board will be voted upon employed by the Company or its subsidiaries in an executive capacity;

   b. is not an executive officer, an employee, and does not have an immediate family member who is an executive officer or employee, of an organization that makes payments to, or receives payments from, the Company in an amount which, in any single fiscal year, exceeds 2% of such other organization's consolidated gross revenues;

   c. is not a significant advisor or consultant to the Company (including its subsidiaries), does not have direct, sole responsibility for business between the Company and a material supplier or customer, and does not have a significant personal services contract with the Company;

   d. The Director is not, and has not been within the past three years, employed by or affiliated with a firm that provided independent audit services to the Company; the Director is not, and does not have an immediate family member who is a current partner of a firm that is the

Company's external auditor; and the Director or an immediate family member was not within the past three years a partner or employee of the Company's external audit firm and personally worked on the Company's audit within that time.

e. The director does not have an immediate family member who is a current employee of the Company's external audit firm and who participates in that firm's audit, assurance or tax compliance practice.

f. is not, and has not been in the past three years, part of an interlocking directorship involving compensation committees;

g. is not a member of the immediate family of Peter Booth Wiley, Bradford Wiley II and Deborah E. Wiley, or management, as listed in the Company's proxy statement.

When determining the independence of a Director, the ownership of, or beneficial interest in, a significant amount of stock, by itself, is not considered a factor.

III. Composition of the Board

Under the Company's By-Laws, the Board has the authority to determine the appropriate number of directors to be elected so as to enable it to function effectively and efficiently. Currently, a ten-member Board is considered to be appropriate, though size may vary. The Governance Committee makes recommendations to the Board concerning the appropriate size of the Board, as well as selection criteria for candidates. Each candidate is selected based on background, experience, expertise, and other relevant criteria, including other public and private company boards on which the candidate serves. In addition to the individual candidate's background, experience and expertise, the manner in which each board member's qualities complement those of others and contributes to the functioning of the Board as a whole are also taken into account. The Governance Committee nominates a candidate, and the Board votes on his or her candidacy. The shareholders vote annually for the entire slate of Directors.

Any nominee Director who receives a greater number of "withheld" votes from his or her election than "for" votes shall tender his or her resignation for consideration by the Governance Committee. The Governance Committee shall recommend to the Board the action to be taken with respect to such resignation.

IV. Director Eligibility

Directors shall limit the number of other board memberships (excluding non-profits) in order to insure adequate attention to Wiley business. Directors shall advise the Chairman of the Board and the Chairman of the Governance Committee in advance of accepting an invitation to serve on a new board. Whenever there is a substantial change in the Director's principal occupation, a Director shall tender his or her resignation and shall immediately inform the Board of any potential conflict of interest. The Governance Committee will recommend to the Board the action, if any, to be taken with respect to the resignation or the potential conflict of interest.

The Board has established a retirement age of 70 for its Directors. The Board may in its discretion nominate for election a person who has attained age 70 if it believes that under the circumstances it is in the Company's best interests.

V. Board and Management Communication

The Board has access to all members of management and external advisors. As appropriate, the Board may retain independent advisors.

The CEO shall establish and maintain effective communications with the Company's stakeholder groups. The Board schedules regular executive sessions at the end of each meeting. Non-management directors meet at regularly scheduled sessions without management. The Chairman of the Board presides at these sessions. In addition, the independent directors meet at least once each year in an executive session presided over by the Chairman of the Governance Committee.

Employees and other interested parties may contact the non-management directors via email at: non-managementdirectors@wiley.com, or by mail addressed to Non-Management Directors, John Wiley & Sons, Inc., Mail Stop 7-02, 111 River Street, Hoboken, NJ 07030-5774.

VI. Board Orientation and Evaluation

The Board annually conducts a self-evaluation to determine whether the Board as a whole and its individual members, including the Chairman, are performing effectively.

The Board sponsors an orientation process for new Directors, which includes background materials on governance, law, board principles, financial and business history and meetings with members of management. The Board also encourages all of its Directors to take advantage of educational programs to improve their effectiveness.

VII. Director Compensation

The Governance Committee periodically reviews and recommends to the Board its members' annual retainer, which is composed of cash and stock grants for all non-employee Directors. In determining the appropriate amount and form of director compensation, the Board regularly evaluates current trends and compensation surveys, as well as the amount of time devoted to Board and committee meetings. As a long-standing Board principle, non-employee Directors receive no compensation from the Company other than for their service as Board members and reimbursement for expenses incurred in connection with attendance at meetings.

Share ownership by each Director is encouraged. To this end, each Director is expected to own, at a date no later than three years after election to the Board, shares of common stock valued at not less than three times that Director's annual cash compensation to which the Director is entitled for Board service.

VIII. Board Practices and Procedures

The Chairman of the Board and the CEO jointly set the agenda for each Board meeting. Agenda items that fall within the scope and responsibilities of Board committees are reviewed with the chairs of the committees. Any Board member may request that an item be added to the agenda.

Board materials are provided to Board members sufficiently in advance of meetings to allow Directors to prepare for discussion at the meeting.

Various managers regularly attend portions of Board and committee meetings in order to participate in and contribute to relevant discussions.

IX. Board Committees

The Board has established four standing committees: Executive, Audit, Compensation, and Governance. The Audit Committee and the Compensation Committee are composed of independent Directors only. The Audit Committee has the sole responsibility for retention and dismissal of the Company's independent auditors. The Governance Committee is composed of independent directors and a member of the Wiley family, as permitted under the New York Stock Exchange's rules applicable to "controlled companies." The Board believes that the family's participation in the Committee will result in a collaborative process to promote the highest standards in the recruitment of new directors and governance generally.

The Governance Committee recommends to the Board the members and chairs for each of the committees. The chair and membership assignments for all committees are reviewed regularly and rotated as appropriate. The chairs of the committees determine the frequency, length and agenda of meetings for each committee meeting. As in the case of the Board, materials are provided in advance of meetings to allow members to prepare for discussion at the meeting.

The scope and responsibilities of each committee are detailed in the committee charters, which are approved by the Board. Each committee annually reviews its charter, and the Governance Committee and the Board review all charters from time to time.

With the permission of the chairman of the committee, any Board member may attend a meeting of any committee.

X. Periodic Review

The Governance Committee and the Board review these Principles annually.

Adopted by the Board of Directors
John Wiley & Sons, Inc.
September 15, 2005

Appendix F

Sample Code of Ethics

One Sarbanes-Oxley innovation is the requirement that companies adopt a written code of ethics to help management, boards, and rank-and-file employees from rationalizing themselves over the line when ethical dilemmas arise and tough choices must be made. Here is a sample code adopted by the company that publishes this book, John Wiley & Sons, Inc.

Business Conduct and Ethics Policy

Policy

It is the Company's policy to manage and operate worldwide business activities in conformity with applicable laws and high ethical standards. Both the Board of Directors and management are determined to comply fully with the law, and to maintain the Company's reputation for integrity and fairness in business dealings with others.

Scope

This policy applies to all employees, officers and directors at all Company locations.

Responsibility

All employees, officers and directors are expected to adhere to all ethical and legal standards as outlined in this policy and to preserve the Company's integrity and reputation.

Provisions

1. Financial Record-Keeping

It is the policy of the Company to fully and fairly disclose the financial condition of the Company in compliance with the applicable accounting principles, laws, rules and regulations and to make full, fair, accurate, timely and understandable disclosure in our periodic reports filed with the Securities and Exchange Commission ("SEC") and in other communications to securities analysts, rating agencies and investors. Honest and accurate recording and reporting of information is critical to our ability to make responsible business decisions. The Company's accounting records are relied upon to produce reports for the Company's management, rating agencies, investors, creditors, the SEC and other governmental agencies and others. Therefore, our financial statements and the books and records on which they are based must accurately reflect all corporate transactions and conform to all legal and accounting requirements. Our system of internal control is designed to provide this information.

All employees have a responsibility to ensure that the Company's accounting records do not contain any false or intentionally misleading entries. Information on which our accounting records are based is the responsibility of all employees.

We do not permit intentional misclassification of transactions as to accounts, departments or accounting periods. In particular we require that:

- all Company accounting records, as well as reports produced from those records, are kept and presented in accordance with the laws of each applicable jurisdiction;
- all records fairly and accurately reflect the transactions or occurrences to which they relate;
- all records fairly and accurately reflect in reasonable detail the Company's assets, liabilities, revenues and expenses;
- the Company's accounting records do not contain any intentionally false or misleading entries;
- no transactions are misclassified as to accounts, departments or accounting periods;
- all transactions are supported by accurate documentation in reasonable detail and recorded in the proper account and in the proper accounting period;
- all Company accounting financial reports be prepared in accordance with generally accepted accounting principles; and
- the Company's system of internal accounting controls, including compensation controls, to be followed at all times.

2. Improper Payments

No payment or transfer of Company funds or assets shall be made that is not authorized, properly accounted for and clearly identified on the Company's books. Payment or transfer of the Company's funds and assets are to be used only as specified in the supporting documents.

No employee, officer or director may authorize any payment or use any funds or assets for a bribe, "kickback," or similar payment that is directly or indirectly for the benefit of any individual (including any government official, agent or employee anywhere in the world), company or organization in the United States or any foreign country, and which is designed to secure favorable treatment for the Company. Under federal legislation it is a felony to make payments of this kind to foreign government officials.

3. Political Contributions

It is the Company's policy not to contribute any Company funds or assets to any political party, committee, organization, or candidate for any office (federal, state or local) in the United States or any foreign country. Employees may, on their own time, support individual candidates or political committees, all subject to applicable laws, and may make voluntary contributions to such candidates or committees, including any Company-related political action committee.

4. Acceptance of Payments

Employees, officers and directors may not seek or accept either directly or indirectly, any payments, fees, services, or other gratuities (irrespective of size or amount) outside the normal course of the employee's business duties from any other person, company or organization that does or seeks to do business with the Company. Gifts of cash or cash equivalents of any amount are strictly prohibited. The receipt of common courtesies, sales promotion items of nominal value, occasional meals, and reasonable entertainment appropriate to a business relationship and associated with business discussions are permissible.

5. Business Entertainment

All solicitations or dealings with suppliers, customers, or others doing or seeking to do business with the Company shall be conducted solely on a basis that reflects both the Company's best business interests and its high ethical standards. The Company does permit the providing of common courtesies, entertainment, and occasional meals for potential or actual suppliers, customers, or others involved with the Company's business, in a manner appropriate to the Company's relationship and associated with business discussions. Expenses in this connection must be reasonable, customary and properly authorized.

6. Conflicts of Interest

The Company expects all employees, officers and directors to exercise good judgment and the highest ethical standards in private activities outside the Company that in any way can affect the Company. They shall at all times exercise particular care that no detriment to the interest of the Company may result from a conflict between those interests and any personal or business interests which the individual may have. In particular, every employee, officer and director has an obligation to avoid any activity, agreement, business investment or interest or other situation that might, in fact or in appearance, cause an individual to place his or her own interest, or that of any other person or entity, above his or her obligation to the Company. The words "in appearance" should be noted particularly since the appearance of an action might tend to impair confidence even if the individual may not actually do anything wrong.

To this end, employees, officers and directors must avoid any investments, associations or other relationships that could conflict with the staff member's responsibility to make objective decisions in the Company's best interests. Any potential conflicts of interest must be reported immediately to the senior officer of the staff member's division or subsidiary, and the Company's General Counsel. In the case of an officer, conflicts of interest must be reported immediately to a senior officer or the Company's CEO as applicable, and its General Counsel. In the case of a director, conflicts should be reported to the Chairman of the Board, the CEO, and the Company's General Counsel.

7. Corporate Opportunities

No employee, officer or director of the Company shall for personal or any other person's or entity's gain deprive the Company of any business opportunity or benefit which could be construed as related to any existing or reasonably anticipated future activity of the Company. Employees, officers and directors who learn of any such opportunity through their association with the Company may not disclose it to a third party or invest in the opportunity without first offering it to the Company.

8. Confidentiality

All employees, officers and directors are responsible for safeguarding and keeping confidential any information that the Company considers to be of a confidential or sensitive nature. Such information includes, but is not limited to financial records and reports, marketing and strategic planning information, employee-related documents, unpublished manuscripts as well as information relating to potential mergers and acquisitions, stock splits and divestitures, and other materials that the Company would not want disclosed to a competitor or any unauthorized recipient, or that might be harmful to the Company or its customers if disclosed whether or not such information is marked "confidential." Confidential information also includes information concerning possible transactions with other companies or information about the Company's customers, suppliers or joint venture partners, which the Company is under an obligation to maintain as confidential. Employees, officers and directors may not use Confidential Information for their own personal benefit or the benefit of persons or entities outside the Company, and must exercise caution and discretion with respect to any appropriate temporary removal of confidential or sensitive information from the Company's premises, and should safeguard the information from unintended disclosure or loss. Employees must at all times adhere to the Company's policies regarding the transmission and storage of the Company's confidential and sensitive business records.

9. Compliance With Laws and Regulations

The Company requires its employees, officers and directors to comply with all applicable laws and regulations in countries where the Company does business. Violation of domestic or foreign laws and regulations may subject an individual, as well as the Company, to civil and/or criminal penalties. Employees have an obligation to comply with all laws and regulations and policies and procedures and to promptly alert management of any deviation from them.

(a) Antitrust Laws

It is the Company's policy to comply with the letter and spirit of all applicable antitrust laws. If the legality of any contemplated transaction, agreement or arrangement is in doubt, employees, officers and directors must consult with a Company staff attorney.

Discussions with competitors regarding the Company's prices, credit terms, terms and conditions of sale, strategies or other confidential, sensitive or proprietary information are not permissible. This applies both to individual discussions and to participation in trade and professional associations and other business organizations. If a competitor initiates such a discussion, the staff member should refuse to participate or request that counsel be contacted. Staff members should seek guidance from a Company staff attorney when appropriate.

(b) Insider Trading

No employee, officer or director may trade in securities while in possession of material inside information or disclose material inside information to third parties ("tipping"). Material inside information is any information that has not reached the general marketplace through a press release, earnings release or otherwise, and is likely to be considered important by investors deciding whether to trade (e.g., earnings estimates, significant business investments, mergers, acquisitions, dispositions and other developments, expansion or curtailment of operations, and other activity of significance). Using material inside information for trading, or tipping others to trade, is both unethical and illegal. Accordingly, no employee, officer or director of the Company may: (a) trade securities of the Company or any other company while in possession of material inside information with respect to that company; (b) recommend or suggest that anyone else buy, sell, or hold securities of any company while the employee is in possession of material inside information with respect to that company (this includes formal or informal advice given to family, household members and friends); and (c) disclose material inside information to anyone, other than those persons who need to know such information in order for the Company to properly and effectively carry out its business (e.g., to lawyers, advisers and other Company employees working on the matter). Of course, where material inside information is permitted to be disclosed, the recipient should be advised of its non-public nature and the limitations on its use. Any questions as to whether information is material or non-public should be directed to the Company's General Counsel.

10. Fair Dealing

Each employee, officer and director should endeavor to deal fairly with the Company's suppliers, competitors and employees. No one should take unfair advantage of another through manipulation, concealment, abuse of privileged information, misrepresentation of material facts, or any other unfair-dealing practice. Information about the Company's competitors must be used in an ethical manner and in compliance with the law. Under no circumstance should information be obtained through theft, illegal entry, blackmail, or electronic eavesdropping, or through employees misrepresenting their affiliation with the Company or their identity. Any proprietary or non-public information about the Company's competitors should not be used if it is suspected that such information has been obtained improperly.

11. Employment of Relatives

The Company's policy is to require advance approval before a relative of an employee is hired by the Company, or is engaged as a consultant or independent contractor of the Company, if the relative of the employee will be in the same department or chain of command of the Wiley employee. Such approval should be sought from the requisite member of the Wiley Leadership Team (for US locations) or the Managing Director (international locations) and the most senior Human Resources officer at the location. A relative of the Wiley Leadership Team and the Managing Directors of international locations may only be hired or engaged with the advance review and approval of both the CEO of the Company and the Senior Vice President–Human Resources. A "relative" may include a member of the employee's family (spouse, child, parent, sibling, in-law) but may also include, for purposes of this Policy, any individual who is living with or otherwise in a significant relationship with the employee, or a relative of such an individual.

12. Duty to Report Violations

Each employee, officer and director is responsible for promptly reporting to the Company any circumstances that such person believes in good faith may constitute a violation of this policy. Except as provided in the next paragraph, suspected policy violations are to be reported (including confidential and anonymous reports) to the Company's General Counsel and its Chief Audit Executive.

Any complaint regarding accounting, internal accounting controls or auditing matters must be reported (including confidential and anonymous complaints) to the Company's General Counsel and its Vice President, Internal Audit, who will be responsible for reporting as appropriate to the Chairman of the Company's Audit Committee Alternatively, complaints may be mailed directly to the Chairman of the Company's Audit Committee at P.O. Box 1569, Hoboken, N.J. 07030-5774.

No retribution against any individual who reports violations of this Policy in good faith will be permitted. However, the reporting of a violation will not excuse the violation itself. The Company will investigate any matter which is reported and will take any appropriate corrective action.

13. Violations of Policy

Violations of any of the foregoing provisions may expose the Company and the individuals involved to lawsuits and possible criminal action. Staff members who violate this policy are subject to appropriate disciplinary action, up to and including termination. Any alleged violations of this Policy will be reviewed by the Company's legal department and other appropriate staff members.

Appendix G

Sample SAS 70 Report

*W*hat follows on the next two pages is a sample SAS form used by a company called SAS70 Solutions. To view an online version of the form, you can visit the company's Web site, located at www.sas70solutions.com.

INDEPENDENT SERVICE AUDITOR'S REPORT

To [Service Organization]:

We have examined the accompanying description of the controls related to the [system name(s), application name(s), process name(s), service name(s), etc.] of [Service Organization]. Our examination included procedures to obtain reasonable assurance about whether (1) the accompanying description presents fairly, in all material respects, the aspects of [Service Organization]'s controls that may be relevant to a user organization's internal control as it relates to an audit of financial statements, (2) the controls included in the description were suitably designed to achieve the control objectives specified in the description, if those controls were complied with satisfactorily; [If the application of controls by user organizations is necessary to achieve the stated control objectives, insert the italicized phrase following the words "complied with satisfactorily" in the scope <u>and</u> opinion paragraph: - "*and user organizations applied the controls contemplated in the design of [Service Organization]'s controls."*] and (3) such controls had been placed in operation as of [last day of review period]. The control objectives were specified by the management of [Service Organization]. Our examination was performed in accordance with standards established by the American Institute of Certified Public Accountants and included those procedures we considered necessary in the circumstances to obtain a reasonable basis for rendering our opinion.

In our opinion, the accompanying description of the aforementioned [system(s), application(s), process(es), service(s), etc.] presents fairly, in all material respects, the relevant aspects of [Service Organization]'s controls that had been placed in operation as of [last date of review period]. Also, in our opinion, the controls, as described, are suitably designed to provide reasonable assurance that the specified control objectives would be achieved if the described controls were complied with satisfactorily. [If the application of controls by user organizations is necessary to achieve the stated control objectives, insert the italicized phase following the words "complied with satisfactorily" in the scope <u>and</u> opinion paragraph: - "*and user organizations applied the controls contemplated in the design of [Service Organization]'s controls."*].

In addition to the procedures we considered necessary to render our opinion as expressed in the previous paragraph, we applied tests to specific controls, which are presented in Section(s) [Section #'s] (the Matrices) of this report, to obtain evidence about their effectiveness in meeting the related control objectives described in the Matrices, during the period from [first day of review period] to [last day of review period]. The specific controls and the nature, timing, extent, and results of the tests are listed in the Matrices. This information has been provided to user organizations of [Service Organization] and to their auditors to be taken into consideration, along with information about the internal control at user organizations, when making assessments of control risk for user organizations. In our opinion, the controls that were tested, as described in the Matrices, were operating with sufficient effectiveness to provide reasonable, but not absolute, assurance that the control objectives specified in the Matrices were achieved during the period from [first day of review period] to [last day of review period]. [The following sentence should be added when all of the control objectives listed in the description of controls placed in operation are not covered by the tests of operating effectiveness. This sentence would be omitted when all of the control objectives listed in the description of controls placed in operation are included in the tests of operation effectiveness – "However, the scope of our engagement did not include tests to determine whether control objectives not listed in the Matrices were achieved; accordingly, we express no opinion on the achievement of control objectives not included in the Matrices."]

The relative effectiveness and significance of specific controls at [Service Organization] and their effect on assessments of control risk at user organizations are dependent on their interaction with the controls and other factors present at individual user organizations. We have performed no procedures to evaluate the effectiveness of controls at individual user organizations.

The description of controls at [Service Organization] is as of [last day of review period], and information about tests of the operating effectiveness of specific controls covers the period from [first day of review period] to [last day of review period]. Any projection of such information to the future is subject to the risk that, because of change, the description may no longer portray the controls in existence. The potential effectiveness of specific controls at [Service Organization] is subject to inherent limitations and, accordingly, errors or fraud may occur and not be detected. Furthermore, the projection of any conclusions, based on our findings, to future periods is subject to the risk that (1) changes made to the system or controls, (2) changes in processing requirements, (3) changes required because of the passage of time, or (4) the failure to make needed changes to the system or controls may alter the validity of such conclusions.

The information included in Section [Section #] of this report is presented by [Service Organization] to provide additional information to user organizations and is not a part of [Service Organization]'s description of controls placed in operation. The information in [Section #] has not been subjected to the procedures applied in the examination of the description of the controls related to [system name(s), application name(s), process name(s), service name(s), etc.], and accordingly, we express no opinion on it.

This report is intended solely for use by the management of [Service Organization], its user organizations, and the independent auditors of its user organizations.

SAS 70 Solutions

[last day of review period]

Index

• *Numerics* •

10-K annual reports/10-Q quarterly reports
  accessing on EDGAR database, 70–72
  CEO/CFO signoff requirements, 87
  companies producing, 9
  internal control reports with, 36
  mandate for, 43
  SOX-mandated enhancements, 50–51, 131
  viewing, 55
401(k) asset transfers, reporting
    requirements, 53

• *A* •

accelerated filers
  customized software for, 201
  defined, 50
  Section 404 compliance requirements, 87
accounting adjustments, reporting
    requirements, 35
accounting firms. *See also* auditors
  coercing, prohibition against, 146–147
  consolidation of, 21
  cooling-off periods, 84
  defined, 155
  document retention requirements, 86
  income from Section 404 audits, 166
  increasing accountability of, 31
  influencing, prohibition against, 147–148
  inspection of, under Title I, 18
  internal supervision requirements, 96
  international, regulation of, 97
  limits on services, 14, 33, 83, 272–276
  permission requirements, 85–86
  regulations governing, 11, 14, 17, 79,
    90–97
  self-regulation, failure of, 78, 89–90
  small, regulation of, 97
  time limits and rotations, 86
accounting methods
  in financial reports, 64
  reporting changes in, 62

Accounting Standards Board (ASB), 91
accounts, identifying for Section 404
    audits, 171
accredited investors, 43
actuarial services, 85, 107, 273
Adelphia Communications corporation,
    misconduct at, 30, 115, 132
Advisory Committee on Smaller Public
    Companies (SEC), 11
advisory services, 45, 83, 109
affiliated persons, exclusion from audit
    committees, 104
American Institute of Certified Public
    Accountants (AICPA)
  accounting standards, 13, 17, 79–80,
    90–91
  Code of Professional Conduct, 95
  self-regulation failures, 78, 90
  Web site, 281
American Stock Exchange (AMEX), 48
analyst integrity, regulations protecting, 20
annual accounting support fee, 94
annual reports
  from audit committees, 263–264
  how to read, 67–70
  identification of audit committee
    members in, 110
appraisal and valuation services, 85,
    107, 273
Arthur Andersen, LLP (accounting firm)
  history and chronology of collapse, 76–77
  impact of Enron misconduct on, 14
  litigation against, 28, 77, 235–236
ASB (Accounting Standards Board), 91
assertions
  defined, 170, 221
  entering in SarbOxPro software, 221
  identifying for Section 404 audits, 170
  testing approaches, 190
assessments of internal control, 126
assets, registration requirements for, 47
Atkins, Paul (SEC Commissioner), 161

attestation reports, 91, 175–176
attorneys
  noisy withdrawal rule proposal, 15
  standards for professional conduct, 37
audit committee
  annual reports by, 263–264, 333–334
  changes in, announcing promptly, 264
  charter for, 102, 262, 323–332
  communication by, importance of, 263
  compensation of members, 104
  engaging advisors, 109
  enhancements of under SOX, 18, 99
  Enron's, independence of, 13
  exclusion of affiliated persons, 104
  financial experts, 105, 261–262
  funding for, 34, 100
  interfacing with auditors, 106
  limits, 13
  maintaining good relations with, 175, 269
  members, 104, 259–260
  naming of members on, 110
  for not-for-profit companies, 249
  questionnaires for members, 262
  roles and responsibilities, 13, 33–34, 99,
    100, 102–103, 105–109
  sample charter, 323–332
  subcommittees, 260–261
  tracking complaints, 262–263
audit interlopers, regulations governing,
    147–148
*An Audit of Internal Control Over Financial
  Reporting Performed in Conjunction
  With an Audit of Financial Statements*
  (PCAOB), 88
audit report standards, 17
Auditing Standard No. 2 (PCAOB)
  and compliance costs, 160
  control deficiency definition, 174
  effective oversight definition, 175
  key provisions, 168–176
  Web site and information about, 88
Auditing Standard No. 60 (PCAOB) on
    material versus other deficiencies,
    134–135
Auditing Standard No. 70 (PCAOB) on
    requirements for third-party reports,
    191–192

auditors
  auditor committee interface with, 106
  banned activities, 14, 84–85, 272–276
  changing, reporting requirements, 53
  cooling-off periods, 84
  document retention requirements, 17, 86
  findings and opinions, 80, 83–84 175–176
  impact of SOX on, overview, 32–33
  independence requirements, 14, 18,
    81–83, 86–87, 170–171
  management disclosure to, 128–129
  for non-profit companies, 249
  permissions for non-prohibited
    services, 85–86
  regulation of, 14, 75–76, 78–79, 147
  responsibility of management to, 134
  role of, 89, 166–167
  rotation of, 18, 33–34, 86, 109
  and Savings and Loan crisis, 14
  Section 404 compliance testing, 189–190
  self-regulation, failure of, 89–90
  two-partner sign-off requirements, 17
  walkthroughs by, 169–170
audits, goals of, 32. *See also* SAS 70
    reports; Section 404 audits
authorization procedures, as key control,
    190–191

● *B* ●

balance sheets
  examining during Section 404 audits, 168
  general format, 62–63
blackout periods
  exemptions from, 114
  limits on, 35, 144
  for stock trades, 19
  30-day notice requirement, 145
Blue Ribbon Committee on Improving the
    Effectiveness of Corporate Audit
    Committees, 101
blue sky laws, 48
board of directors
  as audit committee members, 104
  bad, examples of, 113–115
  compensation setting responsibilities,
    118–119

compensation-related regulations, 112
corporate governance guidelines, 111,
    119, 335–339
independent, 13, 115–117
majority-independence, 112
nomination process, 112, 117–118
for nonpublic companies, 120
for not-for-profit companies, 121
NYSE and NASDAQ exempt
    organizations, 121
off-balance sheet transaction
    approval, 113
performance evaluations, 119–120
prohibited payments and activities, 116,
    144, 145
role and responsibilities, 112
SOX-mandated structure, 12
support from for Section 404
    compliance, 182
Boesky, Ivan (insider trader), prison
    sentence, 132
bonuses
    bogus or erroneous, returning, 19, 35,
        146–147
    cautions about, 255
    SEC authority to freeze, 38
bookkeeping services, 84, 107, 272
broker-dealer services, 85, 107
bureaucracy, impact of SOX on, 11
business conduct policy, sample, 341–347

• **C** •

capital investment, impact of SOX on, 11
capitalized expenses, WorldCom
    example, 100
CEOs. *See* chief executive officers
certification requirements
    keeping current with, 268
    Section 302 certification checklist and
        sample, 126–129, 319–320
    Section 906 certification sample, 321
    subcertifications, 136, 321–322
    versus controls, 269
Certified Public Accountants (CPAs)
    advisory services, 83
    and auditor independence, 81–83

on PCAOB, 93
CFOs. *See* chief financial officers
charter for audit committees, 102, 262,
    323–332
chief executive officers (CEOs)
    certification responsibility, 108
    lawsuits against, as individuals, 229–230
    responsibilities, traditional, 124
    responsibilities under SOX, 15, 127–128
    signoff requirements, 87
chief financial officers (CFOs)
    certification responsibility, 108
    ethical standards for, 140
    lawsuits against, as individuals, 229–230
    responsibilities, traditional, 124–125
    responsibilities under SOX, 15, 127–128
    signoff requirements, 87
chief information officers (CIOs), 203
COBIT. *See* Control Objective for
    Information and Related Technology
    standards
code of ethics
    amendments and waivers to, 141
    checklist for, 142
    code of business conduct, 341–347
    objectives, 140
    publishing, 140
    SOX requirements for, 139–140
    stock exchange requirements for, 141
Code of Professional Conduct (AICPA), 95
Collins, Mac (Congressman), opposition to
    SOX, 11
Committee of Sponsoring Organizations
    (COSO) framework
    AICPA checklist, 186
    compliance requirements, 159
    documenters' need to understand, 183
    exceptions to rules governing, 145
    history of, 208
    internal control components, 192–193
    SEC endorsement of, 135
    software standards, 207–209
    software tools for complying with, 199
    Web site, 159, 193, 282
compensation
    for audit committee members, 104
    for directors, 112, 118–119

competitiveness, impact of SOX on, 11
complaints. *See also* whistle-blower complaints
  about compliance costs, 11
  handling of, 100, 103, 108, 262–263
compliance requirements. *See also* Section 404 audits; Section 404 (SOX)
  costs of, controlling/reducing, 11, 159–163
  monitoring using information technology, 203
  tools for meeting, 212–213, 225
Compliance Week (magazine), 278
Complyant Web-based compliance tools, 225
conflicts of interest
  on audit committees, 262
  identifying, 264
  protecting against, 18
consultants
  on audit committees, 249, 261
  for IT systems, 272
  SAS 70 audit-exempt, 247
contingent liabilities, reporting in financial statements, 63
control environment (COSO framework), 192, 207
control objective (COSO framework), 193
Control Objective for Information and Related Technology (COBIT) standards
  documenters' need to understand, 183
  purpose and function of, 194
  software and IT systems for, 194, 210
control procedures (COSO framework), 193
controls. *See* internal controls
cooling-off periods, 109
Cooper, Cynthia (WorldCom General Auditor), 100
corporate governance guidelines
  NYSE versus NASDAQ requirements, 119
  sample, 335–339
corporate tax returns, signing, 22
corporations
  impact of SOX on, overview, 12
  Securities Act of 1933 and, 10
COSO. *See* Committee of Sponsoring Organizations framework
Cost Advisors, Inc. SarbOxPro software, 212

costs
  of goods sold, in income statements, 61
  of SOX compliance, 11, 15, 159–163, 184–185
  tracking using IT systems, 206
CPAs. *See* Certified Public Accountants
credibility and implementation of SOX standards, 56
credit ratings
  rigging of, Enron example, 27
  SOX-authorized investigations of, 21
criminal liability, triggers for, 21–22, 131–133. *See also* penalties

● *D* ●

data security versus internal controls, 23
day-to-day operations, requirements for, 12
de minimus exceptions, 107
deadlines
  for compliance with Section 404, 154
  importance of meeting, 270
  for Section 302 filings, 130
debt, outstanding, reporting in financial statements, 63
debt securities, regulations governing, 45
deferred prosecution, 237
deficiencies, significant, 174
delegated functions, documenting, 256–257
delisting, 250
directors. *See* board of directors
disclosure committee
  advantages of forming, 137, 265–266
  meeting schedules, 266–267
  reporting schedules, 266
  SEC recommendations for, 128
disclosure requirements
  accounting adjustments, 35
  auditor opinions, 80
  changes to code of ethics, 139
  controls and procedures, 156–157
  emphasis on in SOX, 31
  off-balance sheet transactions, 35–36
  real-time reporting of key events, 36
  under Securities Act of 1933, 41
  senior management stock ownership, 142

SOX Title IV overview, 19–20
of stock sales by senior executives, 142–143
disclosure systems versus merit systems, 40
discontinued expenses, 62
disgorgement of profits, 19, 239
documenters
  process documentation, 183–189, 193
  skill and knowledge needs, 182–183
  software tools for, 212–213
  time tracking projects, 183–184
Douglas, Bill (Cost Advisors, Inc.), 212
Dun & Bradstreet Web site, 66
Dynergy corporation, misconduct at, 132

• E •

earnings per share (EPS), 62
Ebbers, Bernard (WorldCom), 29, 132, 145–146
EDGAR database (SEC). *See also* Securities and Exchange Commission
  accessing, 10, 65
  company filings in, 70–72
  registration statements in, 55
  Web site, 55, 181–182
effectiveness evaluations
  of disclosure controls, 157
  of internal accounting controls, 158–159
  of internal control design, 171–173
Employee Retirement Income Security Act of 1974 (ERISA), 145
employees
  impact of SOX on, 16
  listing using SarbOxPro software, 220
  protections for, 50
  and Section 404 compliance, 181
  SOX-defined duties, 12
  subcertification, 136, 321–322
Enron corporation, misconduct at
  history and chronology of, 26–28
  impact on Arthur Andersen, 14
  prison sentences associated with, 132
  role of board of directors, 13, 113–115
  SOX as a response to, 9–10, 101
EPS (earnings per share), 62
ERISA (Employee Retirement Income Security Act of 1974), 145

Ernst & Young (accounting firm), SEC penalties against, 236–237
escrow funds, 238–239
ethics policies/ethics codes
  changes in, reporting requirement, 53
  checklist for, 142
  sample, 341–347
  SOX-mandated standards for, 139–141
European companies, SOX standards for, 249–250
events, reportable, 206, 256
exceptions (COSO framework), 207
executive officers. *See also* chief executive officers; chief financial officers; senior management
  prohibition on personal loans to, 144
  stock ownership disclosure requirements, 142
exempt securities, 10–11, 49
exhibits, including with reports, 268
expenses from operations (income statements), 61
expert opinions, banning of auditors from, 85, 276
extraordinary items, 62
extraordinary payments, freezes on, 22

• F •

failing Section 404 audits, reasons for, 176
False Claims Act, 240, 241
falsifying records, penalties for, 21
Fastow, Andrew (Enron), 28, 30, 132
Fastow, Lea (Enron), 28, 30
federalization of corporate law, 12
Financial Accounting Standards Board (FASB), 13, 91
financial asset purchases, reporting requirements, 53
Financial Executives International (FEI)
  reducing SOX compliance costs, 163
  Web site, 282
financial experts
  inclusion on audit committees, 105
  tips for finding, 261–262
financial information, corporate
  SEC definition, 127
  sources for, 65–70

financial officers. *See* chief financial
officers (CFOs)
financial statements
certification by CEOs/CFOs, 125
reading, 60–65
testing for SOX compliance, 180
"financially literate," defined, 93
fiscal year and reporting deadlines, 155
Flake, Jeff (Congressman), opposition to
SOX, 11
flowcharts, 186, 189
footnotes (financial statements), cautions
about, 63–64
foreign companies
audit committee requirements, 110
SOX-related standards for, 249–250
Form 8-K reports (SEC)
accessing on EDGAR database, 72
for ethics code changes, 140
for intended blackout periods, 145
reporting requirements, 36, 44, 53,
126, 256
safe harbor provisions, 53–54
SOX-mandated enhancements, 51–52
viewing in EDGAR databases, 55
Form 10-K annual reports (SEC)
companies producing, 9
internal control reports with, 36
SOX-mandated enhancements, 50–51, 131
viewing, 55
Form 10-Q quarterly reports (SEC)
SOX-mandated enhancements, 51, 131
viewing, 55
Form 13-D (SEC stock ownership
disclosure), viewing, 72
Form 20-F (SEC foreign company annual
report), viewing, 72
Forms 3, 4, and 5 (SEC), SOX-amended
stock sale disclosures, 143–144
401(k) asset transfers, reporting
requirement, 53
fraud
audit committee monitoring for, 109
detecting, 135
involvement in, ambiguities about,
128–129
penalties for, 22

• G •

Gemstar case, 238–239
general ledgers, 187, 214
Generally Accepted Accounting Principles
(GAAP)
adherence of auditors to, 13–14
adherence of financial statements to,
64–65
departures from, 80
documenters' need to understand, 183
Generally Accepted Auditing Standards
(GAAS)
adherence of financial statements to,
64–65
components, 81
incorporation into PCAOB standards, 95
on role of internal controls, 134
Global Crossing corporation, misconduct
at, 29, 114
going public, impact of SOX on, 57–58
Gonzales, Alberto (U.S. Attorney General),
on KPMG prosecution, 238
Grassley, Charles (Senate Finance
Committee Chairman), 248

• H •

headhunter services, banning of auditors
from, 274–275
healthcare industry, SOX-related software
for, 201
HealthSouth Corporation
prosecutions under SOX, 132
Scrushy trial, 230–232
Hoovers Online Web site, 67

• I •

implementation problems, 10–11
implicit waivers, 141
income statements, 60–61
independent audit boards. *See* audit
committee
independent auditors. *See* auditors
independent directors, locating, 115–117
industry-specific software, 201

information technology (IT) systems
for COBIT compliance, 210
COSO framework standards, 193, 207–209
evaluating, checklist for, 204–206
IT staff role in Section 404 compliance, 181, 203
prohibition of auditors from consulting on, 84–85, 272
testing controls for, 180, 203
value of investing in, 256
Inside Sarbanes-Oxley Web site, 281
interlopers, audit, regulations governing, 147–148
internal audit outsourcing services, 85, 107, 273–274
Internal Control, An Integrated Framework (Treadway Commission), 135, 192. *See also* Committee of Sponsoring Organizations framework
internal controls
benefits of, 12, 134, 189
certification requirements, 156–157
control deficiencies, 174
COSO framework for, 135, 192–193
design effectiveness, 171–172
disclosure committees and, 137
disclosure controls and procedures, 156–157
documenting and testing, 180
evaluation and review procedures, 128
for information technology system, 203
inventorying, 137
key controls, 190–191
management assessments of, 168–169
management responsibilities for, 19, 128
operating effectiveness, 172–173
for outside vendors, 191–192
penalties for failing to implement, 131–133
process documentation, 188–189
reporting requirements, 36, 129, 133, 135
Section 404 requirements and audits, 17, 153, 158–159, 167–168
software for documenting/tracking, 205, 207, 220–221
testing approaches, 172–173
versus certification, 269
versus data security, 23
Investment Advisers Act of 1940, SOX amendments to, 45

investment advisor services, 45, 85, 275
investment banks/bankers, 20–21
Investment Company Act of 1940, amendments to under SOX, 45
investment contracts, 46
investors. *See* shareholders/investors
issuers
annual accounting support fee, 94
defined, 41, 46–47
security registration requirements, 47
SOX regulations governing, 130
IT. *See* information technology systems
IT Control Objectives for Sarbanes-Oxley (IT Governance Institute), 194, 202–203, 210

• K •

Kane, Madeline Begun (humorist), Web site, 233
key controls
authorization procedures, 191
and materiality, 190
reconciliation, 191
segregation of duties, 190
software tools for, 205
kManager software, 223–224
knowledge of wrongdoing, difficulty proving, 231–235
Kopper, Michael (Enron), 28
Kozlowski, Dennis (Tyco International), 115, 132, 143
KPMG (accounting firm), indictment and deferred prosecution, 235–238
Kranitz, Richard (attorney), 49, 57

• L •

lawsuits/litigation. *See also* penalties
against audit interlopers, 148
against auditors, 80
impact of SOX on, 12, 229
against Kenneth Law (Enron), 233–235
noisy withdrawal rule proposal, 15
pending, reporting in financial statements, 63
preventing, 57, 253–257
against Richard Scrushy (HealthSouth), 230–233
against the SEC, 54–55

lawsuits/litigation *(continued)*
  by shareholders, 12, 35
  under SOX Section 304, 239
  statute of limitation extensions, 21
  tips for avoiding, 253–257
Lay, Kenneth (Enron)
  exemption from blackout period, 114
  indictment and lawsuit against, 233–235
  role at Enron, 26, 28
  trial, 132
  unethical stock sales, 142
Leavitt, Arthur (SEC chairman), 100–101
legal services, 85, 107, 275
liability insurance for directors, 15
like-kind exchanges, 273
litigation. *See* lawsuits/litigation
loans to senior management, prohibition
  of, 144
look-back period, 115–116

• *M* •

majority-independent boards, 112
management accountability. *See also*
  senior management
  blackballing of violators, 38
  certification requirements, 18–19, 168–169
  freezing/seizing personal assets, 146
  as goal of SOX, 31, 34, 153
  for internal accounting controls,
    157–159, 186
  required reports, 126
management services, banning of auditors
  from, 85, 274
Management's Discussion and Analysis
  (MDA) section (annual reports), 70
material deficiencies, reporting
  requirements, 134–135
material errors, 189
materiality scoring, 190, 220
McDonough, William J. (PCAOB chairman),
  90, 235–236
meeting schedules, importance of, 266–267
merit systems versus disclosure
  systems, 40
Milken, Michael (junk bond trader), prison
  sentence, 132
misappropriation, preventing, 12
modifications of SOX law, need for, 10

monitoring function (COSO framework),
  193, 199–200, 209
monitoring role (audit committees),
  105–106
Morningstar Web site, 67
Murray, Brenda (SEC administrative law
  judge), Ernst & Young penalties, 236
mutual funds, 45, 55
myths about SOX law, 22–23

• *N* •

NASDAQ SmallCap Market
  audit committee requirements, 99
  board nominating procedures, 118
  code of ethics requirements, 141
  compensation regulations, 119
  corporate governance guidelines,
    101, 119
  listing requirements, 103
  rules for foreign companies, 249–250
  rules governing director independence,
    116–117, 121
net revenue (income statements), 61
New York Stock Exchange (NYSE)
  audit committee requirements, 99, 103
  board nominating procedures, 118
  code of ethics requirements, 141
  compensation committees, 118–119
  corporate governance guidelines,
    101, 119
  exempt organizations, 121
  listing requirements, 103
  mandatory meetings, 117
  rules governing director independence,
    116–117
  rules governing foreign companies,
    249–250
nonaccelerated filers
  defined, 155
  extension of compliance deadline, 11
  Section 302 filing deadlines, 130
  Section 404 compliance requirements,
    87–88
nonaudit services, 107
nonoperating expenses, 62
nonpublic companies, SOX-related
  standards for, 120

not-for-profit companies (NFPs)
  board of director requirements, 121
  SOX-related standards for, 16, 247–249
NYSE. *See* New York Stock Exchange

• *O* •

Occupational Health and Safety
    Administration (OSHA), handling of
    whistle-blower complaints, 240–243
off-balance sheet transactions
  disclosure requirements, 19, 35–36
  Enron use of, 26–27
  identifying, 63
  legitimate, 113
Olis, John (Dynergy), prison sentence, 132
"other" income and expense category
    (income statements), 61
outsourced functions
  applicability of SOX to, 23
  internal control requirements, 191–192
  SAS 70 reports and audits, 245–247
oversight, effective, 175
over-the-counter traded companies,
    disclosure requirements, 110

• *P* •

Panel on the Nonprofit Sector activities, 248
paper work retention requirements, 17
passage of the SOX law, 9–11
Paul, Ron (Congressman), opposition to
    SOX, 11
PCAOB. *See* Public Company Accounting
    Oversight Board
Peat Marwick (accounting firm), SEC
    penalties against, 237
penalties. *See also* lawsuits/litigation
  for accounting firm violations, 97
  application to senior managers' personal
    assets, 146
  blackballing of violators, 38
  for failing to implement internal controls,
    131–133
  for fraud and conspiracy, 50
  for mishandling or falsifying records,
    15, 21–22

  for retaliation against whistle-blowers, 21
  for violating Securities Exchange Act, 22
  for white-collar crime, 21–22, 37
pension liabilities, banning of auditors
    from consulting on, 273
PeopleSoft, Inc., impact of Ernst & Young
    accounting errors, 236–237
Physmark software for the healthcare
    industry, 201
Pitt, Harvey (PCAOB chairman), 90
POB (Public Accounting Oversight
    Board), 91
policies and procedures. *See also* code of
    ethics
  for accounting, 167–168
  code of business conduct, 341–347
  revising and updating, 267
policing role (audit committees), 105–106
PricewaterhouseCoopers accounting firm,
    30, 235, 272
private placement, 42–43
privately held companies, 9, 56–58, 110
processes
  controls for, costs of testing, 180
  documenting, 180, 184–189
  managing using IT software, 220
  reports on, 206
  time tracking, 183–184
ProCognis software, 199–200, 205, 209
professional conduct standards, 37
profits, disgorgement of, 239
project managers, 181, 183
project planning guidance (COSO
    framework), 193
project teams (Section 404 projects),
    187–188
prospectuses
  requirements for under Securities Act of
    1933, 10, 41
  viewing in EDGAR database, 55, 72
proxy solicitations, 44, 55
Public Accounting Oversight Board
    (POB), 91
public companies. *See also* audit
    committee
  application of SOX to, 9
  registration requirements, 41, 43
  viewing financial information from, 65–70

Public Company Accounting Oversight Board (PCAOB). *See also* Securities and Exchange Commission (SEC)
accounting firm supervision, 96
adoption of GAAP/GAAS, 79–80
An Audit of Internal Control Over Financial Reporting Performed in Conjunction With an Audit of Financial Statements, 88
Auditing Standard No. 2, 160, 168–176
Auditing Standard No. 60, 134–135
Auditing Standard No. 70, 191–192
authority, 97
board members, 93
changing interpretive standards, 11
disciplinary sanctions, 18
document retention supervision, 96
funding for, 94
impact on investors, 32
inspections by, 95–96
responsibilities, 17, 79, 89–92, 93, 96
SEC oversight over, 98
standard-setting authority, 14, 88, 94–96, 153, 183
tasks overview, 32
Web site and standards information, 88, 153–154, 281
public offerings, registration requirements, 41, 43

• *Q* •

qualified or adverse audit opinions, 80, 177

• *R* •

receivership, reporting requirements, 53
reconciliation, as key control, 191
records and documents
  destruction of at Enron, 27
  internal controls for, 135
  penalties for altering or tampering with, 21–22, 133
  retention requirements, 37, 86, 95–96, 206, 254
  SOX-related requirements for, 50, 180, 182–183

registration requirements for stock issues
  applicability of, 10, 47
  exemptions from, 43, 49
  under Securities Act of 1933, 41
  universal, under SOX, 49–50
registration statements, reviewing in EDGAR database, 55
Regulation D (Securities Act of 1933)
  exemptions from, 49
  Rules 504–506, 43
Regulation S-X 2-02 (f) (SEC), attestation/auditor reports, 175–176
regulatory confusion following passage of SOX, 11
regulatory process, outline of, 82
reports. *See also* Section 404 audits
  by audit committee, 263–264
  exhibits with, 268
  generating using IT software, 218, 222–223
  on internal controls, 20, 36, 153
  reviewing before signoff, 267–268
  schedules for, 266
  Securities Exchange Act requirements, 43–44
  SOX-based requirements, 35–36, 153
  by third-party providers, 191–192
restatements and bonus forfeits, 19
retained earnings (income statements), 61
reviews, mandatory, under SEC rules, 54
Rigas family (Adelphia), 30, 115, 132
risks
  assessing in COSO framework, 192
  controls for, testing approaches, 189–190
  documenting, 207
  from processes, identifying, 189
Rule 201(c)(4) (SEC), banned auditor activities, 84–85
Rules 504–506 (Securities Act of 1933, Regulation D), 43, 49

• *S* •

Salary.com Web site, 10
Sarbanes-Oxley Act forum, 281
SarbOxPro software
  data tree structure, 216–218
  features and uses, 199, 200, 216

monitoring control activities using, 208
software implementation checklist,
216–217
SAS 70 reports
requirements for, 191–192
sample, 349–350
and SAS 70 audits, 246
summary of, 246–247
Savings and Loan (S&L) crisis, 14
SB-series form (SEC), when required, 47
Scrushy, Richard (HealthSouth), 132,
230–232
SEC. *See* Securities and Exchange
Commission
SEC v. WJ Howey Co., 46
Section 16 (Securities Exchange Act of 1934)
insider trading prohibition, 44
SOX-mandated enhancements, 143
stock ownership reports, 142–143
Section 201 (SOX), banned auditor
activities, 84–85, 272–275
Section 301(4) (SOX) whistle-blower
provisions, 16
Section 302 (SOX)
certification form, sample, 319–320
certification requirements and checklist,
126–129, 268
civil penalties for false reports, 230
disclosure controls and procedures,
156–157
filing deadlines, 130
forms applicable to, 131
internal controls in, 156–157
management accountability provisions,
34, 125
questions raised by, 129–131
Section 303 (SOX), 34, 147–148
Section 304 (SOX), 35, 239
Section 306 (SOX), 12, 35
Section 401(a) (SOX), accounting
adjustment provisions, 35
Section 403(a) (SOX), insider trading
provisions, 44
Section 404 audits. *See also* audit
committee; auditors; Section 404 (SOX)
audit committee role during, 175
audit fees, 180
auditor's role during, 166–167
control evaluations, 167–168, 170–172,
189–190

documentation and testing requirements,
180, 182–183
flaws and weaknesses, identifying and
correcting, 174, 177
management assessments, evaluating,
168–169
management's role during, 166
manpower and staffing needs, 181–182
for outsourced functions, 246
PCAOB oversight of, 96
process inventories, 185–186
qualified or adverse opinions, 176–177
reporting of findings and opinions,
175–176
standards for, 14, 168
viewing positively, 254–255
walkthroughs, 169–170
work by company personnel,
evaluating, 173
Section 404 (SOX). *See also* Section 404
audits
CEO/CFO signoff requirements, 87, 133
compliance costs/benefits, 57–58,
159–163, 180
compliance requirements, 11, 87–88, 154
function, 153
internal controls in, 20, 36, 153,
156–159, 165
key phrases in, 152
management reports, mandated, 126, 153
PCAOB oversight of, 153
potential amendments to, 155
recertification requirements, 24
Section 406 (SOX), ethics code disclosures,
140
Section 602(d) (SOX), professional conduct
standards for attorneys, 37
Section 802 (SOX), 50, 133
Section 806 (SOX)
lawsuits under, 239
whistle-blower protection, 16, 240–241
Section 807 (SOX), universal applicability, 50
Section 902 (SOX), universal applicability, 50
Section 906 (SOX)
CEO/CFO certification requirements, 125
criminal penalties for fraud, 125, 230
final rules, 268
internal control implementation failure,
penalties for, 131–133

Section 906 (SOX) *(continued)*
  and knowledge of wrongdoing, 232
  sample certification, 321
Section 1102 (SOX), universal
  applicability, 50
Section 1103 (SOX), prosecutions under,
  238–239
Section 1107 (SOX), universal
  applicability, 50
securities
  definitions, 45–46
  identifying, questions to ask, 46
  registration requirements, 47–50
Securities Act of 1933
  enforcement, 10
  goals and regulations, 40–41
  insider trading prohibition, 44
  Regulation D, 42–43
  Regulation S-X 2-02(f) (SEC),
    attestation/auditor reports, 175–176
  SOX-mandated enhancements, 143
  stock ownership reports, 142–143
Securities and Exchange Commission
    (SEC). *See also* EDGAR database;
    Public Company Accounting Oversight
    Board; 10-K annual reports/10-Q
    quarterly reports *and specific forms*
  accounting oversight prior to SOX, 90
  Advisory Committee on Smaller Public
    Companies, 11
  auditors, regulations governing, 78–84
  enforcement function, 10
  establishment of, 42
  Form 3, 4, and 5 amendments, 143–144
  funding for, 20
  general certification form, 130
  harmonizing with NYSE/NASDAQ
    governance rules, 101
  internal controls policies, 135
  mandatory review rule, 54
  noisy withdrawal rule proposal, 15
  notification of pending investigations, 98
  personnel turnover at, 11
  registration exemptions, 10–11
  reporting requirements, 43–44
  reviews by, SOX-mandated, 31
  rulemaking authority, 38, 42–43, 183
  standards used by, 11, 13, 135
  Web site, 10, 280

Securities Exchange Act (1934)
  enhancements to under SOX, 22, 78, 120
  establishment of Securities and Exchange
    Commission, 42–43
  insider trading provisions, 44
  stock exchange supervision
    regulations, 99
securities exchanges. *See also* NASDAQ
    SmallCap Market; New York Stock
    Exchange
  how they work, 48
  regulation of, SOX-related updates, 10,
    39–42, 47, 99
securities violations, disgorgement fund
    for, 19
security tools, 206
segregation of duties/responsibilities
  examination of during Section 404
    audits, 168
  as key control, 190–191
self-evaluation by boards of directors,
    119–120
self-regulation by auditors/accounting
    firms, 78, 89–90
Senate Banking Committee, management
    oversight provisions, 139–140
senior management
  insider trading prohibition, 44
  loan restrictions, 19
  meeting schedules, 266–267
  responsibilities under SOX, 15
  role in Section 404 compliance activities,
    166, 182
  signing officers, 126–129, 134
  stock ownership disclosure
    requirements, 19
  stock trades during blackout periods, 145
shareholders/investors
  accessing ownership information, 72
  civil lawsuits by, 232–233, 239
  exclusion from audit committees, 104–105
  informational Web sites for, 66
  redress available to, 12
  SOX-based protections for, 13, 31–38
  stock ownership disclosure
    requirements, 47, 142
significant deficiencies, 129, 174
Skilling, Jeffrey (Enron), 26, 28

small businesses, small-cap companies
impact of SOX on, 11, 15–16, 88
and SEC registration exemptions, 10
SOX-related software for, 199
software development activities,
exemption from SAS 70 audits, 247
software, SOX-related. *See also* SarbOxPro
software
for COBIT compliance, 210
for COSO framework compliance, 207–209
customized, for accelerated filers, 201
evaluating, checklist for, 206
kManager software, 223–224
monitoring tools, 199–200
purchase decisions, 202–203,
211–212, 256
for Section 404 compliance, 169
for small companies, 199
task-specific software, 201
for tracking documentation and financial
records, 204, 212–215
trends in, 197–199
S-1 forms (SEC stock offering prospectus),
viewing on EDGAR database, 72
SOX For Dummies SOX-update Web site, 280
SOX-online Web site, 278–280
special purpose entities, Enron use of,
26–27, 114
SpectorSoft monitoring software, 199, 201
S-series form (SEC), when required, 47
staff, temporary, exemption from SAS 70
audits, 247
standard certification form, 130
standards. *See* American Institute of
Certified Public Accountants; code of
ethics; Generally Accepted Accounting
Principles; Generally Accepted
Auditing Standards
start-up companies, impact of SOX on, 16
state governments
accounting oversight prior to SOX, 90
reduction of power over corporations, 12
regulation of small accounting firms, 97
statement of management
responsibility, 126
statute of limitation extensions, 37
stock exchanges. *See* NASDAQ SmallCap
Market; New York Stock Exchange;
securities exchanges

stock trades, 19, 143–145
studies, SOX-authorized, 21
subcertifications, 136, 269
Swartz, Mark (Tyco International), prison
sentence, 132

● *T* ●

tax services by auditors, limits on, 23
tender offers, 44, 55
10-K annual reports/10-Q quarterly reports
accessing on EDGAR database, 70–72
CEO/CFO signoff requirements, 87
companies producing, 9
internal control reports with, 36
mandate for, 43
SOX-mandated enhancements, 50–51, 131
viewing, 55
testing internal controls, COSO guidance
for, 193. *See also* Section 404 audits
theft, preventing, 12
Thompson, Huston (Federal Trade
Commissioner), 40
time tracking of projects
benefits of, 270
process for, 183–184
Titles I-XI (SOX), overview, 17–22
top-down approach to control testing, 172
tracking systems, examining during Section
404 audits, 167–168
transaction authorization
as element of internal control, 135
examining during Section 404 audits,
167–168
transaction monitoring, software for, 204
transfer agents, reporting requirements, 44
Treadway Commission. *See also*
Committee of Sponsoring
Organizations framework
Committee of Sponsoring
Organizations, 159
Internal Control, An Integrated Framework,
135, 192
trial balance
defined, 214
generating reports on, 214
tracking software, 214–215, 220
triggering events, 256

Trust Indenture Act of 1939
amendments, 45
two-partner audit sign-off requirements, 17
Tyco International, Ltd., 29–30, 114, 132
Type 1/Type 2 audits (SAS 70), 246

• U •

unqualified opinions, 175–176

• V •

Visio flowchart software, 188

• W •

waivers of code of ethics, disclosing, 141
walkthroughs for Section 404 compliance,
169–170, 188
Web sites
American Institute of Certified Public
Accountants, 281
COBIT standards/information, 194, 210
Complyant compliance tools, 225
COSO Control Environment checklist, 186
COSO standards/information, 159, 193,
282
Dun & Bradstreet, 66
EDGAR database, 55, 181–182
Financial Executives International, 282
Hoovers Online, 67
Inside Sarbanes-Oxley, 281
Madeline Begun Kane humor, 233
Morningstar, 67
NASDAQ, 103
NYSE, 103
Panel on the Nonprofit Sector, 248

PCAOB standards/information, 88,
153–154, 281
Physmark software, 201
Salary.com Web site, 10
Sarbanes-Oxley updates, 155, 280
SarbOxPro software, 212
SAS 70 report form, 349
Securities and Exchange Commission,
10, 280
SEC-required reports, 43–44
shareholder information, 66
SOX-online, 278–280
SpectorSoft monitoring software, 199, 201
Visio flowchart software, 188
whistle-blower complaints
for COSO framework compliance, 207–209
defined, 38
documenting handling of, 263
locating data for investigating, 204
OSHA handling process, 241–243
taking seriously, 137, 255
valid versus invalid, 240
whistle-blower protection
penalties for retaliation, 21
pre- and post-SOX regulations, 16, 38, 240
universal applicability, 50
Wikipedia Web site, Enron entry, 27
Winnick, Gary (Global Crossing), 29, 142
WorldCom corporation, misconduct at
capitalizing of operating expenses, 100
history of, 29
prison sentences associated with, 132
role of board of directors, 114

##

Xerox corporation board of directors, 114

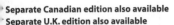

SPORTS, FITNESS, PARENTING, RELIGION & SPIRITUALITY

0-7645-5146-9

0-7645-5418-2

Also available:

Adoption For Dummies
0-7645-5488-3

Basketball For Dummies
0-7645-5248-1

The Bible For Dummies
0-7645-5296-1

Buddhism For Dummies
0-7645-5359-3

Catholicism For Dummies
0-7645-5391-7

Hockey For Dummies
0-7645-5228-7

Judaism For Dummies
0-7645-5299-6

Martial Arts For Dummies
0-7645-5358-5

Pilates For Dummies
0-7645-5397-6

Religion For Dummies
0-7645-5264-3

Teaching Kids to Read For Dummies
0-7645-4043-2

Weight Training For Dummies
0-7645-5168-X

Yoga For Dummies
0-7645-5117-5

TRAVEL

0-7645-5438-7

0-7645-5453-0

Also available:

Alaska For Dummies
0-7645-1761-9

Arizona For Dummies
0-7645-6938-4

Cancún and the Yucatán For Dummies
0-7645-2437-2

Cruise Vacations For Dummies
0-7645-6941-4

Europe For Dummies
0-7645-5456-5

Ireland For Dummies
0-7645-5455-7

Las Vegas For Dummies
0-7645-5448-4

London For Dummies
0-7645-4277-X

New York City For Dummies
0-7645-6945-7

Paris For Dummies
0-7645-5494-8

RV Vacations For Dummies
0-7645-5443-3

Walt Disney World & Orlando For Dummies
0-7645-6943-0

GRAPHICS, DESIGN & WEB DEVELOPMENT

0-7645-4345-8

0-7645-5589-8

Also available:

Adobe Acrobat 6 PDF For Dummies
0-7645-3760-1

Building a Web Site For Dummies
0-7645-7144-3

Dreamweaver MX 2004 For Dummies
0-7645-4342-3

FrontPage 2003 For Dummies
0-7645-3882-9

HTML 4 For Dummies
0-7645-1995-6

Illustrator CS For Dummies
0-7645-4084-X

Macromedia Flash MX 2004 For Dummies
0-7645-4358-X

Photoshop 7 All-in-One Desk
Reference For Dummies
0-7645-1667-1

Photoshop CS Timesaving Techniques
For Dummies
0-7645-6782-9

PHP 5 For Dummies
0-7645-4166-8

PowerPoint 2003 For Dummies
0-7645-3908-6

QuarkXPress 6 For Dummies
0-7645-2593-X

NETWORKING, SECURITY, PROGRAMMING & DATABASES

0-7645-6852-3

0-7645-5784-X

Also available:

A+ Certification For Dummies
0-7645-4187-0

Access 2003 All-in-One Desk
Reference For Dummies
0-7645-3988-4

Beginning Programming For Dummies
0-7645-4997-9

C For Dummies
0-7645-7068-4

Firewalls For Dummies
0-7645-4048-3

Home Networking For Dummies
0-7645-42796

Network Security For Dummies
0-7645-1679-5

Networking For Dummies
0-7645-1677-9

TCP/IP For Dummies
0-7645-1760-0

VBA For Dummies
0-7645-3989-2

Wireless All In-One Desk Reference
For Dummies
0-7645-7496-5

Wireless Home Networking For Dummies
0-7645-3910-8